Basic Safe Travel and Boreal Survival Handbook

Gems from Wilderness Arts and Recreation Magazine

Mors Kochanski

Basic Safe Travel and Boreal Survival Handbook
Gems from Wilderness Arts and Recreation Magazine

Text © 2013 by Mors Kochanski
Illustrations © 2013 by Mors Kochanski
Photographs © 2013 Randy Breeuwsma
Cover 2013 © Marissa Kochanski and Mike Siek

ISBN: 978-1-894453-68-4

All rights reserved. No part of this book may be reproduced by any means whatsoever without written permission from the publisher, except brief portions quoted for the purpose of review. All survival scenarios by nature are life-threatening. Some of the information presented in this book, if used incorrectly, could help kill you. Anyone who provides training that guarantees your safety during an outdoor survival situation is either a fool or a liar. Neither the author, the publisher, nor anyone else assisting in the creation of this book is responsible for your ultimate fate upon using the material contained within these pages.

Karamat Wilderness Way
www.karamat.com

FORWARD

The guide was compiled for the benefit of Outdoor Educators and the Alberta Junior Forest Wardens movement when the articles in Wilderness Arts and Recreation magazine went out of print. The magazine was published in the early 70's and many of the articles were the basis of the content of the book BUSHCRAFT. As the Forest Warden's developed their own handbooks the Woodstravel Guide faded from the scene but continued to be popular with Outdoor Educators and other enthusiasts as it contained information not found elsewhere. Some articles are earlier versions of some chapters found in "Bushcraft" and it seems many readers enjoy the difference between the two. The Guide is being made available through the efforts of Karamat Wilderness Ways.

Mors Kochanski

April 15, 2013

CONTENTS

Copyright

Forward

Contents

I. Wilderness Living Skills   1

A) Site Development   1

1. Shelter   1

2. Latrines   7

3. Garbage Disposal   10

4. Food Storage: Bearproofing   10

5. Outdoor Classrooms   10

B) Equipment   17

1. Clothing and Survival   17

2. The Sleeping Bag   32

3. The Functional Bush Knife and Its Use   66

4. The Five Most Important Try Stick Notches   90

5. The Multipurpose Bush Axe   94

6. The Saw   124

C) Wilderness Fire Lighting Skills in the Spruce Moose Forest   130

1. Approaches to the Use of Fire   131

2. The Question of Impact	135
3. Some Different Types of Fire Users	136
4. Abuses of Fire	141
5. Where Campfires are Out of Place	142
6. Justifying the Use of a Campfire	143
7. Points of Basic Fire Ecology	144
D) Basic Map and Compass Use	**185**
1. The Map	185
2. The Compass	205
E) The Basic Survival Lean-To and Bed	**222**
1. Open Fronted Lean-To Principles	222
2. Open Fronted Lean-To Made of Flexible Materials	233
3. Bough Beds	235
F) Outdoor Cooking	**242**
1. Introduction	242
2. The Australian Cooking Crane	243
3. Steam Pit	246
G) Wild Edible Plants	**249**
1. Plants	249
2. Looking at Edible Mushrooms	273
II. Wilderness Survival	280

A) Defining Survival 280

1. Basic Existence Skills 280

2. Wilderness Survival 283

3. In Survival You Have No Guarantees 285

4. Living Off the Land 286

5. The Advantages of Fasting (on water only) 286

6. Problems with Fasting 287

B) Introduction to Wilderness Survival 289

1. Preparedness 289

2. Panic 289

3. Survival in a Nutshell 290

4. Fire 290

5. Shelter 291

6. Dehydration 291

7. Hypothermia 292

8. Signals 292

9. Conservation of Mental and Physical Energy 292

10. Lost? Finding Your Way 293

C) Water and Human Survival 297

1. Body Water Needs 298

2. How Much Water? 298

3. Thirst	299
4. Local Thirst	299
5. Boiled Water Recommended	300
6. Undetected Water Losses	300
7. Water Loss Through Lungs in the Cold	301
8. The Mechanism of Water Absorption	301
9. Dehydration	302
D) Handling Stress	306
1. Responding to Stress	307
2. Your Only Three Options	307
3. Limiting Factor	307
E) Survival Kits	309
1. Survival Kits: The Basics	309
2. The Personal Kit	312
3. The Basic (Two Kilogram) Universal Kit	321
4. The Personal First Aid Kit	323
F) Caching of Supplies and Equipment	330
G) Signaling with a Mirror	331
H) Signal Fires	334
1. The Choice of Site	334
2. The Simple Signal Fire	335

3. The Standard Signal Fire	336
4. The Large Signal Fire	340
I) Vehicle Survival	342
1. Vehicle Operation Kit-circa 1985	342
2. Vehicle Survival Kit	344
J) Aircraft Survival	346
K) Helicopter Safety	348

III Wilderness First Aid — 350

A) Cold Injuries	350
1. Introduction	350
2. Hypothermia	353
3. Cold Hazards: Frostnip and Frostbite	360
4. Dehydration	362
5. Snow Blindness	365
B) Diarrhea	368
C) The Heat Illnesses	370
1. Introduction	370
2. Water Loss	372
3. Burns, Scalds and Fluid Loss	374
D) Knife Cuts: How to Avoid Them	375

IV. Wilderness Travel Skills — 378

A) Leading Your Group	378
1. Travel Hints	378
B) River Crossing	379
1. Crossing on Foot	379
2. Rope Crossing	382
C) Effects of Travelling at Higher Elevations	385
1. Conditions Resulting in High Altitude Pulmonary Edema	385
2. Conditions Above Tree Line	386
V. Wilderness Environment	388
A) Annoying Insects	388
B) Bears are Dangerous	389
C) Lightning	412
D) Breaking Through the Ice	414
E) Quicksand or Mud	414
VI. Ropework	416
Author	453

I. Wilderness Living Skills

A) Site Development

There may be some merit in avoiding the development of permanent sites for carrying on outdoor programs. Such sites usually involve considerable expense and if left unattended are often subjected to vandalism.

An easily movable facility can be relocated when the current site is becoming over-worn or the local fuel supply is running out. It can also be folded up and stored in the off-season.

As time goes on, roads are built, and as other local developments are carried out, better sites may become available to move to.

When money is scarce many programs never get started because of the prohibitive initial outlay that is required to develop a permanent facility. If considerable development is undertaken at a given site one may be committed to using it for a long time because of the money, time and labour tied up in it. Should local interests wane or be suspended temporarily, little is lost.

The readily moveable facility may provide a more practical experience for the users as an example of a type of comfortable sheltering in disaster, or other crises

1. Shelter

The proposed shelters use as much locally available materials as possible. This saves on costs and the effort in bringing in outside materials. The simplest and most effective shelters are the teepee and elongated teepee types which use nothing but straight poles in their construction. They have a low overhead volume for easy heating, yet have enough of a floor space to accommodate a large bed space and may utilize a wide variety of cover material depending on the amount of money available. This type of shelter is also just as useable in the winter as it is in the summer.

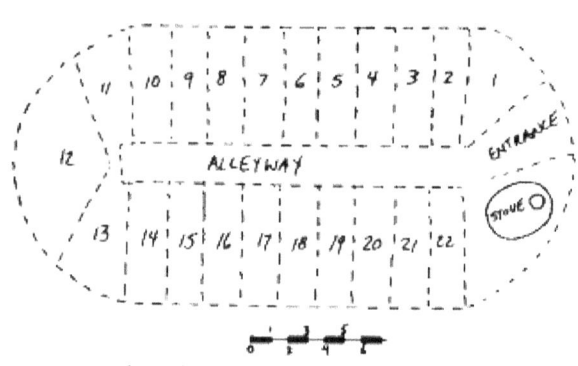

FLOOR PLAN - SLEEPING SPACE FOR 22 PEOPLE

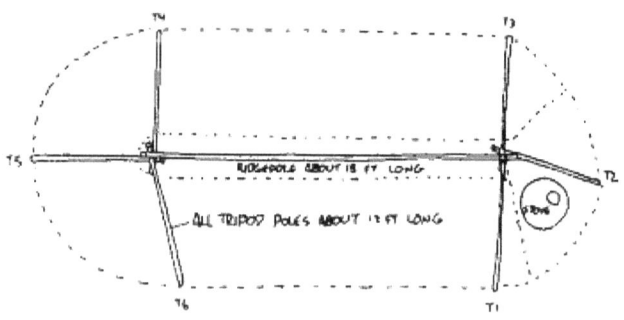

Basic Safe Travel and Boreal Survival

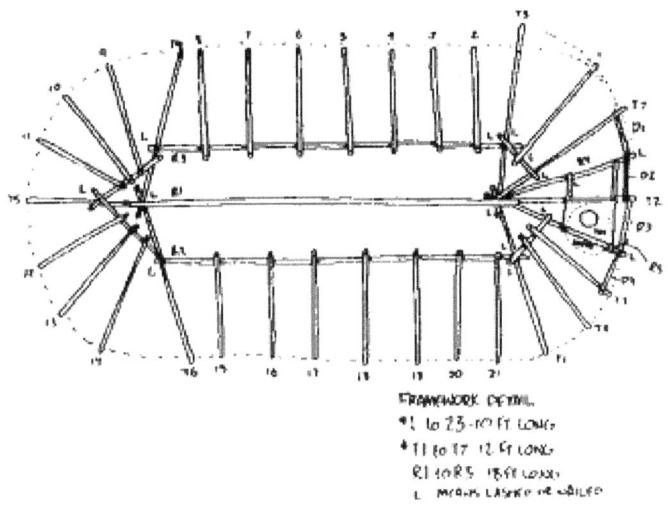

a) The Sleeping Platform

The sleeping platform, which is generally about chair-seat high, is constructed of poles about the length of the tallest user and spaced about a palm width apart. Some platforms may use a layer of boughs if these are available. It is simpler however, to use only the poles in conjunction with 3 inch thick open cell foam combined with a 1/4 inch closed cell foam. This will provide a very comfortable mattress and do away entirely with the need for boughs. This way you are not limited to spruce, so that aspen and pine will be adequate.

Where transportation to the site is not a problem, and where the expense is allowed, 1/2 inch plywood may be used instead of the numerous poles.

b) Heating Stoves

The teepee structures can be heated with common airtights, or in the interest of greater economy, with

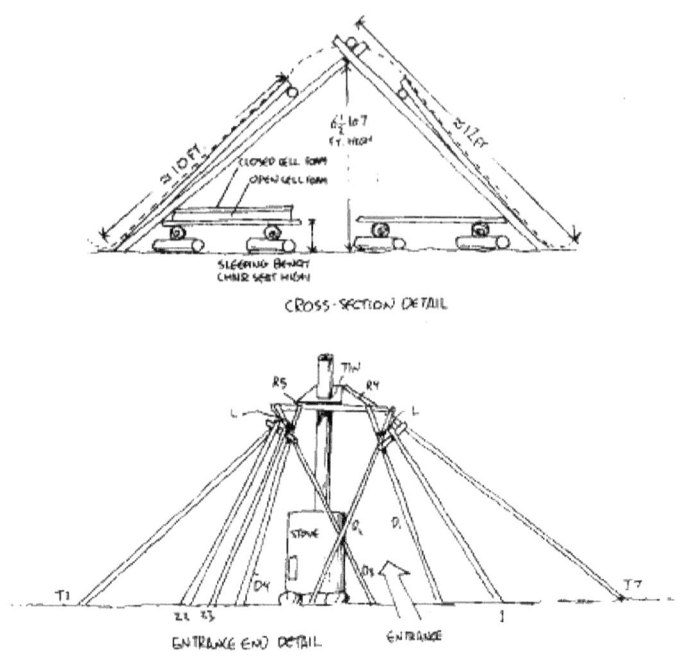

homemade stoves fabricated from 45 gallon barrels. The use of stoves wherever possible may reduce the fuel consumption considerably, especially where it has to be hauled in. The simplest stove is a barrel stood on end with an opening cut out of the side, which may be left open to create the effect of an open fireplace. If a close fitting hinged door is put on the barrel stove, it will operate more like a conventional airtight stove. For winter, a more effective stove is made when the barrel is laid on its side with the door cut in one end. Longer wood can be used and the stove can be filled more compactly.

For smaller shelters (1-6 people) smaller barrels or 5 gallon pails may be used for stoves. Unfortunately, many metal pails are being replaced by plastic ones so that these types of stoves may not be feasible in a few years.

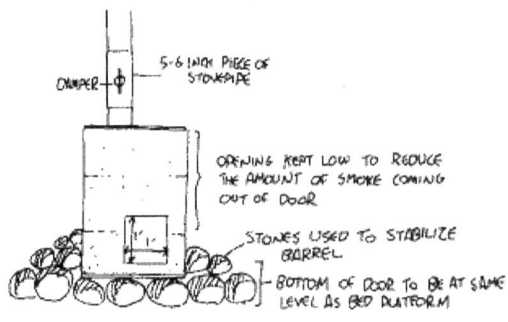

Detail of 45 Gallon Barrel Fireplace

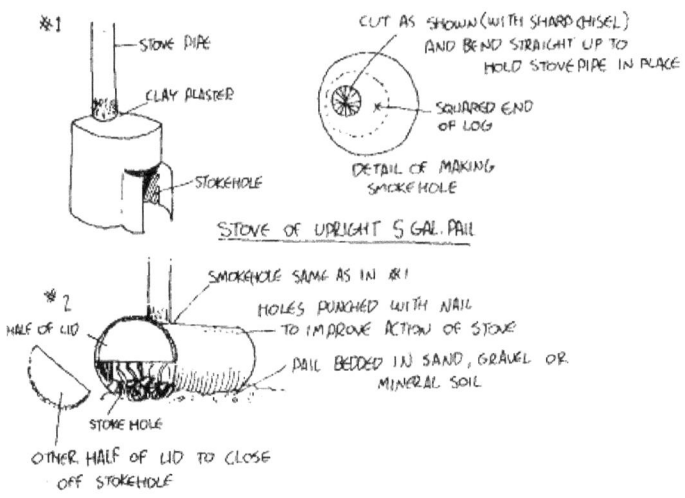

Stove of on-the-side 5 gallon pail

A cooking stove for use out-of-doors may be made from a half barrel. Cooking with pots and bringing water to a boil can be accomplished by use of an Australian crane. A barrel cooking stove will be more fuel efficient and will allow you to work closer to it when using a frying pan.

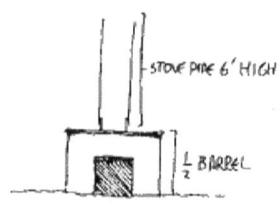

Detail of Cookstove

ATTENTION-SAFETY ISSUE: All the barrel stoves have a smokestack or stove pipe to carry the smoke away above the head. In the interests of stability and safety, a collar has to be attached to the barrel so that the stove pipe will not come off easily. This collar may be welded or bolted on. It is a small detail that should have considerable attention paid to it or the result is usually more smoke leakage and the occasional separation of the stove pipe from the stove.

Whenever possible barrel stoves should be set up on rocks or on inorganic soil, with some rocks piled around the base to improve the stove's stability. Any organic material under or near the stove may smolder and fill the shelter with smoke, or worse yet burst into flame and damage the shelter or any equipment nearby.

Air-tights may be more feasible than home made stoves in some circumstances. A suitably large airtight comparable to a barrel stove will likely cost at least $150.00. It's life expectancy is remarkably short, especially if it is allowed to get wet; it will then rust through very rapidly.

There are water heaters that are made of two 45-gallon barrels. The lower barrel is the stove and the upper barrel is the reservoir where water can readily be drawn by the use of a tap. Some rustic residential camps use these for making warm wash water.

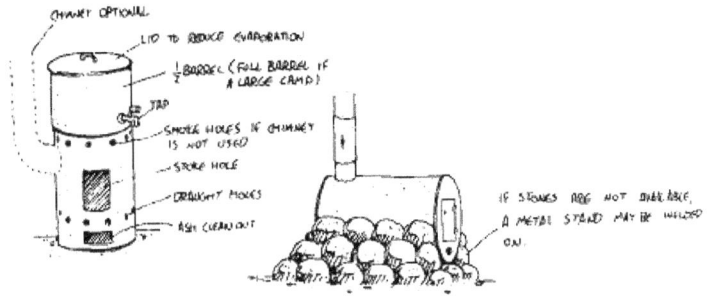

Camp Water Heater

2. Latrines

For the movable camp the following latrine arrangement may be more portable than the omnipresent outhouse. It is essentially a fly proof box that sets over the hole dug for the toilet. The top of the box is removable or hinged in order to more properly apply wood ashes or lime to the contents of the hole, especially when it is under heavy constant use. The latrine is protected by a tipi that has an opaque cover.

a) The Slit Trench Latrine

A more fundamental latrine is the simple slit trench. The slit trench is perhaps the most practical latrine because of its simplicity and ease of construction. A trench a metre long, by twenty or thirty centimetres wide, by about a metre deep will meet most needs. The surface sods are saved for refilling the trench. The excavated earth is piled at both ends or to one side to cover any excreta by scraping it into the trench with the foot or by the use of a small paddle made for the purpose. If the hole has been pre-dug before the ground is frozen and the excavated dirt is also frozen, wood ashes from the previous day's fire are made available to cover excreta. The cone chips from squirrel middens can be used in the same way. When the hole begins to fill, the chips can be at least partially burned up by lighting a fire in the hole and stirring occasionally.

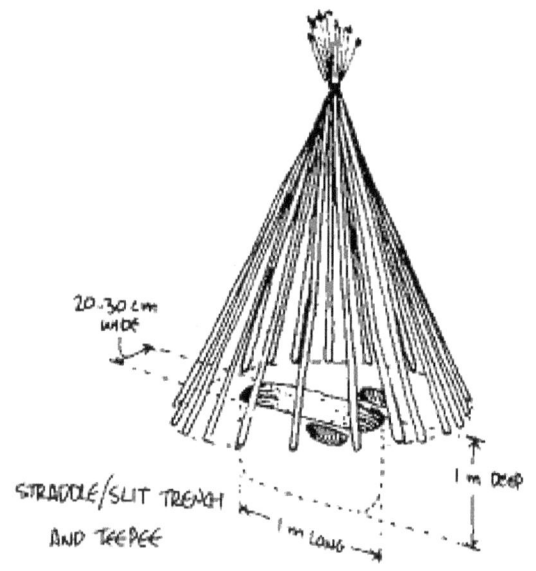

Straddle/Slit Trench and Teepee

If the sides of the trench are crumbly then thin poles are laid along the edges for users to stand upon. When the trench is filled within thirty centimetres of the top, it should be completely filled in and the sods replaced. If another trench is required it is constructed parallel to the first, a metre away. With this type of latrine no disinfectants are necessary.

In the winter when the ground is frozen, a fire can be built where the slit trench is to be dug. In a few hours the ground should be thawed enough to dig a proper trench.

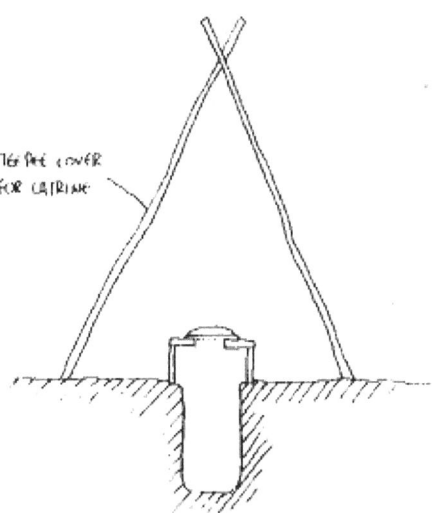

Cross-Section of Box Latrine

b) Choice of Site

The latrine should be to the leeward side of camp, as far as possible from the cooking area. It should have easy access, especially at night. Utmost care should be taken not to contaminate any water supply. If at all possible the bottom of the latrine should not intercept the water table. The Latrine should not be dug where the subsoil drainage will lead into any water, standing or moving.

If ashes are used to "sweeten" the latrine, then a 5 gallon tin pail is very useful for the purpose. Camp users are instructed to fill a 5 gallon pail with ashes from campfire or stoves first thing in the morning before new fires are lit.

3. Garbage Disposal

The smell of burning garbage can bring bears that are down wind from miles away.

All cans should have any label removed and be thoroughly rinsed immediately after being emptied. The tops and bottoms should be cut out and the can neatly flattened so that it can be more easily carried out. If every group that uses the camp carries out their own garbage no one will be stuck with the job.

4. Food Storage: Bearproofing

A recent recommendation in bear-proofing food is to wrap food caches in new 6 mil polyethylene. Moth balls or crystals in the toes of old socks hung around camp may deter bears. Bears cannot smell food through the polyethylene and the smell of the plastic itself masks any odours that may escape.

5. Outdoor Instruction Areas

An outdoor instruction area is essentially a fireplace surrounded by a circle of benches. It may have some means to quickly and easily erect an overhead tarp or parachute to provide protection against rain. It may also have a small storage shelter close by that would store and protect equipment and crafting supplies.

The benches are situated from two to three metres from the fireplace. The fire should be used only when necessary in cold or stormy weather. Ideally the benches should provide accommodation for two or three times the normal group size. That is, if a group size is 12 participants then the benches should seat from 24 to 36 people. This will allow room for movement away from the more smoky side of the fire. The benches should be about chair-seat high and be lashed together to minimize any chances of collapse.

As there is a tendency for everyone to use the benches as tables, you may provide a "table" for this purpose out of poles.

The number of instruction areas will depend on the number of groups of participants being accommodated at any one time. Where heavy usage is expected there may be an outdoor instruction area associated with each demonstration area.

Normally an outdoor fire will accommodate 12 people. Each group of 12 people should have a fire of their own and the seating provided is for 24 people so no one has to face any smoke.

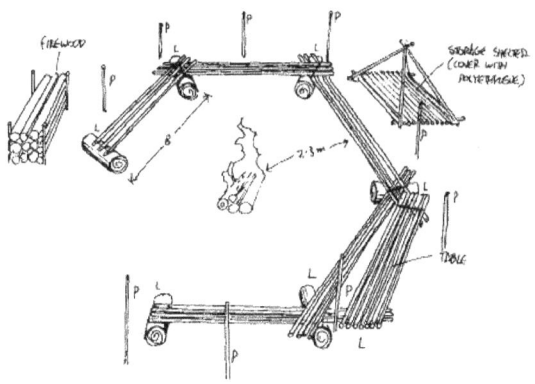

L = Lashing
P = Posts for erecting rain canopy
B = Benches about two metres long

Detail of Typical Outdoor Classroom

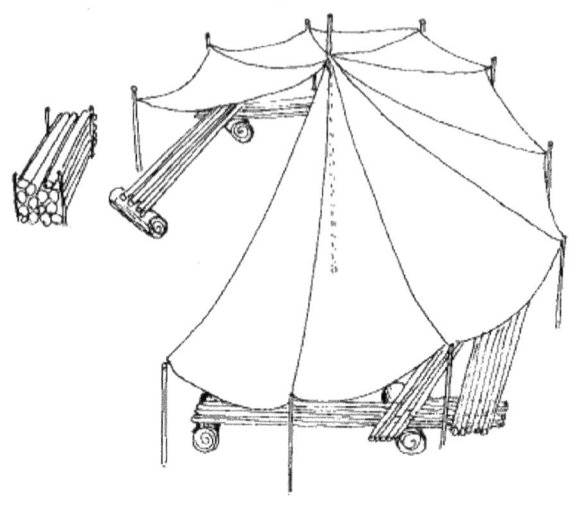

Parachute Rain Canopy in Place

a) Demonstration Areas

The demonstration areas may be situated in the general vicinity of and in some cases may be located where required raw materials are in abundance, such as in the Fire Skills area. The intent is to make it more convenient to instruct certain aspects of wilderness living skills. The following are some suggested areas:

i) Basic Survival Camp

- Basic bough lean-to and bed
- Re-emitter (reflector) fire
- An example of an overnight (winter) fuel supply properly positioned
- Signal fire
- And, nearby but not set to be triggered, except when being discussed:

- Ojibway bird snare
- Squirrel snare
- Wire rabbit snare
- Lifting pole string rabbit snare
- Survival fishing pole
- Grouse snaring pole

ii) Survival Kit Camp (2 kilogram kit)

- Super shelter and bed
- Roycraft "A" packframe
- 1 pair Roycraft emergency snowshoes
- Buck-saw frame

iii) Fire Skills Area

Choose an area that has a thin organic layer (such as amongst aspen or pine) and that has enough space for each individual in an instructional group to have a small clearing for fire lighting skill development and competitions.

- Have laid out a demonstration of the common fires and suspension systems used in the out-of-doors.
- An example of a properly put out fire and an improperly put out fire for comparison.
- A series of fires (guarded by a small fence), one for each year of the operation of the camp to show how fires may regenerate.
- For instructional purposes: a signal fire layed out in stages.
- Class sets of:
  - pots for water boiling competitions (for example jam cans or tobacco tins-all the same size)
  - flint and steel sets-group sets-rocks, strikers, tinderboxes and appropriate tinder materials
  - bow drill sets

- Comparative demonstrations of all the locally available fuels. (Teepee fuel piles of each example).
- Comparative demonstrations of locally available kindling.
- Axes and Saws: a 1/2 group size set of axes and or hatchets and a 1/2 group set of saws. If axes are not used a full group size set of saws for wood cutting for camp needs and skill development.

iv) Shelters Area

This area may have a demonstration of every feasible shelter that may be constructed in your particular area, and the materials for participants to construct conventional shelters and tents.

- Enough poles and materials (tarps, polyethylene, cord) for constructing a group set of shelters (groups of one to six) that participants may use to build shelters to stay overnight.
- Examples of:
    - use of boughs
    - shrub and grass thatch
    - various arch shelters etc.
- Brush teepee

v) Knots, Ropework, Cordage and Netting Area

An area where horizontal bars for the making of cordage and ropework, the tying of knots and lashings and other related applications may be facilitated.

- Knot tying and netting bars
- Poles for lashing and bridge building
- Spanish windlass demonstrations
- Rescue line throwing demonstration

- Display boards on knots, bends, hitches and lashings
  - eg. Parbuckle tie down
  - Prussic

vi) First Aid Training Station

- Materials for building stretchers
- Materials and equipment required for teaching basic first aid

vii) Traps, Deadfalls and Snares

- Functional Models or Full Sized: Examples of native traps, deadfalls and snares.

viii) Natural Crafting Area

- Where stock piles of natural craft materials are kept- black poplar bark, willow, etc.
- Examples of various crafts, primitive looms, primitive lathe, primitive vice and other primitive tools.

ix) Orienteering and Map and Compass Area

It is possible to obtain blow-ups of aerial photographs of the general area and put up markers of reasonable accuracy to teach map and compass use or to engage in the sport of orienteering. The chapter on maps describes how to obtain the blow-ups.

Perhaps 20 strategically located points may be permanently located and marked with gallon cans or 5 gallon pails painted red and white.

x) Nature Trail

A marked trail that can facilitate the identification of many of the locally available plants in the immediate local area. Specimens may be marked with a tripod and name plate. Parts of the nature trail can be used as a jogging trail.

xi) Satellite Survival Camp

The consumptive aspect of survival training puts a heavy demand on firewood and other materials. It may be more appropriate to keep this sort of activity away from the main camp.

xii) Moss Blazed Trail

Lay out a trail exemplifying methods of blazing (preferably without injuring trees) and leaving various conventional trail signs. Include a laid-out example of the moss-marking procedure to use when lost.

B) Equipment

1. Clothing and Survival

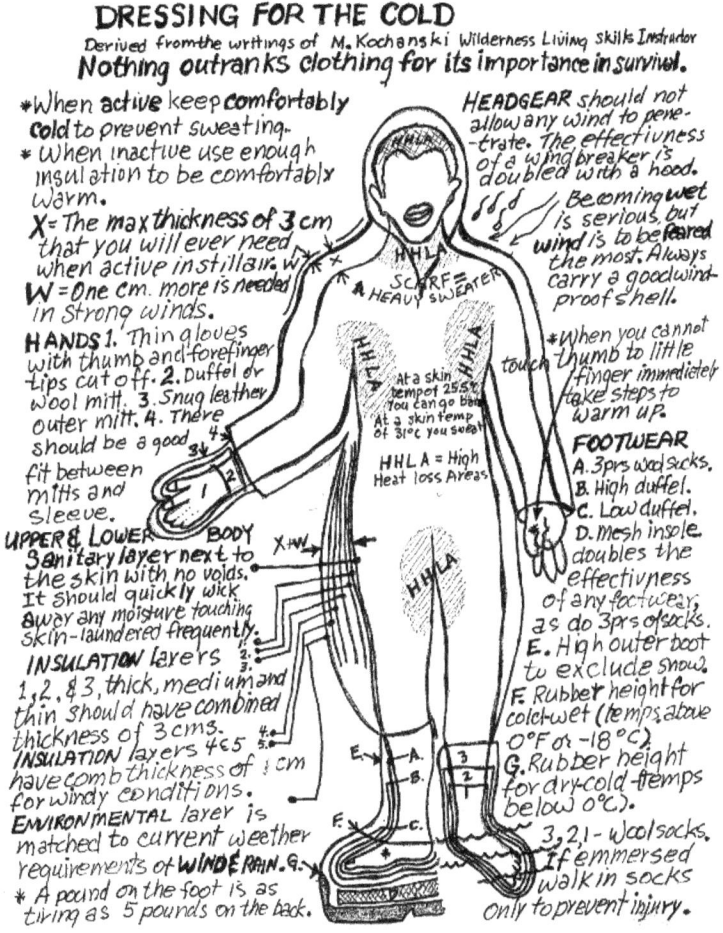

A thumb-nail definition of survival is "keeping your body, or at least keeping your vital organs, at 37°C - the temperature at which the body works best". Actually, 37°C is the usual body temperature for most of us but anywhere between 36.5 and 39.5 would still be considered normal. Further, temperature varies rhythmically in all people, generally increasing about a half degree between morning and evening.

Your body's resting heat production is about 90 calories per hour, while under hard work it may go up to 550 calories per hour. One calorie would be the amount of energy that would warm a kilogram of water 1 °C, or put in another way, the equivalent of four kitchen matches (5 cms long, that are burned up completely). To maintain a steady temperature the body has to employ a highly controlled mechanism to dissipate this heat so that the body stays as close to its normal temperature as possible. The body's high heat capacity allows it to stay at this temperature without any sudden changes. With the body having a specific heat of 0.83, it takes .00083 of a calorie to raise one gram of body tissue 1 °C. To keep warm in cold surroundings the body allows only the excess heat to escape.

a) The CLO

To better explain and comprehend heat retention and heat flow we should establish a convenient unit that translates these factors into mathematical figures. One such unit is the clo which approximates the insulation provided by a summer business suit. It is the amount of thermal insulation that a person sitting still would need to stay comfortable on a summer's day at about 21°C. For a very cold winters day one may need 16 clo.

The clo can be used in describing the thermal insulation of sleeping bags and body tissues as well as clothing.

b) Heat Loss Control Through Vasoconstriction

With normal activities the body has an insulative value of 0.2 clo because it does not conduct heat like a normal solid object, mainly because it is a living thing where a higher figure would be expected. The circulation of the blood rapidly transports heat to all parts of the body or diverts it wherever necessary by a muscular constriction of the blood vessels (termed vasoconstriction - V.C.). For example, V.C. will occur when cold water remains in contact with the skin causing the insulative value of the skin to rise to 0.5 clo. In a very fat person where the skin-fat is about one centimetre thick as opposed to a quarter centimetre in a normal person another 0.5 clo may be added.

c) Shivering

An alternative to V.C. is an uncontrollable heat generating muscular activity near the skin, called shivering. Shivering requires vasodilatation. This may amount to three times the heat as would be generated by the body at rest.

d) Clothing as a Means to Obstruct Heat Loss

The effectiveness of clothing depends on the thickness of the air layer trapped against the skin. Good insulative materials are those that have from one tenth to one fifth fibrous material with the rest being entrapped air. The entrapment cells have to be small enough (no larger than a centimetre, ideally a millimetre) so that the air in them cannot circulate or the insulative effectiveness will be diminished.

Just outside the surface of clothes is a still layer of air that seems to adhere to it, which will provide about 0.8 clo in still conditions and 0.2 clo in the wind regardless of the actual clo to begin with.

The value for dead air is 1.8 clo per centimetre thickness or about one clo per .56 cms. It has been established that clothing layers thicker than about 4 centimetres (or 1 1/2 inches) would seriously restrict movement thereby placing a limit of a maximum of 6 clo that one would expect from useful layers of clothing where normal movement and active function is desirable.

The following chart, based on studies conducted by the U.S. Army Corps of Engineers, translates temperature and thickness of insulation for various activities. The cooling effect of the wind is not taken into account.

TEMPERATURE Degrees Celsius	SLEEPING Cms	LIGHT WORK Cms	HEAVY WORK Cms
15	2.50	1.25	0.2
10	3.25	1.50	0.3
5	4.00	1.75	0.4
0	4.50	2.00	0.5
-5	5.00	2.50	0.6
-10	5.50	2.75	0.7
-15	6.00	3.25	0.8
-20	6.75	3.50	0.9
-25	7.25	3.75	1.0
-30	7.75	4.25	1.1
-35	8.50	4.50	1.2
-40	9.00	5.00	1.3
-45	9.50	5.25	1.4
-50	10.25	5.75	1.5
-55	10.75	6.00	1.6

e) The Effect of Wind

A penetrating wind of 40 kilometres per hour can reduce the insulation by 1.5 clo. In such a wind you may feel as if you have no clothes on for anything thinner than a centimetre unless a suitable outer layer stops the wind. A good design of the garment would also seal off the neck, wrists and ankles to prevent undue loss at these openings.

f) Effect of the Wearer's Movement on Dead Air

Any movement tends to displace dead air, and has associated with it muscular activity that generates more heat. To maintain comfort you usually have to get rid of the warmth produced by movement.

Sweating: Sweating is the fastest method of ridding the body of excess heat. The ideal fabric would allow sweating without losing its ability to insulate, in spite of the presence of any moisture regardless of its origin - sweat, rain or river.

Wool ranks as being one of the more suitable cold and wet weather fabrics because it can take up more moisture than most other fibres without losing its springiness, thereby maintaining its ability to retain its dead air. Cotton on the other hand, goes limp on wetting and loses its dead air spaces with the result that it feels cold when it is wet.

Wearing a cotton T-shirt in a summer's rain invites hypothermia whereas bare skin would not.

The passage of vapour through clothing is a complex process which may take considerable study and mental effort to understand. Vapour pressure, diffusion heat of sorption, or sorption and desorption are some participating factors that would have to be understood, but for the time being are too complex to go into in an article as practical as this.

One major concern is the accumulation of frost in one's clothing in very cold conditions. This frost build-up will impair the effectiveness of the insulation and add weight to the clothing.

Being well dressed in the European tradition in wool clothing, you may be initially wearing about eleven kilograms, which in about five days would accumulate an additional seven kilograms in frost. It was common knowledge about fifty years ago that the above condition would develop in the bitter cold reducing life expectancy to about five days if there was no means to dry out. This is one of the reasons why fire skills are classified as the second most important survival skill after knowing how to dress well.

g) Basic Principles of Keeping Warm

i) Defense Against Cold: Wool as an Insulator

Your body must be protected from losing heat to the surrounding air. The prime defense is properly chosen clothing to keep body heat from escaping by insulating the body against cold air and preventing heat loss due to trapped moisture. The clothing should be an excellent insulator, be moisture permeable, and at the same time be non-restricting and easy to put on and take off. Several thinner layers of clothing are preferable to one thicker layer, because of their ability to create more dead air spaces and the ability of the wearer to better regulate body temperature during active and inactive periods by adding or removing layers. Cold weather clothes should be made of materials with a loose fabric. These should be thick enough to prevent penetration of the cold to the warm layer next to the skin, but not thick enough to restrict mobility.

They should be fairly close fitting without being restrictive, especially at the neck and arms.

The active person will not need more than 3 centimetres of insulation while awake and active and an additional centimetre plus a wind break in strong winds. This maximum of 4 centimetres must be made up of less than 5 layers of insulation.

You may have always known that wool was a good out-of-doors fabric but you may not have known why. The superior qualities of wool clothing for cold and wet weather have been known for at least 7,000 years.

As the hair on the sheep grows out of the follicle, it develops into a spiral that gives the hair a waviness or a built-in crimp. These hairs tend to intertwine very readily to form yarns or felts. This also lends a certain elasticity to the fabric that allows it to spring back when stretched or flattened. The crimpy fibres resist laying closely to each other; this creates countless air pockets in every centimetre thickness of yarn.

Even the most tightly woven wool fabric is about 60 percent air pockets and the fluffiest weaves can reach the ideal of 80 percent air. A good insulating fabric has from 80 to 90 percent air.

The insulative air pockets are maintained by the springiness and resiliency of the wool fibres so that wool tends to be warm even when damp, a property retained by wool fabrics even when worn out to a thread-bare state.

This is in contrast to cotton which becomes limp when wet and imparts a cold feel because any voids in the fabric more or less collapse. Cotton clothing, such as blue jeans, can provide so little insulation in cold and wet conditions that their inappropriate use could be classed as a hazard to life.

Wool and Moisture: Wool has a tendency to shed any moisture falling on it, as well as readily transmitting vapour, such as sweat or other moisture evaporating off the skin, outwards. However, if wool is saturated it can absorb considerable amounts of water into the yarn as well as into the fiber itself. When the fiber takes on water it liberates significant amounts of heat, which helps contribute to one's comfort in wet conditions. As the wool dries out, heat is absorbed by the fiber. The rate at which this occurs makes any chilling action virtually unnoticeable.

When thoroughly dry, wool can develop considerable static electricity, which to a certain extent is countered by the wool's affinity for moisture. A reduction of static electricity lessens the tendency for the wool to pick up dust and lint.

Safety Around Fire: Wool is also noteworthy in its resistance to burning. If a flame is played on it, it will burn, but it will go out as soon as the flame is removed. The terrible stink produced should warn you that you are too close to the fire.

Wool is, therefore, a good fabric around open fires because sparks landing on it tend to fizzle out, usually with minor damage. In contrast, synthetics melt into holes before fizzling out and cotton may glow from one small spark until totally consumed.

Wool is not the strongest of available fabrics but its resiliency, elongation and elastic recovery makes up for its low strength.

Using Shrinkage to Advantage: The spiral that contributes so much to making wool into yarn can be a problem in some respects. This spiral is believed to be due to a bilateral discontinuity in the protein in the cortex of the fiber. Hot water makes the protein shrink at different rates which results in an even greater tightening of the curl. Add to this an agitating action, as in a washing machine, and the curl becomes pronounced enough to significantly shrink a pair of socks or a sweater. This can be used to advantage in making more compact and fuller fabrics, or in making boiled mittens.

Before the invention of the insulated rubber glove this was the main way that Atlantic fishermen kept their hands warm. Mittens were made overlarge to compensate for any shrinkage and put into boiling water until the desired compactness was achieved. In use the mittens were dipped in hot water and used wet. The wool kept the water next to the skin warm.

Wool Blankets: Blankets made of wool can be a versatile addition to a survival kit. You may sleep on a blanket, under it or use it as a shelter tarp. As a poncho, a good blanket may keep you as dry as will most conventional raingear.

There are numerous references in the literature to old-timers sleeping out in the open in very cold weather with only a couple of blankets. I could never understand how they managed until I had the opportunity to examine a blanket made by Parks Canada Historical people as authentic reproductions of the blankets used in the fur trade. It was very thick and fluffy, with a long nap. I believe the Parks Canada representative said that it cost $600 each to make a large number of these blankets!

If you find wool next to the skin irritating, try a finer weave. There are far more people allergic to nylon than who are allergic to wool.

Dressing from Head to Toe: The following outline suggest one way of dressing adequately for the cold.

Head: There should be an effective cover for head and ears, windproof and waterproof where necessary (balmoral, tam, beret, toque, fur cap, balaclava, etc.

Neck: Wear a scarf of wool or nylon that affords complete protection for the neck. A scarf an arm span long (finger tip to finger tip of the outstretched arms) that can wrap around the neck twice is recommended. (Made of rip-stop nylon, double thickness, 30 to 60 centimetres wide.)

The head and neck area can account for 70% of the body's heat loss because many of the blood vessels going to the brain are very near the surface of the skin in that region and the pumping action of the body's movement can force out a great deal of warmed air if there is a poor closure at the neck.

Upper Part of the Body: Four insulation layers of wool on the upper part of the body will allow considerable versatility from the snowy mountain top to the sweltering valley by simply adding or removing layers. Special attention should be paid to an important heat radiation in the area of the upper chest, which is the region you instinctively cover with the upper arms when cold.

- Underwear (two piece jersey: 95% wool and 5% nylon): Wear nylon or thin cotton underwear against the skin if you are allergic to wool. Some people can tolerate finely woven wool fabric, where they would be allergic to coarse wool. Polypropylene underwear is readily available at reasonable cost. It has the property of wicking moisture and sweat away from the skin very effectively. It is, however, very heat sensitive, easily melting from the heat of a good campfire.

- Shirt: Thin wool.
- Jack shirt or thick wool sweater: fairly bulky.
- Wool coat or heavy wool shirt: The sleeves should be long and snug enough to keep the wrists from being excessively exposed.
- Windproof outer-shell: The previous 2 items could be replaced with a parka in the winter time.

Lower Part of the Body: The legs should have two layers of wool with perhaps an outside windproof, snow-proof covering. The inner thighs should also receive special attention as they are another area of significant heat radiation. The cuffs should close snugly against the ankles.

- Underwear bottoms of wool.
- Heavy wool pants.
- Nylon outer pants: optional but advantageous, as snow does not stick to nylon like it does to wool.

Another approach is to use a maximum of 5 sweaters to produce 4 centimetres of thickness combined with a tightly woven shirt that can fit over all the sweaters or between any layer desired.

Feet: Footwear must not be restrictive in any way, yet it should not be so loose as to cause problems such as chafing, distortion of the last, or cause socks to come off or accordion up. There is no one footwear combination that will be adequate for all conditions, and that will be found suitable to the personality and physical make-up of everybody. The choice of footwear has to be carefully matched to the user. For example, under certain cold weather conditions it is difficult to surpass three pairs of good woolen socks without any outer footwear for comfort. At other times a pair of light rubbers over the socks is necessary. Then there are times when this combination becomes inadequate.

There are two major forms of footwear: one for temperatures warmer than -14 °C (wet cold) eg. rubber boots and the other for temperatures under -14 °C (dry cold) eg. Canadian military mukluks not rubberized on the inside or the outside.

When the rest of your body is cold it is not easy to keep your feet warm. There are many reasons why your feet may be cold. Your footwear may be too tight, restricting circulation. You should be able to wiggle your toes and flex your feet inside your footwear. You may not have enough insulation around your feet and your footwear may be very cold conductive. Your feet may perspire excessively. Some people suggest using an antiperspirant on the feet. Your feet may be poorly acclimatized to the cold. You may walk barefooted in the snow until your feet become numb, then thaw them out well. Repeat a few times a day for a few days at the beginning of winter. Smokers have poorer circulation and may suffer colder feet as a result. If you have ever suffered frost bite to your feet you may have greater problems keeping your feet warm for the rest of your life because of the altered circulation.

Some suggested combinations are as follows:

1) One pair of good woolen socks (if allergic to wool, wear nylon socks next to the skin).

- One pair buckskin moccasins to fit snugly over socks.

- Two pairs duffle liners made to be worn one inside the other. In warmer weather use one liner and in colder weather use two liners.
- Fit snowmobile boot to the above after discarding liners. Suggested boot - MINER (Canadian Made) with rings for lacing instead of zipper.

2) One or two good wool socks.

- One pair buckskin moccasins with nylon mesh insoles.
- Good moccasin rubbers.

3) Three pairs good wool socks with a cotton sock on the outside.

- Good moccasin rubbers with a nylon mesh insole.

4) Two or three pairs good wool socks only. This can be found to be surprisingly comfortable and the paragon of dry cold footwear compared to all other footwear. It is best used when the snow is not melting, but it is still passable in wet and moist conditions.

If the footwear you are using is causing your feet to be quite cold, almost instant relief is experienced by taking the boots off and walking around in your socks. Stepping into water seems to present no problems, because the snow quickly soaks up excess water. There is usually a slight sensation of dampness which does not become uncomfortable in using this type of footwear. With this, as with most footwear, there is usually no problem with cold feet, as long as you are not standing still. When a person is standing still, the feet tend to get cold, starting with the heels, which compress the material under them to virtually eliminate any insulation from the cold snow or ground. Of course, standing on ground thawed by a fire presents moisture problems and the grime can be hard on the socks.

Hands: Mitts are preferred to gloves which are usually colder. A good combination is a soft leather outer and a good woolen duffle liner. The combination must be loose and easy to put on or take off. An elastic sewn in the underside of the wrist will help to keep the mitt on and the cold out. The mitt must be tight enough, so as not to easily fall off the hand. Losing a mitt can be very inconvenient. You can prevent loss by using the cord arrangement that is used in keeping children from losing their mitts.

ii) Defense Against Moisture

Moisture, be it in the form of rain, immersion by falling through ice, melting snow or excessive sweat, is all the same in its effect: the rapid conduction of heat away from the surface of the skin. The thermal conductivity of water is 240 times greater than air. That is, wet skin may lose heat 240 times faster than dry skin.

Sources of moisture such as rain should be contended with by an external waterproof or repellent layer of clothing. This outer layer must block the entrance of outside moisture and also allow venting of internal moisture derived from perspiration. Sweat can dampen insulation as effectively as water and it must be controlled. As perspiration evaporates, the body tends to chill. This situation is controlled by the design of your clothing and how you manipulate it.

When skin temperature reaches 31°C the body reacts by sweating. In general, you control overheating by opening or removing clothing. You may also regulate your exertion so as not to produce excessive sweating by keeping the skin comfortably cool or almost cold. Traveling at a slow, comfortable pace, may be more sensible than making a dash for your objective and then exerting extras effort in gathering that much more fuel to keep warm because of having arrived sooner in a heavy sweat.

When you know you will have to exert yourself, you must take steps to prevent excess heat and moisture before any buildup occurs. This is something you have to learn through experience. You can follow this sequence:

1. Uncover ears (take off hood)
2. Uncover neck (remove scarf)
3. Uncover one hand
4. Uncover second hand
5. Open clothing at neck
6. Remove head gear altogether
7. Remove layers of clothing

If you find removing a layer of clothing is too much you may re-establish certain parts of the sequence, such as covering the ears, using a neck scarf , or replacing your mittens after you have taken off your parka.

Your hands and feet should be considered the indicators of your body's state of heat balance. Feet, because they perspire more readily, are difficult to keep warm. If your feet are warm and your body is dry, you are well off. If at all possible, your hands must never be allowed to get cold, as you need your hands to light a fire and to carry out other operations relevant to your survival.

It is very convenient to have clothing that provides a quick means of ventilation, such as having fronts that open for those short, hard spurts of activity. This is a shortcoming in the pullover style of clothing.

iii) Defense Against Wind: Wind Chill

Clothing that is generally adequate under most conditions becomes very inadequate in strong winds due to increased convection and moisture evaporation. If windproof clothing is not available you should immediately seek shelter from the wind and wait it out. Wet and wind are to be feared and respected the most.

2. The Sleeping Bag

Next to clothing, nothing contributes so much to your comfort as a properly chosen sleeping bag. If you can meet your body's water needs and sleep well at night you are well off even in a survival situation.

New concepts and advances in synthetic insulation and 'space age' fabrics all seem to show promise in revolutionizing sleeping bag design. This article will deal with the commonly available sleeping bag types that we feel we have come to understand through usage.

Like many other fundamental items concerning the out-of-doors, the more you learn about a subject the better that knowledge can serve you on both a day-to-day and emergency basis. When the time comes to buy a sleeping bag you may make the most effective choice by saturating your mind with the subject until you feel that you are no longer encountering any new information.

a) Choosing a Sleeping Bag

There are so many variables involved in choosing a sleeping bag that it may be foolhardy on your part to expect someone else to make the choice for you because you will be left without the necessary and valuable background knowledge at a time you need it. If you must ask someone else to help you make any decisions concerning the type of bag you need, you may not be ready to own a good one. A poor bag used by a knowledgeable person may function adequately whereas even a good bag in the hands of a novice may not.

Some of the more obvious factors to consider when choosing a sleeping bag are as follows:

ROLE OF YOUR BAG: Are you a trapper, backpacker, canoeist, bicyclist, fall or spring camper, winter camper, summer camper, mountaineer or a pilot concerned with bush survival?

COMFORT RANGE: What are the temperatures for which to bag is going to be used? A good bag can span a twenty-five degree temperature range in which it can be comfortable. You have to decide which twenty-five degree span is applicable to your needs.

FILLER: What is the insulative material that will work the best under the circumstances? Is it down or synthetic? Your choice of role and comfort range may determine the type of filler you will need. Also consider your financial resources.

FABRIC: Your personal preference will determine what fabrics you choose in the construction of your bag. Allergies may require the avoidance of certain fabrics or insulation.

SIZE: What sort of personal space do you need inside a bag to feel comfortable? Some special needs may have an influence on the choice of bag size. The worst choice is a bag that is too small.

SHAPE: What shape of bag most adequately matches your role, comfort and financial circumstances? Four common shapes are generally available to choose from-mummy, tapered, rectangular, or barrel.

CONSTRUCTION: You should understand how the construction of a bag affects its comfort, warmth, durability and cost.

ACCESSORIES: Certain accessories may extend the comfort range, versatility and the longevity of a bag, such as hoods, covers, liners, foot space -flared or boxed and various zippers to name a few.

COST AND QUALITY: The greater the quality of the work, the more you should expect to pay.

Other Considerations:

- Do you use a tent or an open-fronted shelter? Will you be camping in open, windy country? The interior of a tent can be five degrees warmer than that of an open-fronted shelter. Wind may reduce the effectiveness of a bag considerably.
- Are you acclimatized to the cold? Subjects in a Swedish study were able to sleep in temperatures approaching 0 degrees Celsius with their normal clothing and a blanket to keep them warm. Some people sleep 'cold' and some people sleep 'warm'. There may be at least a 2 centimetre of insulation thickness difference at -40°C or F.
- Are you out-of-doors constantly or are you an office worker who likes to camp on week-ends?
- Are you physically fit? The more fit you are, the better your body can adjust to the cold.

How fat are you? Body fat may be a good insulator as long as it, itself, is warm.

- Do you sweat easily? Are you a nervous person, always in a sweat? Unfit people sweat more freely.
- Your day-to-day tolerance of the cold will also vary according to your health, when and what you have last eaten, and so on.
- How are you affected by fatigue, dampness, high altitude, etcetera?

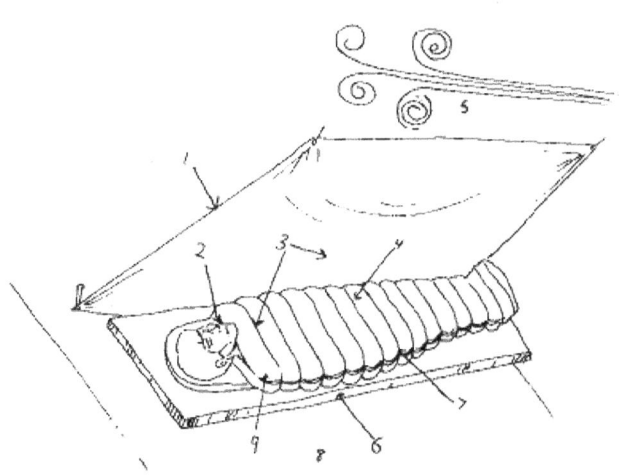

Some factors that can affect your comfort in a bag.

1. No shelter, open shelter, enclosed shelter.
2. What and how much you have just eaten?
3. How much moisture is in your bag and in the air?
4. Your metabolism.
5. How much wind and exposure? What is the orientation of your bag to the wind?
6. How adequate is the insulation under you?
7. How physically fit or fatigued are you?
8. Effect of altitude.

9. How acclimatized to cold are you?

b) Roles: Uses for Your Sleeping Bag

Under normal circumstances, if you've chosen your sleeping bag well, there will probably be very few bags in your outdoor life-perhaps three or four if you are an active out-of-doors recreationist. No one bag can fulfill all roles adequately and if you are a person who indulges in a variety of outdoor actives, then you may have to have a bag for each role, or a combination of bags to suit each role. The role of a bag may be more related to its efficiency than any other factor. Efficiency is being able to save as much warmth per gram of weight as possible.

Consider the following specialized roles:

THE MOUNTAINEER: Because of the great effort required to carry anything up a mountain, the greatest efficiency is sought. That is, weight and bulk must be pared down by all reasonable means. Bags suitable for mountaineering may have all frills minimized in the interests of the greatest warmth for the least weight. A favourite choice would be a pure down-filled mummy bag with little or no zipper and the least possible internal room.

THE BACKPACKER: Here efficiency is desirable but not to the extreme of the mountaineer. There is more compromise between efficiency, comfort, convenience and cost. Frills that allow greater comfort are allowable. Weight beyond two kilograms is not acceptable to the spring-summer-fall backpacker. A mummy that is neither too small nor too large, synthetic insulation with a full zipper going around the foot may be a popular choice here.

WATER TRAVELLERS: Canoeists, sailors and boaters who travel rivers, lakes, and oceans have weight and bulk needs that are not as critical as that of backpackers. However, they are always exposed to becoming wet. Whatever the style of the bag, the most suitable filler is one of the better synthetics, as it can provide an adequately warm bag, even when wet, and can dry quickly when wet.

THE WINTER CAMPER: The winter camper has much the same needs as the backpacker, except that a heavier bag is needed. There are certain construction techniques that are best avoided in the interests of efficiency. The bag's ability to allow the passage of the body's moisture produced by sensible and insensible perspiration is more critical. A slightly more roomy and longer bag may be necessary so that your clothing and boots may be kept inside to dry out or to keep from freezing or you may choose to wear your clothes if the bag is not warm enough by itself.

THE BASE CAMP AND VEHICLE CAMPER: These campers do not camp far from their means of transport. Campers who use horses, some canoeists, winter campers using toboggans, and aircraft survivalists where storage space is not a problem may come under this classification. The sleeping bag is seen as a greater convenience than moving normal bedding around. The prime consideration is comfort and luxury, where a little extra weight is not a problem. Sleeping robes or rectangular bags are feasible here.

THE POTENTIAL (AIRCRAFT) SURVIVALIST: The sleeping bag packed for survival purposes should be adequate to cope with colder temperatures. It should have a full length zipper both for venting and for accommodating injured people. A cover should be provided that is fire resistant in case the bag has to be used in conjunction with a fire in extreme cold. The filler should be able to take extensive abuse and little maintenance without losing efficiency. A mummy bag with a down filler would be a good choice. Many synthetics are easily damaged by being used near a fire because of their low melting point- especially the filler and the plastic zippers.

c) Comfort Range

The comfort range is the maximum and minimum temperatures that a bag is good for. The comfort range that is given on any bag should be taken only as a general guide. Above maximum the bag will be too warm. You may swelter in it, and in attempting to cool yourself you may chill those parts of your body that are outside of the bag. Given time you may be able to acclimatize to a bag so that you will not sweat as much if at all.

Below the minimum temperature the bag will be too cold. As long as the heat loss is slow enough that it can be compensated by the heat produced by the body, you may stay warm.

The warmth retaining capability of a bag is related to the thickness and quality of the insulation in it. The total thickness of the top and bottom parts of a bag is termed the loft. There is a rough relationship between loft and warmth.

Loft	Probable Comfort Range
5 cm	0° to +25°C
10 cm	-10° to +15°C
15 cm	-20° to +5°C
20 cm	-30° to -5°C
25 cm	-35° to -10°C

d) The Filler

i) Down

The ideal filler should be light and compressible for portability and it should hold out wind effectively, at the same time allowing body moisture to pass out. The material that can achieve the greatest difference between its compressed and free expanded state is down. A gram of acceptable down will compress into about 10 cubic centimetres and will expand to about 260 cubic centimetres. A term that may not readily change with metrics is 'lofting power'. This term is derived from one ounce of down being compressed (to about 20 cubic inches) and released to fully expand. If the new volume is 500 cubic inches then the lofting power of that particular sample is 500, which is reasonable. If it is 550 it is good, 600-very good; 650-beware of exaggeration; 750 is possible but very seldom encountered. In metric conversion the 750 lofting power would be the same as one gram of down yielding 360 cubic centimetres.

Down is the fluffy part of the plumage of a goose or duck that does not have a shaft, or quill (if it did it would be called a feather). Numerous down filaments are combined into a loose pom-pom-like configuration known as a pod or plumule. The filaments are what cling together to form the almost infinitesimal number of tiny trapped air pockets that inhibit the outward movement of the 'warmth' produced by the body and the inward movement of 'cold' from the outside. (Hopefully you can tolerate this simplistic explanation).

The best down comes from geese that have been raised in cold climates to full maturity. The mature goose has the largest down pods, hence the greatest loft. The pod of an

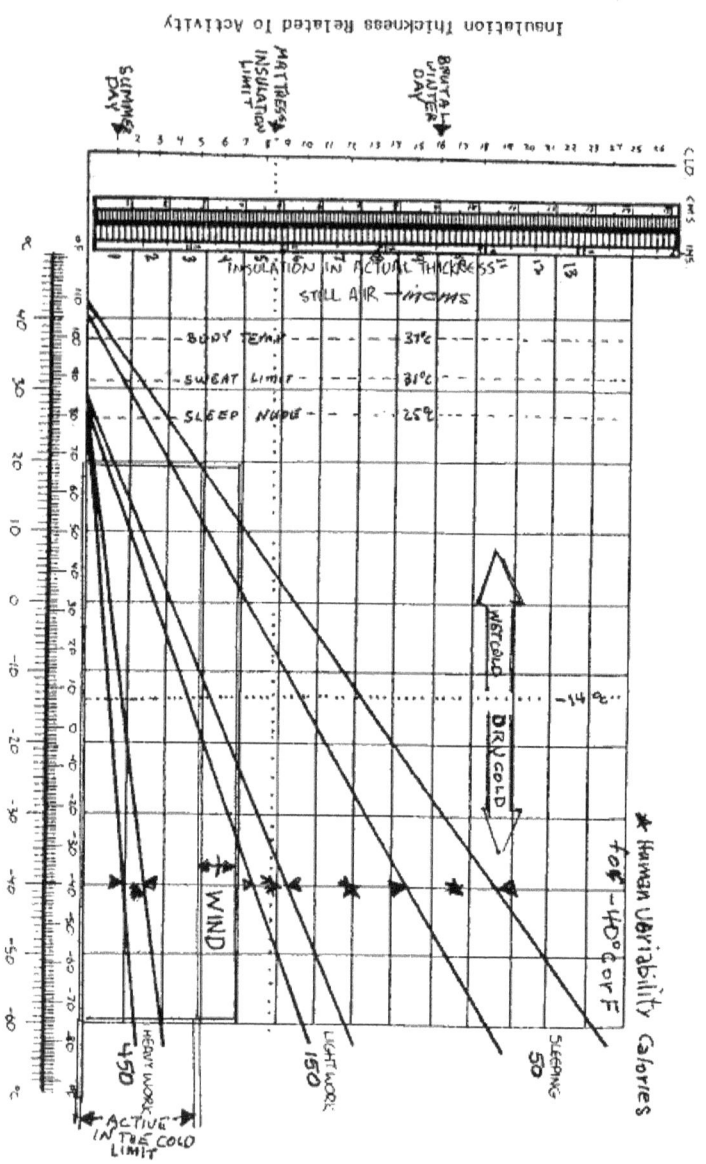

immature goose is about the same size as that of mature duck and be considered the same. Very little of this highest quality goose-down reaches the market as most geese are usually slaughtered before reaching maturity. Custom allows goose down to demand a higher price than duck down. For general backpacking duck down may be the better buy.

It is important to remember that the down must come from birds raised in a cold climate.

Down Pod and Feather Used in Sleeping Bags

Because of the way geese and ducks are raised their plumage may contain more than just down and feathers. Straw, mineral and organic soil, flakes of shredded epidermis and so on, may be included and may not be that easily separated from the down. The feathers, being on the surface, are usually pulled out first and kept separate from the down. However, it is not possible to remove all the feathers without it becoming excessively time consuming; in fact some feathers are so tiny and fluffy (at the base) that they are almost half down anyway. When the machinery for processing down was either primitive or non-existent, the industry was allowed (and likely still is) to include these hard-to-separate materials under the term "100% down". Actually 100% down may be about 85% actual down and even as low as 75% down. A label indicating 80% down and 20% feathers will have 75% of 80 or 60% actual down. the 20% feather content, because it is not specified as water-fowl feathers, can be plumage of any origin. If the label says down and feathers, you can expect 51% down and 39% actual down. If it states feathers and down then it must contain not less than 20% down which translates into 15% actual down.

One way to check the quality of down filler is to feel for the feather shafts or quills. If you can feel quills of the size of a pencil lead you definitely have a lower quality of down. The less noticeable the quills the better the quality providing it does not come from a duck raised in a warm climate.

Check and compare bags in you area's stores by the squeeze and pinch test and compare the feel with the stated price to see what relationship can be discerned, if any.

Advantages of Down

- Down is the warmest of fillers for the weight.
- Clean down is supposedly non allergenic.
- With careful use a down sleeping bag may last a lifetime.
- It's properties have been proven by long usage.
- Down is relatively durable, being able to maintain its loft indefinitely.

Disadvantages of Down

- Down is very expensive.
- Its insulation is reduced considerably when wet. ***But you should be severally taken to task for allowing your down insulation to become wet. Think ahead!!***

- A great deal of expense is involved in the construction aspect in keeping down where it belongs.
- It is difficult to dry on the trail.
- Down escapes readily when the enclosing fabric is torn.
- Down does not fare well in humid situations. It is subject to mildew.
- Down is prone to moth and rodent damage.
- Down is compressed to virtually nothing under the sleeper.
- Down requires special care in cleaning and washing.

ii) Synthetic Fillers

Down is for the purist who is looking for the lightest and very best and can afford it. Some synthetic fillers (polyester) have proven themselves to be worthy insulators. These materials have become more and more sophisticated enough to rival down.

Advantages of Synthetic Fillers

- Polyesters are less expensive.
- They wring out and dry easily.
- They retain most of their insulative effectiveness even when wet.
- They do not compress as much under the user.
- Laundering tends to increase loft.
- Synthetics are simpler to keep clean than down.
- Synthetics fare better in damp conditions.

Disadvantages of Synthetic Fillers

- Polyesters undergo resilience fatigue sooner than down.
- After 3 years even with the best of care there is significant deterioration in loft.

- Polyesters are heavier than down for the same insulative value.
- They do not conform to every body contour like down does.
- They are very sensitive to heat stress.

There are some tried and tested synthetic fillers that are worth considering for their historical aspect.

POLAR GUARD: This is a continuous filament batt that is spun like cotton candy. It is similar to Dacron II but is flammable. No longer produced by the original manufacturer but imitated by others who are making a similar continuous filament polyester.

DACRON FIBERFILLE II: This is made up of masses of short fibers that have been matted together and quilted. In comparing this filler to polar guard, there is no strong case to prefer one over the other. Both are from 20 to 40% bulkier than down.

DACRON II: 1.4 kilograms of Dacron II has the same insulative quality of 1 kilogram of down. Its compression factor is 90% that of down. Dacron II can be easily damaged by heat. Its plasticizing point is only 60 degrees C, the point at which its fibers lose strength and springiness. Laundering should be done in water that is barely warm to the touch. Some fillers will melt if used near a fire even though the outer shell remains undamaged.

e) Fabrics

Of the many fabrics used extensively in various applications of outdoor equipment and clothing the following are the most common.

i) Nylon

Nylon is one of the more popular fabrics for the out-of-doors. For a particular weight nylon will be stronger and take more wear than any other fabric. It does not mildew and it can be woven tightly enough to effectively confine down. Because of its low melting point (250 degrees C) nylon is easily damaged by fire. It does not burst into flame when brought near a source of intense heat, but shrinks away from it. A spark smoulders on the fabric and make a small hole.

Like the nylon cord that is notorious for not holding a knot, nylon fabric is noted for rapidly loosening and fraying at the edges, a process that can be arrested somewhat by melting the fiber ends together. This process is called hot cutting, which is found only in custom bags. In making your own bag you would accomplish this with a candle. Without hot cutting a generous seam allowance must be provided or the fabric unravels at the seam which then gives way. The edge of the fabric should be finished, preferably, by a zigzag stitch. You should be able to feel through the fabric to see if a generous seam allowance has been provided.

Some people claim that the silky feel or slipperiness of the fabric is advantageous especially for crawling in or out of a bag. Others find it objectionable because the nylon shell on a sleeping bag causes it to slip off the nylon cover of a mattress so easily. Nylon is a hard, round fiber that is a poor deflector of rain and does not take water repellents well. In sub zero weather, nylon tends to frost up on the outer shell of a sleeping bag from body moisture. Nylon against the bare skin feels cold for a few seconds but it is easy to become accustomed to.

Nylon fabrics used in sleeping bags are mainly ripstop and taffeta. Ripstop nylon has two heavy, twisted threads woven into the fabric about a half centimetre apart into half centimetre squares. This feature makes the fabric three or four times more resistant to tears. Nylon taffeta is nicer to the feel than ripstop. In the past it seemed to be less fashionable than ripstop although it is just as strong.

ii) Cotton

Cotton is still a valuable fabric in sleeping bag construction. It condenses less than nylon, is more readily made water repellent and has less static build-up. It can also be more wind resistant. The disadvantages are its low tear strength and its tendency to mildew. Although cotton does not melt at camp-fire heats, it can burn up if it is not made fire proof. A spark landing on the fabric can cause it to glow into a large hole and sometimes to be consumed entirely.

A fabric that may be quite suitable is a blend of 50 polyester, 25% nylon and 25% cotton. Having a number of different brand names, this fabric is softer and has less of the cold feel of nylon.

THE OUTER SHELL: The outer shell of a sleeping bag should be light in weight so as not to reduce loft, and should be tear and abrasion resistant.

The higher the thread count, the better. If nylon it should be at least 65 grams per square metre. If you make a double fold in the outer shell, and on applying the mouth, you can easily blow through it, the weave is too coarse.

THE INNER SHELL: The inner shell may be made of a lighter weight cloth. Ripstop nylon initially feels cold.

Nylon taffeta has a nicer feel than ripstop. Poplin and balloon cloth (cotton) have a silky feel and are highly absorbent fabrics that may interest those who are allergic to nylon. Cotton flannel is generally found in the less expensive bags. A cotton flannel inner shell with a cotton flannel liner will help keep the liner in place better.

f) Size

If a size is given on the label check out if it is the actual size. It is best to try out the bag. Wear clean clothes, take off your shoes, get into the bag and do it up completely. Stretch out the toes as far as possible and cross your arms comfortably. Turn over completely inside the bag (by placing hands near the hips, spread the bag as wide apart as possible, bearing down on the elbows and lifting the body and turning. For bags used in winter camping an allowance should be made for wearing of clothes in the bag as well as room at the feet for storing boots (wrapped in something appropriate) to keep them from freezing.

When in doubt choose the larger bag. If a bag is too large, there is more interior to heat, more weight and more cost, all unnecessary. If the bag is too small it will not keep you as warm as it should by not collapsing enough to reduce the voids. It will be cramped and the bag will be prone to damage as you try to stretch.

The size of the bag in which you can feel comfortable is a personal thing. You should pick a bag that makes you feel comfortable at the time of acquisition without making the assumption that you will eventually get used to any awkwardness of fit.

g) Bag Shape

i) The Mummy

In the mummy bag, the body's contours are followed closely so that the minimum of material is used in the construction of the bag and the minimum of interior space is allowed. This type of bag is for the coldest weather and the lightest weight, as it provides the greatest thermal efficiency for every gram carried. You find that you are confined like an insect in a cocoon and because of this many people find it difficult to feel comfortable so constricted. Down is a common filler but synthetics are also used. Other features that go well with this bag are a full length zipper with a draft tube, with extra insulation and more room at the feet (flared or boxed foot). The head covering is an integral part of the bag; only the user's nose and mouth are exposed. If a liner is used, it should be made of slippery material for greater manoeuvrability.

Follow these steps to get into a mummy bag without a zipper: Pull the bag onto your feet until the foot end is reached and the remainder of the bag is against your buttocks. Lift onto your heels and shoulders by arching your back and pull the bag up as far as possible. Then, sit up and pull the bag up around your shoulders.

ii)Tapered Bag

The tapered bag is midway between the rectangular bag and the mummy, having some of the advantages and disadvantages of both. It is not as heavy as a rectangular bag and it is more roomy than a mummy. This bag usually does not have an attached. hood.

iii) Rectangular Bag

The cheapest bags, both material and construction-wise, are found in this class. They are a favorite for mobile-type camping and for use as quilts and comforters in base camps, campers, trailers and holiday cottages.

This type of bag with its rectangular dimensions, is more comfortable and luxurious than any other bag. The use of this bag closely resembles sleeping in a normal bed. Due to its larger size it will have to have more voids to warm. It has to be heavier and bulkier to provide the same thermal efficiency as a mummy bag. Some people feel that the disadvantages are worth enduring for the additional comfort and luxury afforded by this shape. Since we spend a third of our life 'in a sack' this is a good place to add comfort to our lives.

The rectangular bag features a zipper running down one side and an end so that it can be spread flat to be used as a quilt or be joined to another bag.

iv) Barrel Shape

This bag is most specifically used by people who sleep in the fetal position. It is similar in many respects to the mummy.

v) Other Shapes

There may be various modifications, combinations and adaptations in shape. You should study sleeping bags enough to judge these for yourself.

h) Quilting

i) Simple Quilt

The sewing through the inner shell, the insulation and the outer shell holds everything in place. The thin spots that are created by the sewing reduces the effectiveness of the insulation at these points. This form of construction is valid and useful in warmer climates but not suitable for cold weather applications.

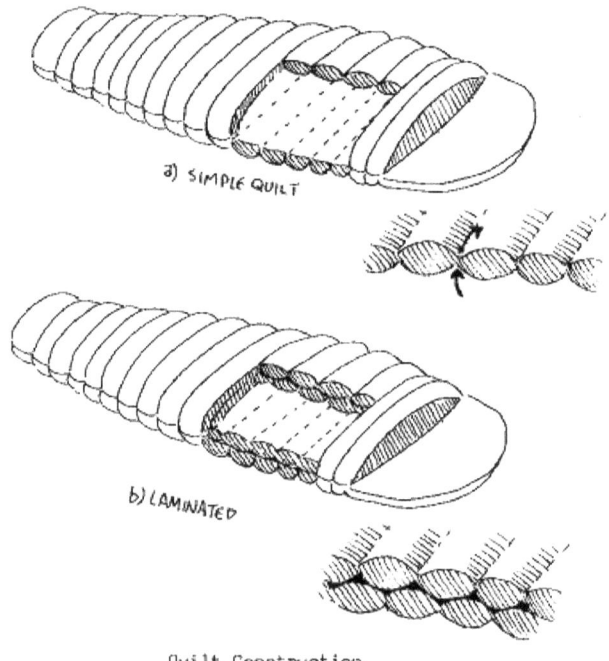

Quilt Construction

ii) Laminated

In this construction there are two quilted layers with offset rows of stitching and dead air spaces. The four layers of fabric used to enclose the insulation creates a heavier bag, it is often employed for heavy-duty applications at very low temperatures.

i) Baffling

The better quality bags use a construction where fabric dividers are used between inner and outer shell to hold the insulation in place.

Parallel walls or partitions are put between the inner and outer liners to create tube-like compartments sometimes known as channels. Baffles that occasionally block of the tube-like compartments are called channel blocks. The baffles are usually made of the thinnest cloth used in the bag, or sometimes netting to which down clings. Small baffled compartments may hold the down in place more effectively, but large compartments allow the down to reach maximum loft. Baffles should not be more than 20 centimetres or about a hand span apart. Some people are of the opinion that the best spacing between baffles is about 15 centimetres or less.

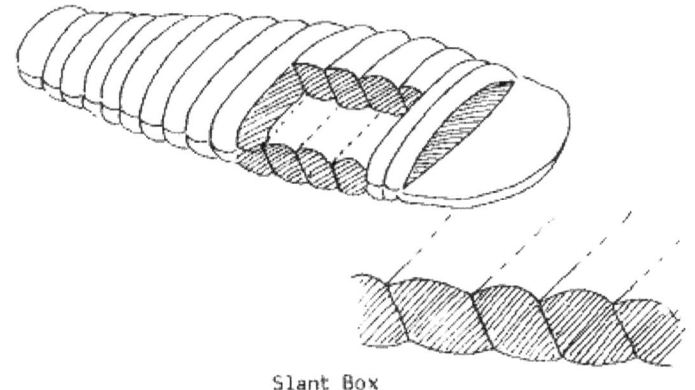

Slant Box

i) Slant Box

In the past this type was the most common type of construction. Manufacturers feel this method of baffling allow the least formation of cold spots.

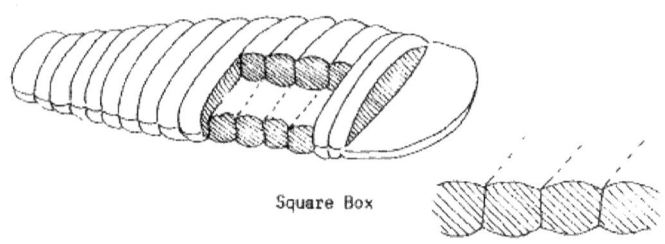

Square Box

ii) Square Box

There the walls are at right angles to the inner and outer shells.

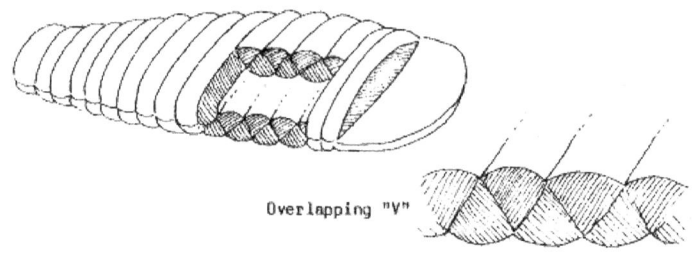

Overlapping "V"

iii) Overlapping 'V'

This allows the least shifting of the down but entails extra weight and extra work, thus extra expense. The major cost of a bag is the sewing of the baffles.

iv) Baffle Orientation

The baffles can be arranged in three ways. In the circumferential construction the baffles are arranged like rings around the body. In the longitudinal arrangement the baffles run parallel to the body where down filling tends to gravitate to the foot of the bag. It also does not display well when hung up in the store. The third method is the chevron, which is midway between the other two, neither going around the body or lying parallel to it. There may be little difference between any of the bag outside of down's tendency to shift foot-ward in longitudinal construction.

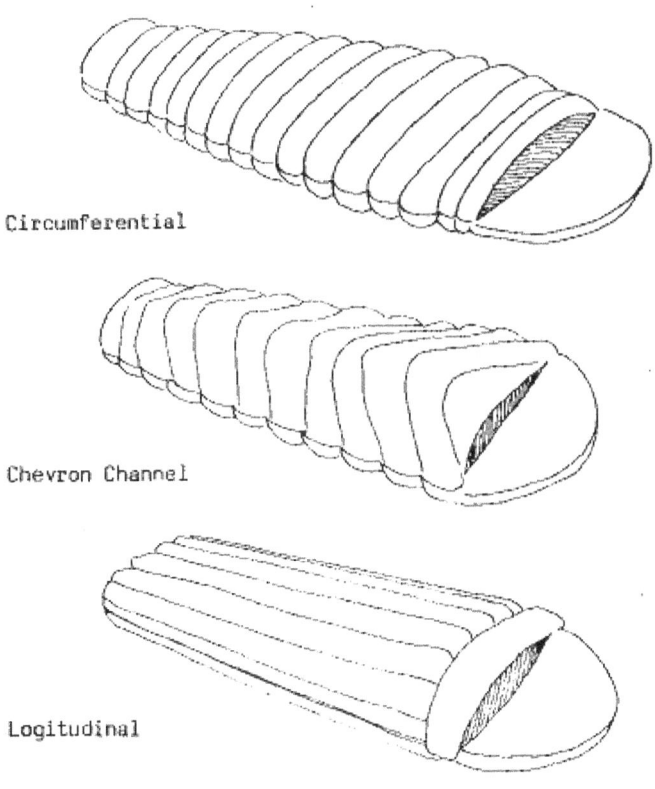

Circumferential

Chevron Channel

Logitudinal

v) **Channel Block**

The channel block is placed on the side opposite the zipper in circumferential and chevron bags to keep the down confined to its own half of the bag. In other words it keeps the down from shifting from top to bottom.

Some people feel that if the channel block is left out they can shift down from the lower part into the upper part when needed on colder nights and vice versa on warmer ones. However, when down is shifted around this way in cold conditions you will have to keep from turning in order not to expose your now more vulnerable underside.

j) How Synthetic Fillers are Kept in Place

Most synthetic fillers come in flat sheets of matted fibers, known as batts, that only have to be anchored down rather than to be confined in compartments (like down).

i) Sewn-Through Quilted Construction

The sewn-through construction is used in the less expensive bags and has similar disadvantages and advantages as down. It is less acceptable in cold usage and perhaps preferred for hot climates.

ii) Edge Stabilized Construction

This is another inexpensive construction technique: the layered batts are stitched to the edge of the bag's shell (at the zipper attachment and across the foot and head of the bag). The batt floats freely between the inner and outer shells of the bag. A disadvantage of this type of construction is that the bag tends to lose its shape, on account of the shifting of the batts in relation to each other when stuffed or laundered. The bag can be reshaped but this becomes tedious after a while. Although this construction may avoid a sewn-through seam the batts may eventually break loose and shift out of place, creating cold spots.

Edge Stabilized Construction

iii) Sandwich Construction

This is a combination of the advantages of both quilting and edge stabilization. Two to four layers of batts in both the top and bottom halves of a bag have the outer layer quilted to the outer shell and the inner layer quilted to the inner shell. The middle layers are edge stabilized. Everything is nicely kept in place, at the same time allowing full lofting. You may expect this type of construction in the better synthetic bags.

We are led to believe that synthetic fillers are now being developed that will be loose like down, requiring the same methods of confinement. This attempts to maximize on the good points of both.

iv) Shingle Construction

Another method for holding batts of synthetic insulation in place is call 'shingle' construction. This construction tends to resemble the Slant Box construction used with down. Batts of insulation are sewn to both the inside and outside fabric shells in an overlapping sequence. By varying the amount of overlap the weight and loft are controlled. This is proving to be a durable and efficient form of construction.

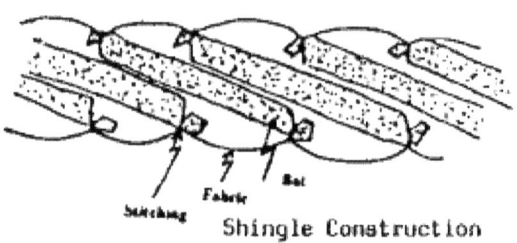

Shingle Construction

k) The Cut

The cut is the size relationship between the outer and inner shells of a sleeping bag. There are three alternatives:

i) Both shells may be exactly the same size (generally known as the straight cut).

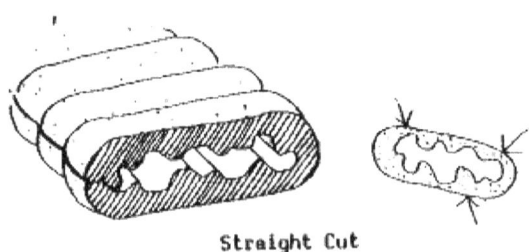

Straight Cut

ii) The inner shell may be smaller than the other shell.

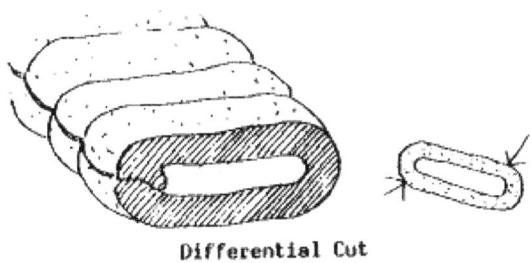

Differential Cut

iii) The inner shell may be larger than the outer shell.

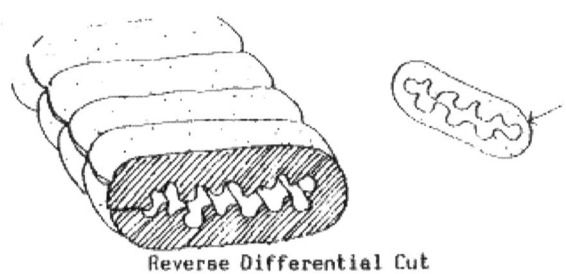

Reverse Differential Cut

1 and 2 are commonly available in sleeping bag construction. 3 can be achieved by turning (ii) inside out, as this type is not made intentionally by anyone as far as is known.

With the straight cut, down insulation tends to tuck around the body more effectively. With the synthetics, which are much stiffer, this may be inconsequential. The differential cut in which the inner shell is larger, is supposed to assist in preventing the compression of the insulation at the shoulders, elbows and knees. Sleeping bag users familiar with both cuts feel the difference to be so small as to be inconsequential and would opt for the less complex straight cut. Some claim that a differential cut bag is more effective when turned inside out, probably by more effectively filling any voids between body and bag.

l) Side Openings

The fewer side openings a bag has the fewer cold spots, the less weight, the less expense and the less versatility. A bag without side openings is more awkward for getting in and out of, is more difficult to vent in warmer conditions, unusable as a quilt, and can't be joined to other bags. Getting into such a bag is awkward if you are injured.

With all the variations to be found in a bag opening, three stand out. An opening the full length of the bag and across the bottom will facilitate laying it out flat for drying, airing and joining to other bags.

Another desirable feature is having the opening on the side of the bag rather than on the top, to minimize the reduction of loft and for better venting.

The third feature is a draft tube flap to more effectively close off and insulate the opening.

m) Closures

The side opening may be closed by a zipper, or more rarely snap fasteners. Snap fasteners are more dependable and versatile than a zipper, but are more awkward and time consuming to open and close.

THE ZIPPER: The best zipper is the coil zipper. It is the most expensive but it is the most snag-proof and jam-proof of all zippers and is self repairing.

The bigger the zipper teeth the better. Plastic is the best material for the teeth, with brass the next best and aluminum the worst. Some plastic zippers will melt and weld together if used near the fire. Imagine yourself being trapped in your bag.

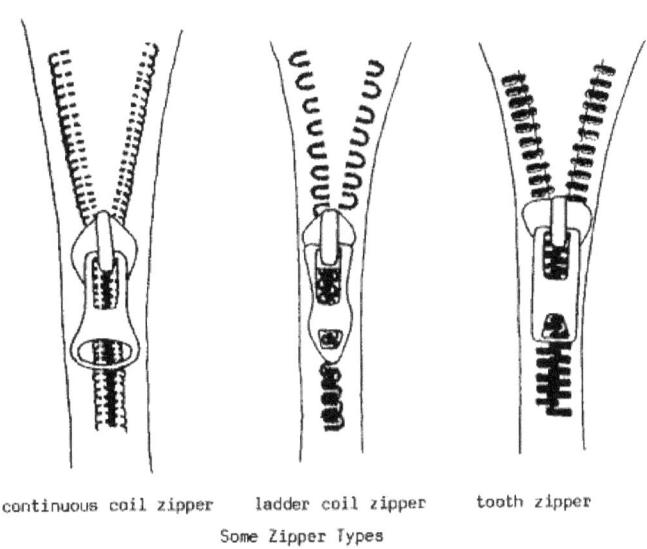

continuous coil zipper   ladder coil zipper   tooth zipper
Some Zipper Types

The zipper pull should be usable from both inside and outside and the zipper should be capable of opening from either end. There should be gussets at the foot end of the zipper with snap fasteners or Velcro tabs to close off the head end of the zipper. The acid test for zipper quality is to open and close the zipper at least a half dozen times to determine the smoothness of operation and the ease of closure. Any sticking or jamming may be taken as a sign of an inferior bag.

If there is any chance that the teeth may jam by grabbing some of the fabric of the bag, a flap of stiffer material should be sewn next to the zipper.

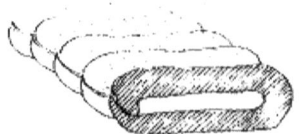

Integral Draft Tube

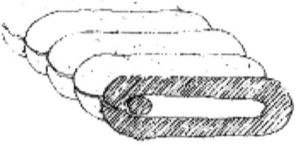

Sewn on Draft Tube

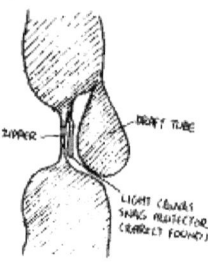

Detail of Sewn on Draft Tube

Bags used in cold weather must have a down-filled draft tube flap next to the zipper. the tube should hang down and be longer than the zipper. In a high-loft bag the tube should be densely packed with insulation.

The integral draft tube is preferred. A draft tube attached by sewing through the bag, as opposed to being attached to the inner shell, is of an inferior construction.

When matching bags that are to be zippered together, the draft tube of the right-handed bag hangs down by the action of gravity. If the draft tube on the left-handed bag is not positioned correctly so as to hang down, as often happens, will be less efficient as it pulls away from the zipper by gravity.

Bags to be zippered together must have paired zippers being of the same type and brand. A bag with a zipper on the right is paired with a bag with a zipper on the left.

n) Foot Section

The foot section should be generous in size and be uniformly insulated. Check the thickness of insulation, with a hand inside and the other outside, by gently pressing the hands together. A down bag should have horizontal baffles across the foot to keep the fill from collapsing to the bottom.

o) Hoods

A properly made and fitted hood is a definite advantage by extending the range of a bag 5 to 8 degrees Celsius. A poorly designed hood will be neglected as it may simply be too uncomfortable to use (especially with synthetic filler). Properly designed hoods are tedious to make, therefore expensive. Hoods may only be worthwhile with down fill and more economically avoided with synthetic fills. A hood must feel comfortable, be easily and quickly drawn around the face, and stay where you want it.

p) The Liner

Sleeping bag liners have their positive and negative points:

1. The use of a liner will significantly reduce the number of times a bag may have to be washed or cleaned. You may go four times as long between washings or cleanings. The liner protects the bag from soiling by

skin oils, grime and perspiration. If need be the liner should be of a material easily laundered on the trail.
2. A liner may extend the comfort range of a bag by at least five degrees Celsius.
3. The sliding action of some liner fabrics makes movement easier inside the bag.

On the negative side, the versatility associated with the liner is obtained at the expense of additional weight. Liners and certain people, because of their sleeping idiosyncrasies, can never work together. Uncomfortable twisting and tangling and damage to the bag may result.

An alternative to a liner are night clothes which keep a bag as clean as any liner, with greater comfort when you have to get up in the night.

q) Outer Cover

In some circumstances a thin nylon outer cover for your bag may be worth its weight and bother in usage. It may protect the outside of the bag from grime, spruce gum and other sticky substances. If the bag is used near a fire, it may act as a spark arrestor. In an open shelter it adds additional wind protection to your bag.

r) Sewing

Examine all stitching, especially seams enduring stress such as along zippers and draw strings. These areas should be double stitched.

A superior bag will not have any stitches that hold the baffles in place exposed to wear and tear on the surface, because the baffles will come loose eventually and allow the insulation to shift. One way to cope with the problem is to tuck the baffle stitch line under a pinch of surface fabric.

The hardest part of the bag to sew is the inside of the foot. The quality of the work here will likely reflect on the rest of the bag.

The thread should be of nylon or Dacron. Four stitches per centimetre is very good, three is acceptable and two is poor.

s) Cost and Quality

In buying a good bag you will find that you get what you pay for. Quality materials and quality work are not free. Half the expense is in the materials and the other half is in the labour of construction. It is highly unlikely that a poorly constructed bag will be stuffed with superior down. Similarly, a well constructed bag is not likely to be filled with poor down. It helps to seek out a reputable manufacturer.

Bags that are similar in construction, weight of down used and loft size, and comfort range should be somewhat similar in price. If a bag is similar in everything but price, the cheaper bag may have a poorer quality of filling.

Comparing bags by their weight of insulation is only useful if both bags have exactly the same surface area. A cheaper bag is usually more poorly sewn together, is probably made with a lighter weight of nylon, has no two-way zipper, has a cheaper zipper, has inadequate foot room, and will have poorer hood design and closure. The cheaper bag may use a design that facilitates the ease of construction rather than ease of bag use.

t) Suggested Checklist to Use When Buying Your (First) Sleeping Bag

1. Become conversant with the information in this article.
2. Send away for various catalogues that carry sleeping bags and study the information provided by the manufacturers.
3. If possible visit local stores and examine and compare various bags by using as many of your senses as possible.
4. Decide on the features you would like in a bag.

    1. Are you allergic to nylon? If so, a cotton inner shell may be necessary.
    2. What comfort range will suit you?
    3. What weight of bag can you carry?

5. Sewing: Check every corner of the bag for flaws. The less stitching that is visible the better. In the best bags the stitch lines holding the baffles in place may be tucked under a pinch of surface fabric. Are the stitch lines even? Are the seams backstitched to secure them? There should be at least three or four stitches per centimetre. A good indicator of quality of work is the inside foot of the bag-one of the more difficult parts to sew.
6. Standing up, put the bag over your head and examine the seams against the light to see if any sewn-through seams exist. The light will shine through them.
7. Seams: Feel around the seams to see if a generous seam allowance has been provided, especially if the bag is synthetically filled.
8. Filler: If down, roll the filler between your fingers to see how much quill may be included. When examining stitching also look for light spots indicating a void in the fill, especially in the foot area.

9. When comparing bags which have synthetic fillers, look for greater loft, lighter weight, easier stuffing in stuff sack, and softness of drape. It is difficult to determine the thickness of fill with synthetic insulation.
10. Zipper: Open and close the zipper six to twelve times. It should have interior and exterior pulls and be able to be opened top or bottom. A well designed draft tube is necessary to avoid snagging. The continuous coil zipper is the best, but all zippers are likely much the same in operation. Poor zippers do not survive in the competitive market.
11. The best designs and materials are a waste if the bag is shoddily made.
12. Care: What direction does the manufacturers provide with regard to the cleaning and care of the bag?

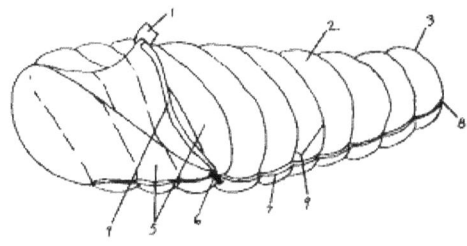

Points to Look for in a Bag

1. Velcro closure at top of zipper.
2. All seams and threads hidden.
3. Fully baffled box foot.
4. Draft tube extends full length of bag.
5. Ripstop nylon or nylon taffeta inner or outer shells hot cut of treated to prevent fraying.
6. Zipper pull can be used inside and outside of bag.
7. With of channels should be 15 cms. Or less.

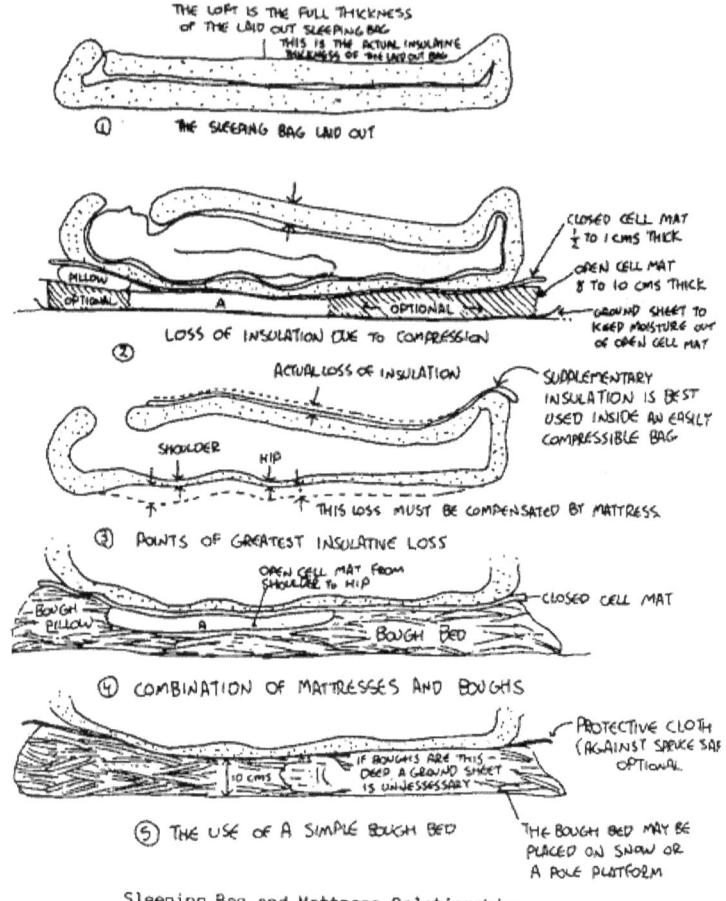

Sleeping Bag and Mattress Relationships

3. The Functional Bush Knife and Its Use

The one tool that may surpass the knife in basic existence skills and survival is the axe. The knife, however, is the more constant and unobtrusive companion, which for its weight and size is still one of the more functional tools of choice for the jobs that are too small for the axe. As well, it is adequate for spring, summer and fall survival needs. The well trained user should find that the knife alone is an adequate tool for winter survival as well. A well designed hatchet, however, would still be the more useful tool in bush survival if a choice between the two has to be made.

a) The Mora Knife

There are many kinds of specialized knives, such as butcher knives and filleting knives, which could have a legitimate place in basic existence. This chapter is confined to the common and readily available Mora. It will hold its own whether you are sharpening a pencil or butchering a moose.

Case-Knife Central Lapp 1901

Made in Mora, Sweden, a region renowned for its stable and exceptionally fine grained steels, this knife goes back a long way in Scandinavian traditions, a style tested by time. It is commonly available, quite inexpensive (considering the high quality of material and workmanship), usually sharp enough to get at least ten to twenty hours of normal usage before sharpening, and is simple to teach how to sharpen properly. The knife happens to be an inexpensive mass production item but nonetheless is very functional design.

A discussion of the desirable features in a bush knife may be helpful in determining the quality of the design of any knife at hand.

b) Function Design

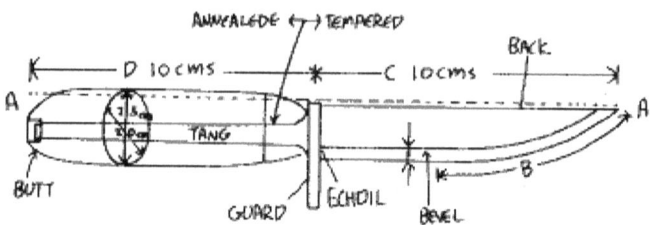

1. The most functional knife tip in a general purpose knife is shown above. The top edge of the knife handle should be in line, or very nearly so, with the top edge of the blade as shown.
2. This curved portion of any knife blade is the easiest to sharpen to a razor's edge. This part of the blade will make the best shavings in planning or making a feather stick. A good woodworking knife would have a blade only as long as the (B) portion, or be about five centimetres long or the width of one's palm.

    When doing fine work with a long bladed knife, the hand may have to creep up on the blade as shown in the diagramon page 74 for more precise control. A knife with a continuous curvature right to the hilt (or choil) may be the best yet.

3. Length of Blade: The longer blade (but only up to 10 centimetres) provides a larger target when the back of the knife is struck with a heavy stick (in the baton usage of the knife) to make heavy cuts. No portion of the back of the blade should be sharpened or the baton will get cut to pieces, the two corners however should be as sharp as possible.

4. Handle Size and Shape: The heavy usage that may be demanded of the knife in a survival situation can raise large painful blisters in the palm of the hand, usually at the junction of the thumb and forefinger and occasionally at the base of the little finger. The handle should not be too small, too large, too round or too sharp cornered.
5. Guards: Some knives have a guard that projects above and below the handle. The part that projects above serves only to interfere with a comfortable usage of the knife and should be cut off and filed smooth. The lower projecting guard can fit between the fingers when the hand creeps up on the blade for greater control, but it will be in the way when the knife is used as a shear. In the Scandinavian tradition the preferred knife has no guard.
6. Bevel: The Mora knife may have a flat or a slightly hollow ground bevel. This predetermined bevel simplifies learning correct sharpening. Simply hold the bevel absolutely flat against a stone or sharpening board and move the knife back and forth. The whole bevel face should begin to shine (like a mirror eventually), if you are using the right abrasive and the correct procedure. The new knife is usually sharp enough for about 10 to 20 hours of use when carving wood. It makes better sense, however, to touch up the edge every half hour of use in order to avoid a major sharpening job from a few days of hard usage. To maintain the edge, the only sharpening device needed is a board with 600 grit wet-and-dry sandpaper affixed on it with carpet tape.

Most Mora knife blades consist of a high quality steel sandwiched between two layers of more shock absorbing steel. This tends to make the blade less brittle, more easily sharpened and allows a higher quality steel to go further. This steel is also good enough to produce sparks for the flint and steel method of fire lighting.

7. Weight: The knife should be no heavier than necessary, without sacrificing strength. In this respect the Mora knife is weak at the juncture of the handle and the blade. It will bend if care is not used with the baton or in using it as a shear when making heavy cuts. It also has a tendency to fracture within the handle at the junction of the annealed and tempered part of the tang. This is probably the single major negative aspect of this knife.

The Skookum Survival Knife, An example of a "pry bar" that works wood very very well.

1. A blade as long as the palm is wide.
2. A handle that fits a hand comfortably made of an indestructible material.
3. Blade of continuous curvature for its full length and of a Scandi grind for easily maintaining a sharp edge.
4. A thick, strong, full tang blade.

5. A metal butt plate to protect handle and to pound with.
6. Hole for a lanyard to prevent loss.
7. Back blade corners, very sharp for scraping.
8. Netting needle.
9. Netting gauge.

If a survival knife cannot carve a netting needle in 5 to 10 minutes it will not be able to assist in constructing many wooden projects in survival.

c) Wood Shavings: Feather sticks

Any good knife proves its worth by making fire lighting easier. In conditions adverse to fire lighting, the knife should easily shave off fine, easy to ignite kindling. Being able to make regular fine shavings from dry wood in the form of a feather stick is a minimal knife skill.

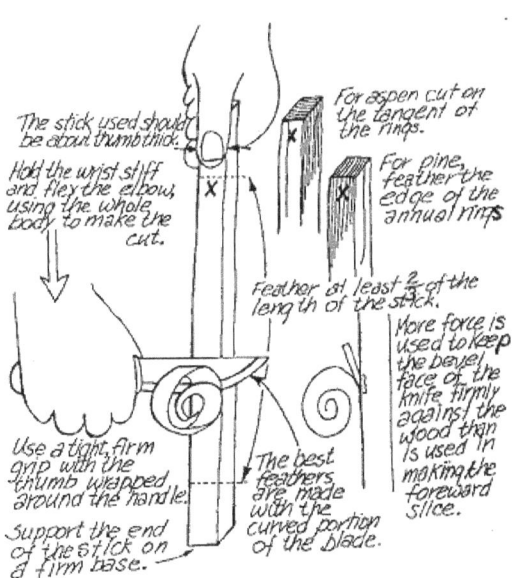

Feathering

The standard feather stick is about elbow to fingertip long and about as thick as the thumb. The feathers that are shaved off should use up at least three quarters of the length of the stick and leave about one quarter of the thickness remaining in the completed feather stick. The best shavings will not break off easily when handled and will burn well.

Support the end of a knot free and straight grained stick on the ground or on a log. Make a few shaves with the knife for the full length of the stick. This will prepare a more regular area to work on that is fairly parallel to the grain. Using the curved portion of the blade and keeping the bevel as flat as possible against the wood, take as fine a shaving as you can. Keep the wrist rigid and work with the shoulder and elbow. For longer cuts, the wrist and elbow may be held rigid and the movement of the knife blade made by moving the whole body up and down by the use of the knees and waist. As the knife is brought back, attempt to glide the bevel back on the wood as flat as possible. The force used in pressing the knife against the wood in the forward and reverse strokes may be greater than the force needed to make the shavings.

The grain of the wood can influence the way the shavings will cut. In pine, the best shavings are usually cut off the edges of the annual rings; in aspen, shavings are usually made tangent to the annual rings. Trial and error occasionally determines that the opposite works better.

Make all the shavings of the same length. At the end of the cutting stroke, bend the shaving away from the stick by rotating the knife blade about forty-five to ninety degrees away from the stick. The best feathers are ones that tend to be flat and have the feathers at one end.

Basic Safe Travel and Boreal Survival

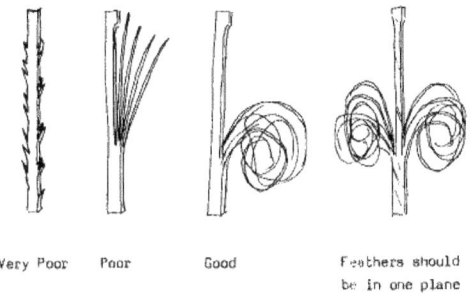

Very Poor   Poor   Good   Feathers should be in one plane

Types of Feathersticks

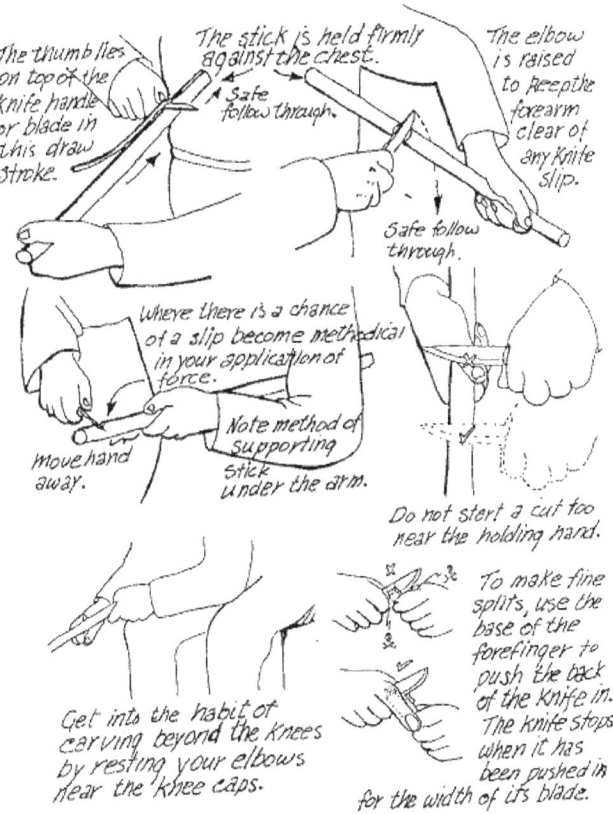

Safe follow through and avoiding the most common knife cuts while carving.

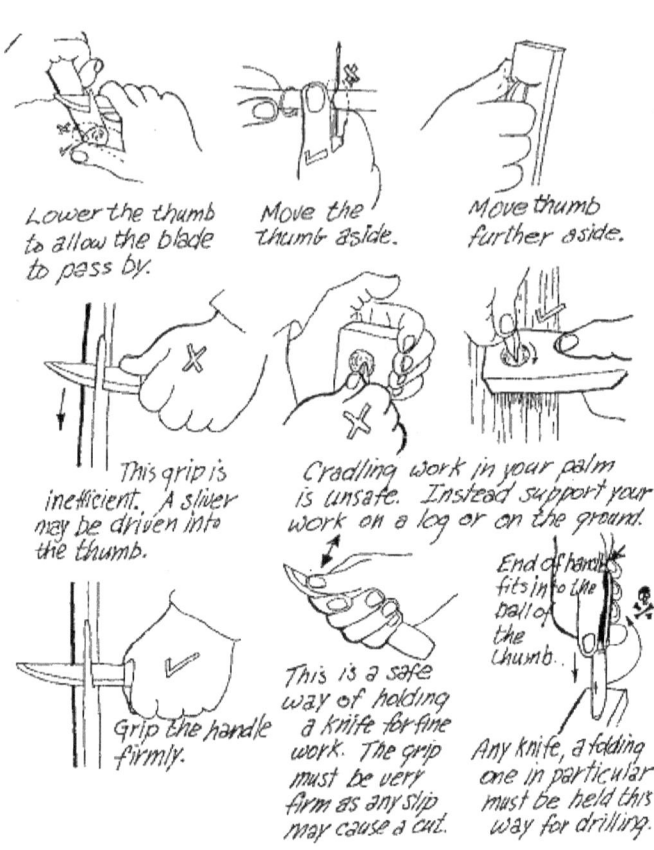

Avoiding the most common cuts while carving.

d) Cutting Down Trees with a Knife

Almost any green tree that is wrist thick or less can be bent, and usually can be easily cut down with a knife. Some soft wooded trees like Populus balsamifera (black poplar or cottonwood), up to ten centimetres in diameter, have been cut down by this technique. A frozen tree is more difficult to cut but it is more easily broken by starting the break with a cut. Stiffer and larger trees can be made to bend more readily by flexing back and forth; more mechanical advantage can be gained by taking a grasp nearer the top of the tree.

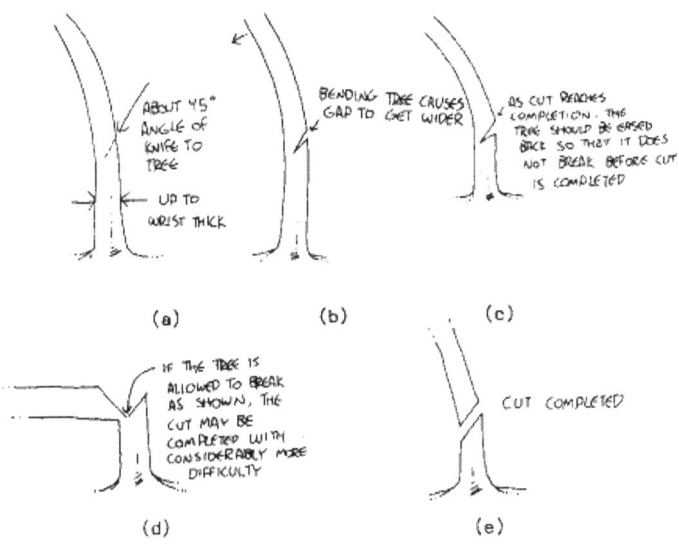

After the tree is bent the knife is applied at about a 45 degree angle to the part of the trunk that is at the middle of the bend. The bending action opens up the cut so the knife blade meets less resistance as it proceeds through the wood. The wood fibers that are put under tension in this way seem to cut easier. As the cut nears completion, the tree should be restrained from breaking by easing up on the bending action and occasionally even restraining the tree from falling of its own weight. If the tree should break, providing it is not frozen, completing the cut is usually made the more difficult. If the wood is tough or the tree is a larger one, the knife is rocked back and forth longitudinally to help make the cut. One way to cut off the top of the tree, is to stand on it and flex it over the thigh to produce the desired bend.

Care must be taken to avoid cutting into some part of the leg when using this technique.

e) Using the Knife with a Baton

Most knives make poor chopping tools as they have so little weight to utilize inertia. The effectiveness of a knife for limbing or cutting through smaller diameter saplings and larger trees can be increased by the use of a stick or 'baton' that imparts its inertia to the knife as it strikes it. Also, a dull knife may be made to function passably well this way. The baton is any stick found or made on the spot, about elbow to fingertip long and about wrist thick or less in diameter. The heavier it is the better, as long as it is comfortable to hold.

The best knife to use with the method is one that is strong enough at the juncture of the blade and handle to resist bending. Over exuberance in pounding too hard will result in the bent handle. Using a folding knife puts a severe strain on the pin holding the blade.

Larger trees of up to ten centimetres in diameter (that can't be bent) can be cut down with a baton by cutting out vee notches and enlarging them. Choose a knife that can stand the abuse. The knife tip can be driven into the cut at 90 degrees to the grain and worked back and forth to cut more fibers with less effort than vee notching. Pounding hard on the end of a Mora knife handle, as it is presently made, especially those with the spring clip, either damages or splits the handle.

When limbing with the knife, the butt end of your pole may be placed on the shoulder for trees that point upward. This will help to speed up the process. The reverse is used for black spruce. As you work your way up the pole, it will eventually stand straight up or the butt end will flop down behind you. In this case you might continue limbing above eye level.

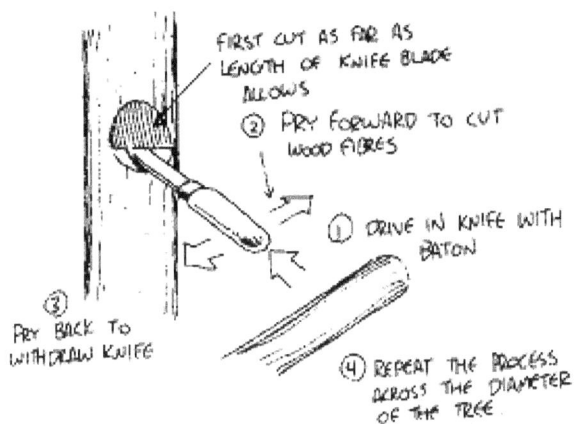

Cutting tree by pounding tip into wood

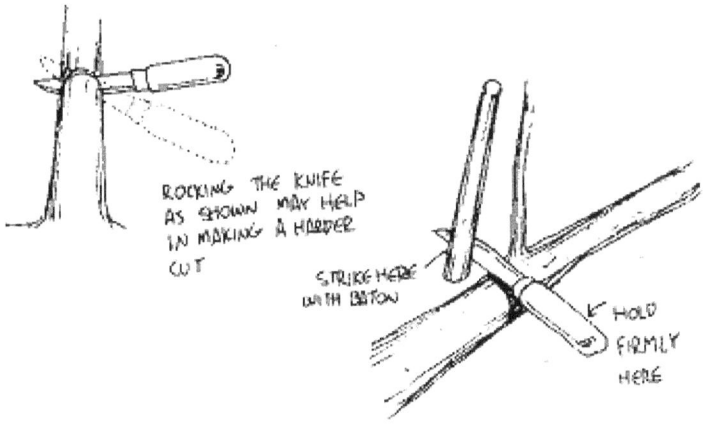

The baton method is useful in cutting through the brisket of a large game animal when you have need to field dress it. In my experience a rather solid heavy baton has to be used for the larger game animals.

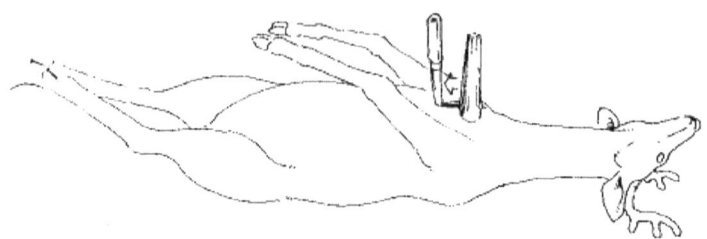

Cutting through brisket of deer

Many operations with the try stick may be speeded up with the baton as well as taking the stress of heavy knife use off the palm of the hand holding the knife. Women readily adopt the baton technique as their wrists and hands are not as powerful as that of men. For example, the pot hook in the following figure can be made in about 30 seconds or less. The vee notches cut on the butt end of the sticks making up the Roycraft Emergency snowshoe are executed faster and less awkwardly with a baton.

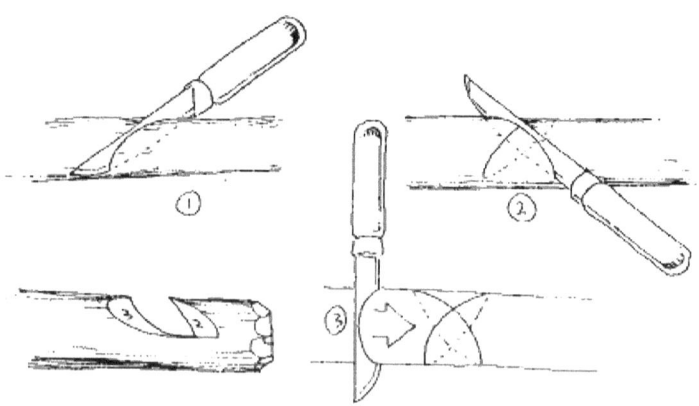

Procedure in making pot hook with baton

f) Knife Shear

The knife shear can be used in rapidly making short pieces of sticks. These can be used when cones or pebbles are not available to tie down plastic and parachute material or to cut plugs when making whistles out of cow parsnip. The shear can also be used in trimming wands and spokes in basketry or in collecting samples of twigs for plant identification. A suitable green stick is found that is about 30 centimetres long with a knot or fork at one end that would tend to resist splitting. The knife tip is driven through the stick slightly below the knot. A vee notch is cut into the stick about a finger width away from the edge of the knife to grip whatever is being sheared as shown in the diagram below. Use care with this device as it could easily cut off a finger. If a knife is being used a lot as a shear it is suggested that a hole be drilled in the knife blade about one or two centimetres back from the tip so that a small nail can be inserted to help keep the knife from backing out of its slot. With the Mora knife care should be taken not to use too much force in bearing down on the handle or the knife may be bent.

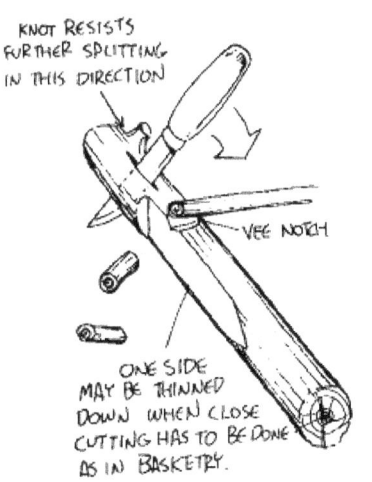

g) Knife Plane

When a spoke shave or planing device is needed to smooth down a shaft or a canoe handle, a device may be carved that can act as a plane with the knife blade being the plane iron.

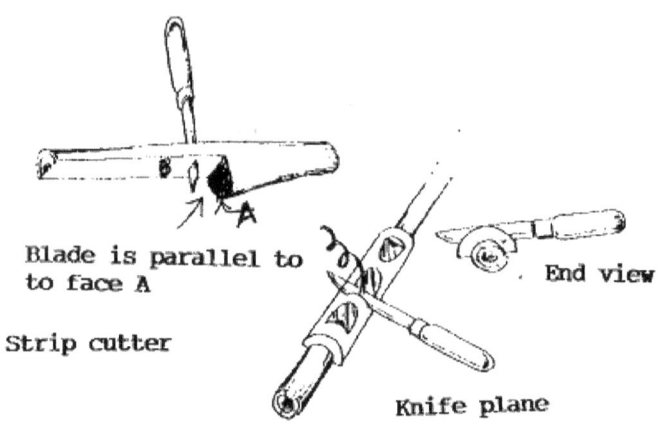

h) Strip Cutter

A forked willow stick can be used and carved out to produce another useful tool. Faces A and B are ninety degrees to each other. The knife tip is driven into the stick so that it is parallel to face A. The width of the strip is determined by the space between the knife tip and face A. The device may be employed in cutting strips in spruce basketry, cutting leather or rawhide strips and in rabbeting wood. To cut perfect circles a variant of the incisor is made into a beam compass with a nail acting as a pivot. This is useful in cutting round lids for birch bark boxes and for constructing sextant's.

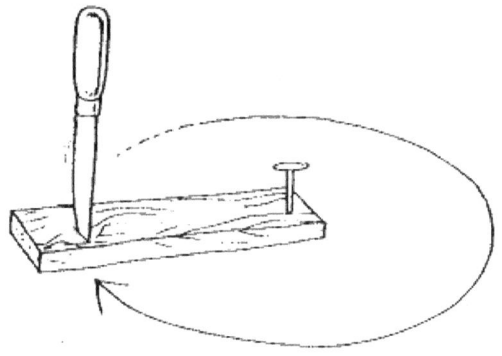

How to cut circles with a knife

i) Router or Groover

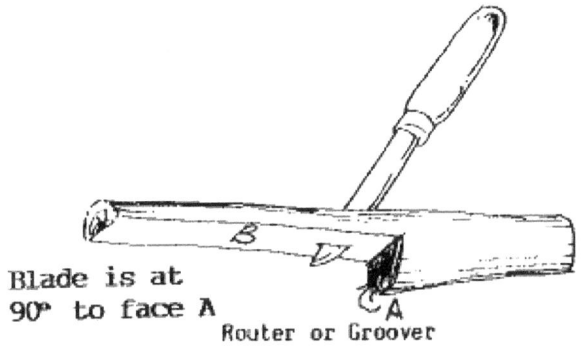

Router or Groover

If the blade is driven in so that it is ninety degrees to face A, it may be used to scrape grooves in the edge of boards.

j) The Tail: Increasing Visibility and Preventing Loss

The handle may be sanded smooth and painted fluorescent orange, or at least taped with fluorescent orange tape (found in hardware stores and in automotive parts sections) to increase visibility.

One form of common loss of the knife is from accidentally falling into soft snow and disappearing. If a tail of nylon cord about thirty centimetres long with a fluorescent tag on the end is attached, the tag should still be visible on the surface even though the knife is buried. A small hole is drilled near the end of the handle to accept the nylon cord. If loss of the knife could be critical, the cord can attach the knife to a belt or belt loop. In working over water, in high places or other situations where dropping the knife could be critical, the knife could be attached to the wrist.

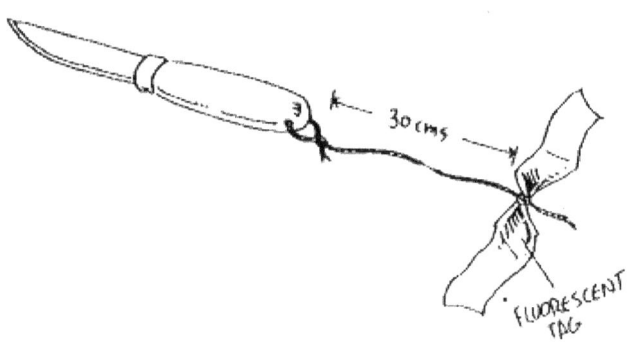

There are numerous stones and devices for sharpening knives. These are often expensive, fragile and awkward to carry around. A passable, inexpensive substitute are abrasive surfaces that are made with carborundum paper, emery cloth, wet and dry sand paper stuck on to plywood or boards with pressure sensitive or carpet tape. They are relatively inexpensive, light and present a large working surface. This method is a good way to master the basics of sharpening, after which you will be able to make a better decision as to what you really need in the way of sharpening tools.

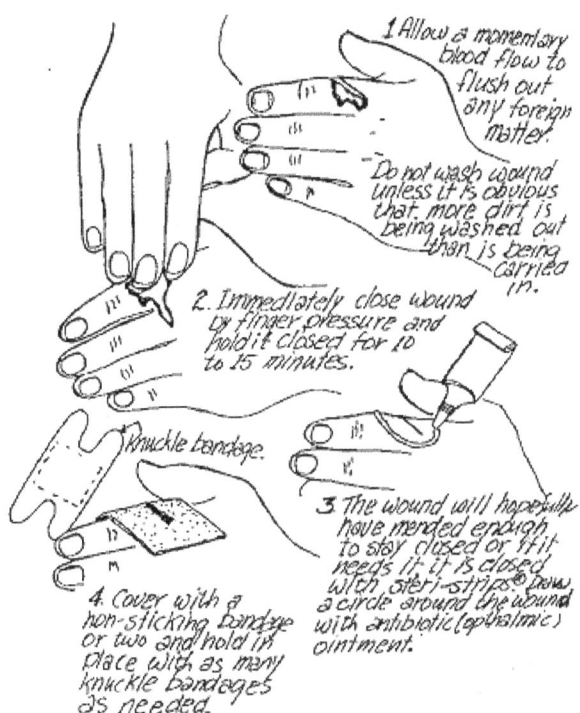

The basic method of handling knife cuts.

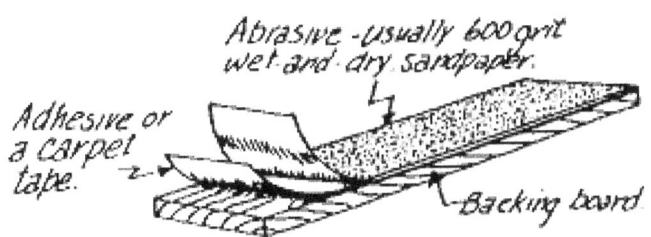

Depending on your needs, you may mount the full sheet of abrasive or any convenient fraction of it. Full size sheets are useful when sharpening large knives (like kitchen, butcher or long bladed filleting knives), while a board five by fifteen centimetres is handier to carry in your back pocket if you like to touch up the edge of your pocketknife frequently.

The main disadvantage of sharpening boards is that the thin abrasive surface can be cut up if too much pressure is used in sharpening. Compared to sharpening on stones, lighter strokes are used and more strokes have to be made to compensate for the lack of pressure. The coarse surface boards will wear out faster than a stone but the finer surfaces become more valuable with use, because as they wear they approach the hone in surface texture, which is the second last stage in sharpening. This does away with the need to make hones out of crocus cloth.

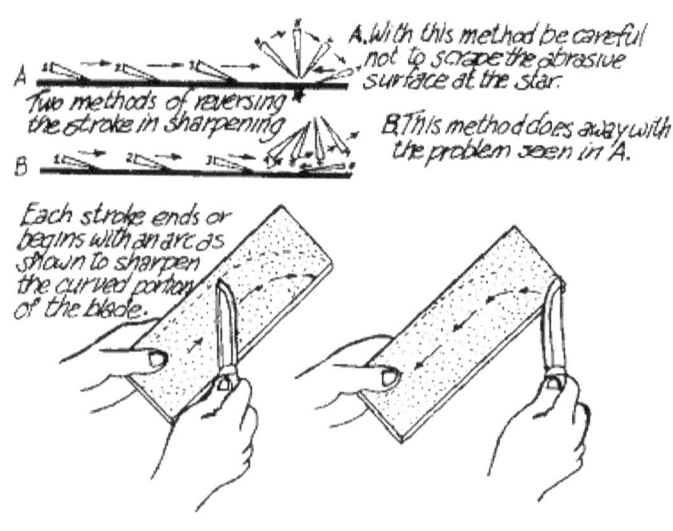

If a dull edge is magnified, it will be found to have a flat, rounded configuration where the sharp edge should be. Sharpening removes the metal at one or both sides of the blade to re-establish the new edge. This is accomplished by the use of abrasive surfaces that grind away the unwanted metal. This may be done in five stages: course, medium, fine, hone and strop.

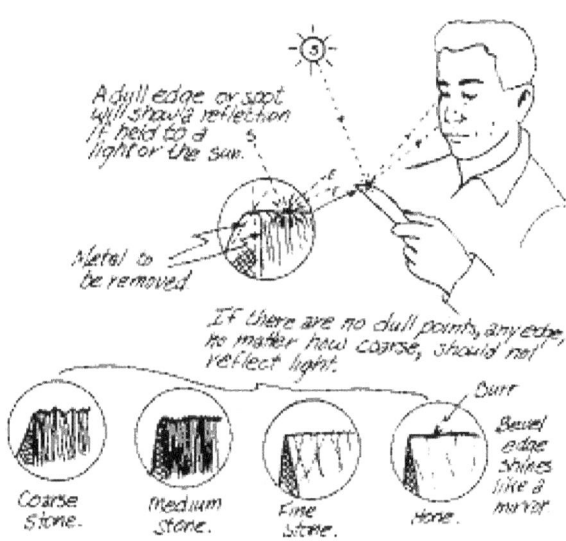

Magnified representations of an edge at various stages of sharpness

A coarse abrasive will remove metal relatively rapidly, but leaves a rough bevel face and a saw-like edge where the serrations from one side of the blade meet those of the other side. Initially, this saw-like edge seems to cut well when used for skinning or to cut meat for a few minutes and then it has to be wiped to regain its sharpness. This is likely because fat and fibres are caught between the teeth. Such an edge seems to dull rapidly for the same reasons when working with wood. The teeth also break off more rapidly and so this type of edge dulls faster than a straight edge.

Using too fine an abrasive too soon prolongs the sharpening process. The fine art of sharpening required that the switch to a finer abrasive surface be made at the right time, as persisting at a courser surface places needless wear and tear on both the blade and sharpening surface.

Once the coarse surface establishes the edge, the medium surface replaces the coarse serrations with its own. Then the fine surface erases the serrations of the medium surface. By now the teeth at the edge are becoming very fine, to be subsequently replaced with a straight edge by the very smooth and hard surface of the hone.

The action of the hone, more so than the previous stages, produces a fine hinge of metal that defies removal by its hard surface. This fine hinge of metal is known as the burr. It is produced when the steel in the blade reaches a certain critical thinness that makes it very flexible so that it flops over to the side opposite from the hone, until it gets so long that it gets torn off.

As the burr is generally difficult to see with the unaided eye, most people ignore it. In the first few cuts that the edge makes, the burr is torn off with the undesirable consequence that it takes some of the good edge with it, or it may also leave the edge in a disturbed state so that it dulls more rapidly than it should. Some sources claim that the burr formed when the edge leads while being sharpened is much finer than the one produced when the edge is dragged. This more substantial burr takes with it more of the edge when it is torn off. It is commonly observed that when the burr is properly removed with a strop, the edge seems to stay sharp longer.

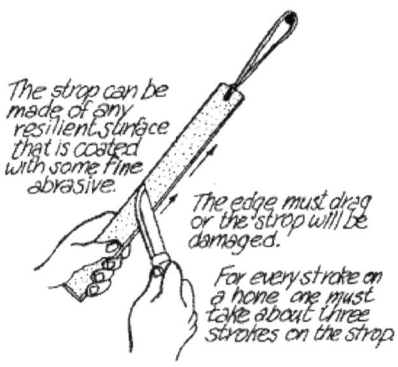

The strop can be made of any resilient surface that is coated with some fine abrasive.

The edge must drag or the strop will be damaged.

For every stroke on a hone one must take about three strokes on the strop.

The strop is the final stage of sharpening, which, with its resilient surface and very fine abrasive action, manages to effectively remove the fine metal hinge by bulging up behind the rigid edge of the blade as it is dragged along the strop. The edge must be dragged on the strop or the strop will be cut to pieces.

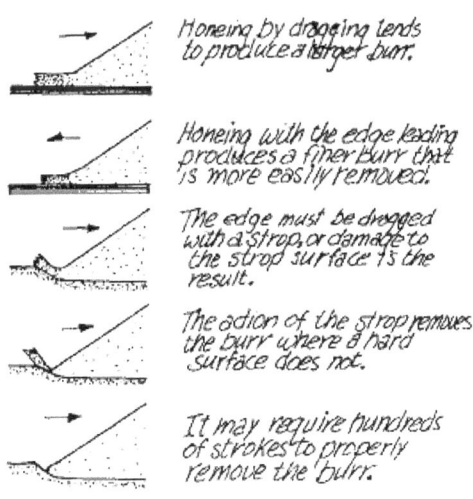

Honing by dragging tends to produce a larger burr.

Honing with the edge leading produces a finer burr that is more easily removed.

The edge must be dragged with a strop, or damage to the strop surface is the result.

The action of the strop removes the burr where a hard surface does not.

It may require hundreds of strokes to properly remove the burr.

Although the hand can be utilized as a strop, it is too slow for general usage. An old leather belt makes an excellent strop. A fast working strop can be made from belting or webbing that has been saturated with abrasive powder or metal polish.

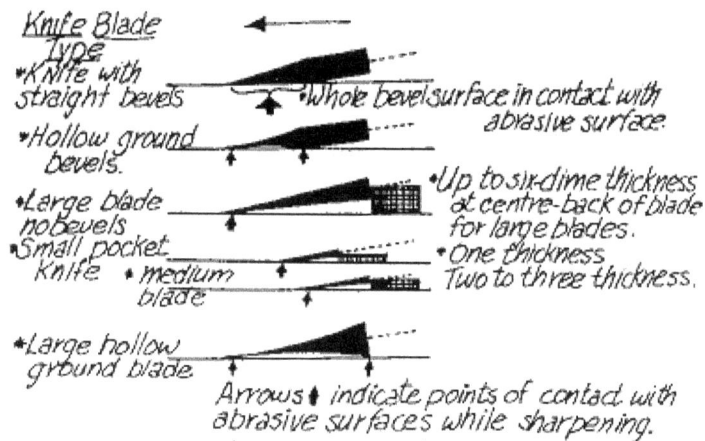

The angles used in different blade configurations

The angle at which the blade edge is held as it is drawn across the abrasive surface has a strong bearing on how that edge will cut. For the general purpose bush knife, that angle is about eight to twelve degrees. This angle may be more precisely determined if it is related to the thickness of a dime. The measurement is made to the middle of the back edge of the different widths of blade. A blade a 1.0 centimetre wide uses one dime; 1.5 centimetres, two dimes; 2.0 centimetres, three dimes; 2.5 centimetres, four dimes; 3.0 centimetres, five dimes and finally 3.5 centimetres wide requires six dimes.

The dime test should prove that knives that have a distinct bevel next to the cutting edge need only to have a bevel face flat against the abrasive surface to achieve the proper angle for the cutting edge, which is around twenty degrees. This type of knife is easy to sharpen correctly. When the whole bevel face shines like a mirror, you have likely produced a good edge.

When sharpening a knife, it is important to hold your correct angle as constantly as possible while you make your strokes back and forth. With a curved cutting edge, the stroke must also be curved or some part of the cutting edge will not come in contact with the abrasive surface. At the end of the stroke the blade is raised sufficiently off the board so as not to scrape the edge on the abrasive surface and accidently destroy the good edge.

Holding the blade at its precise angle is more important than speed. As dexterity develops the motions will naturally speed up.

Once the edge is established by a coarse abrasive surface, the number of strokes taken by the medium surface multiplied by three will be the minimum strokes required by the fine surface and so on. If the medium surface required 30 strokes the fine requires 90, the hone 270 and the strop 800.

The minimal test for sharpness for woodworking is being able to cut ordinary writing paper cleanly. For skinning, meat cutting and surgery, the minimum is being able to shave the wetted hair on the forearm cleanly and painlessly with one steady stroke.

When nothing else is available or affordable, a knife's edge can be maintained with smooth naturally found stones and sand. Trial and error will determine what surfaces and materials will work well in the coarser levels of grinding. For fine work, sand may be used mixed with grease on a flat board. The sand may have to be crushed and used with grease for finer work.

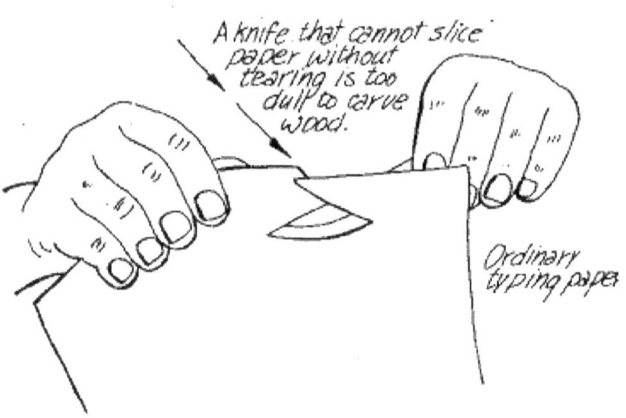

4. The Five Most Important Try Stick Notches

The purpose behind the try stick is to practice and demonstrate the skillful use of the knife as a wood carving tool, as well as to learn some of the practical operations that may be used in wilderness living.

Some of the carving operations may be of very practical application, others are meant to tax the skill of the carver and some may be used for decorative purposes.

Any straight-grained, knot-free wood will do for the stick with one of the better woods being a straight piece of willow (Salix). Although it may be used green the willow is at its best if it is peeled and dried. A stick two to three centimetres in diameter and armpit to fingertip long may accommodate most of the carving operations.

The Pot Hook: The hook should not be carved any closer to the end than three or four centimetres or it may split off in use. The throat of the hook should take up about two thirds of the stick.

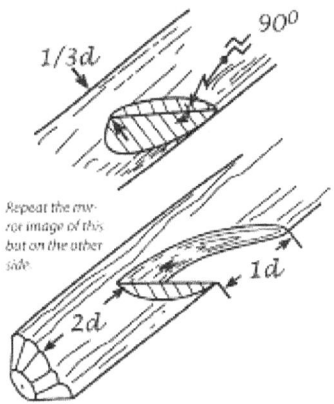

The Round Notch: This notch is one of the simplest common notches in round log buildings. The notch should be the same diameter as the stick, going half way through the stick and be perfectly round.

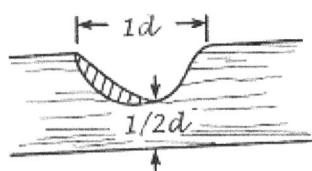

The "V" Notch: The opening of the "V" should be the diameter of the stick and the notch should go halfway through the stick.

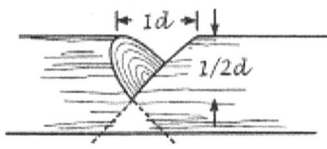

The Spear Notch: This notch is used for fitting an arrow head or spear point on a shaft, for making the Bow String notch on an arrow, for making a netting needle (use a green willow and tie the notch shut until it is dry), and many other applications. "V" notches "a" and "a-1" opposite each other should not be any deeper than one third of the diameter of the stick or the stick will break from "a" to "a-1". The shallow notches "b" and "b-1" should be made to a depth of about one quarter of the stick. With the knife tip cut the fibers 90 degrees to their grain and as deep as possible. The stick is then laid on a flat surface supported at the general region of points "b" and "b-1" as shown in the figure, and given sharp blows with the hand or a stick, gradually increasing the force until the snap is heard. The stick is turned over and the process repeated to break out the other side of the notch. The stick is then worked back and forth to further loosen it, and the notch is then broken out.

The Knife Tip Mortice (Hole Through Stick: Whenever a hole through a stick is wanted and the knife is the only available tool to make it with, the following procedure is used. The stick first has to be thinned down. If you do not thin the stick down enough you will have difficulty in making a hole through it with the knife, and if you make it too thin the stick may be too weak for your purposes. The easiest way to make the hole is to make it square or rectangular by cutting the fibers at 90 degrees from both sides and prying the chips out. Trying to drill a round hole with a knife tip usually results in a fuzzy mess. The hole through the stick is used in the bow for the fire drill, for choke bars in some snares, and for constructing the Ojibway bird snare.

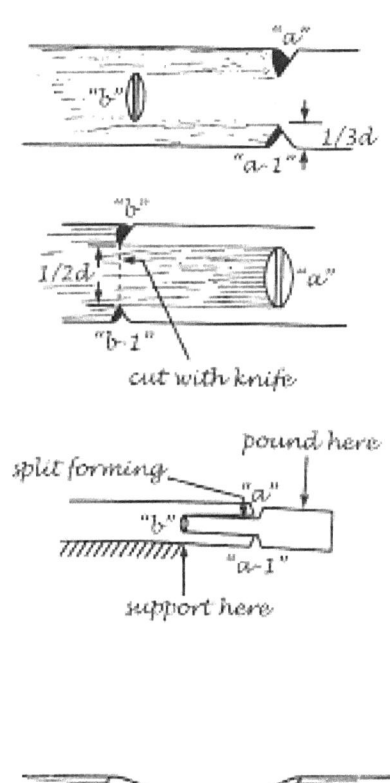

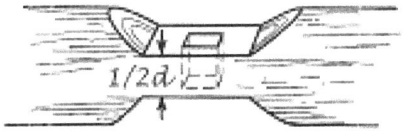

5. The Multipurpose Bush Axe

The axe is the most important bush tool there is. Outside of fire, nothing may contribute more to your comfort and leisure than a well chosen axe. The good axe should feel comfortable to swing. It should bite easily into the wood being cut and cause chips to fly out of the cut with no noticeable binding. The blade should cut to its maximum depth, yet not bind in the cut and never have to be pried out.

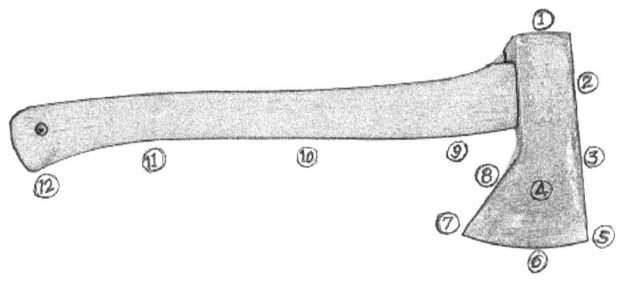

1. Poll
2. Eye
3. Front
4. Face
5. Toe
6. Bit
7. Heel
8. Back
9. Throw
10. Belly
11. Bend
12. Knob

The larger the axe the safer it is in the hands of an inexperienced person. In the long run it requires the least effort to chop the most wood. A heavier axe is a definite advantage in cold weather work or in continuous felling. However, for many situations a big axe may be too cumbersome.

A heavier head is less tiring to use, but heavy axes are not popular because they are so cumbersome to carry. The size and weight of the axe used is a compromise between the amount of work it is put to and its portability.

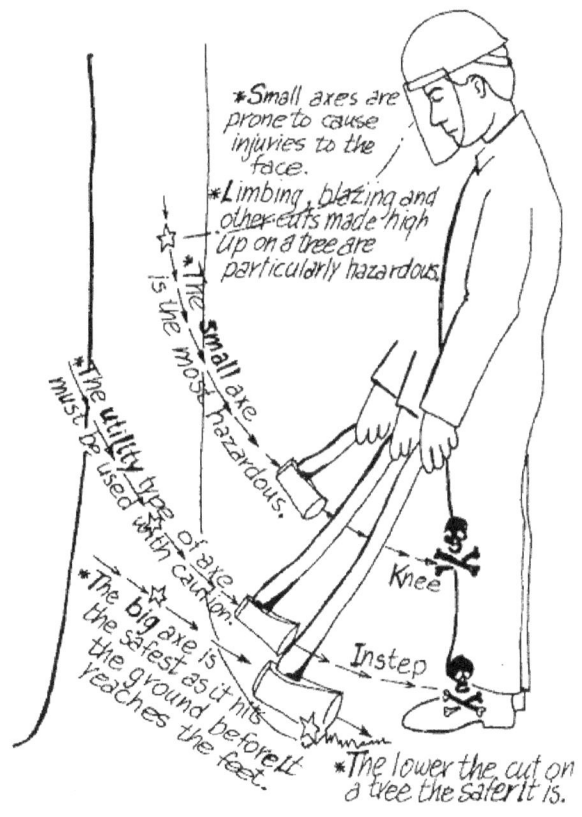

The relative safety of various sizes of axe

a) Axe Size and Safety

Axe handles can vary in length from 30 to 100 centimetres. There is the small camp axe or hatchet with its main targets of injury being the knee area or the forehead. Some consider it to be the most hazardous of the axe family.

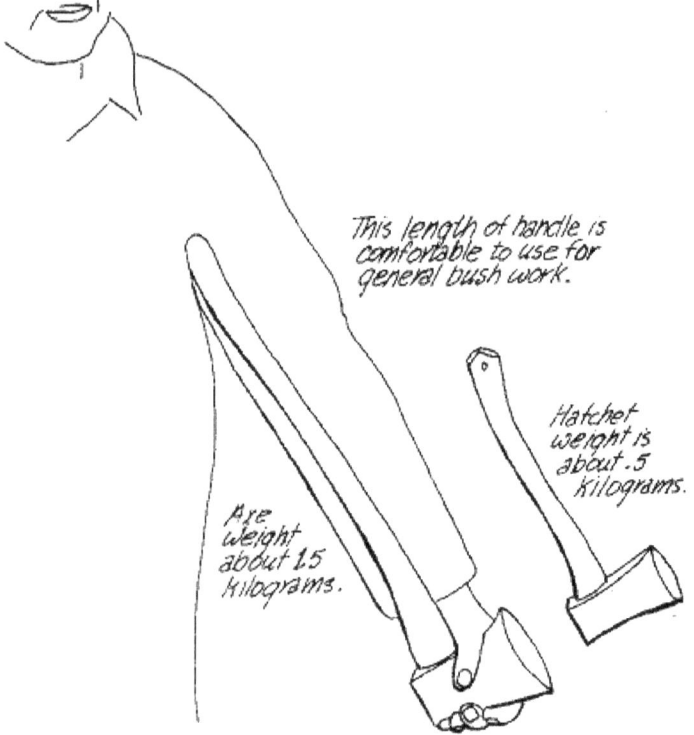

If you hold the head in your hand you should be able to put the end of the handle in your armpit. This is the favorite size of axe of the wilderness survivalist, trapper, and carpenter. If misused, this axe can still cut you in the face, but instead of the knee it favours the instep and the foot.

A blade that has a slightly convex face seldom binds, throws chips well and has more strength in frozen wood than one that is absolutely flat. The heel of the axe blade should be thin enough to "set" easily into a light block of wood that is being split into fine sticks. In examining the profile of the axe blade, its curvature should not be very pronounced.

The eye is usually the weakest point of any axe. If the eye is too small, then the handle may be too weak at the eye. If the eye is too short, the handle cannot maintain a good grip in the head. It is very easy to distort the eye if the axe is used as a wedge in pounding the back of one axe with another. The metal of the eye is generally more malleable to resist cracking.

The strongest handle must have a grain parallel to the flat shape of the handle.

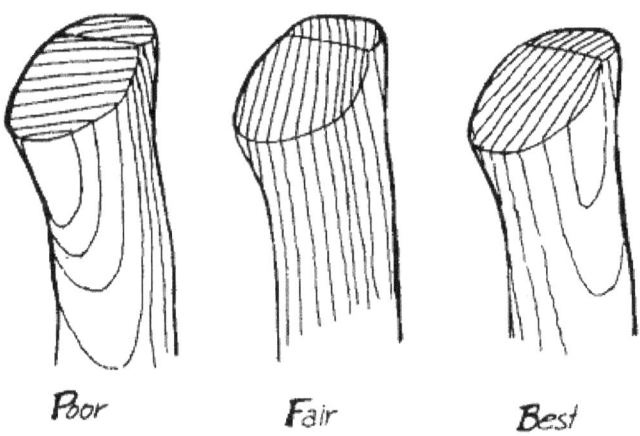

Poor   Fair   Best

A good handle should fit the user's hand, being slim enough so as not to jar when the blade hits hard, and not so slim as to flex easily.

Sight down the blade edge to see how it lines up with the centre line of the axe handle.

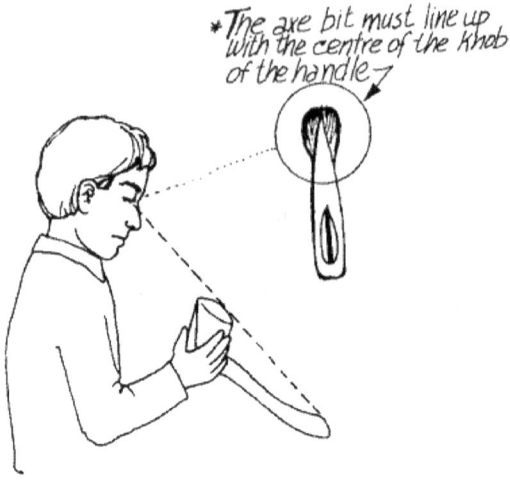

If the knob of the handle and the axe blade both are made to touch a flat surface, the blade should make contact with the flat surface from one third of the way from the heel of the blade to the mid point of the blade.

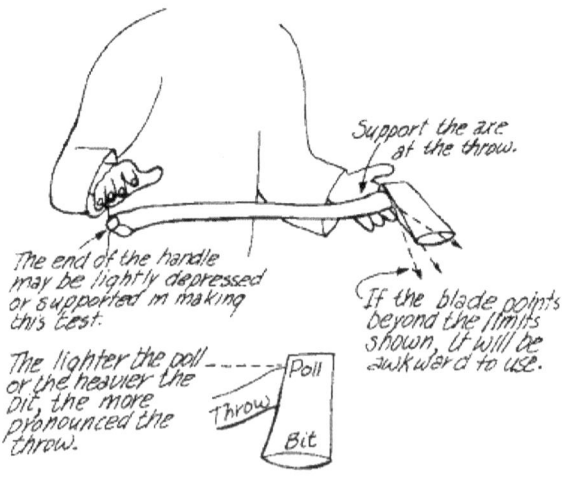

b) Sharpening the Axe

A dull axe is less efficient, is tiring to use, and tends to glance more readily. An axe should be touched up on a regular basis, perhaps every half hour of use or every time a tree is cut down. Some users are satisfied with only a file for maintaining the edge of the blade. Others finish the edge with a coarse and fine whetstone. When an axe is new it may need thinning down with a file. After this initial sharpening the file may never have to be used again, unless the blade is nicked.

Sharpening can be broken down into a number of stages:

1. The first stage is usually the removal of gross material by file, grindstone or coarse whetstone. These tools cut fast, but leave a somewhat roughened surface.
2. The second stage produces the edge by the use of a fine whetstone. Many axe users go no further than this, considering it adequate for their needs.
3. The third stage could be termed very fine grinding akin to polishing, accomplished with a very hard and fine stone, sometimes called a hone, that should produce a mirror finish on the edge.

In working with a file, apply just enough pressure to get a light even cut. Use less pressure and more strokes, utilizing the full length of the file. Heavy downward pressure tends to break off teeth.

Dragging and applying pressure on the backward stroke causes file teeth to break off very easily.

A whetstone is normally used in such a circular motion that the whole surface of the stone is worn in an even fashion. Properly used, a good stone may last a lifetime.

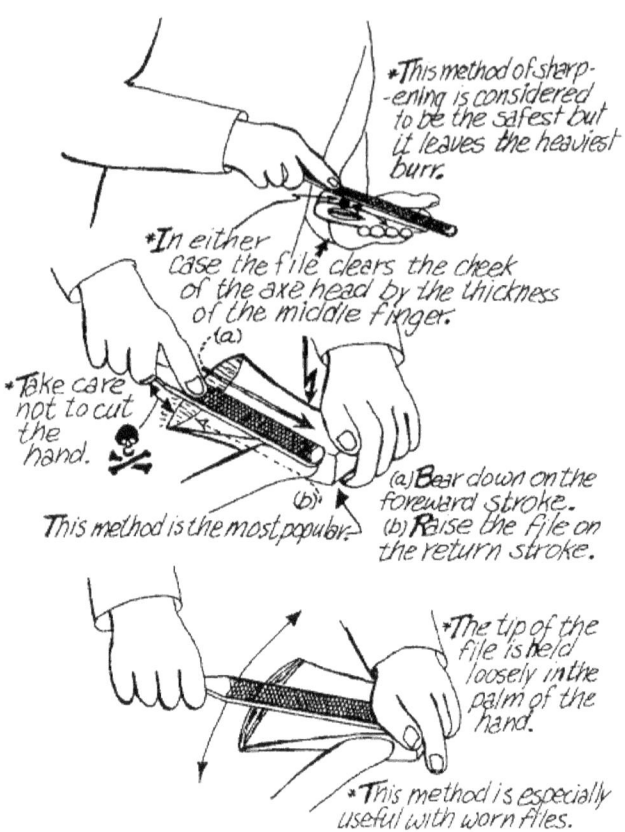

Some methods of filing an axe.

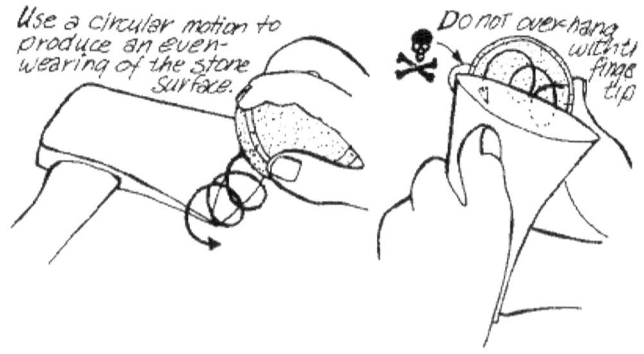

c) Replacing an Axe Handle

When an axe handle breaks, one of the major problems is removing the broken handle. If possible, pry out any metal wedges. If some of the handle remains it may be thinned down enough to drive it forward through the front of the eye. The head is supported on each side of the eye and the handle hammered through. It helps if the head has been dried thoroughly to shrink the wood a little. If this is done near a fire, care must be taken not to overheat the metal or the axe may lose its temper. If you cannot comfortably hold the axe head in your hand you may be overdoing the heating.

A metal drill bit may be used to remove as much wood as possible out of the eye. If the bit is allowed to cut into the metal of the eye, the eye could be weakened.

Putting a head on an axe handle correctly can be a complicated affair. Start by cleaning and grinding the axe head to perfection. File out any lips, burrs or any other irregularities in the eye and on the pole. Place the axe head on the handle to determine how much of the handle to trim off. Allow a centimetre of extra length and saw off the remainder. Rasp, carve or shave down the handle so that it fits the eye snuggly, taking care to remove the same amount of material from both sides of the handle. Try the handle frequently to make sure you do not take too much wood off and end up with a loose fit. Broken glass makes an excellent tool to remove surplus wood. Saw a slot on the long axis of the handle that you would estimate to go two thirds of the way into the eye. The wedge need not be one piece, but it must extend for the full length of the long axis of the eye. The eye must be completely filled with wood.

Except for about a half a centimetre, trim off any excess length of handle and wedge protruding out of the eye. If necessary, metal wedges are now driven in. Long experience in the matter has proved that the best method to drive in the wedges is between the faces of the wooden wedges and the wood of the handle.

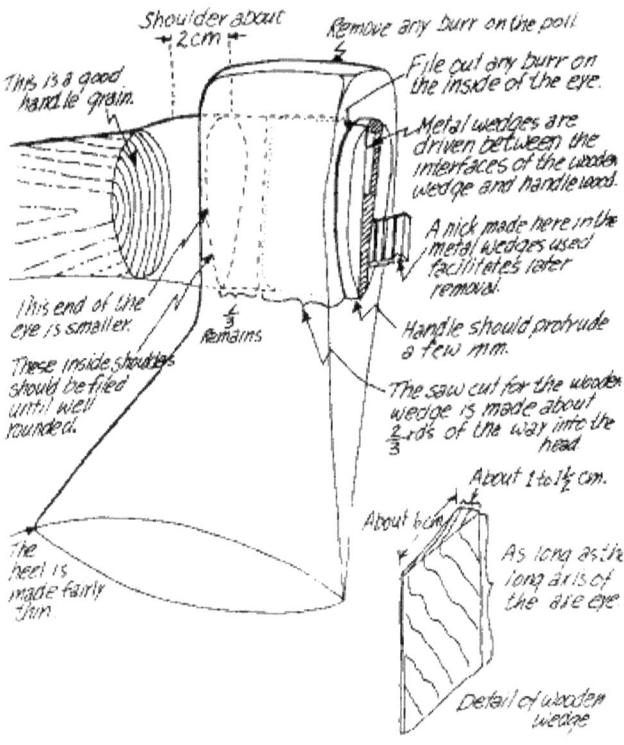

Detail of an axe head

Basic Safe Travel and Boreal Survival

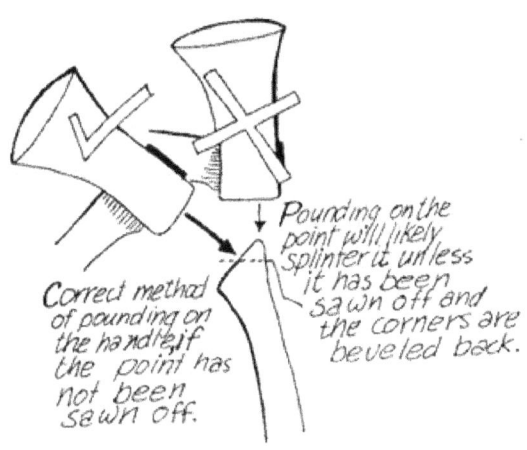

Correct method of pounding on the handle if the point has not been sawn off.

Pounding on the point will likely splinter it unless it has been sawn off and the corners are beveled back.

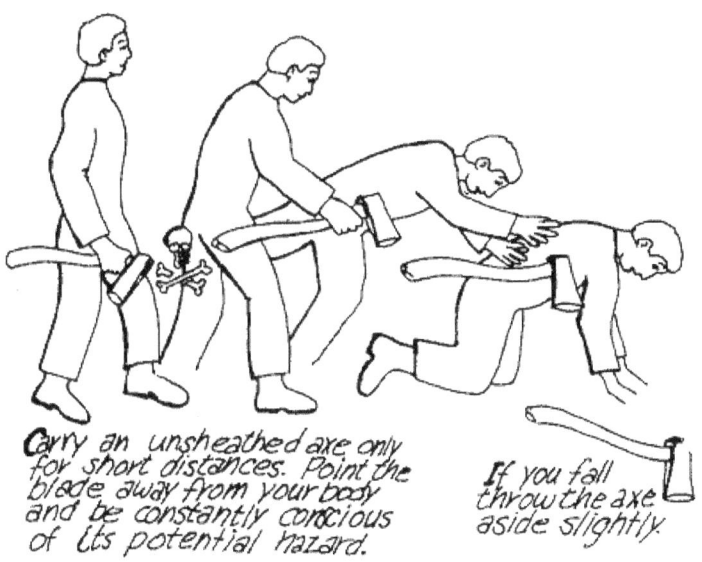

Carry an unsheathed axe only for short distances. Point the blade away from your body and be constantly concious of its potential hazard.

If you fall throw the axe aside slightly.

Carrying the axe on your shoulder is inviting a cut to the neck or back, as well as being a hazard to anyone near you. Wise outdoors persons always carried their axe in a sheath.

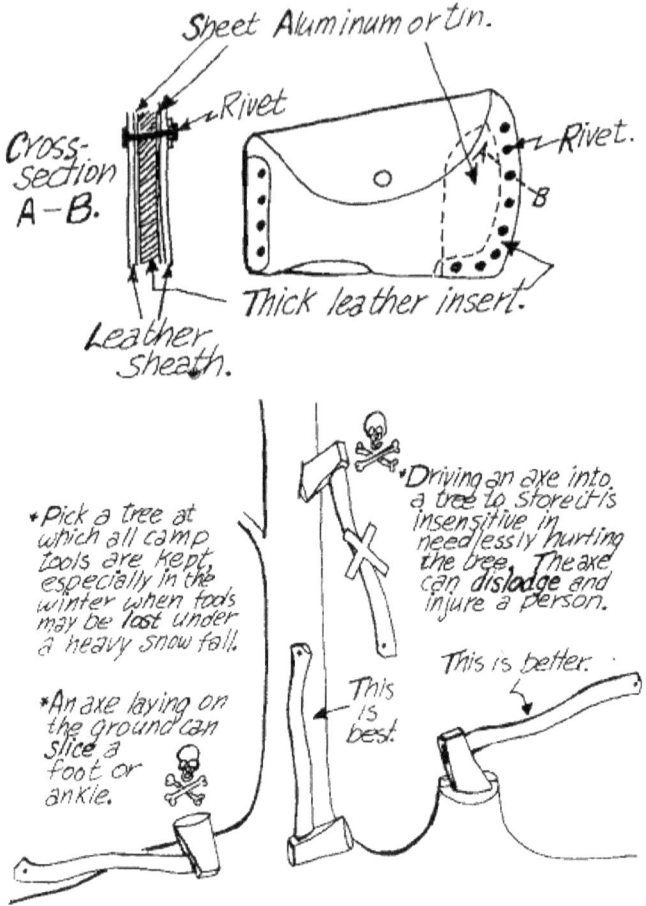

d) Safe Axe Use

Safety should be the major preoccupation in axe use. The misused axe can be very dangerous to the user. The axe itself, no matter how small, is a significant hazard in itself. Combine what the axe does, the fall of a tree with its tremendous kicking and crushing action, you have the ingredients that make a sudden death or severe injury possible. Safe axe use requires that you understand the actions and reactions of both the tool you are using and the tree that is falling. A considerable part of tree falling is based on guess work. The more experience that you have, the better your guess will be. The discipline of axe use may require that you remember many things and be able to recognize a hazard before it becomes your fatal step.

The CAMP AXE or HATCHET: There are two ways of using this small axe.

1. Stay well away from the tree and support yourself against it with your free hand. Chop the trunk as close to the ground as you can without actually cutting into the ground. The shoulder and the arm both participate in the chopping action. At the point in the swing where the head is about 30 centimetres from impact, both the head and the hand travel together in a parallel motion. It is as if the hand is thrown forward before the moment of impact. The axe should bit into the wood at an angle of 30 to 45 degrees downward. Attempting to chop upward could result in the axe flying into the face. The angle is exactly the same for the lower and upper part of the cut. The resulting stump will look rather jagged, but any other method of cutting will not be any safer or faster.
2. The cut may also be done from a kneeling position, leaving both hands free to hold the axe. Stay about one or two axe handle lengths from the tree and use the same pre-impact maneuver just described.

In cutting limbs on standing trees the parallel action of axe head and hand can serve to make that type of cut safer as the follow through can be controlled or arrested more effectively. Another ploy is to reach partly around the trunk of the tree. The resultant follow through should be off to the side, well away from any part of your body.

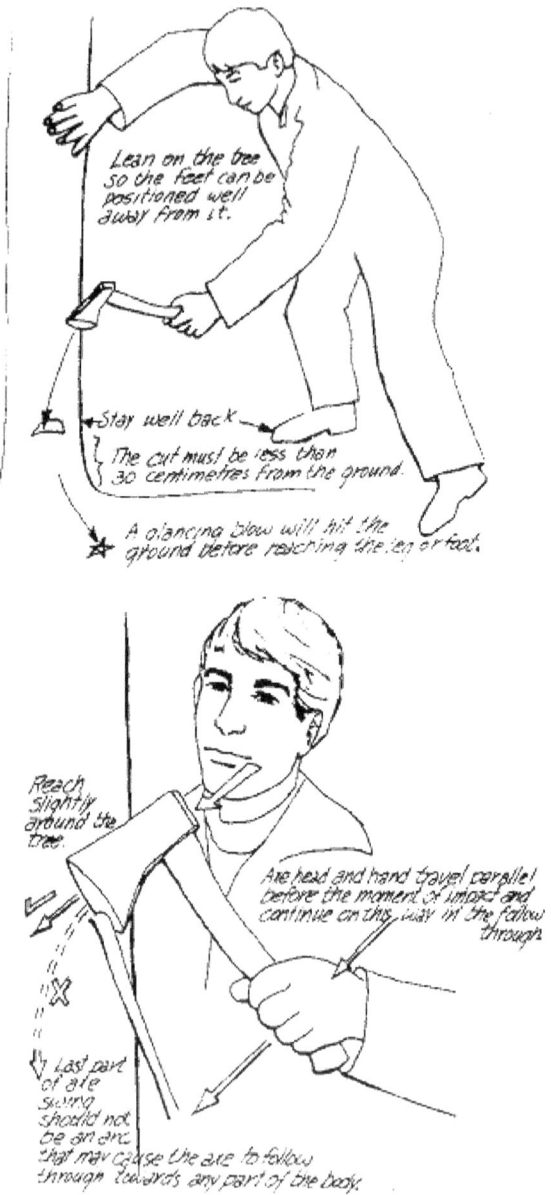

Basic Safe Travel and Boreal Survival

Make cut no higher than 30cm above the ground.

Stay an axe handle distance away from the tree.

In bending the back and reaching for the tree in this manner, the deflected axe would have to travel a considerable distance to strike the feet. Most deflections, if there are any, would end up in the ground. For additional safety, the axe should be swung in such a way that the end of the handle and the head travel in parallel paths in relation to each other for the movement preceding impact. By the time the axe stops moving, the handle ends up parallel to the level ground or at 90 degrees to the trunk of the tree.

Using the axe well is mostly a matter of co-ordination. The axe must hit exactly where wanted, at the correct angle, precisely into the previous cut, or effort is wasted in cutting the same wood over and over again. The mark of competence is large chips, few in number, while the inexperienced axe user makes a large amount of fine chips.

It is important to keep stumps low in axe work. If the point of impact is over 30 centimetres, a glancing blow may not

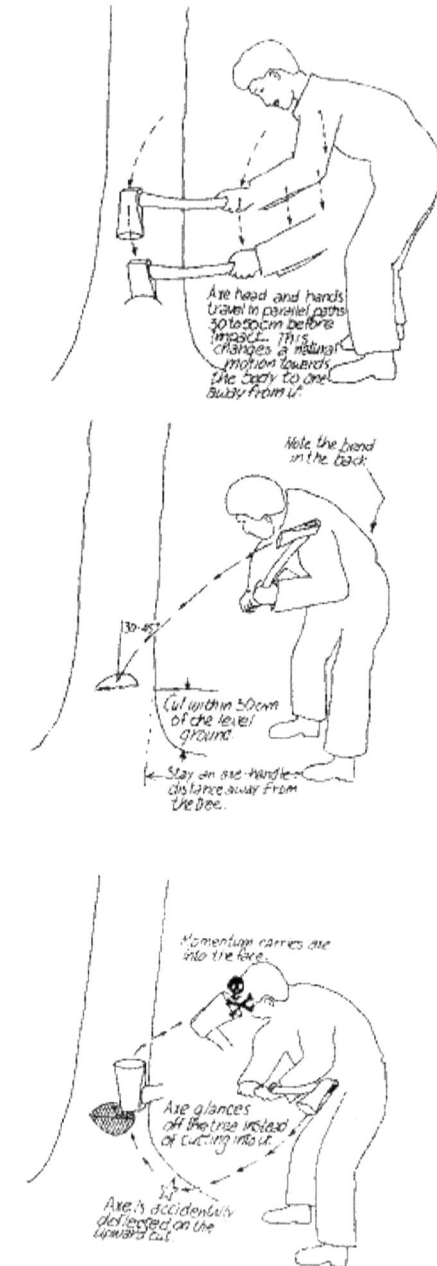

catch the ground. Whenever a higher cut has to be made it should be done with an awareness of the additional hazard involved. When experience is lacking it may be prudent to avoid the unusual at first, such as trees over 30 centimetres (reach around the tree with your right arm, if you cannot touch your left shoulder it is too large) in diameter, crooked, crowded and leaning trees and trees growing on slopes. With no experience or opportunity to work with someone knowledgeable while you gain some basic experience you may confine your efforts to trees no larger than what you can circle with the fingers of both hands, or about 15 centimetres in diameter.

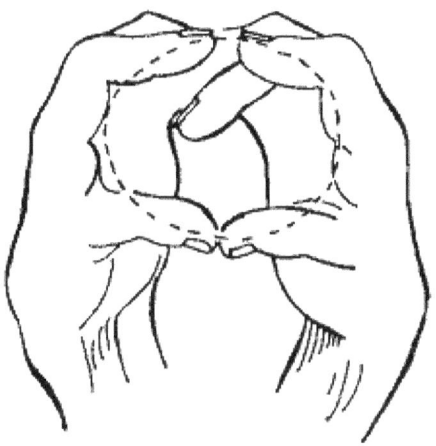

e) Safety-Cutting Down Trees

Before attempting to cut down a tree you must have a clear space to work and a sure footing. Low branches, brush and anything else that may catch your axe should be cleared away.

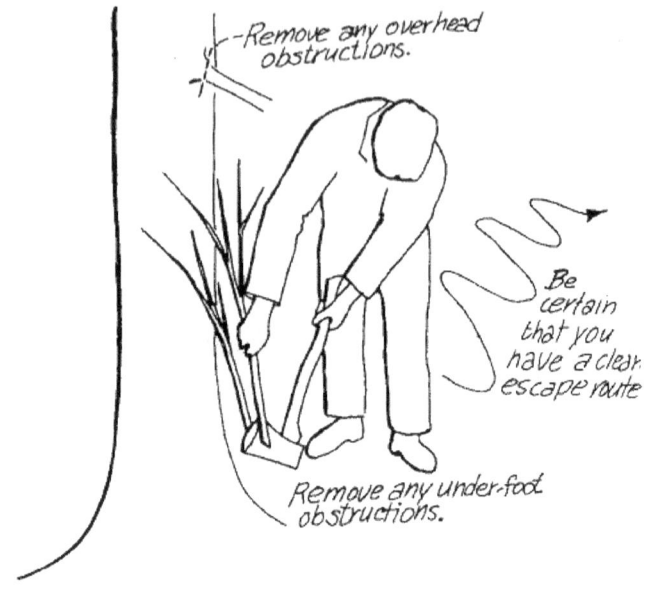

Low overhead branches can spring back an axe into the head or the back. A good axe swing hooked on a low branch can cause your feet to be lifted clear of the ground in such a way that you may land flat on your back. When doing axe work near camp beware of lines such as clothes lines or guy lines, which if caught by an axe can cause severe injuries to the head. Clothes lines and wood piles should be kept well separated.

THE FACTORS THAT INFULENCE A TREE'S FALL: There are many factors that may influence the way and the direction that a tree may fall. Understanding these factors should help you in determining the safest way to fall a tree, or how to fall it where you want it. Unless there is a pronounced lean to the contrary, expect to fall a tree with the wind. A tree is much like a sail in the wind, especially when it is an evergreen or a deciduous tree in summer foliage. A tree of two degrees lean or less can be made to fall in any direction on a still day. An experienced faller, with or without wedges may fall a tree against a lean as

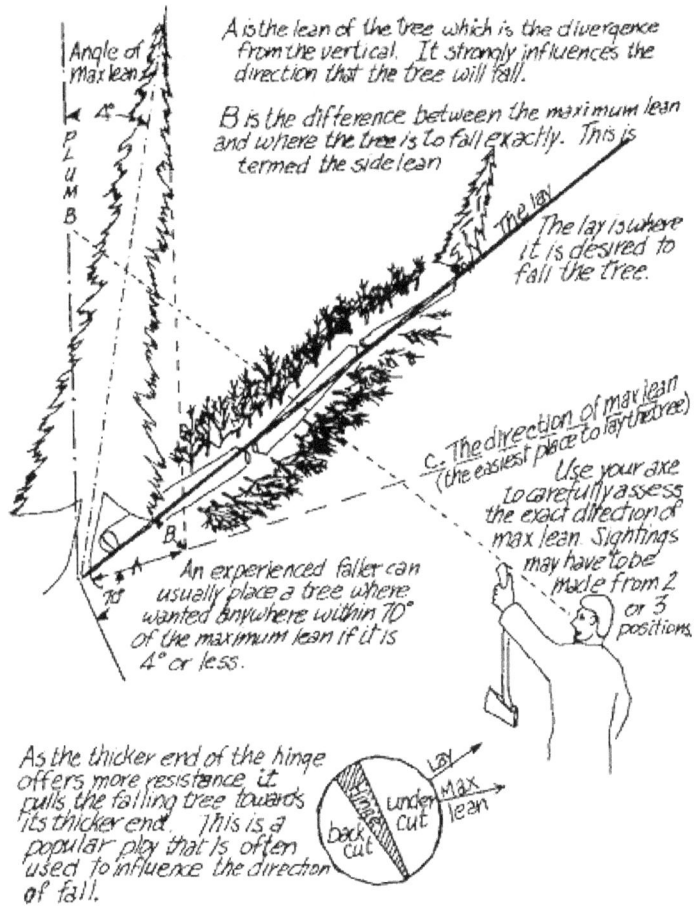

great as four degrees. In the case of a pronounced lean a tree can be made to fall within about 70 degrees to either side of its maximum lean. It is important to ascertain the exact lean, as poor determination of the lean may be the greatest cause of trees falling in unexpected or undesirable directions. When the situation could be critical a plumb line should be used from at least two different angles 90 degrees apart, to zero in on the maximum lean. Trees with heavy branches growing on one side tend to fall in that direction.

HAZARDS ASSOCIATED WITH TREE FELLING:
The same species of tree may have the same outward appearance, but health, grain, locale and age may result in a unique reaction to the feller's axe. The safe assumption is that each tree is different. Evaluate all the problems you may encounter before felling it. Check for the possibility of falling wood from overhead. The chopping vibrations on a tree with an unsound top may cause it to break off especially dry, old, fire killed trees. Strike the tree several times with the back of the axe while watching the top of the tree to detect any wobble indicating weakness. It is easy to side step anything that falls. The advantage of head and shoulder protection is obvious.

Because of the danger of falling branches or cones injuring the eye, one should never look up without first moving away from the tree. The smallest branch falling the height of a tree may do significant damage to the eye if you should happen to look up at the wrong moment. Any unusual configuration of tree or terrain may have a hazard associated with it. Trees that fall up a slope or over a hump, may spring back or lash out sideways with crushing force.

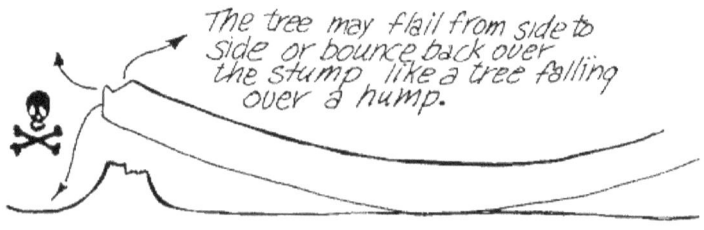

The tree may flail from side to side or bounce back over the stump like a tree falling over a hump.

A tree with a curved trunk, much like the one falling over a hump, may come back over the stump and lash upwards or sideways. As a tree falls its branches may snag those of a neighbouring tree, causing it to rotate and fall in an unexpected direction. A relatively small snag at the top of a tree may have a pronounced effect on the direction of fall.

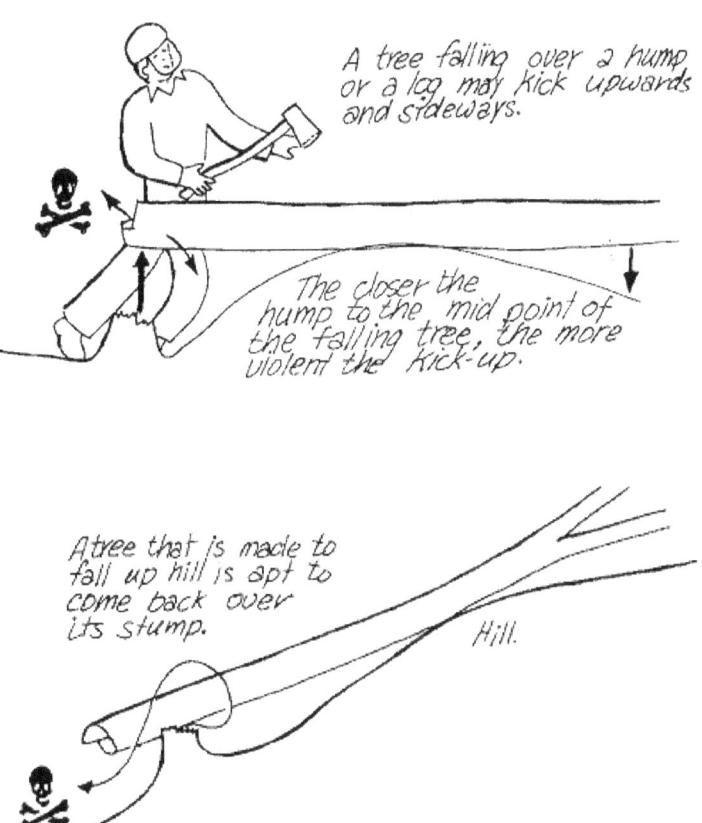

FELLING CHARACTERISTICS OF DIFFERENT TREES: Different species of trees may have their own unique ways of reacting as they fall. The branches of a dense white spruce tree may cause it to rebound back over the stump. Birch is a very flexible tree. If it catches on another tree it may bend severely and break on exceeding its elastic limit, with pieces of wood flying in any direction. A falling tree sometimes catches a smaller birch tree and causes it to bend so severely that shards of birch wood fly about. The springiness of birch is to be guarded against as any careless release of tension can result in injury.

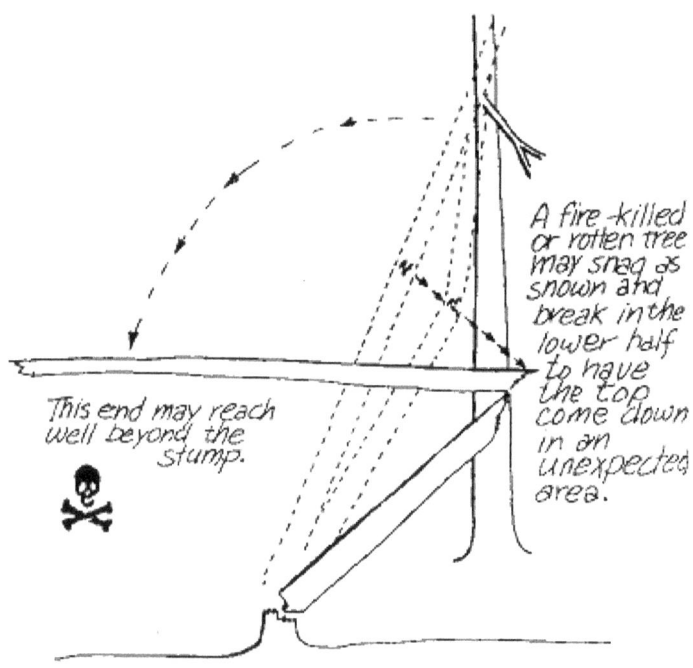

White and black poplar often have rotten cores that may cause them to fall sooner than expected and in the wrong direction. White poplar is particularly prone to hooking a neighbour and turning on the stump as it begins to fall. When a falling tree becomes entangled in nearby trees a hazardous hang up occurs that required caution and experience to be safely handled.

Basic Safe Travel and Boreal Survival

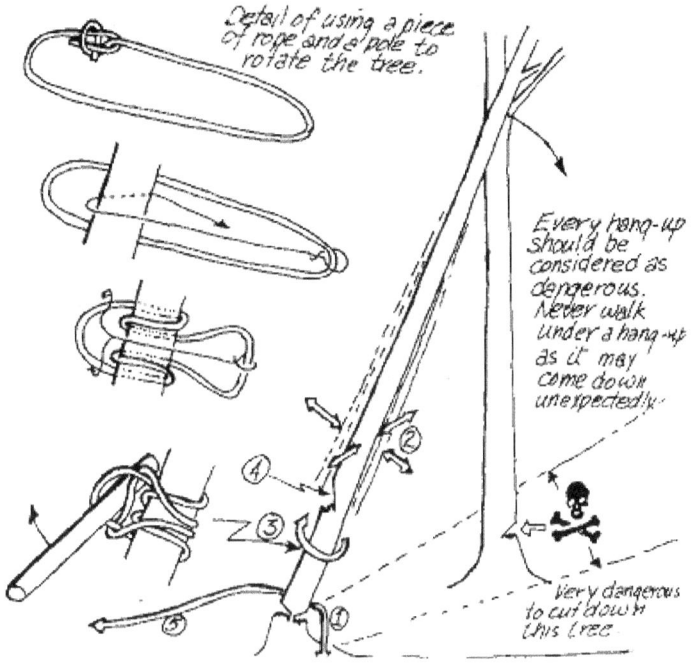

1. If the tree is freed from its stump, the short fall may dislodge it.
2. Rocking the tree back and forth may dislodge it.
3. Rotating the tree may dislodge it.
4. Chopping out a short section of trunk may help. Use care as the tree may be made to fall in an unpredictable direction.
5. If the tree is light enough it may be freed from the stump and pulled outward to dislodge it. As the tree starts to fall, let go and get clear of it before it hits the ground or you may sustain a severe jar to the arms.

If rocking, rotating or prying the butt does not dislodge it, the next expedient may be to chop off a section of the trunk one piece at a time until the tree is dislodged. In any event, the hang-up should be studied closely and approached cautiously. Chopping above waist level should be done with due care because it is more hazardous.

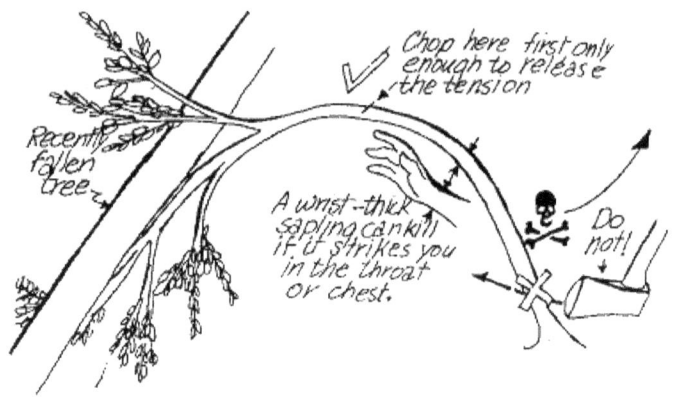

Saplings bent down with their tops pinned under a fallen tree can be very dangerous if cut improperly. The tension must first be taken out of the sapling. If it is cut near the ground the end can lash out with lethal force. A wrist thick tree that is bent into a bow can kill if it hits you in the chest or throat.

f) How to Cut down a Tree

Determine the direction the tree is to fall.

Determine your escape route. Study beforehand where you are going to go if the tree's actions are not to your liking.

Clear away any obstruction around the tree.

Make the first cut, the undercut, in the direction the tree is to fall. In making the undercut, the top part of the cut may be at an angle of forty-five degrees and the bottom part of the cut may be made using cuts at 45 degrees that move through the wood in increments of the depth of the axe cut. This may not look as neat as the straight in cut but is more efficient.

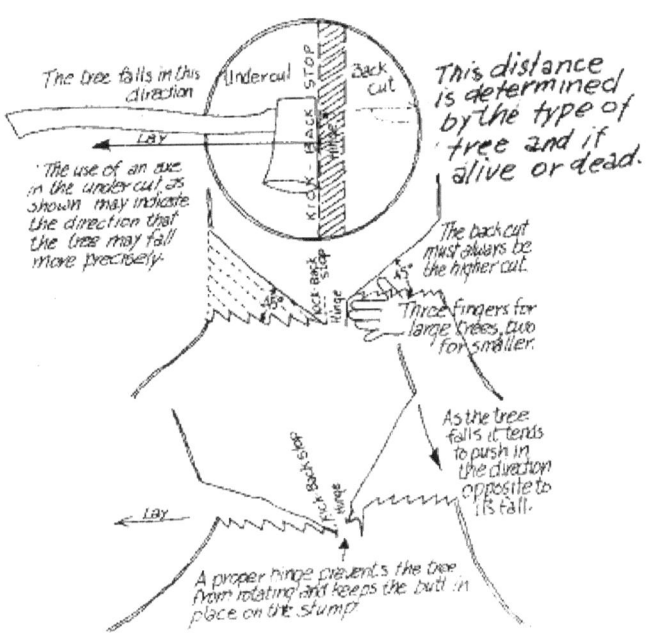

The width of the undercut is approximately the diameter of the tree. The depth of the undercut may vary from one-half to two-thirds of the way through the trunk, depending on the soundness of the tree, the degree of slant, the strength of wind and other factors. If the undercut is made too deep, the tree may fall before the back cut is made, resulting in the notorious "barber chair". This could be dangerous and wasteful. If at all possible, the cut should be made straight across rather than at any slant, which makes a poorer hinge.

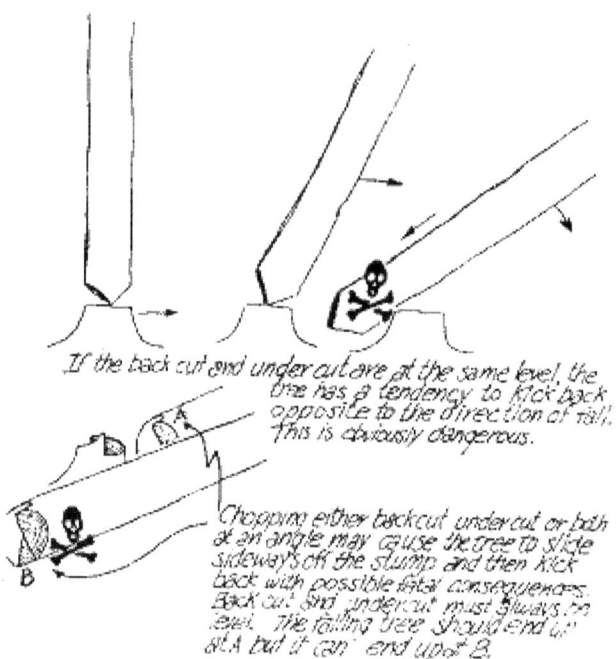

The back cut is then made on the opposite side of the tree a certain distance higher than the undercut, thereby creating a hinge about which the tree will fall, helping to keep it from slipping back off the stump. If the previously made undercut was not made deep enough, or if the back cut was not made deep enough, or if the back cut is too high above the undercut, the tree may fall opposite to the desired direction. The difference in height between the undercut and the back cut may vary with the type of tree, whether it is dead or green or whether you have any special effect in mind.

Basic Safe Travel and Boreal Survival

* Attempting to fall a tree with little or no undercut may cause the tree to barberchair. Any tree with a pronounced lean is apt to fall in the way illustrated.

* The barberchair is considered dangerous as it can happen in an instant catching the faller on the upward swing of the trunk or the highly-raised trunk may spring back and fall on top of him.

* Use great caution in dealing with heavy leaners.
  1. First make the undercut making it much larger than usual.
  2. Cut the corners out as shown to reduce the chances of splintering.
  3. Make the backcut last.

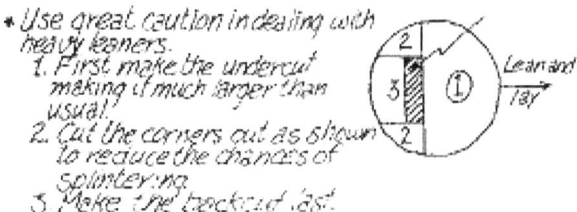

A rough, general purpose distance would be around four fingers. If a pronounced lean has to be counteracted, the hinge is made wedge shaped (when viewed from the top) with the thicker part of the hinge opposite from the lean. This, in effect, helps to draw the tree around in the direction of the thicker part of the wedge. A green tree may fall when there is still a lot of wood between the back cut and the undercut. A dry tree tends not to fall until there is little or no wood between the back cut and the undercut. Towards the completion of the back cut, the tree, if not too big, may be started on its way with a push to make sure it will fall in the required direction. The moment that a tree starts to fall do not take your eyes off of it until it is laying on the ground. That way, should something erratic or unexpected occur, you may be able to dodge it. Never turn your back on a falling tree. The moment that a tree begins to fall, back away from it to a respectable distance, which may be around five metres. Never stand near a tree as it falls. Too many dangerous things tend to happen near the stump.

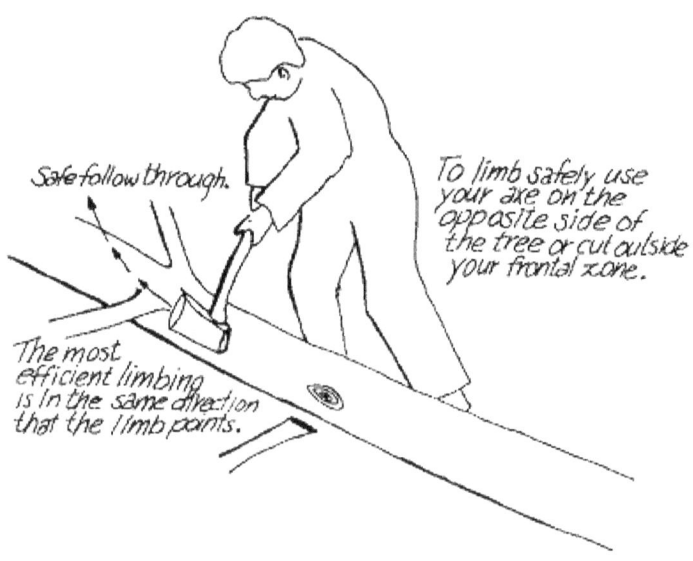

It is easier to limb a tree by cutting towards its top, if the limbs point upward. Black spruce is the exception in that the branches tend to point downward. Any limbing is best done on the far side of the tree, as the tree itself will protect your legs. If your limbs on the same side, chop in such a way that the axe is swung away from you.

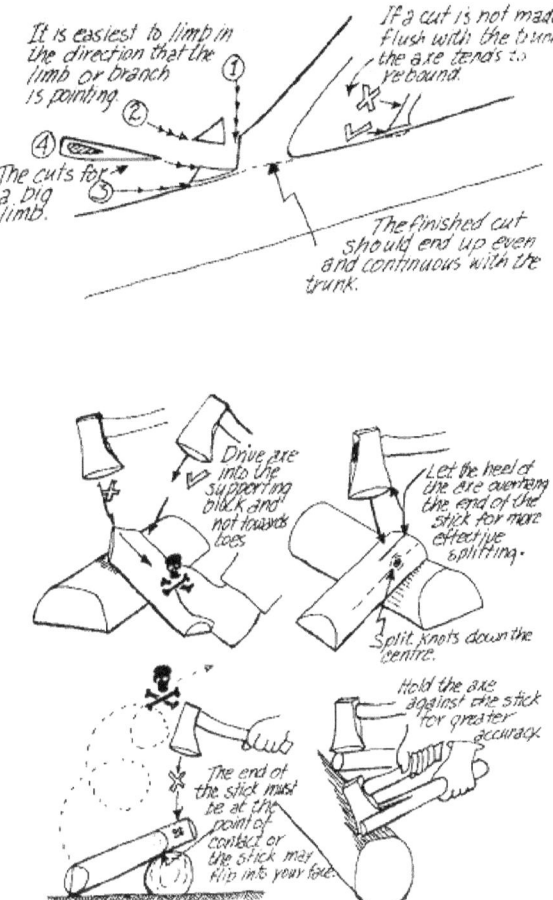

It is easier to section a log by cutting it half way through from opposite sides rather than cutting it completely through from the top. A comfortable stance, with legs well apart, is taken as close to the log as possible, being careful not to have the toes protruding under the log. Inexperienced axe users tend to stand too far back, exposing themselves to the hazard of over shooting the log and chopping themselves in the leg, particularly with a smaller axe. The

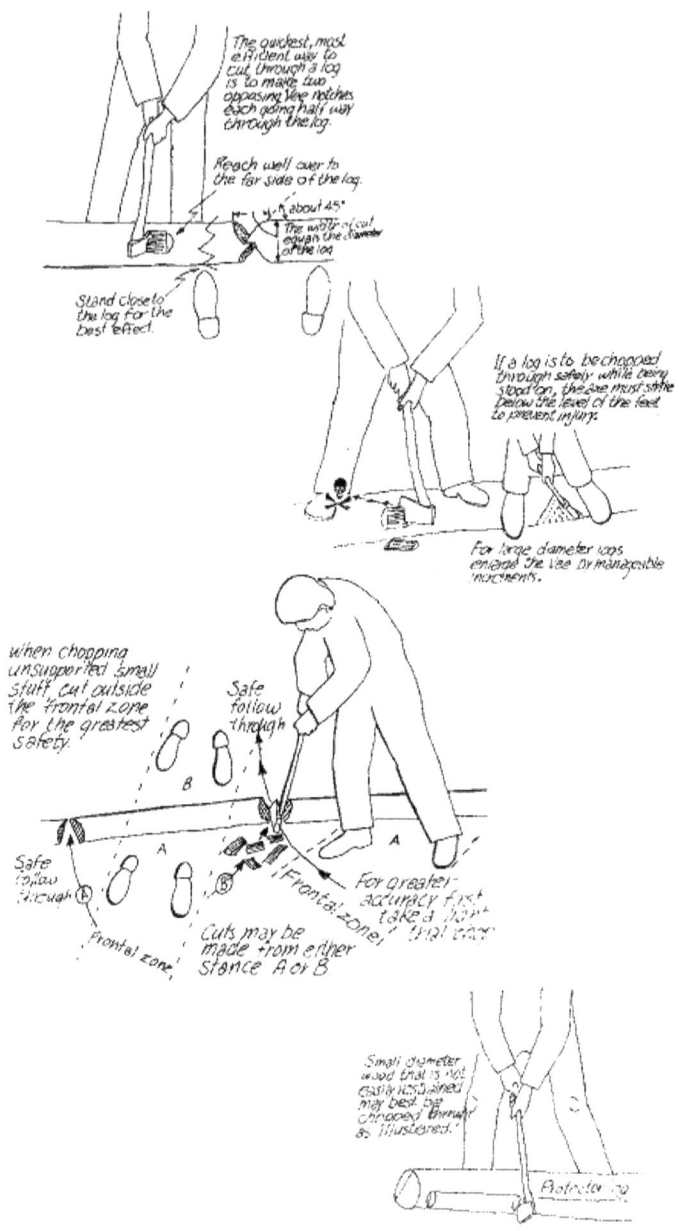

width of the cut is equal to the diameter of the log. The cuts are made at an angle of 45 degrees to the log's surface. If the log is of a large diameter, a smaller notch is made and then extended later, otherwise the chips will not dislodge easily because of the width of the cut.

To complete the separation of the logs a similar stance is taken as used in limbing beyond your feet, a measured swing is made and the cut completed with a well placed blow. Standing on top of a log when cutting through it may leave you open to a cut to the instep. Likewise, when cutting through a short log resist holding it down with a foot. A better way is to use a protective log between the stick to be cut and your feet.

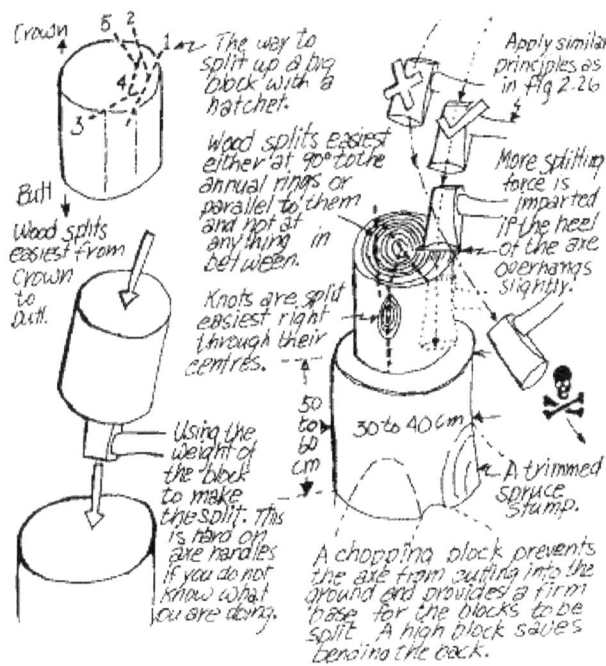

Making difficult splits in wood blocks

6. The Saw

a) The Saw and Axe Compared

The axe may be the first choice if you are limited to only one tool. An axe may fall, limb and section any size of tree. Splitting and shaving wood, making pegs and pounding them in or chopping holes in ice are impossible with a saw.

The more versatile axe is also the more durable tool. A replacement handle can be fashioned with the head alone.

The cutting edge can be maintained with locally-found natural stones.

The axe is the more hazardous tool, taking weeks of constant use to master and is especially dangerous to use after dark. A saw, on the other hand, may be used by a blind person under most circumstances, after a few hours of training.

The depth of a Swede saw's bow limits the size of tree it may cut through. Otherwise it can fell, section and limb a tree with a fraction of the exertion demanded by an axe, in confined or awkward spaces.

Wedges used in a saw cut can fall a tree in directions that are not possible with an axe. A saw makes squared ends with a minimum of waste. The saw is handier for cutting stove wood for wood burning stoves.

A saw blade is quite fragile and is easily trapped in its cut. A twisted or bent blade is impossible to use. With a disturbed set the saw cut becomes dished, sometimes causing the drag to become so great it is impossible to pull the saw back and forth.

A saw frame should be heavy enough to keep its blade under a strong tension.

A saw should have a blade about one metre long (from the nose to the fingertip of the extended hand) and have a throat (distance from the blade to the frame) of about 25 centimetres or a hand span.

Compactness and portability should not be sacrificed for unrestricted function and durability. An inferior but portable fool is useless in serious wilderness living. A big bow saw may be awkward to carry, but will make up for the extra energy used in carrying it, in a half hour of sawing.

All saw blades should have guards to prevent cuts to the hands, clothing, packs, tents and pots. You can be severely injured by falling on a unprotected blade.

With a saw used above the head, you may get sawdust in the eyes, the worst being from dry, brittle branches of spruce or pine. Tamarack sawdust can cause a severe reaction as well. Keep the eyes as closed as possible to help the eyelashes exclude the sawdust.

In a properly working saw the teeth are correctly arranged and the blade is perfectly straight. Avoid any adverse use affecting the teeth such as twisting, kinking, bending, heavy pushing, pulling or downward force.

If too much force is used you will tire quickly. A full length stroke back and forth is worth three short ones that take twice the effort.

The function of the set in a saw blade is to cut a kerf or slot that is wider than the thickness of the saw blade allowing it to move freely in its cut. If the log is supported at its ends the kerf closes behind the blade short of interfering with its movement.

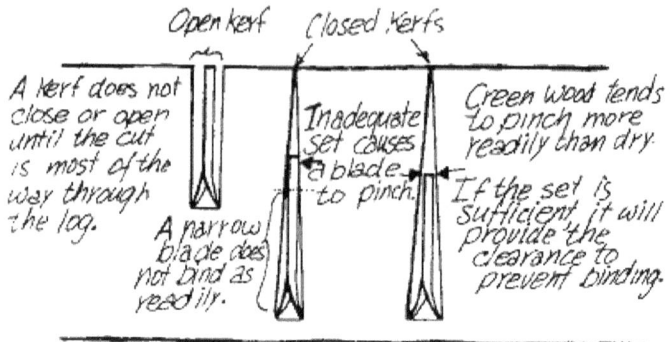

How a saw blade is pinched

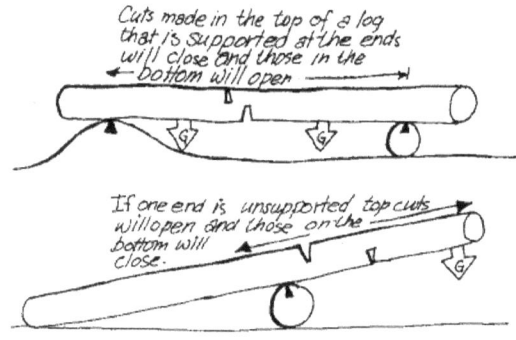

The opening and closing of saw cuts

A log suspended off the ground, or a log supported at the ends, is cut downwards as far as possible, short of the kerf closing and then it is continued from underneath where the kerf will tend to open. When an unsupported end is being cut off, use the opposite approach.

b) Cutting Down Trees with a Saw

Basic Safe Travel and Boreal Survival

The principles of cutting down a tree (falling) with a saw are much the same as those used with an axe. The back cut is made as a notch, allowing the use of wedges to assist a tree to fall in a required direction.

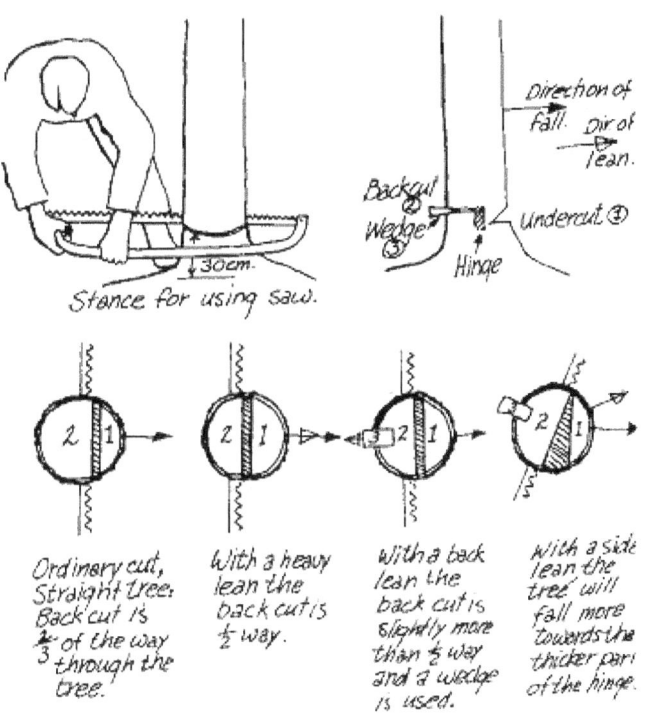

Cutting Trees with a Saw

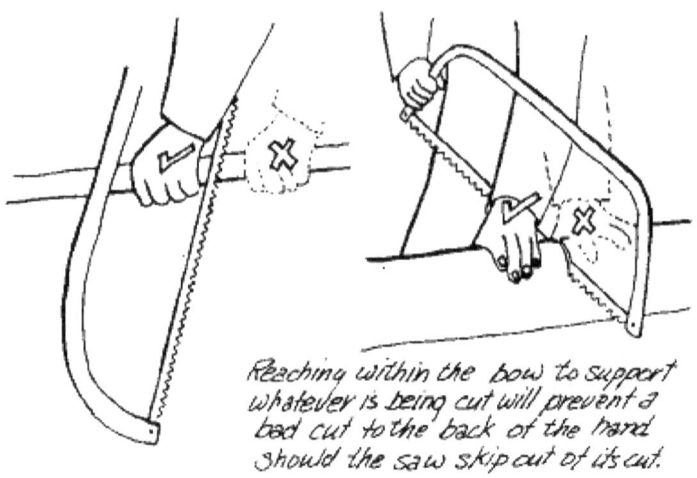

Reaching within the bow to support whatever is being cut will prevent a bad cut to the back of the hand should the saw skip out of its cut.

Avoiding saw cuts to the back of the hand

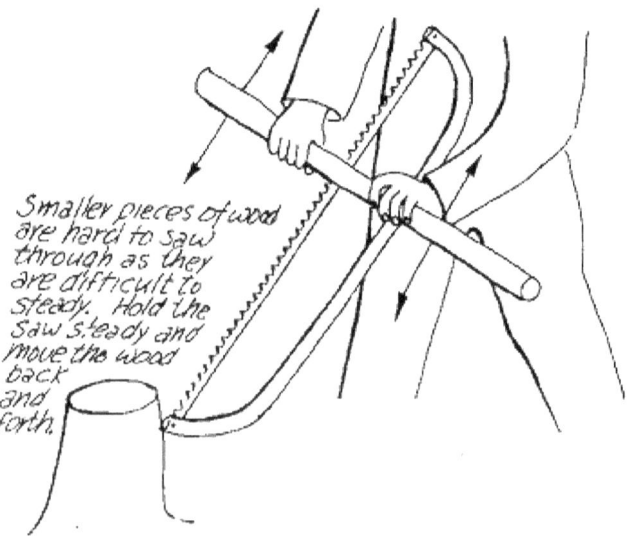

Smaller pieces of wood are hard to saw through as they are difficult to steady. Hold the saw steady and move the wood back and forth.

Using a saw in reverse

Basic Safe Travel and Boreal Survival

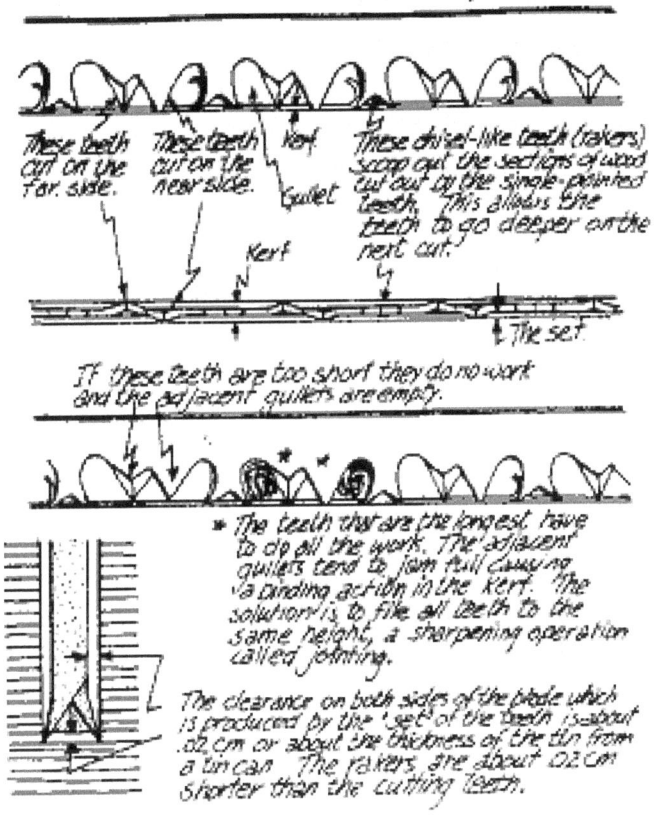

How a saw cuts

C) Wilderness Fire Lighting Skills in the Spruce-Moose Forest

"What is a camp without an evening campfire? It's nothing but a place in the woods where some people have some things."
Ernest Thompson Seton

Has anyone ever sat near a good fire in the darkness and not enjoyed it?

"The Navajo has a different idea of comfort from ours, but according to his likes he can make himself and his companions comfortable with very little. One thing always included in the "very little" is fire. If one is wet or cold, he needs a fire; if the weather is balmy and fair, he needs a fire to cook his humble meal. Perhaps the conditions are pleasant, the wind is warm and he has no food; then especially he needs a fire for company."
From "Weaving a Navajo Blanket" by Gladys A. Reinhard

Some anthropologists feel that the archaeological evidence shows people and fire to have been associated for at least a million years. Today, a concern for the negative ecological implications of campfire usage in recreational camping is prompting us to examine our present practices of fire use in the out-of-doors.

Theodore A. Wertime in Volume 61 of the "American Scientist", pages 670 to 682 succinctly sums up our romance with fire in his article "PYROTECHNOLOGY: MAN'S FIRST INDUSTRIAL USES OF FIRE". He states that the cooking of food has been going on for at least

100,000 years; fire hardening of spears for 80,000 years; the annealing of stones for chipping for 25,000 years and the firing of pottery, smelting of metals, and the making of glass for the last 10,000 to 15,000 years. With each stage the temperature gets higher and the application of fire more complex.

It is assumed that people likely appreciated the warmth of fire before we used its effect on food.

Although "man" is often defined as "the animal that uses fire", our present modern technology allows us so little intimacy with fire that we tend to fear it, misunderstand it and even despise it. Some authorities contend that it no longer is a valid way to enhance enjoyment, as in the use of fireplaces or campfires, because of the impact of using a fire on air quality. In the out-of-doors, concern is expressed over the consumptive aspect of both the fuel materials and the forest floor, especially in light of the increased popularity of camping and backpacking and the resultant pressure on wilderness areas. How fires are used, if at all, will be directly related to the nature of a particular environment, its proposed use for the future, and how heavily it will be used. Heavy populations of users will likely impose a prohibition of all fire usage. There are however, places in the Boreal Forests of the temperate zone where I feel that the open fire may be the least evil of the choices that are available to keep warm, to cook with, to dry clothing and to enhance the outdoor experience from the recreational point of view.

1. Approaches to the Use of Fire

There are basically three approaches to fire use in the out-of-doors as discerned through my experience and through familiarity with the pertinent literature.

1. No fires: (a preservationist approach). Cooking is done on portable stoves and the fuel is carried in. The environment should be preserved in its natural state. Dead wood is part of nature's state and should be left alone.
2. Fires are acceptable as long as they are kept small: (a combination of conservationist and preservationist approaches). In fact, the only good fire is a small fire. It is economical on fuel, produces a small fire bed, creates minimal visual impact and allows one to work close to it. The fire site reverts back more readily to its natural state, on account of its smallness. However, a fire this size will do little to keep you warm at -40°C.
3. The size of fire is determined by need: (a consumptive approach). If it is minus 40 outside, the fire may have to be quite large to keep one comfortably warm. If the use of fire is justified then one should be able to use naturally found wood because of its convenience, low cost and the avoidance of the use of a non-renewable resource. At the same time the forest can be enhanced by the use of thinning principles, the removal of diseased wood and dead wood and with it associated fungal threat, and so on. This type of user should endeavor to become highly sensitive to the environmental and recreation usage by others.

FIRE IN THE BOREAL FOREST
By Mors Kochanski

Next to knowing how to dress properly, the most important bush skill is fire lighting.

A. SOME STANDARDS - 1. You should be able to light a fire under virtually any circumstance in the boreal (spruce-moose) forest. (An ecology that progresses towards a greater degree of combustibility). 2. In a spruce forest, a fire of flames half your height, and boil a liter of water within ten minutes. 3. Sequence of developing skills: (i) learn with large wooden matches first, (ii) paper matches second, (iii) split paper match third. Finally, learn how to use flint and steel.

B. SOME NATURAL KINDLINGS - 1. Birchbark - good ignition with open flames but not flint and steel - very waterproof. 2. Inner bark of black poplar or cottonwood (*populus balsamifera*). 3. Dry Grass - most universally available - if damp, roll up in a bundle and place near the pit of the stomach to dry. 4. Old Man's Beard - good if dry, but hydroscopic in damp weather. 5. Conifer resin. 6. Fine Spruce Twigs. 7. The Feather Stick.

C. USEFUL FUELS - 1. Willow (*Salix sp.*) very tolerable smoke - good coals, easy to gather, but comes in small pieces. 2. Aspen - comes in bigger pieces but is a little smokier than Willow. 3. Alder - smoke pleasant - may even relieve head aches - can be broken into stovewood lengths, but burns fast. 4. Black Poplar Outer Bark exceptionally good coals, but burns up fast. 5. Pine Black and White Spruce - smoke induces headache, wood sparky - especially black spruce. 6. Tamarack or Larch - produces the most B.T.U.'s of all the woods but not common. 7. Birch - seldom found dry either green or rotten like aspen may be burned in green state when other fuel is scarce. 8. Driftwood - regardless of origin, tends to burn fairly hot and fast. Sodden driftwood (dripping wet) is very hot once you ignite it.

D. TECHNIQUES - 1. Start with a very hot fire for the best results 2. In winter, pile of fuel over fire should be a least knee high. 3. The best universal fire is with fuel lying parallel and in line with the wind. 4. Best build on a bump rather than in a hole. 5. Sequence: a) ignite any kindling, which in turn b) ignites a handful of match to pencil thick sticks which in turn c) ignites ten finger-thick sticks which in turn d) ignites two wrist thick sticks then e) two leg thick sticks. f) then anything you have.

E. SOME COMMON ERRORS - 1. Fire too small. 2. Wood too thick. 3. Not enough fine stuff to start fire. 4. Wood packed to close together. 5. Wood too widely spread apart to produce effective inter-reflective action. 6. Allowing a cavity to develop under long logs as they burn. 7. The cure for a smoky fire is to add more good fuel. 8. If you want irritating smoky fire use green pine or spruce or punky wet wood. 9. A good fire thrives on attention - adjust frequently.

The Open-fire burning properties of common boreal forest wood fuels

RANK	Strongest useful point	Disadvantages	Hard to force smoky	Kindling properties	Related areas
Alder [4] *Alnus* Northern species	Easily gathered without tools and easily broken into small pieces.	Burns up the fastest of all woods	Very little smoke - it tends to cure a headache		Alder in the green stage preferred for smoking meat/fish
Birch [11] *Betula* Northern white bark types	The hottest and the most pleasant smelling firewood. Will burn well enough even when green.	Found either green or rotten, therefore generally not used in camping and survival.	Pleasant smoke	Waterproof bark renowned for fire lighting	Source of bog free and false tinder fungi.
Driftwood of all types	Very hot burning even if dripping wet!	Strong sulfur smell.	Moderately smoky		
Balsam fir [3] *Abies balsamea*	The most free of resin of all the conifers.	Rarely available somewhat like birch, very poor radiance.	Moderately smoky		
Jack pine, **Lodgepole pine**	A fast burning wood that can generate strong heat	Bitter smoke that hurts eyes and lungs, imparting strong smoky smell.	Bad. Smoke very sooty	Needles (red) are very waterproof and combustible, yes in saturated branches and wood.	
Black poplar *Populus balsamifera*	The green wood burns the least of all woods for the wall backed fire. The bark makes very good coals for baking.	The wood is about as 'cold' as balsam fir.	Sound wood moderately smoky. Punky wood very acrid	Inner bark a superior kindling in priming ember to flame	Punky wood used to carry fire
Trembling aspen or **white pop**	Available in large long burning logs that is reasonably smokeless. Can be burned green.	Tools req'd to cut up wood.	Only slightly hard on the eyes.	Cured wood feathers beautifully	Ember goes out the easiest of all woods - good for scarce coal situations.
Black spruce *Picea mariana*	Adequately hot fuel that is sometimes the only available fuel.	The most acrid smoke that's the hardest on the eyes. The worst spark thrower.	The worst wood for smokiness that bothers	Resin very good for firelighting. Twigs very useful	A green piece of black sp. will preserve an ember for relighting fire
White spruce *Picea glauca*	Large logs (30 cm) make the most lasting and the most intensely radiant fire (due to glowing surface of coals)	Rarely will throw sparks. Tools req'd to cut up for use.	Bad	Same as Black Sp.	
Tamarack or **larch** *Larix laricina*	About the same as birch in heat value, weight for weight.	Generally only available in winter due to wet environment	Moderate		Roots burn like a fuse for carrying fire and to be noted as a fire hazard near dead trees
Salix or **willow** - many northern species	The most compatible fuel for humans. Pleasant smoke, brilliant flame, good warming heat and excellent coals. Easily gathered without tools.	Burns up rather quickly and comes in small pieces therefore not so useful as a warming fire while you sleep.	The least bitter of all the fuels. A very pleasant smoke that does not bother eyes or lungs.	Splinters from breaking a dry willow stick useful	The most universal useful woods for fire by friction

The open blazing fire is an important part of the quality of their outdoor experience to many people, just as the view may be an important component of a mountain walker's enjoyment, or the challenge of the impossible ascent important to the mountain climber.

It is suggested that there is a time and place for all three types of approaches in most of the vast Canadian Boreal Forest and everyone using the out-of-doors should be familiar with all of them. The mountain walker is definitely justified in promoting the use of the portable stove in sensitive ecologies, but to use the stove everywhere may be just as inappropriate as using open fires everywhere, especially in the Boreal Forest. The group leader that does not know how to use a fire properly in dire emergency is possibly lacking in professionalism.

2. The Question of Impact

Your mere presence in the bush creates an impact of sorts. The weight of your foot may crush whatever living thing may come between the sole of your boot and mother earth. The kink in your back may be nothing compared to the kinks you have imparted to the flora you slept on last night. "Leave nothing but footprints, take nothing but pictures" is close to being an archaic and inadequate concept. The foothills near Hinton, Alberta that have provided the pulp for photographic paper for most of North America have had their share of the burden to bear with their balding hills in meeting the needs of outdoor enthusiasts who may feel proud, even sanctimonious, that they took nothing from their own wilderness little realizing that they were detracting from someone else's.

"If everyone were to light fires where would we be?" is often asked. Go one step further and ask, if everyone were to set foot in a particular fragile alpine ecology what would be the fate that befalls it?

It is readily understandable to restrict fires when the hordes descend because those that are fortunate enough to be first will have something to burn and those that come later have only the bare view.

Fragile ecologies are another matter. Up to what point does any one individual experience his fair share of any fragile environment. If you have fallen in love with the alpine meadows, do you go back there again and again? An ecology too sensitive to bear an open fire may likely be too sensitive to bear the weight of too many feet. Just because you carry everything on your back, don't cut trees, light fires or pick the flowers does not mean that you might have inalienable access.

In the United States in 1980 it is estimated there are at least 10,000,000 backpackers. For every ounce of fuel used to cook one meal, 75,000 gallons of fuel is used up. There are also 20,000,000 day trippers. Surely these people are not all in ecologically sensitive areas at the same time. There is a $400,000,000 industry relating to outdoor recreation in North America.

3. Some Different Types of Fire Users

a) The Minimum Impact Camper

If you are planning to travel in ecologically sensitive areas then you should use techniques that produce no negative impact. This includes areas above or near the tree line, or anywhere that is designated by custom or law to be left in as natural a state as possible, perhaps to serve the needs of many people such as park. In some areas very visible effects are being created simply by foot traffic and by sleeping on the vegetation even with the use of cushioning mattresses. Fires are especially inappropriate in these areas. The slightest impact is so negative that there is little possibility of producing any positive impact at all.

Minimum impact campers carry everything needed to stay completely independent of their environment. Some campers of this type feel that since they choose not to use any raw materials found in their environment they are not required to master such skills as open fire lighting, as they have enough to do in learning how to manipulate their portable stoves. Backpackers may often acquire a false sense of security from the independence that results from bringing with them all that they need.

Those who venture above the tree line often do not realize how unforgiving that type of environment may be. The vegetation is stunted and regenerates slowly for no small reason. For the hiker, the lack of protection from the elements, the lack of raw materials for shelter and fire, the oxygen-rarefied atmosphere and its resultant effect on fire as well as thinking process, the cool temperature, and the sudden weather changes all result in an environment that may demand a higher than the usual degree of competency when dealing with the emergency situation. About 35 Americans perish every year because they venture into areas for which they are not adequately prepared and great numbers of others incur considerable expense in being rescued by the authorities.

An injury that would impede travel, the loss of a ski or a broken ski, an unexpected detention due to being storm or fog bound, a temporary disorientation or even becoming lost, are a few occasions where knowing extra wilderness skills may be the insurance that provides for comfort or for the saving of life or limb. Good fire skills may make up for glaring deficiencies in other areas of knowledge, and in the loss of vital pieces of equipment and in other kinds of emergency.

NEXT TO KNOWING HOW TO DRESS WELL, FIRE IS ONE OF THE MOST IMPORTANT BUSH SKILLS THERE ARE, BECAUSE IT IS ONE OF THE FEW MEANS AVAILABLE TO MAKE UP MOST GREAT DEFICIENCIES.

Now, having to master fire skills does not mean these skills have to be practiced in ecologically sensitive areas even if that is where you always travel. Simulation in more resilient areas is adequate as long as you realize at least these points: High altitudes may have more wind to contend with. Only the driest, most vertical wood will ignite readily. Fires tend not to burn as well in the more rarefied atmosphere. To avoid making any fire where none is wanted make sure you know what you are doing before going where angels fear to tread.

b) The Traditional Wilderness Camper

To justify the use of wilderness raw bush materials this type of camper must use an approach that creates a positive environmental impact through the thinning and cleanup of forest litter. The type of environment chosen for this style of camping should, of course, be one that is resilient enough to absorb this usage. By law it should never be a park unless the required permits are obtained.

The wilderness camper may use the best of both worlds: good equipment combined with the raw materials more conveniently derived from the bush rather than substitutes carried in.

If the creation of a fire place is a problem, a fire pan may be considered, especially for more permanent camps. This metal or tin tray will keep the fire from damaging the vegetation or soil by being suspended far enough above it. Also, the ashes could be evenly dispersed in the environment rather than being concentrated in one spot as is done in an ordinary campfire.

The Right Place: There are many people who might not be able to afford the other types of camping and may depend more on what they know about the bush rather than on what they can buy. Ultimately, this type of camper in my opinion may put less of an imposition on the total environment than better equipped cousins with all of their aluminum, synthetics and non-renewable fuels.

c) The Survivalist

Survivalists look to the environment to provide for their total needs in every way possible, where environmental concerns are generally set aside in the interests of preserving life and limb. However, it is not the blighted unfortunate individual who is enduring an actual survival situation whom we may be concerned about, but the survivalist in training.

Survivalists have acquired a bad reputation in the past because their lack of care in choosing the right environment in which to extend their skills. The teaching and practise of knowledge, insight and sensitivity, as compared to the other forms of camping, as well as a cognizance of the needs of others who may be using the same environment to accomplish other ends. In present circumstances "survivalist's" practicing their skills seems to be the least knowledgeable or sensitive of all the users. Survival skills should be an important part of the safety knowledge of those who indulge in camping, especially off the beaten path. There is likely a false sense of economy displayed by the camper who neglects to practise survival skills, and on getting lost, perishes or has to be retrieved through search and rescue with its associated expenditure of someone else's time and money. If you don't know how to cope with basic wilderness emergencies, maybe you don't have a right to be in the bush unless you directly bear the costs involved in your rescue.

The survivalist should know how to safely use adequately large fires to cope with extreme cold, to build signal fires and know how to light fires under adverse conditions to a certain minimal standard within a certain time limit.

d) The Educationalist and the Social Worker

Another class of wilderness users are those involved in educational and/or mentally and socially rehabilitative bush programs. These are people who are using the out-of-doors as a tool to educate or rehabilitate. Experiencing the natural world takes us in the direction of beginning to understand it. The most basic processes that keep us alive are those used in wilderness living as practiced by our distant ancestors from time immemorial. Of the many disciplines in basic existence skills, few are as natural and important as the mastery of fire. It should be a valid topic for any school curriculum in view of the fact that about 34 out of every million people in Canada (about 800) die of fire every year. In the U.S.A. 55 per million or 15 to 13 thousand die. At least four to six children die every year from tent fires alone in Canada. Fire skills should be taught in outdoor education not only for camping-recreation applications and for fire safety in home and industry.

I have not added to the fatalities previously listed the numbers who would not have frozen to death had they known how to light a fire properly.

Some minimum-trace campers find survival techniques repugnant, attributing may incidents of bush misuse to a "survival ethic". It is unfortunate that many people who choose to practice survival skills, or more likely "minimum expense" camping, have not yet gained sufficient insight into the etiquette of bush use to know enough to avoid ecologically sensitive areas and to keep their activities out of the public eye. Those well versed in fire usage are not the ones that create the eyesores. Survival instruction and practice, as well as the educational and rehabilitative endeavors are an industry and not a recreation in my view, and as such should best be practiced in non-recreational areas, such as logged over areas or those destined to be logged over.

4. Abuses of Fire

Those who do not understand fire are usually the ones who become involved in the abuse of fire and often become its victims. Here are some of the typical ways fire is misused.

1. Escaped campfire burning up the environment due to carelessness in leaving a fire unattended, lack of knowledge in managing fire, or the failure to put a fire completely out. (Often resulting from a lack of understanding and perceiving the conditions that contribute to a high fire hazard).
2. Fires built in fragile environments (high altitudes for example) in which destroyed vegetation may take scores of years to regenerate.
3. Fires built too near to living trees with needless indelible damage to the bark, branches and roots.
4. Firewood gathered in an unsightly way. Stumps not cut flush with the ground. Dead branches taken off so that a living tree is further injured, or disfigured.

5. Poorly chosen fire sites resulting in a noticeable disfigurement of the ground and vegetation. Large holes burned into moss. A beautiful clearing or vista marred by an unnatural looking fire site.
6. Fires put out improperly with highly visible and enduring charred wood remaining in the fire site.
7. Residual garbage materials not being retrieved after being burned out, especially glass and aluminum.
8. Altering the ground for a special fire and not rehabilitating it when finished. Example: cooking beans in a hole, building a trench fire, or using a stone ring to confine fire or stones to support cooking utensils.
9. Not using previous fire places. If the first user does not choose a fire place with enough expertise and care, the subsequent users may build their fires wherever they feel like it so that an extensive area is pocked with fire places.
10. The over-use of a popular area until it is pounded to dust and fire-pocked so that regeneration is prevented by the high concentration of ash.

This list is not complete but it exemplifies what the basic problem may be, which is simply ignorance of skilled fire techniques and fire etiquette.

The misuse of fire is usually about ninety-nine percent a visual problem and one percent an actual environmental imposition. It generally stems from a lack of appreciation for the needs of others that may be using the same areas, and not knowing that there are more acceptable ways to handle the situation.

5. Where Campfires are Out of Place

1. Where they are prohibited by law.

2. Where the environmental disturbance and visual imposition that the fire creates is not justified by the advantages of a fire.
3. Where a natural feature is not enhanced by the placement of a fire. Why do we choose the most beautiful vistas to make our camp, even at the disadvantage of having to drag firewood a long way? Why not camp where the camping is best (near water and fuel supply) and just visit the beautiful vista?
4. Where a fire will cause an environmental imposition that will lead to erosion or an unduly long period of time to revert back to a natural state. It might be worth considering that if an environment cannot stand the imposition of a campfire then maybe it cannot stand being walked upon very much either.

6. Justifying the Use of a Campfire

The way a fire is used and a fireplace created could have positive results that may outweigh any neglectful aspects. Using forest "fire management" principles, with an understanding of the ecology of fire, as well as using good judgement, one should be able to leave the forest better than one found it, at least as far as our needs are concerned.

From an ecological and economic viewpoint a forest could be groomed so that there is no tree nearer to its closest neighbor than approximately two meters or about the distance of the outstretched arms from fingertip to fingertip. This was a condition that seemed to have been maintained naturally throughout most of inhabitable North America before the appearance of the `white man`, who has significantly disturbed the natural forest succession.

THE MICRO ECOLOGY: Another way of looking at the campfire is to examine the notion that in creating a fireplace, in the right context, you create a micro-environment by inhibiting the predominant local vegetation and concentrating the various nutrients through the accumulation of ash. Campfires that have been used for a relatively short period of time, such as three or four days of continuous burning, are usually far from sterile as far as vegetation is concerned. The plants that often colonize a campfire are ones that do not seem to be locally abundant. They are plants from a previous era lying dormant and waiting for an opening such as a simple campfire or in the other extreme a forest fire. The greater the diversity we create, the greater the ecological stability.

7. Points of Basic Fire Ecology

On this infinitesimal speck in the universe known as Earth, all processes follow the three laws of thermodynamics. The first of these is the law of conservation of matter and energy. In simplistic terms, it means that neither matter nor energy are destroyed; they are only changed in form. Burning by any means, be it by a lightning storm or by a psychotic firebug, according to this law does not destroy anything. The owner of a fire gutted home may disagree.

Burning a piece of wood does not destroy the nutrients that should continue to remain available in the soil for the local flora.

Trees get no energy whatsoever from tree humus. Instead they use the sun`s energy through the medium of chlorophyll to breakdown water and carbon dioxide to make simple sugars.

Burn a kilogram of wood and there remains a fraction of a gram of ash which contains the essential materials for the growth of protoplasm in the living cells of the tree, which in turn has to expend energy derived from the sun through photosynthesis to use these nutrients. As opposed to the slow breakdown of humus through natural means, fire causes the mineral nutrients to be released at once and to become readily and instantly available.

A small amount of ash may represent a large amount of wood and generally the ash is the first thing we focus on when we see a campfire. The quantity of ash depends on the quantity and quality of the wood burned, the kind of fuel and the amount of moisture, humidity and wind that were present when the fire burned. The ash is always high in calcium, potassium and phosphorous, and has traces of other mineral elements. In fact, from a health point of view, recent studies have shown that the concentration of heavy metals is often too high to recommend the usage of wood ashes on garden soils. In a forest fire these components would return to the soil right where the organic material burned. A campfire concentrates these materials in one place, perhaps suggesting that the ash from a campfire should be dispersed back into the environment.

E.V. Komarek Sr., in his article "Fire Ecology" which was presented at the first Tall Timbers Fire Ecology Conference, makes this statement: "In nature, fire is a great regenerative force, one might even say rejuvenative force, without which plant and animal succession, in the absence of climatic upheaval or physiographic cataclysm (or at least great climatic or physiographic change), would be retarded so that old, senescent and decadent communities would cover the earth. I have been unable to find a single exception to the rule that fire always changes the succession to a younger stage. The intensity and frequency of fire determines how youthful such a stage will be. Without fire, plant succession ultimately seems to lead to catastrophe, for increased hazard to fire apparently is in direct ratio to age. The older plant communities become more and more vulnerable to fire until finally, unless some violent upheaval occurs, fire rejuvenates the succession, sometimes even to the bare rock itself". (page 105-106)

Thus the boreal forest will, from time to time, be consumed by fire. Over the millennia the forest has evolved to 'expect' this form of rejuvenation. Predictably, the climax forest reverts to a somewhat fundamental community of mosses, lichens, low broad-leaved plants, grasses and shrubs and these bring with them the animals that prefer this habitat, wherein the inexorable process begins towards re-establishing the forest to its climax or last stage of development.

Without periodic fire to remove underbrush, decaying leaf build-up and dead wood from the forest floor, many forests have experienced marked ecological changes to become far more vulnerable to fire than they were before intervention with fire suppression practices. This artificial exclusion of wild fire has produced major changes in many woodland plant communities that were dependent on this fire as a chief regulator of vegetation types. A hundred years ago small fires every ten years or so attacked the turf and underbrush without reaching the crowns of the trees.

Without these fires, this excessive organic build-up leads to a condition that might annihilate the forest when fire sweeps through. Negative implications for tree regeneration, soil fertility, water holding ability and erosion are a few of the potential results of a forest fire.

An interesting book worth referring to with respect to what our North American boreal forests were like before our forefathers came on the scene is YELLOW ORE, YELLOW HAIR, YELLOW PINE: a photographic study of a century of forest ecology by Donald R. Porogulski, photography by Richard H. Showell, published in July 1974. This is Bulletin 616 of the Agricultural Experimental Station, South Dakota State University, Brookings. The cost of the publication is about $10.00.

The most noticeable difference between the forests of today and those of a hundred years ago, is the very crowded trees (known as dog hair stands) and the lack of ground vegetation needed by many wildlife species of today's forests.

It is taking a long time for people on this continent to come to the realization that our ecology (like many other ecology's of the world) is intimately connected with fire.

The natural forest progresses ecologically in the direction of increased combustibility. Genetically the flora is geared to depend on fire to maintain stable ecological relationships by:

- returning nutrients more quickly to the soil;
- producing the seed bed required by some species so that they may regenerate;
- reducing, preventing or cleansing the forest of tree diseases;
- removing senile trees;
- making room for the young, keeping stands of trees pure, and maintaining a healthier spacing.

Proper spacing alone would likely sustain a far greater and more diverse animal and plant population by providing for greater amounts of varied ground vegetation.

In comparison to what has just been said about the natural wild fire that may cover millions of acres at one time, how can a campfire be implicated in being so injurious to the environment?

a) How a Fire Burns

Fresh fuel added to a fire basically passes through three stages of combustion:

1. Moisture is evaporated.
2. Volatile gases, oils and tars are given off and burn usually in the most visible flame.
3. The fixed carbon char is burned by a glowing action about three times the intensity of the more visible flame.

The diffusion flame combustion process that is commonly known as fire is made easier to understand with the use of a graphic model known as the tetrahedron of fire. This approach to explaining fire applies universally to any form of combustible material and is one of the more popular concepts used in fire suppression theory. This theory helps us to understand the molecular processes involved in burning and in fire suppression. It is based on the work of W.M. Haessler, THE EXTINGUISHMENT OF FIRE, Dayton, 1962.

In the four-sided tetrahedron the four entities are adjoined and each is connected with the other three to exemplify their intimate relationship. The four entities represent the four factors in the fire process: fuel (wood), air (oxygen), heat and uninhibited chain reactions. By the use of the four-sided model we mean to imply that each of the four factors are equally related and of exactly the same importance. If any one factor is removed, fire is impossible.

The fire process goes something this this: When heat is applied to a fuel, which in this instance is wood or more specifically cellulose, the rise in temperature starts a breakdown process known as pyrolysis. Some components of the wood are changed into gasses and vapours (amongst other things) and the continuing rise in temperature causes the vapour components to become increasingly agitated until they break up into very active particles, known as free radicals, which are very intent on finding something suitable to latch on to. The free radicals interact amongst each other and go into an uninhibited chain reaction which now involves the oxygen from the air. Fire is the result. The fire now becomes its own heat source, becoming self-propagating and continuing as long as there are properly sized and arranged pieces of fuel to maintain pyrolysis, radical formation, and feed-back heat.

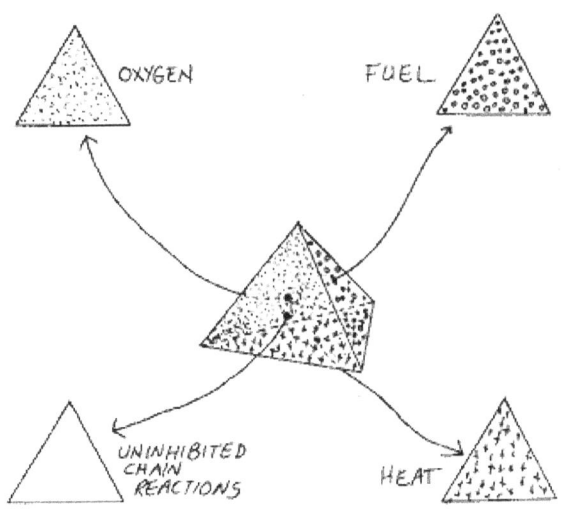

The Tetrahedron of Fire

b) The Fuel/Wood Surface to Mass Ratio

The ease of ignition and the promotion of combustion are greatly affected by the size of the wood used. The finer the wood, the more readily it will burn, and of course the faster it will burn. If a block of wood with a surface area of a square metre was split so that the resulting pieces would have a total surface area of ten square metres, the pieces would burn with greater intensity to a higher temperature, in a shorter time span. However, the amount of heat liberated would be the same for both, the block and the pieces, because this depends on the calorific value of the material. The way to be assured a good start for a fire is to use enough fine material to get the intensities of heat to make the larger sticks burn. Twigs or wood feathers should be about the thickness of a match stick to ensure easy and rapid ignition.

c) Fuel Spacing and Arrangement: Oxygen Access

It is not sufficient that the fuel be thin enough. It also has to be properly spaced in relation to the other pieces near it so that the required heat concentration from the igniting source can be achieved. The oxygen then has access to the combustible gasses that evolve, and when the fuel is burning, the adjacent fuel is involved to extend the fire process. Experience will eventually determine that you can not squeeze your fuel too close together or have it spread too far apart, both when lighting the fire and later in keeping it going.

If the kindling is too close together the mass of the material in the kindling absorbs too much of the match's heat before it can be effective, and it physically obstructs oxygen access. The oxygen-combustible vapour mixture is then too lean to catch fire and produces only smoke. If the convective heat is not allowed up through the kindling because it is such a dense mass, its drying and pre-heating action is much less efficient. At match thickness the spacing of the material should be of the diameter of the material itself. But by the time the material is ten centimetres in diameter, the spacing is only a centimetre.

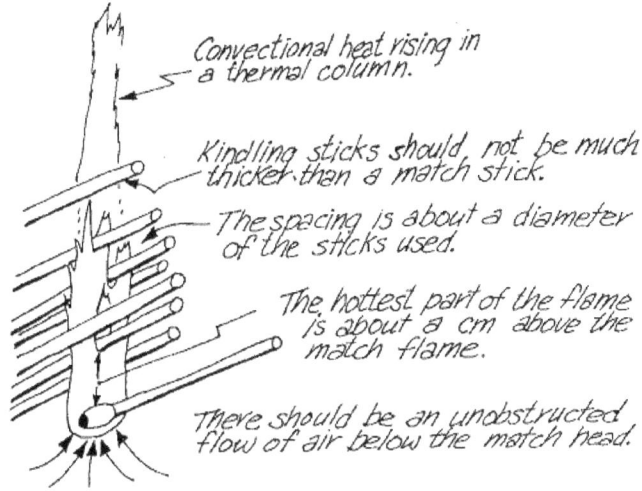

Diagramatic sketch of how a match should be used

It is also helpful to light your kindling well off the ground. The coolest, dampest air is near the ground and there is also more obstruction to the flow of needed air to the site of combustion.

The best fuels are ones that are high in carbon and hydrogen content. The most common elements found in all living things are carbon, hydrogen, oxygen, and nitrogen. Oxygen is not a fuel but it supports combustion. Nitrogen is not a fuel and it does not support combustion; in fact, it tends to interfere with oxygen. Combustion-and breathing for that matter-will cease when the atmospheric oxygen level drops below 15%.

d) The Composition of Wood

Wood is composed of three major constituents: Hemicellulose, cellulose and lignin. Their molecular structure puts them in a class of chemical known as polymers. A polymer is a relatively large molecule that is made up of a number of repeating (poly) smaller units called mers.

When wood burns, the cellulose mostly participates in producing the visible flame and the lignin supports the major part of the glowing.

The cellulose is the main structural part of the cell wall of trees and plants. Wood has such an intricate structure, creating such an enormous surface area, that a cubic centimetre of wood spread out would cover an area of ten million square centimetres.

Wood heated up to 200 degrees centigrade dries out and undergoes slow pyrolysis (breakdown through being heated), evolving some carbon dioxide, formic acid and vinegar. Some heat is given off. At temperatures between 200 and 280 degrees centigrade wood slowly undergoes pyrolysis with much the same evolution of gases as mentioned earlier and the wood is reduced to charcoal without flame. From 280 degrees up to 500 degrees centigrade the mixture of gases are combustible and are readily ignited. Spontaneous ignition occurs at about 545 degrees centigrade towards the end of pyrolysis, as the emission of gas decreases and air can reach the hot charcoal. Above 500 degrees centigrade, carbon monoxide and hydrogen burn as a non-luminous flame and the charcoal burns until white ash is left.

COMPOSITION OF WOOD AND COAL ASHES MATERIAL
Units are in parts per million

Element	Wood Ash From Home Wood Stove	Anthracite Pea-Coal
P	7569	984
K	68217	448
Ca	237557	2563
Mg	15530	133
Mn	2262	9
Fe	365	88
B	262	4
Cu	70	10
Zn	686	43
Al	2048	430
Na	NA*	NA
Hg	NA	NA
Pb	NA	NA
Cd	NA	NA
Cr	NA	NA

NA* = Not available at this time

Credit: Dr. George Estes, Plant Science Department, University of New Hampshire

Wood will readily ignite from a flame at 380 degrees centigrade.

Studies have shown that the average composition of the evolved volatiles remain constant throughout the pyrolysis. The calorific value was constant at about 4 Kilocalories per gram.

Cellulose, which composes about 50% of wood, volatilizes rapidly around 340 degrees centigrade and exhibits typical polymer characteristics by degrading into nearly two hundred different chemical compounds. Numerous simple molecules form and diffuse to the surface where mixing with oxygen occurs. Subsequent ignitions take place if the temperature is at or above the ignition point. All woods have similar ignition temperatures despite appreciable variations in their ignitabilities. Cellulose products burn without melting to form a char.

Rapid heating produces little charcoal, much tar and highly inflammable gases. Some of the compounds evolved through pyrolysis are very toxic, which account for headaches resulting from breathing smoke-especially from black spruce and pine. Some of the compounds you are likely to find are:

- carbon monoxide
- hydrogen cyanide
- carbon dioxide
- creosote
- formaldehyde
- acetaldehyde
- butraldehyde
- nitrogen dioxide
- acreolin

There are also more than a dozen other cancer causing (carcinogenic) compounds.

e) Smoke

Smoke is mostly composed of unburned carbon particles that are less than one millimicron in diameter and can be suspended in a gas. Anything larger would be considered a dust particle. Smoke is composed of clouds of particles, which when taken individually would be invisible, but when taken as a cloud scatter light and are opaque. Smoke results when carbonaceous materials and hydrocarbons, are incompletely burned due to a lack of heat or a restriction in the oxygen supply, unreacted carbon molecules form. Soot is formed when these molecules lump together. When other intermediate gaseous products form simultaneously with the carbon, they may condense on the particles to produce uniquely acrid, toxic and irritating smoke. In a confined space, wood smoke alone can produce lung damage and be lethal long before the heat of the fire would have any effect. Improperly burning wood in stoves results in a serious pollution problem. The particles emitted by wood, in comparison to other particles, are very small and the wood also produces from ten to a hundred times more particles than gas or oil, depending on the quality of the wood. Compared to gas or oil, which is virtually 100% consumed, only 80% of wood is burned up in a fire. Not only are the by-products of a poorly functioning stove more irritating to the lungs but they are more easily drawn into the lungs on breathing. The greatest concerns are the cancer producing compounds that coat or are an integral part of these particles. To minimize the problem, dry wood should be used, smoldering fires avoided and very hot fire lighting techniques practiced.

Intuitively, the relationship of wood smoke and lung cancer should seem virtually self evident. However, some preliminary investigation into connection of wood smoke and lung cancer indicates there may be very little connection. This may be due to our ancient association with wood smoke that has resulted in lung tissue that can readily cope with the carcinogens in wood fire.

When an open fire is producing excessive smoke, it is likely due to the condition of the fuel. It may be too green or too wet, so that so much heat is being used up in drying that there is little left over for volatilizing. The solution is to add good dry fuel on top of the smoky fuel so that the products of incomplete combustion will be more completely burned in the improved fire. As well, the improved thermal column will carry the smoke up above head level faster and more effectively.

Tip of match head made of Tetraphyosphorous trisulfide (very heat sensitive fuel), glass (for increased friction) and glue, usually water soluable

Rest of head made of sulfur (fuel), lead dioxide (fuel), and water soluable glue

Paraffin wax (fuel)

Wood (fuel), often Aspen as, it burns well and does not sustain an afterglow

Common wood match

f) Oxygen

The atmosphere generally contains about 20.9% oxygen and about 79.1% nitrogen. In the presence of oxygen almost all matter undergoes a change, which is often termed oxidation. Oxidation can be as slow as rusting or as rapid as an explosion. With an increase in temperature, the rate of oxidation also increases. For each 10 °C rise in temperature, the activity of the molecules doubles. This accounts for the greater ease with which a fire may be made on a summer's day at 20 °C as compared to minus 20 °C on a winter's day. If the temperature of a fuel is raised continuously it will eventually burst into flame (the production of heat and light), an indication of its rapid reaction with oxygen. This is termed combustion. The rate of combustion is dependent on the ability of the molecules of fuel and oxygen to mix together in the appropriate proportions in spite of the interference from the nitrogen in the air.

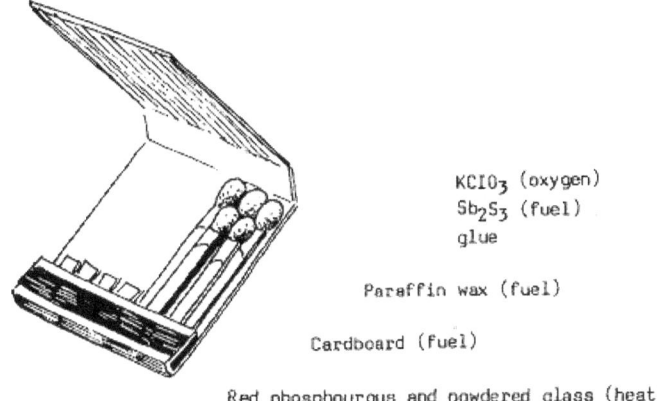

$KClO_3$ (oxygen)
Sb_2S_3 (fuel)
glue

Paraffin wax (fuel)

Cardboard (fuel)

Red phosphourous and powdered glass (heat)

The chemical make-up of paper safety matches

In still air a fire will draw in surrounding oxygen through the circulation created by the hot convection currents (thermal column) rising above the fire. A fire suspended off the ground will burn better than one on the ground. A fire built on a mound will burn better than one in a hole. There is a difference between suspending a fire off the ground and a fire having a void under or in it; the latter is a factor that tends to slow a fire down.

A strong wind will force far more oxygen into a fire than convectional draw could provide and thus will make the fire more intense.

The thermal column formed above a flaming area establishes an airflow so that the oxygen is brought to where it is needed for mixing. The mixture thus formed has a flammable range within which it will burn. If the mixture is too lean in oxygen or too rich in oxygen for a certain concentration of fuel vapour, no combustion will result even if an open flame is present.

The "two rich in oxygen" phenomenon is often encountered in lighting a wood stove. When the door is open there is usually an imperceptible draw through the stove up the chimney. When the fine kindling is lit, the door is closed, the draft is reduced, the kindling roars into flame.

It is interesting to note that when the oxygen supply for any reason drops from its 20.9% to about 15%, combustion ceases due to the smothering action of the nitrogen in the air.

A phenomenon that may be encountered in air-tight stoves is a slow, small form of explosion termed a backflash. The condition is most likely to occur when wood is added to a bed of hot coals and the air supply is inadequate. The wood volatilizes to fill the stove with combustible gases and if the door is opened the sudden influx of oxygen may cause these gases to ignite, sometimes causing a surge of combustion that may force smoke or flames out of every crack or opening, especially the door. It is a wise precaution not to have your face near the door when you open it, as the backflash may singe eyebrows, eyelashes and hair.

g) Ignition Continuity

Once combustion starts and is given ample oxygen, it becomes self-supporting through the following process:

1. As the fuel burns it creates more heat.

2. The increase in heat raises more fuel to its ignition temperature.
3. Additional oxygen is drawn in by the convection column of heat forming above the fire. In a raging conflagration a windstorm can be observed drawing air to the burning source.
4. The oxygen increases the rate of burning and more fuel becomes involved.
5. This chain reaction continues until the fuel has been consumed. This is known as a fuel-regulated fire. Outdoor campfires are fuel-regulated in that you make it big or small by adding or withholding the fuel. In a stove the fire is oxygen-regulated, in that you can vary the air supply to make the fire burn slower or faster.

h) Heat Transfer

In an open fire heat transfer is carried out by either convection (flame created thermal column) or by radiation, with conduction generally being insignificant.

i) Heat Transfer by Convection

Heated air or other gases produced by the burning process, are generally lighter than the surroundings, and flow upward to warm or to dry any fuel above or even bring it to a kindling temperature. This transfer of heat through a circulation medium is termed 'heating by convection'. It is important to realize that when fuel is wet or green it must be put on a fire far enough in advance so that this convective heat can dry it out in anticipation of when it is needed. This form of rapid heating of a chilled person can be done by using small, but not fine high-quality (smokeless) fuel, provided enough wind is present to blow this air warmed by convection at and past any bystander, otherwise the heating effect is only radiant.

j) Heat Transfer by Radiation

Any hot object that sends out invisible infrared waves that warm anything that intercepts these waves (if something is white hot it can emit ultra-violet rays that are even hotter, but this likely will never be encountered in a campfire situation). When you stand near a fire a wind may waft some convective heat your way but it is the radiant heat you would most benefit from. It is much like the warmth that we feel when the sun shines on our skin or on a dark item of clothing. Radiant energy can be blocked by a reflective light colored material that bounces back these rays while the material itself remains cool. A dark surface absorbs the ray which results in rise in temperature of the surface. The dark surface may then produce a sensation of warmth by re-emitting what it absorbed but in a longer weaker wave length.

k) Moisture

Moisture has to be driven off (the process of drying) before anything will burn. While moisture evaporates, it carries away a great deal of heat which causes the combustible material to cool or stay cool. This cooling process is easily understood when you recall the cooling effect of water on your skin. One gram of water requires 540 calories to evaporate.

The experienced firelighters develop a "feel" for fire conditions. They can sense when greater caution is called for as to where to light a fire, how big it should be, how much vigilance they have to maintain over it, and how painstaking they have to be in putting it out. In the other extreme, they can also recognize the conditions and circumstances that affect a fire adversely, that make it difficult to start and to keep it burning. They may seem oblivious to what may be perceived as very hazardous by the inexperienced fire maker.

l) Fire For Warmth

FIRE MAKING: Fire may be the simplest and sometimes the only recourse in protecting yourself from the discomfort of cold, counteracting the effects of hypothermia, or in making up for inadequate clothing, bedding or shelter. If you were dressed in the old European tradition of good wool clothing, you would be wearing about 9 kilograms of clothing for -40°C. In five days the same clothing may weigh about 15 kilograms due to frost build up, if no means of drying is available. This so impairs the efficiency of the clothing that survival may not be possible without fire. Fire lighting is one of the more important bush techniques that should be mastered to at least a minimal level before travelling off the beaten path. It is of primary importance following an accident or whenever you are otherwise detained in the out-of-doors, especially when used in conjunction with a shelter in cold or wet weather.

In cold weather a good rule is to light your fire first before doing anything else. It is always more sensible to keep yourself warm rather than trying to thaw yourself out later. In times of a high fire hazard this rule does not apply so rigidly, because the weather is far warmer and hypothermia is of a lesser concern.

In the cold, when you have decided that an open shelter is necessary, you should try to estimate where the fire should be positioned to end up in front of the completed shelter. This will avoid creating a second fireplace. The fire may then do a number of things for you while you are building the shelter.

1. It will warm you when you need it.
2. The direction the smoke is blowing will indicate to you the proper orientation of the front of your shelter.
3. Long pieces of wood can be dragged over the fire and be made to criss-cross so that in burning through they will create more manageable pieces of firewood without the effort of cutting on your part. Wood too big to move may be burned through where it lies. You could have a number of fires working for you simultaneously.

CHOICE OF SITE FOR CAMPFIRE: The first step in putting out a fire is the careful selection of a suitable site. A fire on a poorly chosen site may take a lot more effort to put out.

High fire hazard demands special care in picking a safe fire site. In a survival situation you may have to build a fire right where you are, if injury or other circumstances prevents you travelling very far to find a suitable site. Knowing how to handle inadequate conditions is an important aspect to good survival training, as you may have to make do with whatever is available in the immediate vicinity.

When there is a high fire hazard it is wise to be extra cautious with regard to controlling your fire, which under certain circumstances may go out of control in a matter of seconds. Leaving a fire unattended is foolhardy in circumstances other than continuous rain; even then, in some jurisdictions this may result in a fine even if there is no hazard. An unattended fire is one where there is no direct visual contact with the fire in the immediate vicinity of the fire. That is, you could be around the bend fishing, sleeping inside your tent or otherwise be occupied where it is obvious that no one is watching the fire regardless of how fire-safe the site or how low the hazard.

In high fire hazard, build fires on sand or gravel bars or on mineral soil. Remove duff to the mineral soil for at least a metre around the fire. As well as keeping the fire small, do no turn your back on it until it has burned a distinct fire circle for itself. Where there is a need to remove duff, first ask yourself if a suitable duff-free area can not be located instead, because this is less disturbing of the natural setting. It may be wise to make the fire so near to a water source that the water can be thrown directly on the fire without having to take a single step. If this is done below the annual flood level, the remaining traces of your fire will be erased on the next flooding of the river.

m) Ground Fire

Duff is the decayed and partially decayed litter or organic matter that is found in varying thickness on the forest floor. If it is more than a few centimetre thick it will often smolder in such a way that it is virtually undetectable. Even when wet it will burn by drying a centimetre or so thickness of fuel ahead of itself. It may surface if the wind blows at the right time so that the litter or non-decayed organic matter on the surface may catch fire.

Fires made on top of deep moss or muskeg for any length of time burn out a cavity; the longer the fire burns, the deeper the cavity. A disfigurement may be created that will last many years before the ground regenerates. Fires built on moss need a lot of water and effort to be put out with certainty, even in the winter time with snow on the ground. In the winter time when the fire caution is usually quite relaxed, a fire may smolder until the snow is gone, only to surface in the next dry, windy spell. Rain will often not penetrate deep enough to put out this so-called ground fire. A ground fire usually reveals itself by the haze or smoke it may produce. It is especially visible early in the morning after a night of very still air, but in other circumstances may remain undetectable until you virtually step in it. It is only under the exceptional circumstances, such as sustaining a broken leg or finding one's self in a muskeg you cannot walk out of, that a fire should ever be built on deep moss.

A divot of moss used to cover a small properly put out campfire usually takes as a transplant and often proves to be one of the more effective ways of hiding a fire site.

If the duff is no more than five to ten centimetres thick, the fireplace will revert back to a natural appearance very quickly. Grassy sites, the heavier the growth the better, revert back the quickest. Aspen and pine stands tend to provide good sites as the duff build-up is rather shallow, and the trees favour soils that makes a good firebase.

Rocky ground tends to retain a great deal more heat than loamy ground and needs more water to cool it.

A small fire should not be situated closer than an arm span or two metres from any living tree and further for larger trees. The radiant energy from a fire that is too close may damage the bark, the heat in the soil may injure the roots and the thermal column may injure the branches, buds or leaves it envelops. Large fires should be built accordingly.

The general area of the fire should be level and free of features that may trip you such as stumps, roots, holes and shrubbery.

The soil should be well drained or have a good grass cover so that it does not churn into mud when it rains.

Ideally, for fire safety and environmental cosmetics, the site should be such that you can light a fire without clearing the site or having to prepare it in any way, be it grass or duff. The fire is built on top of the uncleared site and allowed to burn its own fire circle, all the while being carefully watched. In the case of a fire of short duration (two to three hours), there is surprisingly little heat penetration downwards in non-gravelly or sandy soil so that most grass roots remain viable. Undue disturbance of the soil in this situation creates a more negative impact than the often suggested method of digging up or completely disturbing the soil.

In lighting thousands of fires in this way, under normal conditions, I have not had any problem in any fire getting away and the fire site tends to revert back to the natural state the quickest of all of any method. Complete reversion for a heavily used fire of 24 hours duration may take two or three years.

The forest, and perhaps the tree, may cope with needless injury but those of your own kind may recognize you as a boor by your lack of sensitivity and knowledge of fire etiquette.

n) The Use of Matches

MATCHES: Matches in a protective container should always be carried, if possible, in three places; (a) in your pants pocket, (b) in your coat, and (c) in your pack. Matches should never be carried loose in any pocket. Hundreds of people are burned every year because they ignore this point. In the U.S. about 50 people burn to death from this cause alone. The matches should be in waterproof containers that can be easily opened when the hands are numb. Your hands may be so numb from cold or you may be beginning to suffer from hypothermia that opening the container could be difficult. Your competency should be severely questioned for allowing such a condition to develop. Under these conditions, where the need is most urgent, fire lighting becomes most difficult. You may have to exercise strenuously to restore circulation and heat to the hands before attempting to strike a match, or in your clumsiness you may break the match or strike it and drop it. For this point alone keeping the hands warm is one of the greater priorities in surviving. Allowing the hands to become numb to the point of becoming useless is a hazard to be strictly avoided. Not only is this condition physically uncomfortable, but it can be mentally terrifying as well.

Any so-called water-proof container should always be tested to prove its effectiveness by submerging in an upright position for at least ten minutes.

Some Native people suggest that one should test how cold the hands are by touching the thumb to the little finger of the same hand. As soon as you cannot carry out this exercise you are reaching a dangerous state of incapacity and you should immediately take steps to warm up.

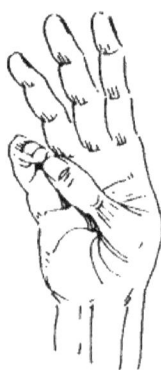

The test for hypothermic incapacity.

THE IMPORTANCE OF PRACTICE: Carrying matches is not enough. Their use must be mastered through considerable practice. There is no magical way to gain proficiency in fire lighting. There are suggested minimum standards that one might strive to achieve in the training or learning process. Under normal circumstances one should be able to gather the necessary materials and get a fire going with flames reaching your own height in five to ten minutes time. First master you lighting skills with wooden (kitchen) matches, then paper matches and finally paper matches split in half. A large kitchen match represents about one B.T.U. when burned up completely.

A BTU is the quantity of heat required to raise the temperature of one pound of water one degree Fahrenheit at a specific temperature. A Calorie is the amount of heat required at a pressure of one atmosphere to raise the temperature of one gram of water one degree centigrade. A BTU is about 25.2 calories or about 10.5 joules.

The flame strength of a paper match is a fraction of the strength of a wooden match and a split paper match is half that again. If you can consistently light a fire with a split paper match there will be few fire lighting circumstances that will give you any difficulty. The essence of lighting fire with matches is to enhance the strength of the match flame with some highly combustible substance as soon as possible. There is no lack of such materials in the boreal forest.

The ecology of the boreal forest progresses through various successive stages towards a higher state of combustibility as it gets order. The forest has more than adequate combustible materials that will allow you to light a fire in virtually any circumstance without anything more than just matches. So-called fire lighting kits tend to elicit a considerable measure of contempt from me, but if it is the only way some people can light a fire then the method has to be accepted. Fire skills for survival are so important and fundamental that a fire starter kit should be considered absolutely redundant in the spruce-moose forest.

o) Twig Method of Fire Lighting

LIGHTING FIRE WITH MATCHES AND TWIGS:
The advantages of this method are: (a) it requires no tools, (b) it is efficient, (c) it is a good method to use in the cold because the twigs can be gathered with mitts or gloves on and the hand needs to be exposed only for a few moments when lighting the twigs and (d) it is the most convenient method of lighting a fire nine-tenths of the time.

1. In winter it is relatively easy to find dry twigs on spruce, willow, (Salix sp.) or poplar (Populus sp.) due to the relatively low humidity, inadequate quantities, and sizes thin enough to be easily ignited by a match. Any fine twigs can be used if they are dry and no thicker than an ordinary match stick at their thin ends.
2. The size of the twig bundle used may vary according to the needs of the moment. It may be a comfortable handful used for most fire lighting purposes, a large handful for emergencies, and a hug size bundle for a fierce hot fire such as in producing a fast signal fire or quickly warming up people on a winter walk or thawing out a cold wet canoeist.

    a. The Common Twig Fire: Gather a small handful of fine spruce branches in the same number as the fingers of your hand (about 5) that are as long as your armpit to fingertip but no shorter than elbow to fingertip. Break these in an orderly fashion into thirds so that you can ignite the finer tips which in turn will ignite the next thickest broken twigs. The broken ends ignite easier than the bark covered twigs. The idea here is to see how little you can get away with and still succeed in lighting your fire, assuming you have an adequate supply of matches. In the interest of laziness and efficiency this method might be used nine-tenths of the time.

b. Survival Twig Bundle: Although the common twig fire will suffice for most ordinary needs the survival twig bundle is the one that should be practiced for emergency applications. If you are low on matches and cannot afford to waste any, this method tends to make fire lighting as fool-proof as possible in that you endeavour to achieve almost absolute success.

The best materials for this method are the fine dead branches of either the white or the black spruce. These should be somewhere between elbow to fingertip, to armpit to fingertip long. The minimum diameter of the bundle should be no smaller when slightly compressed than the circle formed when the thumb and fingers of the both hands are made to touch (10 to 15 cms.). The larger the bundle the more protection it provides for the match flame in windy conditions. Avoid any branches with old man's beard (Usnea, Alectoria, Vulpina, etc) as these lichens tend to be hydroscopic and when you seriously need a fire they are usually at their worst, tending to suffocate any match stuck into them. In dry weather when you need them least they go up like gasoline.

The twigs are neatly gathered so that the butt ends are to one end and more or less even with each other. The thin ends are usually all over the place and as such are not conveniently arranged to participate effectively in lighting the bundle. The remedy is grasping the thin ends together at about the one-third distance of the bundle length from the tips and folded against the main bulk of the bundle so as to better incorporate them into it.

Generally, the bundle may best be manipulated at eye level so that you can see what is happening as you light it. In case the bundle tends to fall apart or spring apart it should be tied after it is folded. This is especially important in a survival situation where the waste of matches is to be avoided. The bundle should be bound with anything handy. This may be cord, grass rope, two interlocking pliant forks of any shrub, etc. When the bundle is well lit any cord used may be salvaged before it burns up.

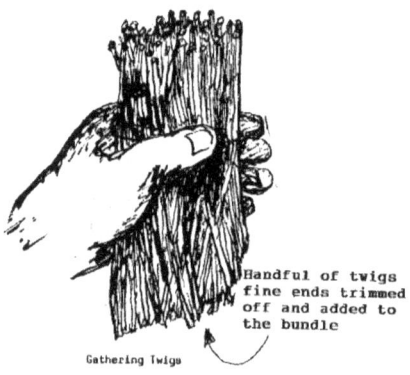

Gathering Twigs

Handful of twigs fine ends trimmed off and added to the bundle

If the hands are numb the bundle may be accidentally dropped, or on being laid down the bundle may spring apart. In both cases the fire will likely go out and another match is wasted.

For the bundle made of dry twigs it is sufficient to find a suitable spot in the thin end of the bundle where the twigs are not too densely packed together or two widely spaced apart. Each twig should be about a finger's diameter away from its neighbours. A cavity may be made where the match is to be inserted before the match is lit so that you know exactly where you want to put the match before you light it.

Some of the twigs in the cavity should be broken up as the broken ends ignite more readily. Twigs packed together too densely act as a solid mass and deny good access of oxygen to the match flame. Again, the principle is to immediately transfer the flame of the match to some highly combustible material that will help the match flame do its work. Kindling is defined as a material that catches on fire from a flame on the count of five.

3. A match is taken from its container and the matchbox is held firmly against the bundle of twigs with the thumb.

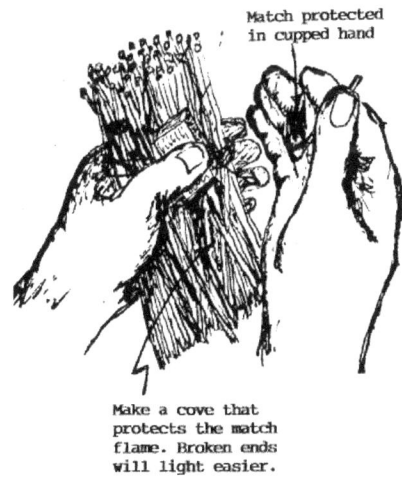

Match protected in cupped hand

Make a cove that protects the match flame. Broken ends will light easier.

Lighting the small handful of twigs.

4. Depending on the wind conditions and the seriousness of your situation, you may go as far as making a wind proof shelter on the ground with your coat draped over a stick poked in the ground or the snow. Under less strained conditions you may turn your back to the wind and hold the bundle in the protection of your coat. In gusty and variable wind conditions, you may have to turn your body to continue providing protection. Once the bundle is ignited you have at least a minute or two to lay it down. This means that you may light your bundle in a protected area some distance from the fire site. The larger the bundle the more protection it itself will provide for the match flame.
5. The match head is held in the cup of the hand and the end of the match is held between the thumb and forefinger with the middle and index fingers supporting the matchstick so that it does not accidentally break at the moment of striking, a common occurrence. The fingers are moved away after the instant that the match ignites and the flame protected from the wind by the cupped hand. The flame is then applied to the broken ends of the twigs in the depression made for it.
6. As Soon as the twigs are burning well, put the match box away rather than allowing it to drop to the ground.
7. The bundle is turned, if necessary to make the flame catch better. Remember that the hottest part of the flame is in the thermal column above it. Rotate the bundle so that the thermal column is engulfing other twigs, and so preheating its own fuel as the flame is likely to go out if no new fuel is ignited. In about a minute, the flame should have caught well enough that any wind will cause it to burn with a greater intensity. In this method the wind, which normally would be an adversity now becomes an advantage. In fact, if there is no wind and the bundle is slightly damp, it may have to be gently waved back and forth to keep it going in the

early stages of ignition. Walking with the bundle provides an excellent draft.
8. For a small fire the burning twigs are now laid on the ground or on the snow, in such a way that the wind blows the flame into the core of the bundle. With the above-sized bundle the fire should not go out even if the ground is wet. For a big warming fire lay down three of the biggest logs at a palm spacing parallel to each other and the wind. After the fire gets going add three more big logs for a fire that may last a few hours.
9. Finger thick sticks are now added. Since you have ten fingers add ten sticks, then at least two wrist thick sticks, two leg thick sticks and then anything no larger than the thigh until the fire is going well.

p) Use of the Bundle in Wet Conditions

If the forest is dripping wet, especially with wet snowfall, special tactics may be required. First, twigs that are as dry as possible are gathered to make the bundle in the normal way except that before the branches are added to the bundle they are flicked or swished violently to remove excess moisture through inertia or centrifugal force. The bundle may have to be protected from further wetting by being placed under one's coat. After the bundle is bound, a core of about a small handful of exceptionally ignitable or dry material is forced into the thin-twig end of the bundle. If nothing else you may carefully search the leeward sides of trees, especially those spruces that are large and crowded to get a small handful of dry twigs. These twigs, when ignited are meant to dry the rest of the bundle sufficiently to continue burning.

An exceptionally effective material to use in this manner is the hardened resin found in most conifer injuries, especially if it is incorporated on a piece of bark. By itself, the resin does not tend to ignite until it reaches a rather high temperature and is much like the wax in a candle that tends not to burn without a wick. The bark and the twigs become little wicks or alternately a pure lump is wedged between the twigs in the heart of the bundle so that when the heat of the match causes it to melt and run, it coats the twigs below it and these twigs then become the "wicks".

Any of the following kindling can be used in the heart of the bundle and some of the kindling are adequate in themselves to start a fire: red pine needles, birch bark and wood shavings.

OTHER KINDLING: Kindling is any material that will light easily by the application of a flame within a count of five. This word seems to be confused with the term tinder which is a material that will begin a glow when an incendiary spark lands on it, specifically when a piece of carbon steel is struck with a rock that is harder than the steel. The tinder is then combined with a suitably fine kindling to produce flame by the use of the breath or the wind.

1. **Pine Needles**: In pine country, when the weather is very wet, a particularly useful form of kindling is the partially dry pine needles that are either found on the forest floor or taken off dead pine trees. In the winter, trees can be found that have been blown or cut down. When the needles have turned at least partly red they are almost as flammable as birch bark. If the tree has not been dead long enough the needles may be more difficult to keep burning. Moisture does not penetrate the needles until they have deteriorated considerably. Any moisture on the surface of the needles can be vigorously shaken off by striking the needles against a tree or one's forearm. Usually you strike the tree to

remove the moisture and the wrist to determine if any moisture remains. If the needles fly off because they have deteriorated too much or are two brittle, they may have to be handled more carefully when shaking any moisture off and be left with a higher amount of moisture on the needles.

A few large handfuls of the needles are collected. It is very important to make a large, compact but not tight bundle of the needles. In adverse conditions where it is important to use as few matches as possible, the bundle should be bound with something because in laying it down the needles almost always spring apart and the flame goes out. Without practice it is difficult to judge accurately the degree of compactness necessary to allow combustion and the amount of moisture that can be tolerated in igniting the needles. This is a method that is not recommended to be tried for the first time under the duress of a survival situation because a large number of matches may be wasted. The effectiveness of the pine needle technique can be demonstrated by submerging the needles for a day under water, removing them from the water and immediately proceeding to light a fire in the above described way.

2. **Birch Bark**: This is one of the foremost kindling found in the boreal forest. Birch bark contains an oily substance that makes the bark impervious to moisture and causes it to burn with considerable intensity. Finely or coarsely shredded bark is easy to ignite with a flame in any weather. Its only disadvantage is that it is not as commonly found as the twigs of conifers. The availability of birch bark kindling in the spruce-moose forest is usually the exception rather than the rule.
3. **Inner Bark of Black Poplar**: This bark is very good when dry, especially when used with the ember in the

bow drill or in the flint and steel method of fire lighting. This is a rather rare - if not the rarest - high-quality kindling. The best is found on trees cut down by beavers during the winter or early spring. The inner bark of aspen is similarly used but is of a much poorer quality.
4. **Dry Grass**: Dry grass is an excellent kindling that is especially available in the winter and is rather scarce most of the summer. Black poplar bark, grass and old man's beard may be dried by tucking some in one's shirt next to the skin in the region of the abdomen a few hours in advance of intended time of use. Those with a sensitive skin should wrap the material in some cloth or a shirt tail. Dry grass is one of the better kindling to use with the flint and steel method of fire lighting.
5. **Old Man's Beard**: Old Man's Beard is a kindling that absorbs humidity from the air making it practically useless in wet weather. It is however, a fairly acceptable kindling to use in the winter time. It can be easily dried out with body heat and does not have to be wrapped with anything. Avoid it when you are making the twig bundle in wet weather as it will tend to smother any match put into it. When you need it in the worst way, it is at its worst. In dry weather it tends to burn like gasoline. When dry it is good enough to use with both the bow drill and the flint and steel.
6. **The Feather Stick**: By using an axe or knife or both, kindling can be made from large wood. The feather stick is especially useful after prolonged rain when natural kindling is difficult to find.

Choose a dry, standing tree (a leaning one will have a high moisture content) with a good check for most of its length. If you can encircle the tree with the thumbs and forefingers of both hands touching, the tree is too small. A tree of lesser diameter is apt to be damp throughout in a prolonged rain. Most of its bark should be loose with patches of wood free of bark. Any dry wood such as aspen, spruce, willow, pine or fir can be used. The resinous dead wood from a damaged conifer, especially pine (often termed a cat face), that is often found in a still living tree, is very good. The wood is dead and the cells are saturated with a resin or turpentine that burns well. Avoid trees with any knots as they interfere with being able to make feathers easily. Black spruce (Picea marianna) is usually poor feather wood because of this point.

After felling the tree, cut out two knot-free sections about elbow to fingertip long that can be split into coarse kindling of thumb thickness. When spruce trees are blown over, and to a lesser extent pine and aspen, there are usually splinters that can be torn off the stump without tools and easily made into feather sticks. Small diameter willow with knot-free sections may also feather nicely.

For thin, long curly shavings a sharp blade is necessary. Ideally, the shavings should be so thin that they form at least one curl. This means the shavings are so thin and flexible that they bend instead of breaking off when handled and also catch fire more readily. At the end of each cut, the knife blade is twisted outward to make the feathers spread out a little.

In making the feathers, better control can be maintained by holding the arm straight and moving the body up and down. The bottom end of the stick should be supported on something stable such as a log or on the ground. You can apply more pressure by pressing the bevel of the knife flat against the wood than by making the knife move forward to make the shaving. At the beginning of the cut the grain should be followed as gradually as possible. Usually the best feathers are obtained by shaving the edge of the annual rings for pine and spruce and on the tangent for aspen and willow, but only trial and error will determine what is best.

A minimum of six feather sticks should be used as this assures a good start for a fire. If the feather sticks are stood into a teepee, the structure is unstable and offers little protection for the match flame. Instead, the feather sticks should be leaned against a log or split log, for support and protection.

Trial and error will reveal what woods (especially willows) will fracture into long fine splinters when broken or can be pounded between rocks to make fine kindling when a knife is not available.

7. **Wood Scrapings**: A very fine form of feather, which can be termed a scraping instead of a shaving, can be made with any non-resin saturated wood when none of the usual fine kindling are available for the flint and steel or the bow drill. Any of the woods suitable for feathering, especially willow, will scrape up into a fluffy mass of material that will ignite from an ember or a metal match.
8. **Dead Pine Branches**: The old, dead lower pine branches, if snapped off near the trunk of the tree, are often found to be saturated with resin. The brittle resinous wood can be chipped up or made into small feathers used like spruce resin.

q) **Frequently Used Fire Lays**

THE PARALLEL FIRE LAY: The more useful fire lay in the bush is the one where all the sticks in it are more or less parallel to each other and in line with the wind if there is any. The smaller the fire required, the shorter the sticks. For winter conditions the sticks are usually fingertip to fingertip or about two metres long. Unless the wood is exceptionally straight fuel longer than 1 and 1/2 arm lengths is too long because the gaps between the burning

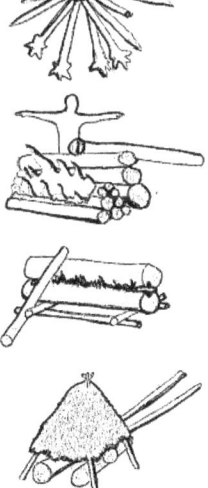

COMMONLY USED FIRES IN BOREAL FOREST SURVIVAL
Derived from the book "BUSHCRAFT" and other works by M. Kochanski

The following are the practical fires used in modern Boreal Forest survival where fuel is plentiful.

THE PARALLEL WOOD FIRE (warming and cooking). Firewood lengths from half to one and a half one's hight are laid parallel to each other and to the wind. Nine times out of ten, this is the fire of choice. The king of fires is three hug sized dry spruce logs the length of your height.

THE CROSSWOOD FIRE (warming, cooking and sectioning). Long firewood is used without cutting it into short lengths. The fire stops burning where wide enough spacing occurs. The ends are stockpiled for night time use if needed.

THE STARFIRE (sectioning). Awkward long logs are burned through into more manageable pieces when no axe or saw is available. When the spaces between the burning pieces of wood are greater than the width of the palm combustion tends to stop.

THE WALL-BACKED FIRE (warming). This is a special version of the parallel wood fire where the wasted energy on the far side is better utilized. The wall redirects most of the warming action to the near side, spreads the flames into a broader sheet and draws smoke higher over the head. This is an especially useful fire in bitter cold.

THE SNOW SURFACE FIRE (Moderate but steady warming). When a fire is needed on top of deep snow and fairly large diameter dry spruce logs are available, this is the longest lasting fire lay known.

THE SIGNAL FIRE (Almost instant smoke signal). This fire generates large volumes smoke within two to three minutes of being ignighted.

exceptionally straight fuel longer than 1 and 1/2 arm lengths is too long because the gaps between the burning logs are usually too wide. If the fuel is less than nose to fingertip in length the gaps are usually too narrow to properly sustain the fire.

THE STAR FIRE: In a survival situation where energy conservation is important there is no advantage to using shorter pieces. Unless you are using a stove, the cutting of your wood into stove wood lengths is not only an unnecessary expenditure of energy and dulling of tools but the chance of injury is increased four or five fold. If a smaller fire is required the long sticks are crossed and the fire will confine itself to the crossing, more or less.

In starting a fire in cold or wet weather the pile of finger to wrist-thick sticks placed on top of the burning bundle should be at least knee high. This will produce enough heat and coals to start the fire off properly so that when any fuel is added it starts to burn immediately with a minimum of smoke. Starting a fire properly is particularly important when only poor fuel is available. A common error amongst most inexperienced fire builders is using too large pieces of fuel too soon.

Fires are much like most humans: they thrive on attention. Frequent adjustment of a fire will keep it going at its best. The adjustments usually consists of maintaining a spacing of the width of any finger by 1) moving together pieces of fuel that are too far apart, 2) parting those that are too close together, 3) filling voids under the fire, or 4) putting fuel into the thermal column early enough for pre-drying and preheating. Often, the cure for a smoky fire is simply proper adjustment. A spread-out fire with inferior fuel always smokes.

THE WALL-BACKED FIRE (WBF) -FORMERLY REFLECTOR- FOR WARMTH: A fire in an open area emits radiant energy in all directions. With a re-emitter or log wall a considerable portion of this radiant energy can be redirected in a more useful direction, thereby using the fuel more efficiently.

The WBF described here was evolved through considerable use and experience. Built properly, it is like a large fireplace radiating heat and light.

If it is not very cold, the WBF is built of green logs so that it lasts longer. A commonly available slow burning green wood is black poplar (populus balsamifera). Logs 25 to 30 centimetres in diameter should last at least one night for any condition above -20 °C. The colder the weather the more massive, up to waist high, the reflector should be. If the weather is very cold, then the WBF can be built of dry logs, which become a source of fuel themselves; their burning surfaces tend to radiate more intensely than green wood. This type of fire may have to be rebuilt or readjusted as well as being stoked every four to six hours.

If very large logs (40 centimetres) are used a wall three logs high is adequate. With smaller logs, four logs high is more satisfactory in performance. Ideally the re-emitter should be about as high as the waist of the user.

A simple measure for the length of log used is the distance from fingertip to fingertip. For more stability, the logs can be hewn flat, on top and bottom-an operation more conveniently done before the logs are cut into sections. With the three log WBF, a brace log can be used to hold the stacked logs in place by its weight, or logs may be piled behind the reflector for added support.

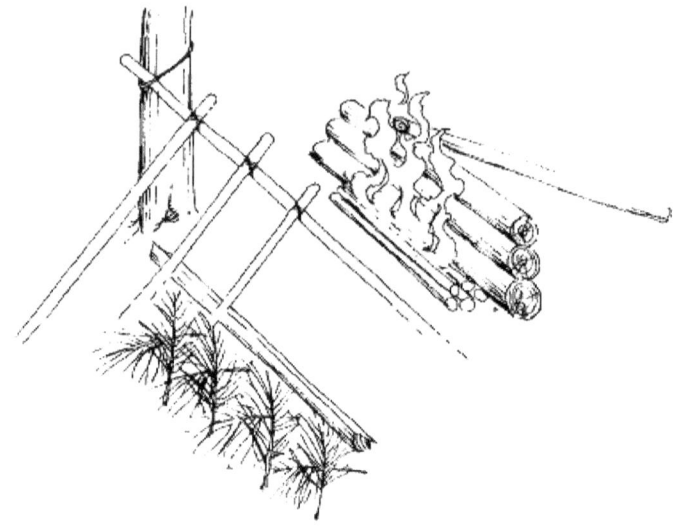

Wall-Backed Fire

The wall is usually built vertically. If the log wall is leaned slightly toward the fire so that if it collapses, it will fall on the fire, a few stoking sessions in the night may be avoided.

The WBF must be built parallel to the wind. The wind direction may vary 15 degrees or so either way, but it must blow across the front of the log wall to properly carry away the smoke and sparks. It is not the heated air that keeps you warm in this instance. It is the radiant energy that you intercept that warms you, much like the warmth you receive from the sun. It should be noted that the fire must be built against the face of the WBF for maximum effect.

The old term for this device was the REFLECTOR. It is likely that very little reflection is done by any log face. The log wall can only burn or absorb the radiant waves emitted by the fire in front of it and then re-emit this radiant energy in a longer wavelength. Reflection would imply that a wave would bounce without any change in length.

r) Burning Poor Fuel

Once a good fire is started, most fuels be they damp, inferior, or green will burn fairly well if at least three logs are stacked on the fire close enough to each other to be about one or two centimetres apart and if the pieces are not loo large. In this way an inter-reflective action and heat concentration is created between the logs as long as they are kept close together. Green wood will burn adequately if first split, then used on a hot fire, and watched closely and adjusted frequently so that the green logs are kept in close proximity with the neighbouring logs. It should be expected that there will be more smoke coming from the fire. Occasionally very straight logs may be used in which case the spacing between the logs can become too small and the quality of the fire can suffer.

The cure for a smoky fire is to put good fuel on top of it. which in turn will increase the thermal column above the fire, carrying the smoke directly up and over the head rather than into the face.

". . . It's dark now, the sky's black! There'll be a storm tonight. Put on more wood!"

I did as she bade me, and threw on a handful of twigs, took the bellows and blew them into flames. Elle had fallen silent, and we both sat watching how the red flames crept along with dark twigs making a gleaming path, soft and warm. It was like the sudden flowering of the dry branch in the sage, a miracle performed before our eyes, a daily miracle happening every moment, a miracle of which we never tired. The brown twigs lay there, dry and dead as if never a flower or bud had bloomed on their withered stalks, then suddenly a red spark glowed into a tiny sun, and the small buds flowered and blossomed one after the other . . . glowed for a moment in their beauty, then fell to pieces dimmed, and died."[1]

"In summing up: Fires have periodically swept through the vegetation of virtually every square mile on this earth that had anything to burn. These fires, both ancient and modern, have helped shape the present day patterns of vegetation. Civilized man has had a tendency to regard fires as the ultimate disaster to vegetation, and by and large tried to eliminate it as a factor in the environmental complex. So well has this disaster aspect been taken that in some of our present day forests, fires can be catastrophic".[2]

---

[1] From Tent Folk of the Far North, by Ester Blenda Nordstrom, (a schoolteacher living and teaching amongst the Lapps), page 166.

[2] First Annual Tall Timbers Fire Ecology Conference, Walter S. Phillips, Fire and Vegetation of Arrid Lands, page 92.

D) Basic Map and Compass Use

If you wish to go from one place to another with some accuracy, or to know exactly where you are at any given moment in unfamiliar country, it helps it you know how to use a map and compass.

1. The Map

A map is a two dimensional representation of the natural features of an area and their relationship in terms of distance and position. The value of a map is that it makes a great deal of information available in a compact form, allowing one to plan one's position and movements over a certain area with regard to distance, time, method of travel, obstacles to be foreseen, etcetera, without painstaking reconnaissance of the ground. Under certain circumstances a map alone will be sufficient to allow you to know where you are at all times and to forewarn you of what is coming up.

a) Types of Maps

There are a variety of maps available:

PLANIMETRIC: These maps show natural and man-made features in their horizontal position only. Relief is not showing in a measureable form. The ordinary road map should be an example.

FOREST COVER: These maps are planimetric, and show a great deal of information about the forest, such as tree species, height, density, maturity and productivity sites. They are generally available in blue line in four, two and one inch to the mile, and lithographed in the scale of one inch to two miles. They are excellent for showing trails and larger streams.

NATIONAL TOPOGRAPHIC SERIES: In general the forest cover maps tend to be more up-to-date in depicting recent roads and cut lines, but do not show contours. Topographic maps show relief, which is the presentation of the vertical and horizontal features in measurable form. Horizontal features are presented planimetrically and the vertical positions are shown by contour lines that are referenced to mean sea level. The general topographic map is favoured by recreational users. The topographic map shows a complete picture of the land including its roads, trails, lakes, streams, forests, bogs, hills and so on. You can obtain a free index map that will help you determine what maps you need for your particular purpose by writing to the following address:

Map Distribution Office
Department of Mines and Technical Surveys
615 Booth Street
Ottawa, Ontario

Many of the features on the older issues of the National Topographic Series maps are much outdated but the maps are invaluable for the detailed contours showing the nature of the terrain. The most useful is the two-and-one-half inches to the mile. Scales of one-and-one-quarter inches to the mile, one inch to four miles, and one inch to eight miles are generally available for the whole province.

ACCESS: This is a popular form of map, much like the ones just mentioned in scales of one inch to four miles and eight miles except that the contours are omitted and more effort is taken to depict all forms of access such as roads, trails, seismic lines, air strips, rivers and so on. Compared to most other maps this information is updated frequently.

OTHER SPECIAL PURPOSE MAPS: These maps have a great variety of special purposes, such as soil and land surveys, geology, oil and gas development, aerial photo coverage, etcetera. They may be of remote or occasional interest to the bush navigator. One special purpose map that may be of interest is the aeronautical chart, which can provide long distance coverage, especially for resections or triangulation on visible distant objects such as Fire and Microwave towers. This map comes in scales of 1:500,000 and 1:1,000,000.

AERIAL PHOTOGRAPHS (A/P): Aerial photography is one of the most important tools in modern map making. Photographs can show a multitude of details, impossible or impractical to show on maps, as well as allowing for three dimensional viewing. A disadvantage of serial photographs is that distances and directions taken off them may not be reliable. Another disadvantage is that photographs are rather clumsy to handle in the field. The commonly available scale is 1 inch equals 3,333 feet, or 1:40,000. Aerial photographs may be obtained from the Provincial Government at the following address:

Aerial Photos, Technical Division
Alberta Energy and Natural Resources
2nd Floor, Petroleum Plaza North
9945-108 Street
Edmonton, Alberta T5K 2G6

Request their information flyer "Aerial Photography and Mosaics" which will outline what is available and the costs involved.

In order to be able to order these with a minimum of confusion obtain the legal description of your desired location.

You may find it adequate to order the less expensive "ITEK" print which is a photocopy of the actual print. For overhead projection a print known as a FILM DIAPOSITIVE may be useful. Both of the above prints are 10 inches by 10 inches in dimension.

Enlargements can also be obtained. Mark off the desired area on an ITEK print and include the desired information. Such enlargements could be used for map and compass training or orienteering (scale 1:15,000). The enlargement sizes range from 10 inches by 10 inches to 40 inches by 40 inches.

b) Care and Handling of Maps

Maps can become a major expense, so it is important to handle them carefully. A hundred mile trek or river trip may require $30 to $50 worth of maps.

FOLDING: The purpose of folding a map is to reduce it to a convenient size for carrying and handling that will minimize damage and normal wear and tear. Proper folding should present a reasonable size of area to work from in the field. The following diagrams illustrate two basic methods of folding.

CONDITIONS CONTRIBUTING TO MAP DETERIORATION: The life expectancy of a map taken into the field is severely reduced, even with special protective methods. The protective methods may not justify the expense involved, or may not be readily available to the average map user. However, a little understanding, care, and attention may double or triple the life expectancy of a map.

- Folding: A map that is constantly folded and refolded becomes ragged very rapidly. Keeping folds to a minimum and having a map conform to its original folds will go a long way in conserving it. Keep your map folded in such a way that you can follow your route easily, without having to unfold the map in full. Placing tape over the folds on the back of the map to reinforce them is beneficial.
- Tears: A map tears readily along its folds, especially when it is wet. A map unfolded in the wind or in a confined space, like an automobile is easily torn. Maps will tear if carelessly removed from a pocket or packsack unless they are in a protective case.
- Wet: A wet map tears easily and also abrades rapidly at the edges and corners or wherever the fingers come in contact with it. A wet map more readily picks up grime. A wet map should be dried at the earliest opportunity.
- Grime: The hands should be kept as clean as possible when handling maps. The map should be kept in a protective case or plastic bag as much as possible when in use (especially in the rain). If a pencil has to be used on a map use H or 2H rather than HB, which smears excessively. Draw the lines as lightly as possible. Using an eraser too heavily may obliterate some of the map.

c) Map Grid References

Many maps carry a superimposed system of squares or grid in kilometres. These squares are formed by vertical lines numbered from left to right (eastings) and horizontal lines numbered from bottom to top (northings).

To give the reference for a particular square, first take the

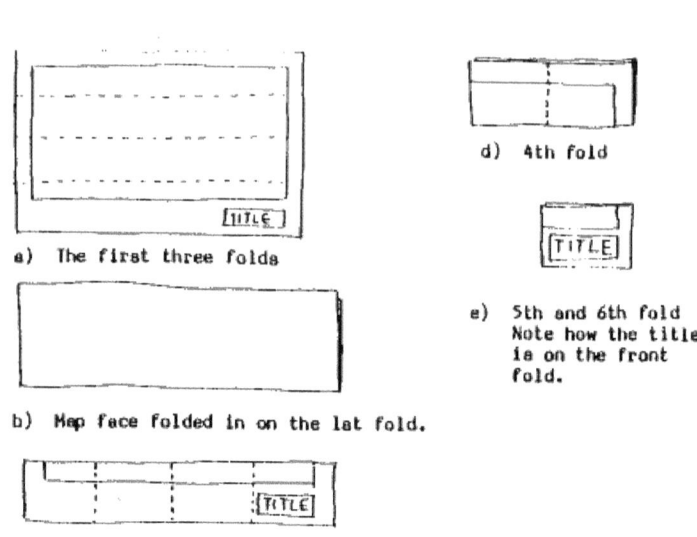

How To Fold A Map - Method One

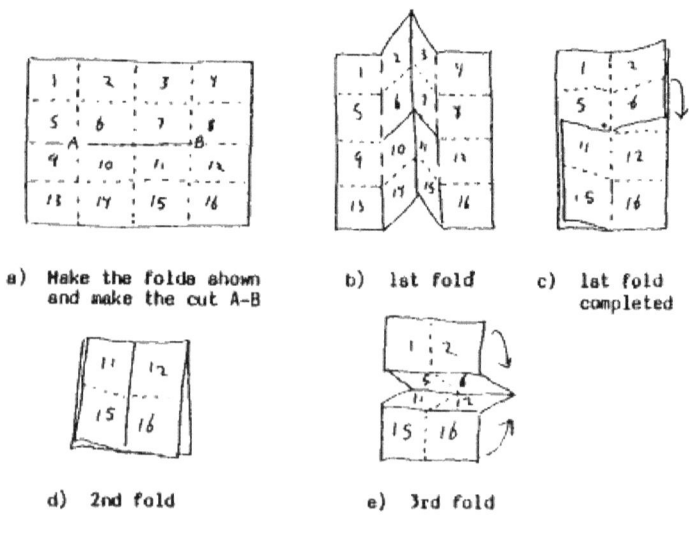

How To Fold A Map - Method Two

number of the line bounding the left hand edge of the same square. This gives a four-figure description of the square.

To give the reference of a point within the described square estimate the distance of the point in tenths from the left hand edge and tack this on to the easting. Likewise estimate the distance from the bottom edge and tack this onto the northing. The description of the point is now a six-digit figure with the easting always expressed first. The chart below illustrates the grid method of map reference. When passing on information it is important to give the name and sheet number of the map when the grid reference is being given. Also give a short physical description of the point, such as "top of hill" or "stream junction".

POINT	GRID REFERENCE
A	105365
B	120380
C	139349
D	097392
E	085345

Using Grid References

A map reference must always have an even number of digits, the first half being eastings and the second half being northings. Since the reference numbers repeat themselves every 100 kilometres (about 63 miles) the complete description requires the letters printed on the face of all gridded topo maps. Point A could then be more precisely NL105365, but it is still not unique although it does not occur again for 2,880 kilometres (1,800 miles). If a reference that is unique the world over is required then get the GRID ZONE DESIGNATION off the edge of your map and prefix it on your reference. 11U NL 105365 describes a point in central Alberta.

d) Some Topographical and Geographical Terms and Their Definitions

Alluvial Fan
    A deposit of sediments, usually associated with mountain streams, marking a sudden reduction in velocity of flow due to a change in gradient from steep to relatively flat.

Basin
    An area of level ground, surrounded or nearly surrounded by hills. A district drained by a river and its tributaries.

Col
    See Saddle

Contour
    A contour is an imaginary line on the surface of the ground at the same height above mean sea-level throughout its length. Contours may also be defined as the plane of the lines at which a water surface (of the ocean for instance) would be intersected by the surface of the earth, where the water level is raised successively in equal vertical steps.

Contour Interval
    The difference in level between two adjacent contours (generally known as the Vertical Interval).

Crest
    The general Line formed by joining the summits of the main ridge of a chain of mountains or big hills.

Declination
    The number of degrees by which a magnetic needle misses true north. In other words, it is the bearing of magnetic north.

Delta
: A built-up deposit of sediments marking the place where a stream enters a pond, lake or sea, whose waters are generally quiet.

Drift
: Glacial eroded material left after the ice has receded.

Drumlin
: A smooth egg-shaped hill composed of till and found on the surface of till plains.

Dune
: A hill or ridge of sand formed by the wind.

Escarpment
: The steep face of a sloping rock formation; an extended line of cliffs or bluffs.

False Crest
: The line along which a lower, steep slope changes to an upper, gentle slope.

Gorge
: A rugged and deep ravine.

Gradient
: The rate of rise or fall of sloping ground expressed as a fraction such as 1/10, which represents a rise or fall of one unit in a horizontal distance of ten units.

Grid
: A system of squares formed by lines which represent progressive distances east and north of a fixed origin.

Horizontal Equivalent (H.E.)
: The distance in plane between two adjacent contours.

Kame
: A small, steep-sided conical-shaped hill formed by glacial melt water near the ice margins.

Kettle
: A small depression formed by the melting of a covered block of ice.

Knoll
: A low, detached hill.

Moraine
: Land forms composed of materials deposited by glaciers.

Permafrost
: Permanently frozen soil.

Plain
: An area of less than five hundred feet of local relief and mostly of low elevations of usually more than two thousand feet elevation, which rises abruptly on at least one side above the adjacent area; an elevated plain.

Re-entrant
: A gully running down the side of a hill.

Saddle
: A neck or ridge of land connecting two hills, lower than the hills, but higher than the surrounding valley.

Spur or Salient
: A projection from the side of a hill running out of the main feature.

Talus
: A pile of rock debris collected at the lower slopes of a hill.

Undulating Ground
: Ground which alternatively rises and falls gently.

Variation
: For the purposes of this article it is the amount of declination changes every year.

Vertical Interval (V.I.)
: The difference in level between two adjacent contours.

Watershed
: A ridge of land separating two drainage basins; the summit of land from which water divides or flows in two directions. A watershed does not necessarily include the highest points of a chain of mountains or range of hills.

e) Map Study

All the clues necessary for the proper use of a map are generally given on the margins of the map itself. Study the marginal information (and sometimes the information on the back) taking particular note of the scale, date and magnetic variation.

A map may be a geographic picture of a part or of the whole earth. Maps have lines, words, symbols, and colors which show the distribution and arrangement of various features.

Since there is a great reduction in the size of the various features and the land area when they are illustrated on a map, it must be drawn to scale in order to be accurate.

1. Scale: A scale is the ratio between distance on the map to the same distance on the surface of the earth. It is often shown on the map as a divided line or bar, with each unit representing so many miles or kilometres. Because there are many maps expressed in inches, feet and miles, the following explanation will be made in the English System.

   Since there are 63,360 inches in one mile, this means that one inch on the map equals 63,360 inches or one mile on the ground.

   In general, small-scale maps (eg. 1:250,000 or four miles to the inch) show large areas with comparatively little detail, while large-scale maps (1:24,000 or two-and-one-half inches to the mile and 1:63,360 or one inch to the mile) depict smaller areas with a corresponding increase in the amount of detail shown. An exception is the "Orienteering" type of map with a scale of 1:15,000 or about four-and-one-quarter inches to the mile. Large scale maps may present more detail than is required for the purpose and on an extended journey many maps may be required. Aeronautical charts may have a scale of 1:500,000 or about eight miles to the inch, mostly useful for giving an over-all view.

2. Date: The date shows when a map was issued and revised. This is important as one may come across features, especially roads, which have appeared since the map was made. Also, some features may have been obliterated, such as trails and old buildings. Old maps (early 1900s) are often unreliable. Maps twenty years old can be rather frustrating to use because of the lack of recently added features which can be confused with those that are shown on the map.
3. Magnetic Variation and Declination: This information is given on the margin of the map and is very important when you are using a compass and a map. It will be covered in the compass use section.

CONTOURS: The most accurate map used for showing the irregularities in the surface of the land, hills, valleys, and slopes, is called a Topographic map. These features are depicted by the arrangement of contour lines.

The use of contour lines is undoubtedly the best method of representing relief on maps. A contour may be defined as a line on a map joining all places of equal elevation above mean sea level. Thus, along a contour line of one hundred feet, all points are precisely one hundred feet above sea level. The vertical distance between any contour and the one below or above it is known as the contour interval. To walk along a contour line is to walk along a level pathway. To leave the contour line, you must either rise or fall in elevation. The elevations are written so that they are read facing up hill.

It is sometimes useful to be able to judge the nature and steepness of a hill from the contour lines. Contours close together mean steep slopes. On a map of one inch to the mile and a fifty-foot contour interval, contours one-half inch apart have a slope of 1/50, one-quarter inch apart a slope of 1/25, one-tenth inch apart a slope of 1/10, and one-twentieth inch apart a slope of 1/5. If the contours are almost touching, the slope is 1/1. A slope of 1/25 is definitely a hill, 1/10 a very steep hill and 1/1 looks almost vertical as does 1/3, 1/4 and 1/5.

Contours that are far apart mean gentle slopes and contours that are evenly spaced mean a uniform slope. When the contour spacing reading from high to low decreases, the slope is convex; when it increases, the slope is concave.

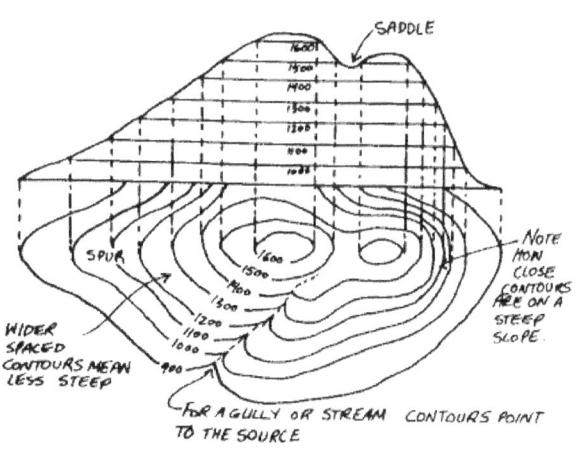

How Contours Are Drawn

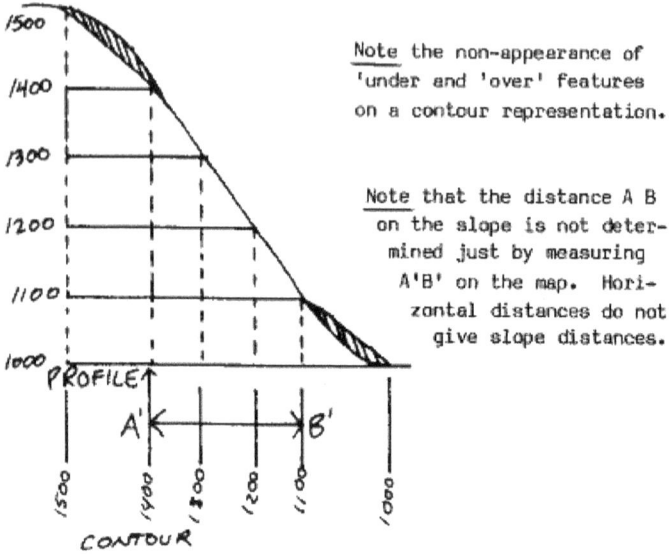

The Non-appearance Of Some Features On A Map

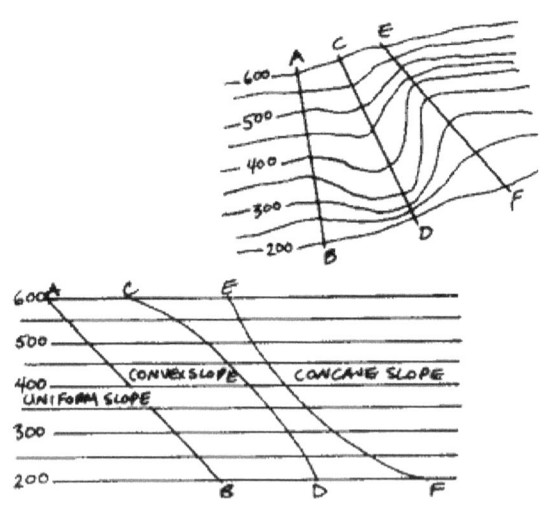

How To Judge The Character Of A Slope

f) Drawing Profiles

Sometimes it may be necessary to draw a profile of a section of map to better determine the gradient, and other pertinent features. The height scale is often exaggerated in relation to the horizontal scale, to accentuate the rise or fall of the ground.

1. Place a piece of paper across the map between the two points A and B.
2. On the paper mark the points where the contour lines meet the edge of the paper. On the paper write the values of the contour lines. (eg. 1,000, 12,000).
3. On a sheet of paper draw enough parallel lines to accommodate the two extremes of elevations encountered in this particular profile.
4. Place the edge of the strip of paper just below the lowest elevation and draw vertical lines to the elevation written on the strip of paper.

Then draw a line joining the tops of the vertical lines you have your profile.

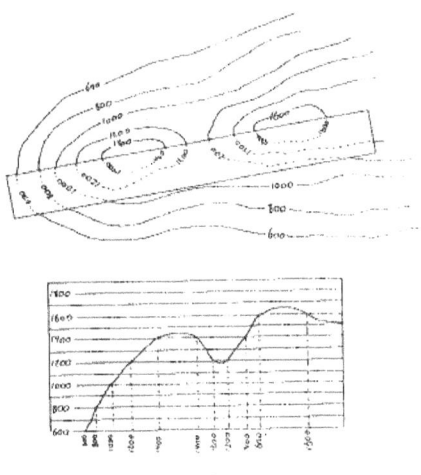

Drawing Profiles

g) Learning to Use a Map

When learning to use maps the emphasis should be placed on developing the ability of visualize the land from the map and the map from the land, and the relationship of contour lines to land forms. The best way to learn map reading is through extensive experience in the field.

1. Select an area with as much diversity as possible. Climb to a height of land which offers the largest view of the area. Orient the map, by being certain the north-south grid lines run true north-south.
2. Select one corner of the map and intensely compare the representation to the actual feature. Note how a meandering stream shows nearly level ground. Note every prominent feature.
3. Now do the reverse by studying a different area of the map until you have formed a mental picture of it. Then look up and note any errors that you have made.
4. Concentrate on studying the contour lines and you will soon realize how much valuable information they represent.
5. The ability to form clear mental pictures from a map comes only from constant practice. There is no better way.

h) Methods of Map Orientation (without a compass)

When looking at a map, it is best to turn it so that the way you see the surrounding features corresponds to the way that they appear on the map. Lines that are straight ahead of you on the map should be straight ahead of you on the ground as well. This is called "orienting the map".

If the map is always oriented, it will be less confusing. You will be able to anticipate which geographical features will appear next and so you will always be more sure of your position. There is a better chance that you will go in the right direction when you come to a confusing junction. You may know ahead of time whether to go right or left. You will quickly realize that as you turn, your map turns as well.

If you always keep the map oriented you may often know more about the surrounding area than you can actually see with your eyes at any given moment. You will know

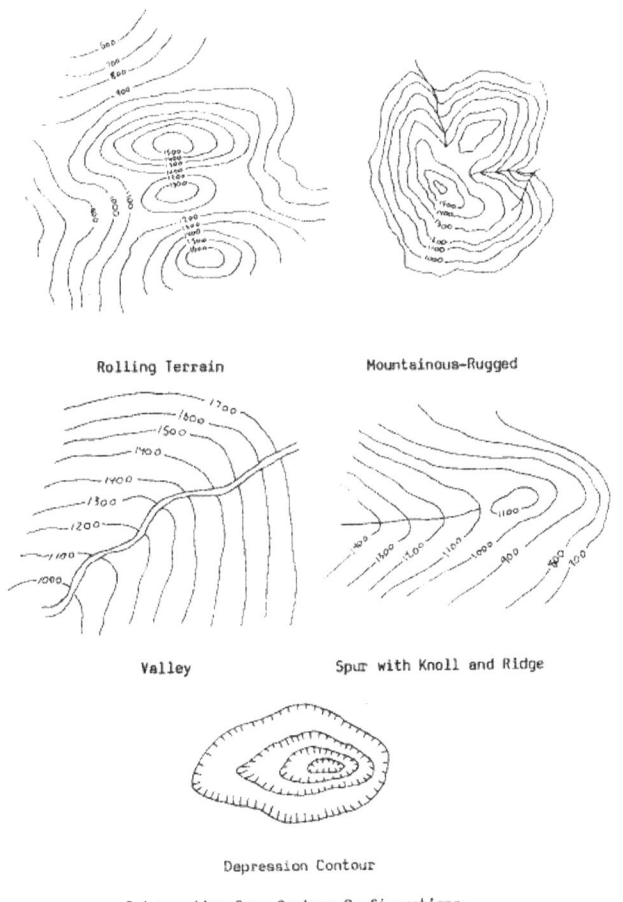

Interpreting Some Contour Configurations

exactly where to look for a feature even though you cannot actually see it.

Orienting a map is turning a map so that True North on the map coincides with True North on the compass. Both of the following techniques will accomplish essentially the same purpose: setting the map so that the map is correctly aligned with True North.

1. If your position is known: Pick a prominent feature and draw a line from your position to it on the map. Turn the map until this line points to the distant object.
2. Prominent lengthy feature: Select a trail, river, etc., and turn map until this feature parallels it.

i) Methods of Estimating or Keeping Track of Distance

In successful navigation, a good map is a great asset but it may not seem so until you develop an accurate method of keeping track of where you are on the map. One of the more fool proof and precise methods is to use intelligent and methodical pacing. The next time you become confused about your position you will realize how important this statement is. You will also find that bush travel is made more enjoyable if you know when you have covered each and every kilometre. Otherwise it may seem that you have covered ten kilometres, but in reality you have covered only four. The tedium of not knowing precisely where you are is many times heavier than the bother of counting your paces.

Pacing becomes more critical when you have no compass.

Many roads and cut lines that are not shown on your map are a constant source of confusion with those that are when they are not verified by pacing.

Knowing how many paces cover a kilometre or a mile should be considered an indispensable adjunct to good navigation and may be worth the trouble of establishing by direct measurement. A kilometre may be laid out by automobile odometer or distinct points picked out on a map and paced. If you do not have the opportunity to determine your pace rate, you may find that a rough rule of thumb may be adequate. An adult of average height will pace about one kilometre in 625 paces and a mile in 1,000 paces.

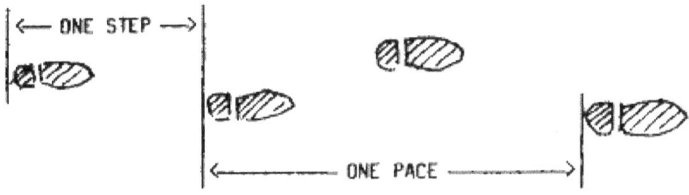

Mille Passus: The odd figure of five-thousand-two-hundred-eighty (5,280) feet to the mile comes from Roman days. The Roman Legions set up markers every 1,000 paces (mille means 1,000). The term was eventually shortened to our term 'mile'. An adult of average height generally comes within a few feet of a mile by pacing with this method. To keep track of the pacing an object (stick, pebble, etc.) is placed in the hand every 100 paces.

Your pace number will be lower if you are walking downhill and higher if you are going over rocky uneven ground or up a hill. Your number will also be higher if you are very tired at the end of a long walk. Under those conditions, you will have to make allowances and adjust your pacing.

The following chart may give a rough idea of some rates of travel. If keeping track of distances is not absolutely critical then the time lapse method may be useful. The chart shows the number of minutes it takes to cover one kilometre. If this method is used then stricter time management has to be applied or distances may be out by a significant factor.

ADULT AVERAGE RATE OF TRAVEL

METHOD OF TRAVEL	TERRAIN	KMS PER HOUR	MINUTES PER KM
Fast Walking	Road	6.0	10
Comfortable Walk	Cutline	4.0	15
Comfortable Walk	Broken-Wooded	3.5	18
Comfortable Walk	Mountain Forest	2.5	25
Snowshoeing	Average Snow	3.5	18
Skiing	Average Snow	6.0	10
Jogging	Road	8-10	6
Jogging 50 paces Walking 50 paces	Road	7.0	8

Travel Rates

For a good 8 hour (day's) travel:

1. Walking on a road, 25 miles or 40 kilometres.
2. Walking in woods, 10 miles or 16 kilometres.
3. By horse on a country road, 35 miles or 56 kilometres.
4. By canoe on a lake, 25 miles or 40 kilometres.
5. By canoe upstream 20 miles or 32 kilometres (depending on current).

6. By canoe downstream 30 miles or 48 kilometres (depending on current).

2. The Compass

The compass works on the principle that the tiny magnet in the form of a compass needle swinging on a free pivot is influenced by the earth's magnetic field so that the needle points towards the center of magnetic attraction.

A good compass should have a dial face that is at least four centimetres in diameter. The compass should have adequate markings on the dial of not less than 2 degree intervals, preferably in azimuth. The Azimuth type of dial makes the directions on a compass simpler as well as more accurate to describe and transfer by dividing the compass circle into 360 degrees.

The degrees marked on a compass start with 0 degrees at north and go clockwise to 360 degrees at the north again. Of the two choices, north has been assigned 0 degrees.

When degrees are used to describe an exact direction, the direction is called a bearing.

The bearing of 180 degrees means the exact direction of 180 degrees from where north is, which is actually south.

The compass should be sturdy enough in construction so as to withstand the rough handling that it is apt to receive in bush work. In a good compass the needle does not swing wildly about, nor does the needle swing back and forth very long before it steadies itself on Magnetic North.

There are various ways that the swinging about and quivering of the needle are reduced; this is termed

DAMPING. Of the various ways damping may be achieved, the most practical and relevant means is liquid damping.

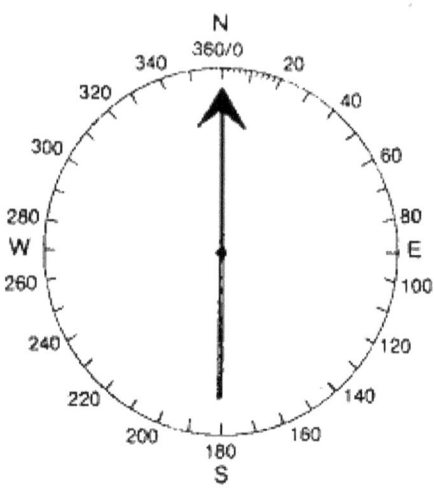

The Azimuth Dial

The part of the compass that houses the needle is often made so that it can be filled with a liquid that has a low freezing point and a high boiling point. Bubbles will occasionally appear in this liquid which are of no concern as far as accuracy is concerned until they are over 7 mm in diameter.

a) Where Every Compass Points To

The map can stand alone to a certain extent. When it is combined with a compass then navigation becomes a precise art. There is, however, a major hurdle to deal with when a compass and map are used together. The compass indicates Magnetic North (MN) and the map shows Grid

North (GN) and the two may be quite different. Except for the line (known as the AGONIC) that runs from the North Geographic Pole (NGP) approximately through Thunder Bay, Ontario and Stolkholm, Sweden, the compass needle will point either too far east or too far west depending on which side of the AGONIC line you are. This is because the strongest point of attraction known as the North Magnetic Pole (NMP) is about 1,500 miles or 2,400 kilometres south of the NGP. Not only that, but the NMP is continually shifting about so that the declination varies continually. Scientific observation has established the direction and rate of shift which is termed the MAGNETIC VARIATION (MV). All modern maps will give the MV, usually on the margin somewhere expressed in minutes and factions of minutes. A degree is divided into 60 minutes; a minute is divided into 60 seconds.

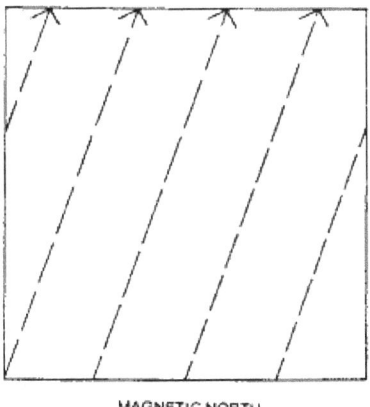

MAGNETIC NORTH

Determine the age of the map and multiply this by the MV. Add this figure to the declination of the map at its date of issue, rounding the total off to the nearest degree. For West Central Alberta the Declination is about 22°E. For the purposes of this article consider 22°E to be the TRUE BEARING of the Magnetic North.

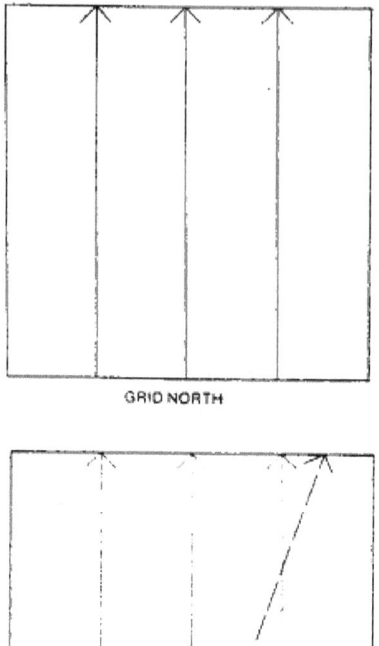

GRID NORTH

DECLINATION

b) The Use of the Protractor Style of Compass

There are a variety of compass styles but the PROTRACTOR type stands out as being one of the more accurate, versatile, easy to use and durable compasses made. It will be the standard against which all other compasses will be compared in this article on compass use. Once you have mastered this type of compass, you may find that you will be able to use most other types of compasses as the need arises by simply examining whatever feature they have.

Basic Safe Travel and Boreal Survival

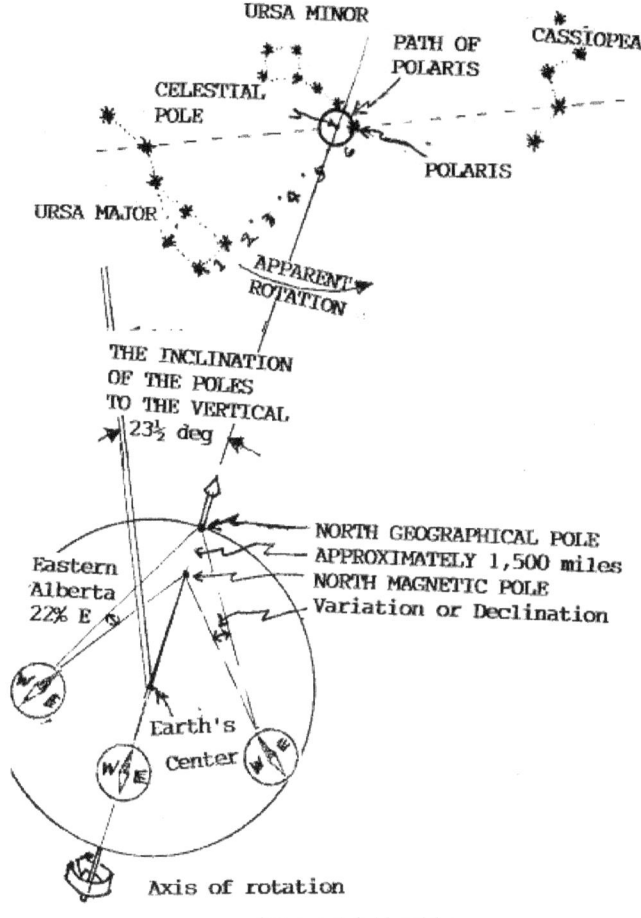

Compass Relationships

c) Parts of a Compass

The compass has three main parts:

1. Compass Needle: When the needle is held level and allowed to swing freely it will eventually come to rest on the bearing that is described as Magnetic North. The red end of the needle should always point toward the

magnetic north unless there has been a reversal of polarity.
2. Compass Housing: This is the part of the dial with degrees marked on the outside ring by the azimuth system as well as containing the housing lines and housing arrow.
3. Base Plate or Protractor: This part of the compass with its edges and the lines parallel to the edges used in conjunction with the Azimuth allows the fairly accurate measurement and/or the application of angles in navigation. The direction arrow inscribed on the Base Plate vertically always points the direction to be taken. The base of the arrow indicates the bearing being taken by the compass.

Study the Following Section Carefully

For a quick mastery of basic map and compass use with the minimum of confusion, study this section carefully; it comprises nine tenths of general navigation.

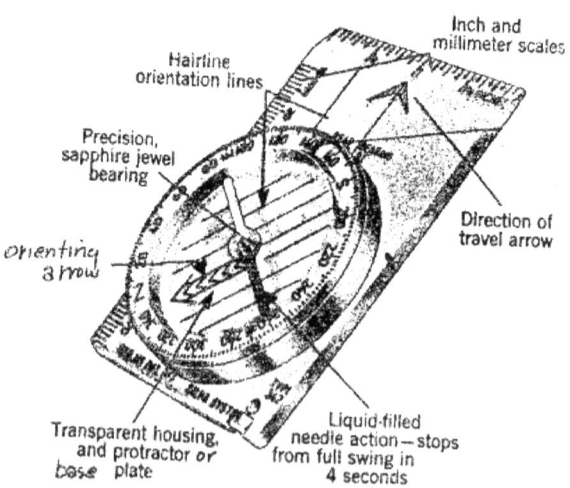

d) Steps in Using a Protractor Type Compass and a Regular Topo Map

1. Determine the bearing (declination of the magnetic north pole for the area of map you are using.

2. Draw a line from where you are (A) to where you are going (B) indicating the direction with a small arrowhead-->--.

3. Place the compass edge or any line on the base plate along the line A-B with the direction arrow pointing in the desired direction of travel.

4. Rotate the housing until the lines in it are parallel to any true north-south lines on the map with the housing arrow pointing to the north of the map. (A reversal here will make you 180° out, which means you may travel in exactly the opposite direction intended). Your compass is now set to point the way.

5. Hold the compass level and squarely in front of your body with both hands at waist level. Hold your elbows symmetrically against your waist to help square you off, and rotate your whole body until the red end of the compass needle points to the (true) bearing of magnetic north, which for most of Alberta is 22°. Raise your head and look straight ahead of you to some land mark or feature on your route of travel. When the land mark is reached repeat this step until your objective is reached.

6. Repeat steps 2 to 5 for the other legs of your course.

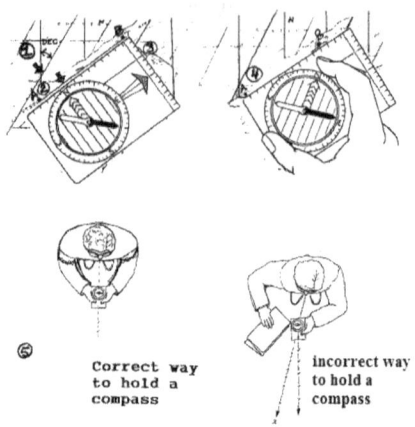

Correct way to hold a compass

incorrect way to hold a compass

e) Using the 'Protractor Style' of Compass as a Protractor

One of the most distinctively advantageous features of the protractor style of compass is the ease with which it can measure or set off angles. Invented in 1933 by GUNNAR TILLANDER, a Swedish orienteer it has greatly simplified the marriage of map and compass.

To use as a protractor use the following steps:

1. Draw or choose a line on which an angle may be drawn, if necessary, placing a dot on the apex of the angle.
2. Set the desired degrees on the direction arrow.
3. Line up the edge of the compass on the dot or place it where the apex of the angle may be conveniently positioned.
4. Holding the edge on the dot across the line, line up one of the housing lines with the line in Step 1.
5. Draw the line along the compass edge going through the dot.

Basic Safe Travel and Boreal Survival

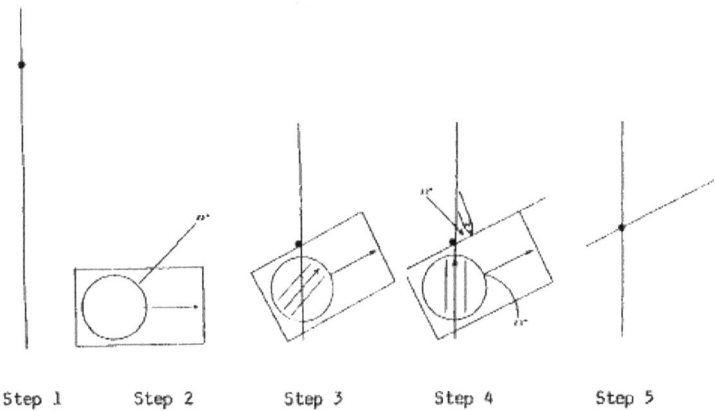

Step 1   Step 2   Step 3   Step 4   Step 5

f) Orienting Any Compass for Grid North

1. Determine the local DECLINATION.
2. Holding the compass level, pan it so that the north end of the needle points to the declination.
3. The compass is now oriented for True North.

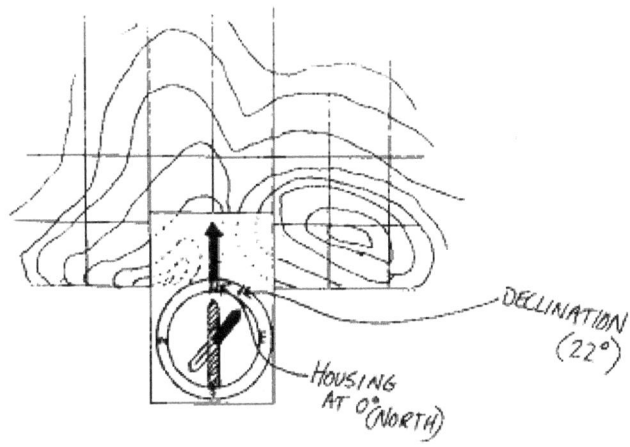

Orient the map with a compass

g) Orient The Map with Compass

Method A

Hold the map flat with the compass on top of it, its straight edge aligned with the vertical grid lines, and the direction of travel arrow pointing to the top of the map. (North of the map is always at the top).

-Set the compass housing at 0° (which is North)

-Turn the compass so that the N end of the needle points to the declination

-The compass must be aligned with grid north, in order for your map to be oriented.

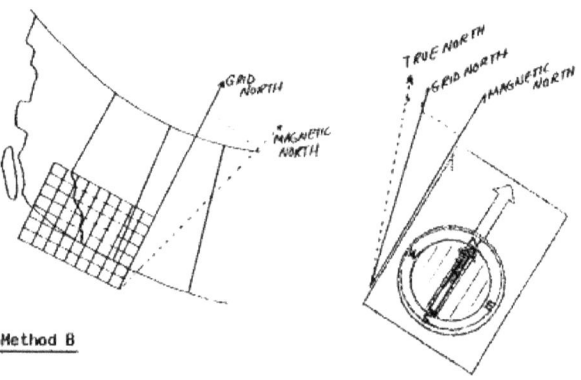

Method B

1. Draw lightly with pencil the declination (magnetic N-S line) in the area of the map you are using.
2. Place the compass on the map and rotate the map until the compass needle matches the declination line. (Be aware of a 180° error if the north of the map and the north of the compass do not match).

h) Causes of Errors in Using Compass

Poor stance in transferring the compass direction to a distant object is a major cause of compass error.

1. Taking a reading while you are too near metal, such as a knife (one metre), axe (three metres), rifle (three metres), vehicle (twenty paces). Photographic light metres have powerful magnets in their mechanisms and are apt to strongly influence a compass needle. The filament coil in some flashlight bulbs when the flashlight is on can have a powerful electromagnetic effect. A slow rotation of the body, while observing the direction of the compass needle, will determine if something on the body is influencing the reading.
2. Compass is not held level, causing the needle to bind.
3. Worn or damaged pivot. The needle should swing smoothly if iron (eg. a knife) is brought near.
4. Unmapped local magnetic disturbance.
5. Magnetic dip (downward pull on the needle) may be so strong in some areas that the compass may have to be tilted, to keep the needle from binding.

Approximate minimum distances to avoid the influence of outside sources on a compass:

- High tension power line – 190 paces
- Telephone and Telegraph wire buried and on posts – 20 paces
- Barb wire – 5 paces
- Vehicles – 20 paces
- Any large object of metal – 50 paces
- Pipe lines – 100 paces
- Light meters – 5 paces

i) Maintaining a Line of March

1. Take a bearing on some distant object that is in the direction you wish to travel, such as a tree, etcetera. The more distant the object, the more accurate your route will be.
2. Travel to that object and ten repeat the process.
3. If in dense bush or in featureless country the compass alone may have to be used, and references to it made frequently.
4. Beware of paying so much attention to the compass that actually you are veering may degrees off course.

j) Locating a Distant Object by Off Aiming

If you attempt to hit an object dead on such as your camp and happen to miss it, it is often difficult to determine on which side of it you are. This is solved by deliberately missing it to one side, for example, to the south, rather than to try hitting it exactly. Then you can search to the north of you once you have travelled the required distance. Otherwise you may have to search for your objective by increasing concentric circles.

This is also used when attempting to reach some point near a linear feature that lies across or near your route such as a road or river. When you miss your objective you will not know which direction to turn unless you purposely miss it to one side. When you reach the linear feature (eg. road, river) you will then know in which direction to turn.

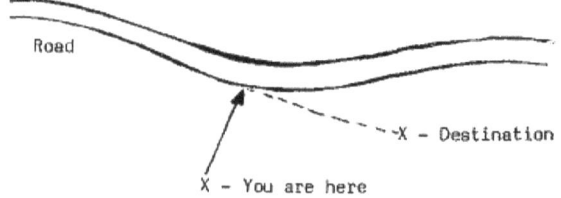

k) Taking a Bearing

When you wish to check a cutline, road, etc. to see if it has the same bearing as a given line on your map, use these steps:

1. Point your direction arrow accurately down your line: you can use your arm as an extension of the direction arrow by holding the compass straight out as far as possible while still being able to see the dial to set the needle on the declination.
2. Holding your compass level rotate your housing until the north end of the needle points to the local declination.
3. Place the compass on your map, with the direction arrow in line with the line being checked and see if housing lines line up with nearby grid lines. The housing arrow should point to the north of the map.

l) Plotting a Bearing (Back Bearing)

If a bearing is to be plotted from a distant object (as in taking a resection or triangulation) the procedure is the same as in taking a bearing but the south end instead of the north end of the compass needle is made to point at the declination. The compass is then placed on the map with the housing lines lined with any N-S line, the housing arrow to the north of the map and the bearing plotted from the object off the edge of the compass.

Back Bearing: To convert a bearing to a back bearing, add 180°. Rather than move the compass housing and risk permanently losing your original bearing, simply turn the entire compass and your body so that the red end of the needle points South and the white end of the needle is made to point to the North on the compass dial. The line of sight or line of travel will be exactly 180° greater than your original bearing and you will be travelling on a back bearing.

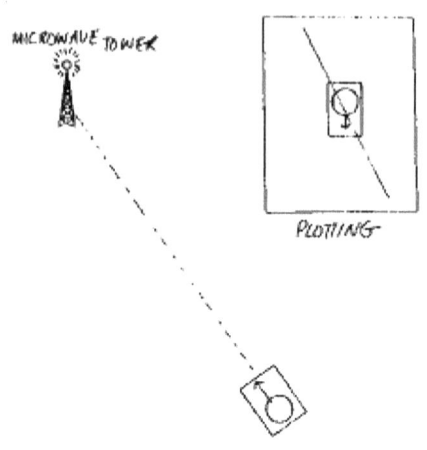

m) Resection: (Obtaining Fixes)

Keeping in mind that if you are doing a proper job of pacing you may not need any fixes. In some cases you know that you are somewhere on a line and you wish to pinpoint where you are on that line. This is termed getting a fix on your position. If a prominent identifiable feature is available take a back bearing, plot it and you have a fix on your line of travel.

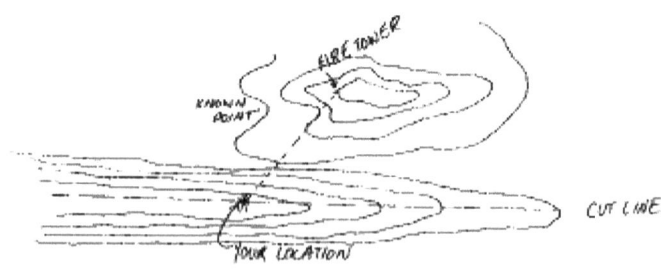

Another method of obtaining a fix, especially when you are not sure of your present location, is to locate two distant objects, take their back bearings and plot them.

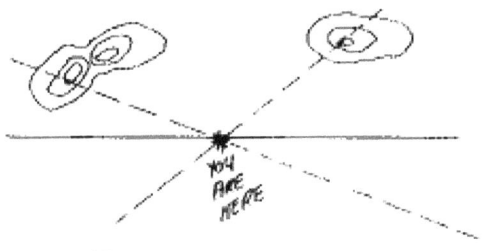

Triangulation uses the same principle but involves three known points of reference. The small triangle turned by their intersection is your location.

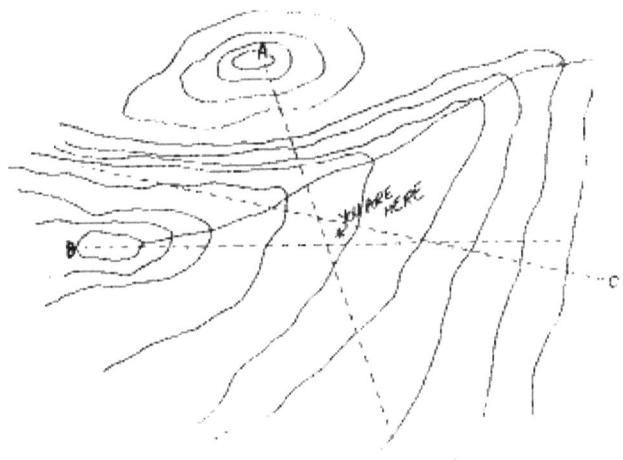

n) Traversing

One of the basic operations with compass and map is traversing. A traverse consists of a number of straight lines of known length which connect each other at angles or bearings. A closed traverse begins and ends at the same point. The lines of a traverse can cross other lines of the same traverse.

The purpose of a traverse is to know your exact position at all times.

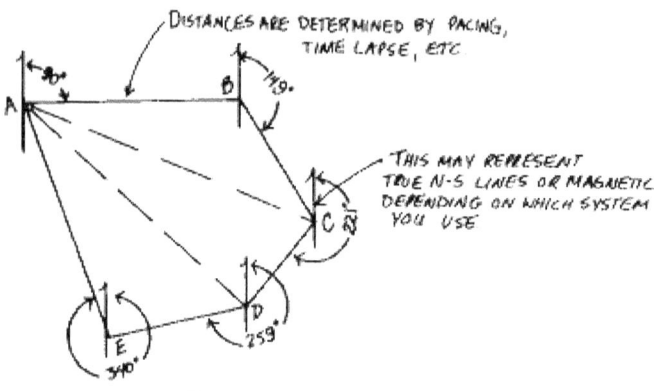

Traversing With A Compass

Measuring Angles of a Traverse: (for the purpose of checking for errors).

1. Lightly draw a north arrow through each station as shown. On a map you would normally use section or grid lines and drawing the north arrow would be dispensed with.
2. Measure the angles.
3. As a check measure all the internal angles and find the sum. Divide the figure into as few triangles as possible. The number of triangles times one hundred eighty (180) degrees should be the same as the sum.

Basic Safe Travel and Boreal Survival

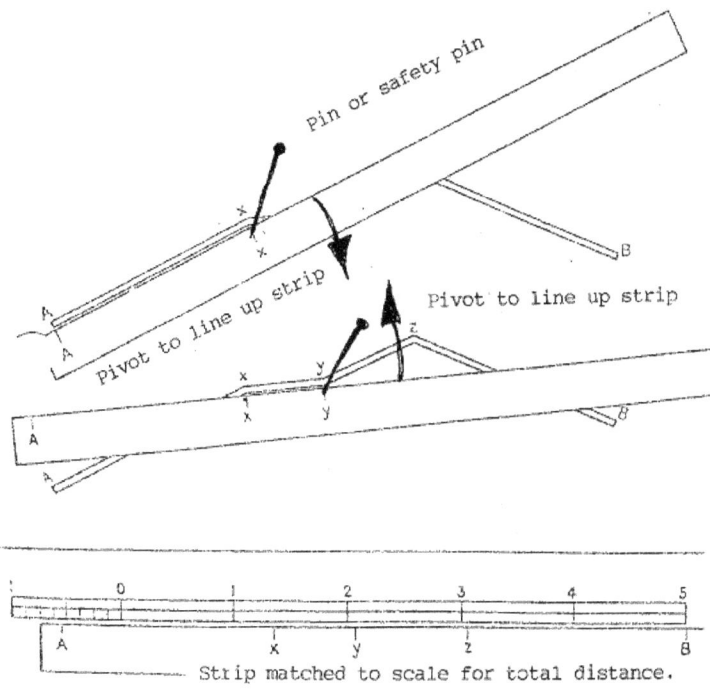

Paper strip method of measuring distance using a pin as a pivot

E) The Basic Survival Lean-To and Bed

The topic of bush shelters is extensive and complex. There are shelters that will specifically ward off rain, snow, wind, and insects, with some shelters fulfilling one role well and others standing up to all the impositions of the environment at once. Some shelters require a fire in front to keep the occupants warm while others are kept warm by the occupants themselves. Shelters may be built above the ground, on the ground, partially in the ground or completely in the ground. The form a shelter takes may depend on the building materials, the tools available, and the expertise and experience of the builder.

A good shelter will deflect the wind, fend off rain or snow and if necessary trap the radiant heat from a fire to provide a warm, dry area to work, rest, and sleep in, as well as providing psychological security in time of survival stress.

1. Open Fronted Lean-To Principles

In essence the shelter's first function is to prevent any air movement through the back and the two ends. Its second function is to intercept any rain or snow from overhead.

Good sites can generally be found near the bases of tall spruces with large overhanging boughs. The ground near the base of the spruce is often spongy, drier in rain, or more free of snow in the winter, as the tree tends to offer considerable protection from above. Overhead protection as well as a bough bed are often unnecessary when a good spruce can be found. You may only need protection from the wind. How often have I gone to a lot of trouble to build a shelter and found my equipment wet, when the ground under a nearby clump of spruces is dry?

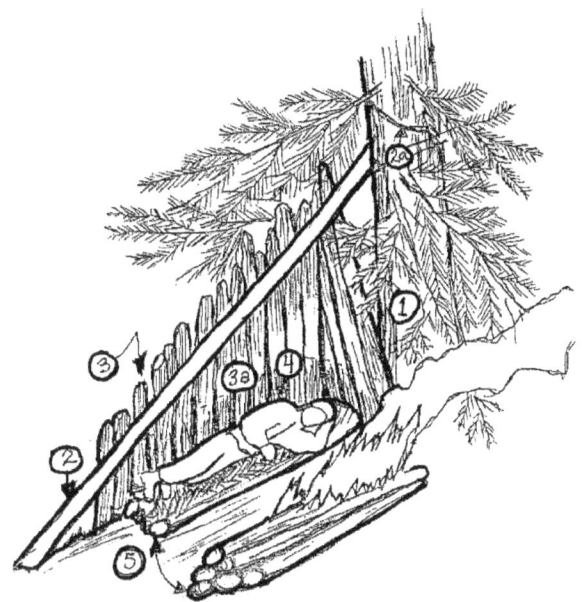

The Simplified Pole Lean-To

Arranging your fuel pile into a shelter.

1. Locate a tree providing substantial overhead protection and build on its down-wind side.

2. A sturdy ridge-pole at least three arm spans long (avoid those lying on the ground as they have a bad reputation of being weak) is placed at a slant and parallel to the wind with the mid point being about shoulder high.

2a. The high end must be propped up or tied to prevent any downward motion if the supporting tree sways in the wind.

3. Lean firewood and rotten wood against the ridge-pole to make a solid wall-roof at least two layers thick.

3a. To windproof it chink with moss for a height of only a meter above the bed.

4. The bed is no wider than the shoulders.

5. The fire is a step away from the bed. Block off only the windward end. Leave the down-wind end open to reduce smoke problems.

A familiar form of boreal forest survival shelter is the lean-to or matchegin. The lean-to is often maligned by those who have not taken the time to understand it. It is one of the many shelters available to the expert survivalist and it should be first type of shelter to be mastered by the novice because of its ease of construction and wide range of applicability.

The lean-to has certain advantages and disadvantages. Its main advantage is that it can be readily built anywhere there are trees. It is an easy shelter to build with the most common readily available materials, such as spruce boughs, and if necessary it can be built without any tools. A person trained in the use of a good Mora knife should easily be able to cut down green trees with it as thick as the wrist for the rafter poles faster than most people can cut them down with a hatchet. The ridge pole, which should be at least ten centimetres in diameter, can be cut down with a knife and baton in about five minutes.

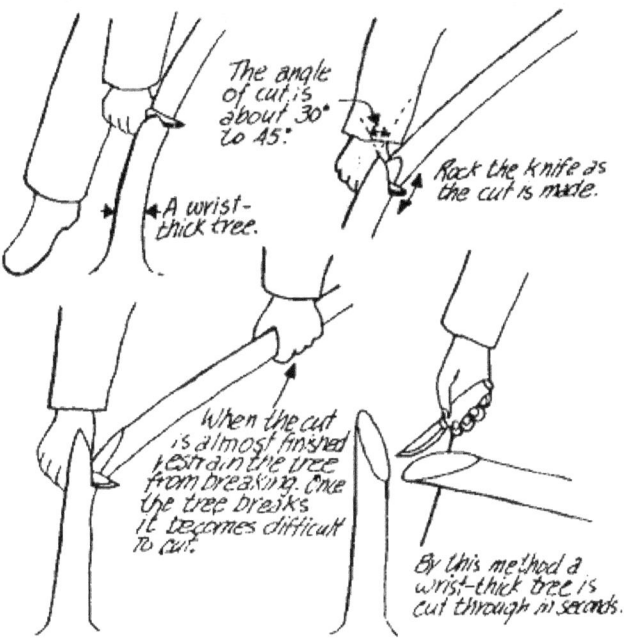

Its main disadvantage is the large fire that has to be maintained in front of it to keep you warm. Gathering of adequate amounts of fuel is exhausting and stoking the fire frequently during the night disrupts your rest. The amount of fuel used for one night would keep a 12-person teepee with stove warm for a week or more. Another disadvantage is the amount of materials and time required to build a cozy functional shelter.

In conjunction with the wall backed fire, the simple open-fronted lean-to is one of the more tried and favoured shelters. Both the lean-to and the wall backed fire are oriented parallel to the wind. A variance of up to 15 degrees from either angle can be tolerated before you begin to experience problems with smoke. The ridge pole of the shelter is placed about one small pace from the face of the wall back when it is very cold, a long pace in moderately cold weather, and two steps away when the temperature is above 0 °C.

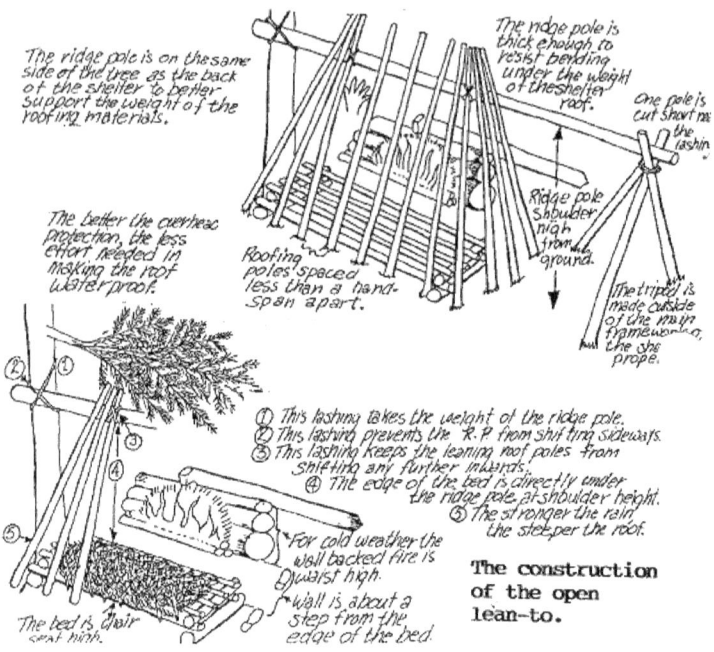

The construction of the open lean-to.

The ridge pole of the lean-to should be sturdy and sound so as to easily bear (without bending) the weight of the poles, boughs, and banked snow used in building the shelter. If the butt end can barely be circled with the four fingers of both hands, it should be adequate. A sound ridge pole is seldom found lying on the ground and so should be made of a standing tree. The ridge pole can be supported between two standing trees, two tripods, or a tree and a tripod. The latter is the recommended method because the tree provides stability and the tripod provides for ease in rearranging the shelter, should there be any wind shift after the shelter is built. The two standing trees have to be used when the shelter is built of poles or split logs because of the great weight that has to be supported by the ridge pole. Tripods are notoriously unstable if there is a heavy lateral force applied to the ridge pole they are supporting.

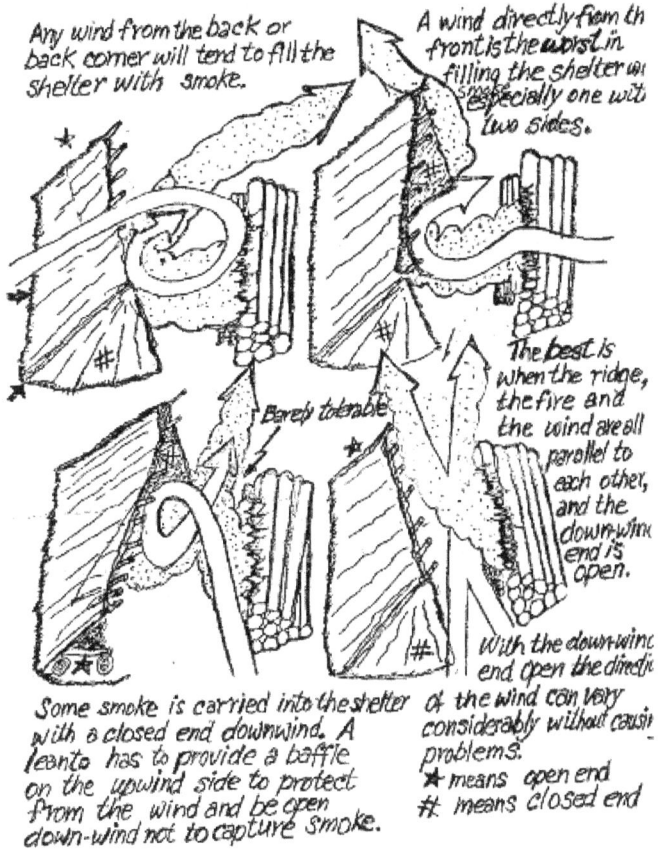

Wind direction relative to shelter back

Cross Section of a Winter Lean-To

1. Wall backed fire is waist high.
2. Fire one good step away from the edge of the bed.

CROSS SECTION OF THE OPEN LEAN-TO

3. Fire made hot enough to force you to stay one step away.
4. The back of the shelter is as close to the fire as possible.
5. The bough bed is at least four fingers thick when compressed.
6. Boughs are thick enough to prevent heat penetration from melting the banked up snow.
7. Snow is banked up to prevent infiltration of cold air.
8. If possible, bank up the whole roof with snow.
9. The ridgepole is substantial enough to hold up the weight of the bough and snow cover. The ridgepole is parallel to the wind. It is about shoulder high off the ground providing room to sit and work under the shelter roof.
10. The core of the bed is made of snow. It is about chair seat high.
11. Snow retaining log prevents the snow from melting out from under the bed.
12. With an elevated bed the ground can be uneven.
13. Face the shelter towards the sun.

14. A clear expanse of snow if front of the shelter provides more warming effect from the sun.
15. Make the shelter under a tree that provides some overhead protection.
16. The snow is cleared away between the fire and edge of the bed.

For ease of handling and for providing a convenient height to work and live under, the ridge pole is erected shoulder high above the ground. Sound poles are selected to make the tripod. To determine the point at which the lashing should be placed, one of the poles is stood upright and grasped head high. The legs of the tripod are spread wide enough apart so that the ridge pole placed on it comes down to shoulder height. If possible, make the ridge pole long enough so that the tripod supporting the end is excluded from the main body of the shelter (it tends to get in the way when building the bough thatch).

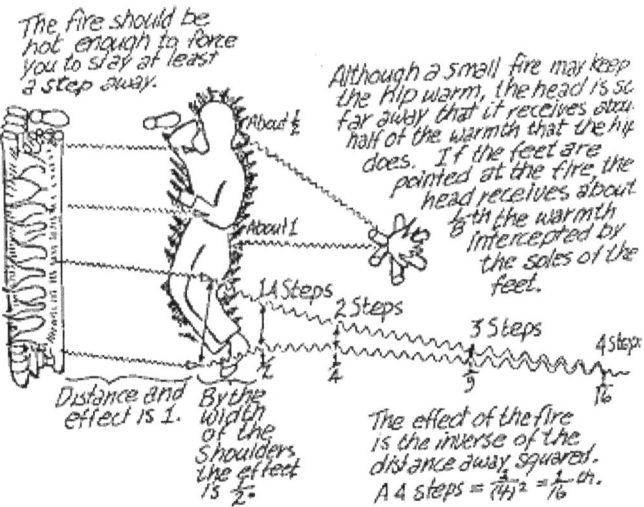

Fire size and distance relationships

The other end of the ridge pole can be lashed or propped up with a stick. In either case, the ridge pole is on the same side of the tree as the back of the shelter. If no lashing material is available in winter a serviceable cord can be twisted from the grass found near the bases of smaller spruces. In the summer roots from almost any tree, especially spruce, can be used.

Occasionally there is a tendency to shift parallel to the ridge pole causing a collapse of the shelter. This is prevented by lashing the ridge pole firmly at the tree support end.

Dry rafter poles for the back of the lean-to can be gathered without the use of the axe. The poles can be burned off to the required length. They are limbed by being run back and forth between two closely spaced trees. When using boughs, the poles are roughly spaced a hand span apart or narrower. The ends are closed to block the wind, especially on the windward side. The poles are leaned against the ridge pole at the shallowest angle possible that still provides adequate over-head protection. The deeper the shelter, the colder the opposite side of the body may be. The closer the shelter-back is to the fire the greater the chance for it to warm up, and in turn, for it to be better able to warm the shelter occupant.

The effect of the radiant energy is the inverse of the square of the distance. That is, if the back is a metre away, the effect could be $1/1^2=1$ at two metres, $1/2^2=1/4$ and at 3 metres $1/3^2=1/9$. That is, doubling the distance away from the fire gives you one quarter the effect. Tripling the distance gives you one ninth of the effect.

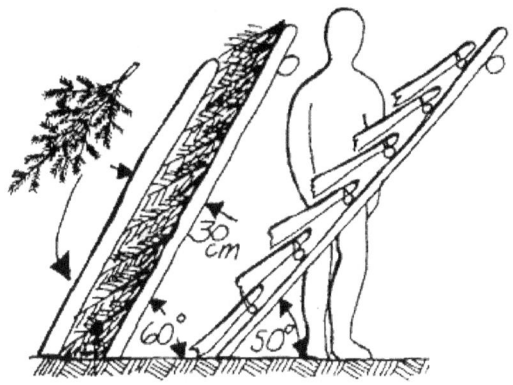

The amount of lean a roof may have

If the shelter has to deflect rain, then the steepness of the rafter poles has to be increased to the point where the boughs shed the rain. In severe rain storms the back of the shelter thatched with conifer boughs may be straight up and down and may have to be higher than shoulder height to provide adequate coverage. The rafter poles used in the back of the shelter should not be excessively long as they may catch the rain and drip into the interior of the shelter.

Boughs are now placed on the back of the shelter. The best boughs are of Balsam or Alpine Fire, with White Spruce being second. Any material including the needle-less lower branches of spruce, leafy alder tips or handfuls of densely packed swamp birch, to name a few.

A layer of about 25 to 30 centimetres is required. In winter the layer of boughs has to support the snow banked on it and at the same time be thick enough so that the heat of the fire will not penetrate through and melt the snow. The snow is usually banked up high enough to be a half metre higher than the top of the bed in the shelter. This assures a still-air space inside the shelter. It is very annoying and disruptive to your sleep to have to frequently turn over to warm up that side which is away from the fire. It bears repeating that this is one of the most essential points in making a comfortable lean-to. Without snow this is more difficult to achieve. The boughs have to be packed as densely as possible and perhaps compressed with logs at the back of the shelter. When it is very cold and no snow is available one of the most effective shelters is made of two layers of closely fitting poles chinked with moss.

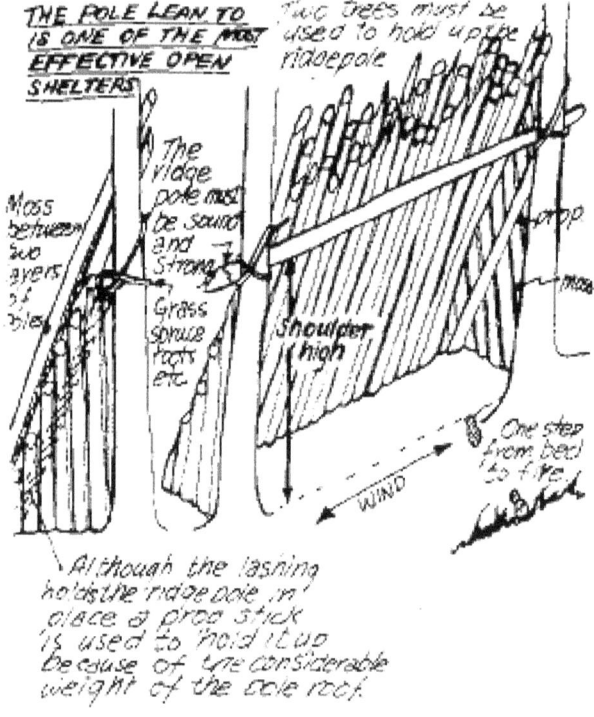

Pole lean-to chincked with moss

If the boughs are to deflect all rain, depending on the severity of the storm, they may have to be piled on quite thick. The first layer of boughs is composed of the biggest boughs available. They are set down stem first, top side out. These boughs provide a foundation for the smaller boughs that are laid on next. The remaining boughs are placed stems up and under sides up, as experience has shown that this provides the maximum shedding effect. After the first layer is applied the stems of the boughs are jammed into it to produce a neat shingled effect. The first layer of boughs can be laid on at a slight sideways angle to help keep the stems of the boughs from reaching into the shelter between the rafter poles.

The roof of the shelter can be made of a great variety of materials, especially in the summer. Two or three layers of straight poles are quite effective. Sheets of bark from dead Birch and Black Poplar trees are good. Green White Poplar splits very easily when frozen and the split halves can be very effectively used to make a lean-to. In summer, any leafy branches can take the place of boughs. Clover, as found on many river banks, is quite effective. Grass thatching is often mentioned in the literature.

2. Open Fronted Lean-To Made of Flexible Materials

On occasion, though poles are not readily obtainable, thinner flexible materials are. When only a pocket knife is available, this shelter is fairly easy to build. The ridge pole and its end supports are replaced by two arches paralleling each other about 30 centimetres apart, spanning slightly longer than one's height. The two arches are brought together at the top and bound together to provide stability. Instead of rafter poles, arches a hand span width apart make up the back of the shelter. The shelter can now be roofed with any of the materials mentioned earlier, especially grass.

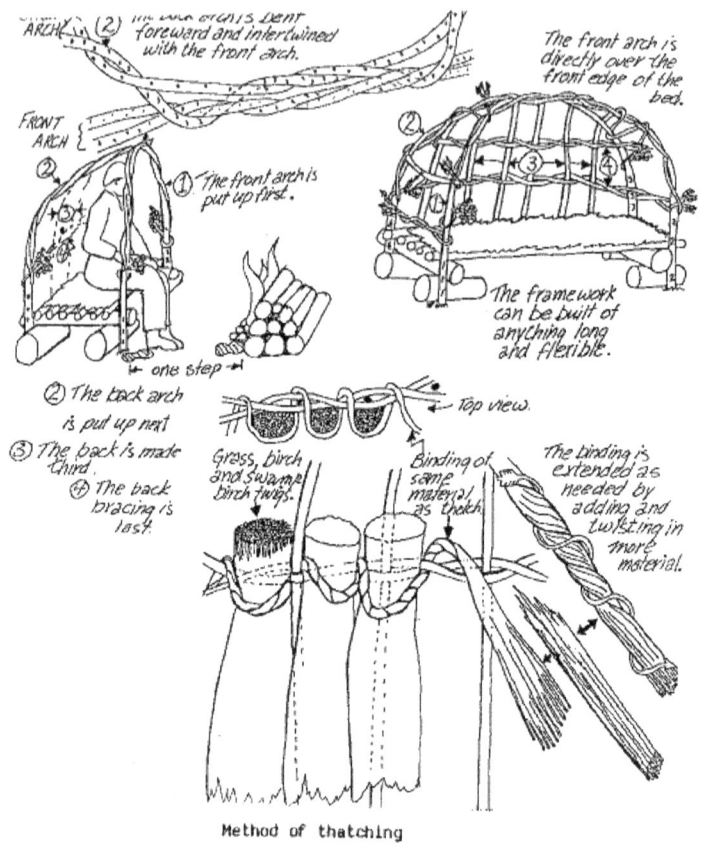

Method of thatching

With one person the lean-to is made large enough to accommodate that person. Two people increase the length of the bed about a third longer and sleep with heads at each end, overlapping heels to hips. With one third more effort a second person is accommodated. A third person replaces the re-emitter fire with a second one person lean-to and a fire is maintained between the shelters. Four people use two of the longer shelters with a fire in between. Five or more people may be better off using a brush teepee which in actuality is a lean-to in a circle with a small fire in the middle.

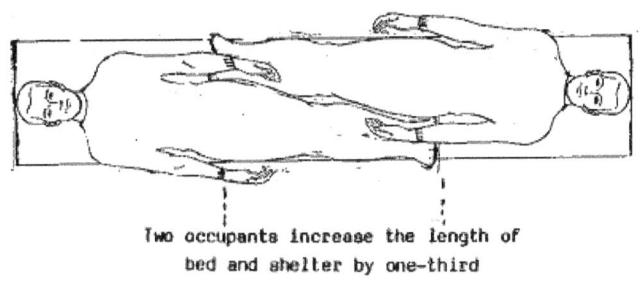

Two occupants increase the length of bed and shelter by one-third

3. Bough Beds

The saying "you made your bed, now sleep in it" may have a bush meaning as valid as the one originally intended for it. It could mean that your comfort is limited only by your lack of experience and knowledge in the use of the materials nature may provide.

The use of the term "bough" bed may be somewhat misleading. I have encountered people who could not make a bed when spruce or fir boughs were not available. Although the spruce boughs are the traditional material for the standard bush bed, they are not the only material that can be used, nor are they necessarily the best. Almost any material will do, if it is fine enough at the tips and no thicker than your thumb at the stem. This could be any shrub such as willow, red osier dogwood, alder or swamp birch, any branch such as aspen, black poplar, birch or pine, with or without needles or leaves, or forbs such as clover, or grass, green or dry. Most of these materials offer a more springy bed than spruce boughs do.

In fact you may avert some criticism with regard to the consumptive aspect of making a bush bed by staying away from the needle-bearing trees and using alder, willow or red osier dogwood more extensively. There are people who may be critical regardless of the material used. I would not begrudge this criticism as long as they recognize that there are times and places where a bush bed may be appropriate.

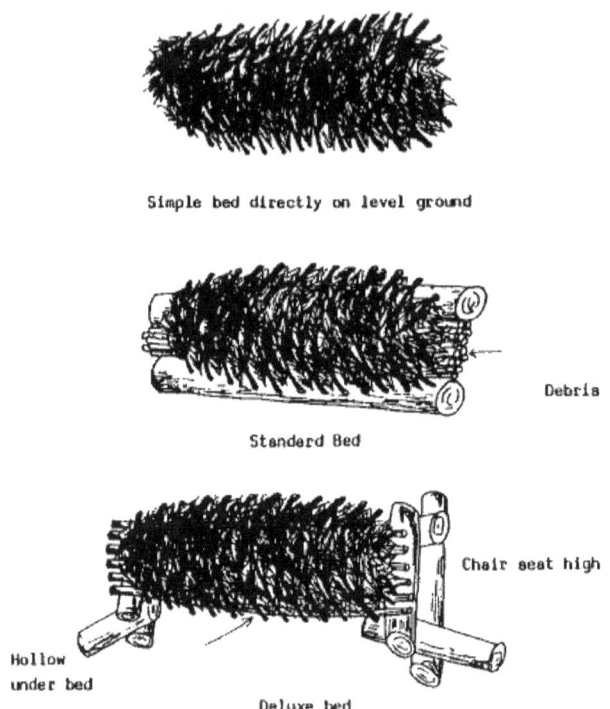

Knowing how to make a good bush bed does not imply that you must always use one. Personally, wherever possible, I prefer to use an open-cell foam about seven or eight centimetres thick under a closed-cell mat about a centimetre thick. This preference is mainly due to the time factor in making a bed. It may take from a half an hour to an hour-and-a-half to make an adequate bed.

Spruce boughs are actually more effective in making acomfortable bed than they are useful in thatching a roof.

The layers of boughs provide a comfortable place to lie down, insulate against cold, and keep the body away from the damp or cold ground. A ground sheet is unnecessary if the bed is at least four fingers deep, when the bed is made directly on the ground.

In very cold weather the boughs are very brittle and should be heated so that the needles do not break off. In wet weather as much moisture as possible should be shaken off the boughs before laying them down. The bough bed, like the shelter, can be made without an axe. The dry boughs often found at the base of a big spruce can be far more efficiently used in the bed rather than by being burned in the fire. This is especially true in the winter.

There are about three basic variations of the single person bush bed that may be useful to consider: The simple, the standard and the deluxe.

The Simple Bed is essentially the upper-most or mattress component of the other two. It may be all you need in the summer or it can supplement a mat and sleeping bag in the winter.

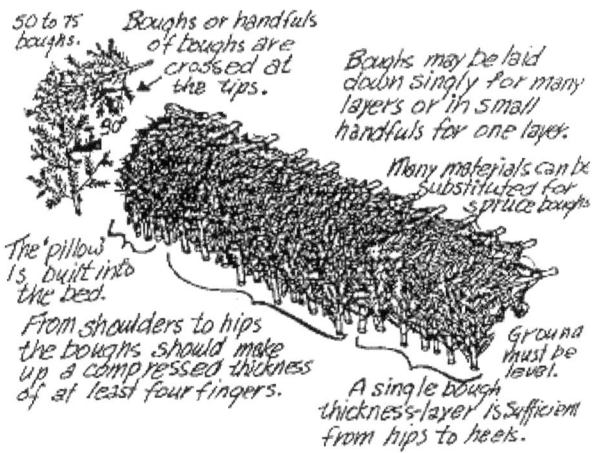

Any material that is fine enough can be used in making the bed. To simplify my explanation, I will only use the term "boughs" for which one could substitute branches, shrubs, clover or grass. All are used in virtually the same way.

If there is no level ground on which to place the simple bed, you may have to use the standard one. In the winter the snow may have to be packed and leveled and the bed constructed directly on top of it. Digging the snow away to the ground serves no useful purpose.

Boughs that are about elbow to fingertip long are laid down in small handfuls so that the tips cross each other in a herringbone fashion. For the greatest resiliency the boughs are laid down the same way they grew on the tree: with the upper-most side up.

The first layer of boughs, which is often more than adequate for a bed, may extend the full length of your body. If a second layer is added, it need only be from you head to your hips. The legs require only one layer for resiliency and insulation value. If more than one layer is used, start with the coarser, lower boughs of the tree, saving the finer boughs for the top layer. Snap off long needle-free stems that add little to the comfort of the bed.

Boughs thicker than the thumb at the stem should only be used in the base layers. Finally, the smaller, shorter branches of pencil thickness may be incorporated into the bed by jamming the ends into the bed wherever needed. That way you do not end up lying on any thicker ends and you get the maximum of springiness. Usually the stems at the edges will curve upwards. If small logs are laid on the edges to hold these stems down, it will be noticed that the centre of the bed rises slightly, again providing a little

Basic Safe Travel and Boreal Survival

added springiness. Also, the log nearest the fire serves to keep you from rolling into the fire while you are asleep.

A "pillow" may be made by tucking handfuls of boughs under the base at the end of the bed.

The Standard Bed incorporates a base that raises the bed 15 to 20 centimetres off the ground. It allows you to build a bed on uneven ground. It also is more resilient than the simple bed and may be more appropriate for long term usage.

Two logs, the larger the better, are laid down about shoulder width apart and leveled if necessary. The space between them is filled and packed with coarse boughs or shrubbery level with the top of the logs and a simple bed is then built on top.

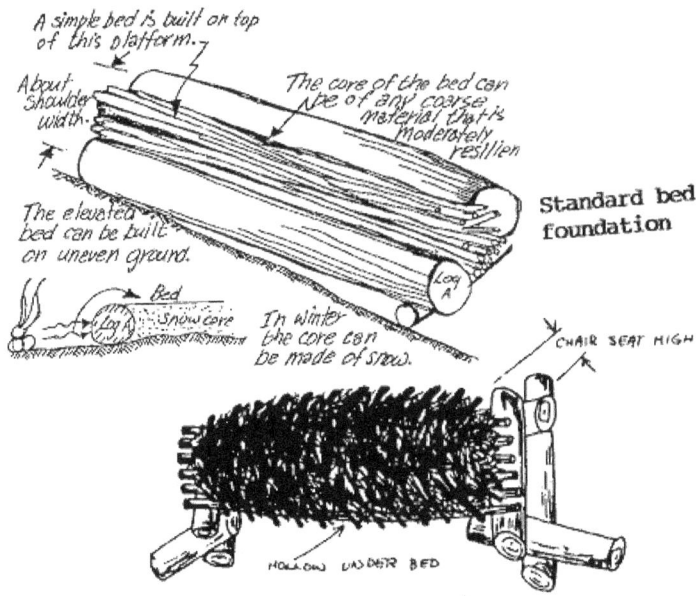

The deluxe bed

The Deluxe Bed would be used when no mattress or sleeping bags are available and where conditions are so adverse that you need to eke out every gram of comfort just to get by. A platform about chair-seat high (30 o 40 cms.) is constructed so that the radiant heat of your fire will go under the bed to assist in keeping you warm. A well made simple bed of at least two layers is then built on top of this platform.

Bough beds tend to lose their resiliency with use and may need to be spruced up every three or four days.

Larger Beds: When a bough bed has to accommodate more than one person, such as in an enclosed shelter or a deep summer tarp lean-to, there may not be enough space for the herringbone bough bed. In this case put a layer of the thickest boughs and dry boughs crossways on the bed, with the second layer going 90 degrees to the first and the subsequent layers at 45 degrees to each other with each new row.

Making a Bed in Winter: Although not that necessary in the summer, an elevated bed may add considerably to your comfort in the winter. The bed provides a comfortable place to sit in front of the fire. It is warmer because the heavier cold air on top of the bed, will flow over the edge of the bench. There the air is warmed and the insulative aspect of the snow and the bed's height will counteract the cold radiating from the ground. The edge of the bed-base is faced with logs to keep your fire from melting the snow from under your bed. The snow in the area where the fire is to be is used to make the base of the bed. Therefore, uneven ground, logs, or stumps do not pose a problem.

After the snow base has been made by leveling and packing the snow, the bough bed is built on top of it. Dry spruce boughs are adequate for the first one or two layers. The first layer may be laid across the bed, the second layer lengthwise and the subsequent layers of green boughs in a herringbone fashion. The elevation also prevents you from rolling into the fire unconsciously while asleep.

Note: Concern with Respect to Using Boughs for Bed Making, Shelter Building, and Signal Fires: Although everyone venturing into the wilderness should be familiar with the use of boughs for shelter, insulation, springiness, and smoke generation, the use of boughs in this way is strictly consumptive. If too much of these activities were carried on in the wrong context, considerable depletion of spruce trees might result. One of the most comfortable beds is made of seven centimetre open cell foam pad under a one centimetre closed cell foam pad. A nylon or canvas tarp will allow you to make a very effective lean-to in minutes rather than hours of construction time.

F) Outdoor Cooking

1. Introduction

Cooked food can become more tasty and digestible. There are several ways to cook foods. Man can be distinguished from other creatures because he mastered fire and used it for cooking. This provided access to a means of improving the digestibility of available food.

Baking

Baking is cooking in an oven or on a hot dry surface with dry heat. Breads, casseroles and pizzas are usually baked. Baking a piece of meat heavier than 1.5 kilograms may not kill bacteria and parasites in the centre of the meat. There is generally a great loss of fat in baking.

Boiling

Boiling is the easiest method of cooking in the bush and usually conserves the most food value of all the methods. Boiling is considered better than baking.

Boiling swells the fibers and cells of the food so that they burst, thereby becoming more tender and digestible. Boiling meat causes less waste than baking. There is less water lost, less fat volatilized and the water can be fully used. Boiled foods may be less tasty than roasted foods, especially when no seasoning is available. For example, a boiled rabbit without any seasoning, especially salt, can not be very appealing. Roasting the rabbit slightly after boiling improves the flavour somewhat.

Carbohydrates usually originate from vegetables. During boiling, carbohydrates expand and burst the indigestible cellulose cell walls to make more food available. The more a vegetable is boiled the more digestible it becomes. However, vegetables that are over boiled tend to lose a great deal of their mineral constituents to the water used in boiling. To regain what is lost, use as little water as possible, then use the water in some way such as in a soup. Proteins, usually of animal origin, shrink when heated; thus, meat becomes less digestible the more it is boiled.

Boiling at 100°C for at least twenty minutes will kill bacteria and parasites but prolonged boiling will destroy essential vitamins. Cook food only long enough to make it palatable and digestible, unless bacteria and parasites are a problem.

2. The Australian Cooking Crane

One of the most effective ways to suspend a pot over an open fire is by the use of a pole arrangement called the Australian Cooking Crane. This crane allows you to cook well without having to watch the pot closely. Pots can also be placed on the fire or removed from it without having to come near the heat or flame. The whole crane can be built simply with dry, straight poles.

The effort to build the crane is well spent if you are cooking for a large number or if you are camping in the same place for an extended period of time. The quickest way to put up the crane is to build it first and then build the fire. It takes about a half hour to build the crane. The crane can also be used in hanging a large pot over a small perhaps unstable portable stove. The following method assumes a fire has been built.

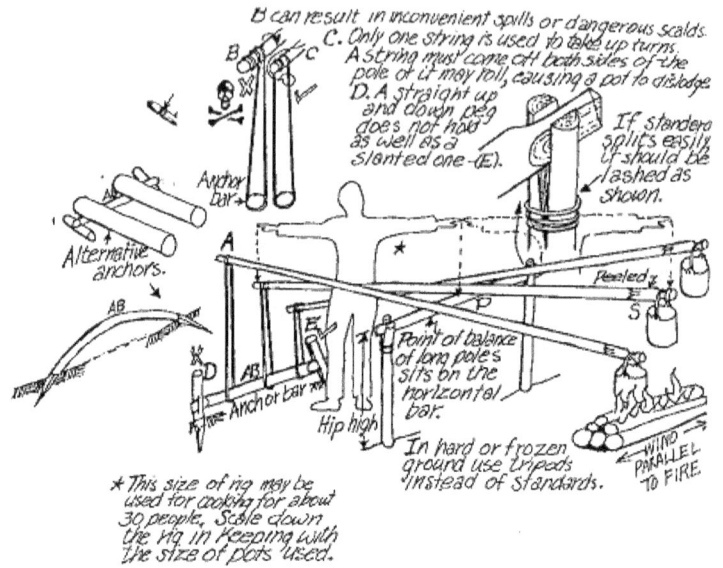

The Cantilever Poles

Step 1: Select either dry or green cantilever poles about two arm spans long. If large pots are used the heavier pole ends should be at least the thickness of your wrist. The bark on the working end of the pole right above the pot should be peeled off or else pieces of charred bark will be continually falling into the pot. To keep the pot from slipping off the end or down the pole, especially with smooth skinned poles such as white poplar, cut a "V" notch completely around the pole about five centimetres from the end. The notch must be cut around the pole because it is hard to tell where the pole will stop rotating and it can rotate with each adjustment of height.

The cantilever pole's point of balance should be very near its point of contact with the horizontal bar; otherwise, a light or partially filled pot may not stay down where desired. To position the horizontal bar, first find the balance point. Hold the pot end of the pole over the center of the fire or where the fire is to be. The horizontal bar should be positioned right below the balance point.

The uprights and horizontal bar are now put up. If the ground allows it, two posts can be driven in, their tops split and the thinned ends of the horizontal bar driven into the splits.

The Horizontal Bar

Step 2: The length of the horizontal bar is generally the length of the fire used for cooking. A metre and a half long bar will easily accommodate the suspension and manipulation of four large pots. Since the cooking fire is usually made parallel to the wind, the horizontal bar should also be parallel to the wind. If the ground is rocky or frozen, tripods may have to be substituted for the posts. If you are cooking for one or two people for a relatively short time, a forked stick can replace the horizontal bar arrangement. This system is slightly less versatile.

The height of the bar should be somewhere between the knee and the point of the hip. Hip level is better for large pots and large group cooking.

The Height Control

Step 3: To anchor the thin ends of the cantilever poles use a sufficiently heavy log, an arch made of a supple sapling, a wand or some other suitable device. To determine the length of string required to control the end of the pole, place a pot on the working end of the cantilever pole and drop it to its lowest required position.

A double string as shown in the figure allows some manoeuvrability along the anchor and also keeps the cantilever pole from rolling as sometimes happens with one string. During use there must be a string coming off each side of the pole, otherwise you may spill the pot or cause a scald injury. If string is at a premium, a taut-line hitch arrangement may be more suitable.

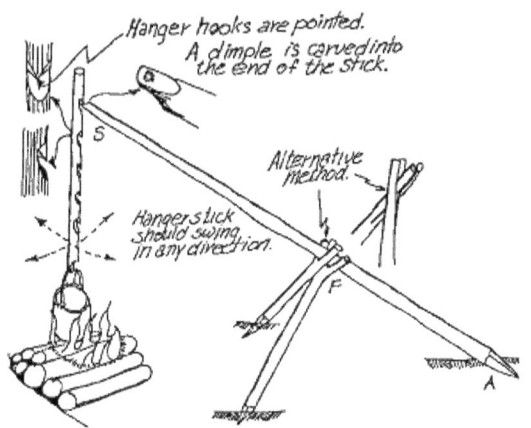

The Burtonsville rig for suspending pots.

3. Steam Pit

Consider using the steam pit when large pieces of meat, especially tough meat, are to be cooked.

Prerequisites

1. Fuel - A good supply of non-resinous wood for heating the pit and the rocks.
2. Rocks - Rocks taken from a stream may break-up too much while being heated. The small pieces are not as convenient to move around.

3. Site - A sandbar that allows the digging of a pit about 40 centimetres deep and that has nearby suitable rocks and good driftwood for fuel would be a good site. Sand retains heat better than any other type of soil and is fairly fire safe.

Cooking Pit Construction

1. A pit is dug with sloped sides 50 to 60 centimetres deep.
2. A good fire is built in the pit by heaping wood in it well above the ground line. Stones are piled on the wood and are heated until they glow. Enough rocks are required to form a layer on the bottom of the pit and a second layer over the food to be cooked. If necessary, more fuel can be piled on top of the stones.
3. Once the rocks are hot and most of the wood has burned up, remove any unburned wood or large embers. A layer of stones is arranged on the bottom of the pit and the rocks that are to be placed on top of the food are temporarily set aside.
4. The thick layer of green foliage is laid down on the hot rocks. This can be clover, alfalfa, sedge, fern or alpine hedysarum tops. Use any greens that neither impart an undesirable flavour nor are poisonous.
5. The food to be cooked can be wrapped in foil, cloth or burlap for further protection against the sand. Lay it down and cover it with a thick layer of foliage. All of the foliage should be thoroughly wet (when cooking for 6 to 8 people, two gallons of water may be used). If good vegetation is not available, such as in the early spring, foil or wet burlap may be substituted. Poking a hole to pour water into the pit as is often described elsewhere usually results in the water carrying dirt into the pit and contaminating the food.

6. The hot rocks previously set aside are arrange into a layer covering the food. A crudely woven willow mat is place on top of the rocks and is covered with a layer of grass to help prevent any sand reaching the food. At this stage, any water required (see previous paragraph) is poured on before the pit is covered over with sand.
7. The pit is quickly sealed with a good layer of sand, packed down slightly, and lightly wetted down to make it more steam proof.
8. When cooking with this method, you cannot spoil food by overcooking. The pit can be loaded in the morning and opened for supper. Meat must be cooked two hours per pound for a minimum of six hours. Trout and average size fish require an hour. The steam pit is also useful for cooking vegetables.

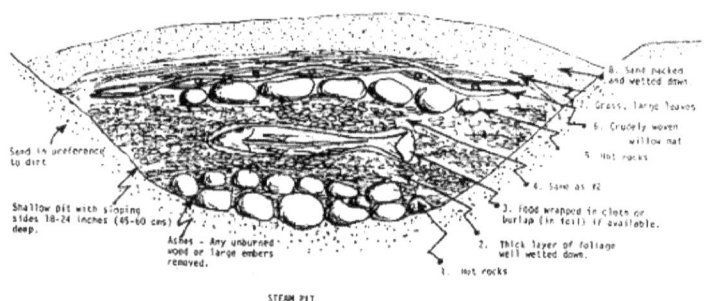

STEAM PIT

G) Wild Edible Plants

1. Plants

a) Some Reasons for Using Wild Edible Plants

1. Wild edible plants can be a hedge against hard times, be they wilderness survival, times of scarcity or outright poverty. The use of wild edibles may be a means of reducing pressure on conventional supplies in times of need.
2. Wild edibles can add variety to an otherwise monotonous diet. This was an important consideration in pioneer days.
3. Most of the plants in this article have an especially high content of vitamins and mineral nutrients. During pioneer days, wild edibles were used to supplement a deficient diet, especially at the end of a long winter when garden plants were months away from being available. Old timers can still be encountered who can recall using cow parsnip, marsh marigold, stinging nettle and cattail as early spring vegetables.
4. Learning to use wild plants as food can help you to better understand how natural communities work. By learning to manage edible plants in a way that ensures the ongoing availability of these plants, you can develop a responsible relationship with this natural resource.

A definite responsibility rests with everyone who uses wild plants, to know enough about them to properly conserve them. You should have some idea as to whether the plant is rare, slow to regenerate or readily eradicated by certain methods of gathering. What forms of harvesting does the plant react to most favourably? Some plants may best tolerate being pulled up while others prefer to be sheared off as if eaten by a rodent or ungulate. Will leaving a part of a plant start a new one? Does the plant readily grow from seed? Can a rare or more desirable plant be encouraged to grow in your garden especially when nearby competition is removed? Once planted it can provide a handsome return for a minimum of tending.

The plants in this article were chosen with the knowledge that they tend to respond favourably to usage and none are rare in Alberta. All the same, they should still be used by the same conservation rules that apply to the gathering of all plants, common or rare.

b) Some Rules for Gathering

1. Gather plants only where you are not prohibited to do so by law. All plants within Provincial and National Parks and Reserves are protected by law. Anyone picking, damaging or transplanting any plants can be prosecuted. Some municipalities have regulations governing the gathering of plants, trees and shrubs in their jurisdictions. Some plants are protected by law. I believe the Western Wood Lily (Tiger Lily) is one.
2. Plants should not be gathered where they serve the public in any way, such as along trails, nature walks or in school study areas.
3. Gather plants where the collecting activity, especially digging for roots, will not contribute to erosion or cerate any other unacceptable effect.
4. Collect only what you can use. If it is the leaves you want, pick only those you can use, leaving the rest of the plant uninjured. When using the roots of perennials be sparing and use cup quantities rather than quarts. When collecting a part other than the root, leave the root intact.

5. Vigorous, introduced plants should be considered fairer game than less competitive native ones.
6. Create as little disturbance as possible to the surrounding vegetation with your foraging activities.
7. When you have determined that your plant is obviously abundant and thriving and you have ascertained that it will tolerate harvesting (through the literature mostly), you may consider collecting it in the following manner. a) First take the overcrowded plants. b) Depending on prevalence and other factors you may take one in five if the plant is common, one in ten if less common and one in twenty if somewhat scarce in any given locale.
8. There are places where plants may not be fit for consumption. Plants near a well travelled road may have a higher than normal lead content. Avoid collecting plants where herbicide use is suspected, such as along some municipal roads, railroad and power line right of ways, and near orchards.

c) Positive Identification

It cannot be overemphasized that you should be positive about the identification of the plants you plan to eat. Your enthusiasm in the use of wild plants should be tempered by a cautious and careful attitude. Although relatively rare, there are plants that can kill. Learning the scientific name of the plants you can use can be very important. A plant can have many common names and many different plants can end up with the same common name, especially in different parts of the country.

The common name is very much like a nickname. The scientific name is the one and only name assigned to a particular plant throughout the whole world. It comes in two parts. The first part, known as the Genus, is always capitalized and is analogous to one's surname. The second uncapitalized part, known as the species, corresponds to one's given name.

Unless you learn to use the scientific name of a plant, there may be many instances where others will not be sure what plant you are talking about when you are seeking assistance in identification or if you are trying to tell a doctor what plant it was that you think made you ill.

Occasionally, you may encounter a statement such as "the Viola species are edible". By this we mean that all plants of the Genus Viola are edible. Although occasionally there are plants where the whole Genus is edible one must not assume that if one plant in the Genus is edible, that all plants in the Genus are. You can have edible and toxic plants in the same Genus. If there is the slightest doubt about a plant's identification get an expert opinion.

d) Direct Mounting of Plant Specimens with Broad Scotch Tape

Plant study is becoming more popular and one aid that instructors or teachers might find very useful is a good collection of mounted plant specimens.

In teaching plants to University students, I soon noted their desperation as we went into our second dozen plants (eventually ending up with as many as a hundred or more plants in a month long course). How were they to remember their names? Even though they took notes furiously while the plant was being talked about, mere words were often not enough to help identify the plant again later. Sketches could be just as incomprehensible when made by the untrained hand and any photographs taken would not be of any use until after the course was over as there was no opportunity to develop any film.

Digital cameras have remedied this. Most resorted to taking a specimen which was a waste as the specimen shrivelled or got lost, not to mention the general devastation of a class of twenty students each picking their own specimens.

The solution that seemed appropriate was to make up a class collection that could be referred to as needed for the rest of the course. Early attempts at carrying a vasculum and newspapers for pressing prompted me to seek other solutions. The weight of the vasculum and the newspapers, and the drying time that caused the specimens to not be ready for use until after the course was over made conventional methods inappropriate.

The original intention was to create a collection that was to be useful for a period of up to two weeks. Four years later, that same collection is still holding its own.

I feel that individual students do not generally qualify to have their own collections unless they fully intend to teach plant identification themselves. If the teaching of plants was started in kindergarten and was done more systematically than it is now, a student graduating out of grade twelve would have no need for a plant collection because they would already know the names of all the plants in their general locale.

That original collection of plants showed the way the plants may be mounted to get the most out of them by having the specimen retaining its original form and color as much as possible. Plants mounted by scotch tape method retain far more of their identifiable characteristics than those mounted by conventional methods and stand handling far better.

The mounting of specimens in this way is almost a science if the following suggestions are followed.

1. **Tape**: The most convenient size of clear tape is about 2 inches wide (5 cms.) that may be found in stationary stores, dollar stores or hardware stores.
2. **Paper**: In my experience a paper I have developed a preference for mounting the specimens on is ordinary typewriter paper-not only is it inexpensive, it also allows moisture to pass through it readily. It also produces a more compact and portable collection. Use something like 20 lb. white bond or something similar.
3. Providing the plant is not damp with dew or rain, mount it immediately on picking. Do not give it a chance to wilt.
4. Tape down the entire plant, even the stems. Any part of the plant not taped down will crumble away and disappear through the constant handling it may endure.
5. There is no need to be too neat with the taping. Functionality is the objective. Preoccupation with neatness at first may cause you to take twice as long to complete your collection (thereby making it twice as expensive).
6. If the leaves are arranged or removed so that there is only one layer, the original color is retained better; otherwise, the specimen tends to turn black and make the collection more bulky. Thick plants may have to be sliced in half to reduce bulk. Some plants may have to be "exploded" or torn apart and the individual components mounted; otherwise, all you will have is a black, difficult to identify, almost useless mass.
7. Do not use the back of the page for mounting another specimen as the moisture trapped between the two layers of tape will cause a color change (usually blacking and in some cases, fading).

8. The plants that present the greatest problems are the bulky ones. The most fragile plants turn out the best, such as buttercups, grass of Parnassus, flax and caraway. Leaves at the back of the specimen may be cut or plucked away.
9. Freshly mounted plants may dry quicker if not bundled together. Some plants with a lot of juice in them may stain adjacent pages (the acid in stinging nettle ate through three adjacent pages in the original collection).
10. Keep the fresh mount away from the sun or any source of heat (like the inside of a car on a hot day) or color change may occur.
11. To arrange plants to minimize layering and to make a more attractive specimen, a glue stick is useful in helping to spread out leaves and hold parts in place until the tape is applied. Another ploy is to make a frame out of coat hanger wire and stretch some tape on the frame. The plant is then carefully arranged on the sticky side of the tape and then stuck on to the paper. The tape is then cut away from the frame with the sharp tip of a knife.
12. What of MacTac? I have seen students using clear MacTac which may be neater, but more expensive.
13. Leaves of related plants may be taped on the same page to show why plants belong to the same family, eg. birch, alder and hazelnut or rose, saskatoon and buckthorn.
14. The mature seed pod and the winter skeleton may be later added to the page.
15. Keep your specimens in a suitable sized box to help your collection last a lifetime.

e) Eating Wild Plants

Generally, the taste of any wild plant is a new experience to the normal palate. Some plants can be uncommonly bitter on the one extreme and completely tasteless on the other.

In comparison to our garden vegetables, the wild plants contain more nutrients gram for gram, mainly because they are on a much lower water content. You may find that eating less than half the quantity expected for a domestic vegetable may adequately meet one's nutritional needs.

f) Acclimatizing to Wild Plant Food

Simply sampling a known wild edible can cause sharp stomach pains in some people. Accepting wild plants and mastering their use is a skill that requires persistence and concerted application. This is likely one of the greatest achievements in wilderness living skills.

By becoming thoroughly knowledgeable about edible plants, you will develop confidence in your abilities to safely use wild plant foods. The plants chosen for this article are similar enough to the taste and texture of familiar vegetables to make their use relatively easy. The other 900 wild edible plants of Alberta may demand a considerably greater effort from both the body and the mind to accept them. You may need to gradually include a plant in your diet before your body can tolerate or properly digest any great quantity of it.

The first step is to begin eating a plant in small quantities until you become accustomed to the taste. Your gut might also require time to develop the flora that may better handle the new food. As you become accustomed to the plant you may gradually increase the amounts perhaps without experiencing any unusual digestive disturbances. It bears repeating that care must be taken to use wild plants in moderation not only as a conservation measure but to avoid excessive stomach pain.

It is a bit too late to begin the process of familiarizing yourself with a plant in an actual survival situation. You may find you've burned up more energy gathering and trying to use it than you've gained back by digesting it.

g) The Plants (more or less in order of importance)

Cattail (Typha species)

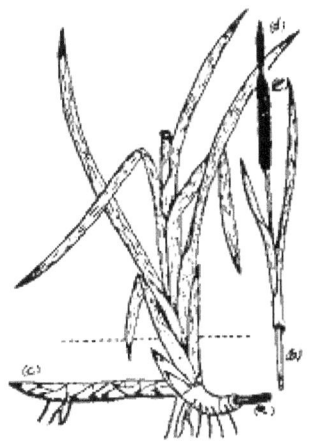

From the tips of its roots to the tip of its flowering stalk, sooner or later some part of the cattail becomes edible.

Root Starch: The thick puffy rind of the root is peeled away to expose a core that may be as thick as a pencil. This core consists of starch packed away amongst rather bothersome strong thin fibers. The fibers may be dealt with by 1) roasting until they are brittle, 2) by chopping the core up into fine pieces, 3) washing out the starch and discarding the fiber, or 4) by drying the core, then pulverizing it by pounding.

Some authorities claim that a heavy growth of cattail can produce about 6,700 kilograms per hectare of starch (or 6000 pounds per acre). No feasible commercial process has yet been developed to exploit this tremendous resource.

The starch can be used in place of flour for cakes and pancakes and can be fermented to produce alcohol.

Shoots: The plant extends itself by horizontally advancing shoots. Although these are more prevalent in early spring, they can be found at any time of the year. There is usually from eight to sixteen centimetres of edible shoot that may be eaten raw or cooked, with numerous shoots on each plant. The first 30 centimietres of the plant without a flowering stalk is placed on glowing coals. The charred outer portion is peeled away and the cooked core is eaten.

Stem: In late spring the stem may be pulled up and eaten raw or cooked. The plants without stems have a lump of starch at the junction of the plant and the root that is cooked like potatoes.

The Head: Heads that are still in the sheath (June) are boiled and eaten like corn. There is a tedious method of extracting the somewhat oily seeds from the head. The pollen bearing spike is a more productive endeavor. Before it matures it is scraped to produce a thickener for soup. The pollen itself is later gathered in early August by enclosing the head in a bag, bending the plant over and giving it a rap to dislodge the pollen. The pollen can be used as a flour substitute or mixed with a small amount of flour to make pancakes.

Bear Root (Hedysarum alpinum)

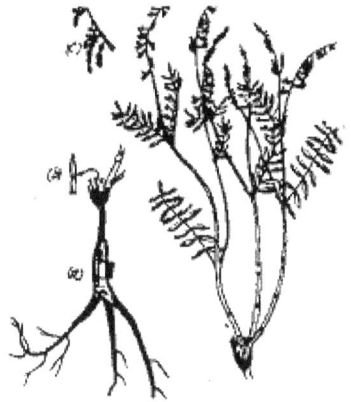

Next to cattail this is one of the most important wild edibles in Alberta. Bear root is available throughout the summer. It's taste changes with the way it is prepared. The raw root tastes like a mixture of coconut and peas. The baked root, like potato chips and the fried root, like parsnip.

Caution: Those allergic to any foods, especially fruits, may react violently to this plant.

Wild Roses (Rosa species, especially R. acicularia)

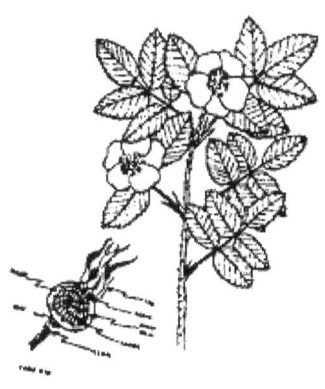

When the first frost occurs, the rose hip (the mature seed container) is at its best. The fleshy part of the hip can be eaten raw or added to other foods and soups. Rose hips are renowned for their vitamin C content: eating five to ten hips may provide you with your daily vitamin C requirement.

Stinging Nettle (Urtica species, especially U. gracilis)

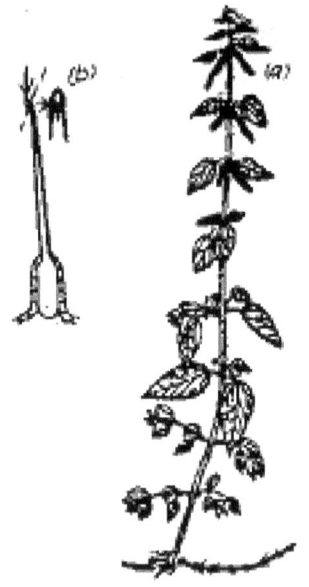

The stinging principle, formic acid, is destroyed by heat in about 15 seconds of boiling. The tops are gathered in May when the plant is no more than 15 centimetres tall and cooked in as little water as possible. This ranks as one of the more tasty and nutritious edibles available that is readily gathered in considerable quantities.

Marsh Marigold (Galtha palustria)

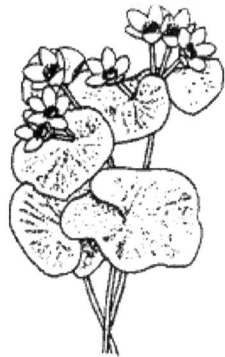

This plant is usually available in early spring (mid April) and is best picked before the plant blooms. The plant contains a toxic glyceride that is destroyed by boiling. A biter component may require the cooking water to be changed once or twice.

Dandelion (Taraxacum officinale)

The tender leaves, make an excellent salad ingredient. Protecting the leaves from the sun with a board produces especially tender, pale leaves. The roasted fresh root is quite tasty. Dried, roasted and ground, the root makes an interesting coffee substitute. Dandelion may be one of the more nutritious plants growing in any garden.

Quackgrass (Agropyron repens)

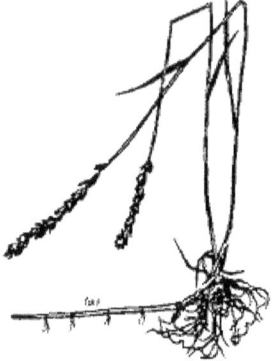

The roots are roasted at any time of the year. Quackgrass is a very nutritious but maligned and neglected edible plant.

Fire Weed (Epilobium angusifolium and E. latifolium)

The shoots are boiled and the core of the mature stalk is eaten raw. The flowering head is used to thicken stews. The dried blossoms and leaves make a tea especially useful as a mix for alcoholic drinks increasing their potency somewhat.

Cow Parsnip (Heracleum lanatum)

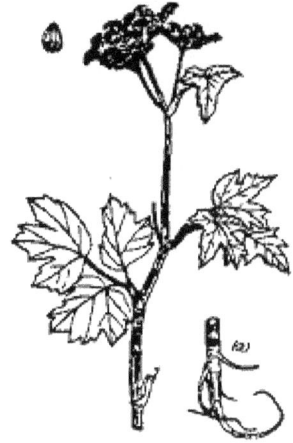

Before the flowers open, the stalks are peeled and eaten raw or cooked. The skin has to be peeled off before being used because it contains a substance which can induce a photodermic rash if eaten. The contents of the seed head, before it opens, are used in salads. The root is supposedly cooked like rutabaga but the author find the taste to overpowering to eat. If you eat a lot of the plant brushing against it with the back of the hand or above the knee caps can raise blisters.

Caution: Be sure not to confuse this plant with a similar looking but notoriously poisonous one known as water hemlock (Cicuta species).

Sedges (Carex species, especially Carex squatillis)

From May until August, the tender hearts of this grass-like plant are eaten raw or cooked.

Timothy (Phleum pratense)

In the fall, the ripe heads are stripped off, crushed and winnowed to extract great quantities of seed resembling miniature wheat. The seeds can be crushed and made into gruel.

Silverweed (Potentilla anserina)

In spring and fall the root is eaten raw, roasted, boiled or fried. The dried root has a pleasant nutty flavour.

Aspen (Populus tremuloides)

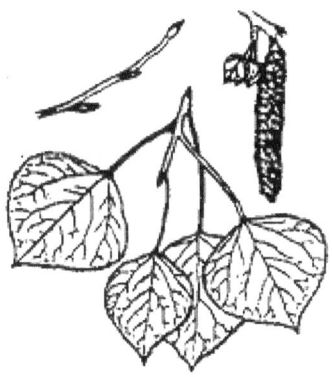

In late May to mid-July when the bark is easily removed from the tree, the surface of the wood or cambium layer is scraped with a knife to obtain a sweet, juicy, stringy material, sometimes call Indian spaghetti. It is eaten raw or dried for future use.

Lodgepole Pine (Pinus contorta)

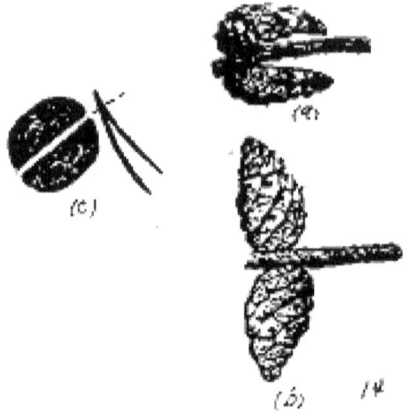

Use it exactly the same way as aspen. (a) Jack Pine (b) Lodgepole Pine (c) Cross Section of Needles

Violets (Viola species, especially Viola canadensis)

From spring to first frost the whole plant can be boiled like spinach.

Thistles (Circium species especially C. hookerianum)

The core of the young plant stem is eaten raw and the roots of the rosette stage are roasted.

Wild Onions (Allium species especially A. schoenoprasum)

The plant must look, smell and taste like an onion or it may be confused with Death Camus (Zigadenus elegans). Use all parts at any time of the year.

Caution: Excessive use could cause anemia.

Coltsfoot (Petasites palmatus)

The young leaves are cooked like spinach. The green leaves can be rolled into tight balls, thoroughly dried on a rock by the sun, piled into a pyramid and burned to an ash, and then used as a passable salt substitute.

Plantain (Plantago major)

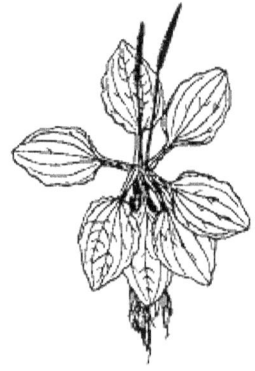

The young leaves with the stringy veins removed are cooked like spinach. The dry roasted seeds are edible. The main part of the root is almost like celery hearts in taste.

Bulrush or Tule (Scirpus validus)

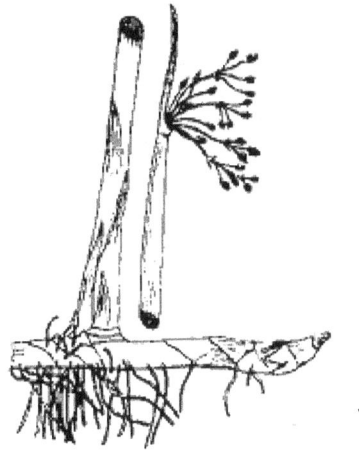

The young shoots are peeled and eaten raw or cooked. The roots are processed similar to cattail roots. The seeds can be ground for mush or flour.

Labrador Tea (Ledum groenlandicum)

At any time of the year, the green leaves may be boiled to produce a Jasmine-like tea or dried and steeped in the normal fashion. Use in moderation until you are used to it or stomach cramps and headaches may result.

Lamb's Quarters (Chenopodium album)

The young plant or the tender leaves of older plants are cooked like spinach. Lambs Quarters has a higher vitamin A and C content than spinach. The tender leaves may be used in salads and the seeds boiled and crushed to make gruel.

Caution: Leaves with reddish patches should not be eaten. Oxalates are particularly high in late summer and fall, so it is best not to use this plant at that time of year.

Curly Dock (Rumex crispus)

In the spring the very young leaves are cooked like spinach in several changes of water.

Mountain Sorrel (Rumex acetopella)*
Sheep Sorrel (Oxyria dignia)*

From spring until fall the leaves are cooked like spinach or made into soups with other ingredients.

Purslane (Portulaca oleracea)

From spring until fall the whole plant is cooked like spinach or used raw in salads. It is very high in iron content.

Common Chickweed (Stellaria media)

From early spring to first frost use the whole plant or sprouts in salads.

*Note: Like rhubarb, Rumex, Oxyria and Chenopodium contain oxalates. Oxalates give a tangy taste and can interfere significantly with your body's ability to absorb calcium from food.

Some Recommended Books

- Harrington, H.D., Edible Natural Plants of the Rocky Mountains, Albuquerque, University of New Mexico. Press 1967, soft or hard cover. This book has over a hundred edible plants that are found in Alberta.
- Lewis Clark's Field Guides to: Forest and Woodland, Field and Slope, Marsh and Waterway, The Arid Flat Lands, The Mountains; Grays Publishing Ltd., Sidney B.C.
- Cormack, R.G.H., Wild Flowers of Alberta

2. Looking at Edible Mushrooms

One of the more common misconceptions about mushrooms is that they have no food value. Many survival manuals suggest that mushrooms should be avoided altogether as the risk is much too great for the small benefit gained. There tends to be a view that mushrooms are a luxury vegetable, providing only variety and an agreeable flavour to otherwise ordinary dishes. Their main justification for use is that they have always been seen as only flavour for soups, sauces and gravies and as a garnish or accompanying dish.

This view is changing. Mushrooms are proving to be a rather significant source of protein. Being about 37 percent protein by dry weight, mushrooms compare favourably with soya beans and peas. Mushrooms also rank high in chromium nutrients as well as being a source of phosphorous, copper, iron, potassium, thiamine, riboflavin and niacin. Mushrooms also contain varying degrees of all the essential amino body building acids, especially the somewhat less common folic acid.

Mushrooms are very low on calories, containing about 235 calories per kilogram. Mushrooms contain little sodium.

Rats can thrive on a diet of nothing but mushrooms.

There are three activities that I personally place in the same class of enjoyment: Panning for gold, fishing for trout, and picking mushrooms.

a) Collecting Mushrooms

If I have sold you on the value of edible mushrooms then I must also sell you on the safe ways of using them and the pitfalls you may encounter.

1. Never eat any mushroom or fungus that you do not know well. Avoid all risk of making a mistake. **PAY ATTENTION. BE CAUTIOUS. BE PRUDENT.**
2. Go slow in adding to your list of edibles. Limit your first efforts to well defined types.
3. Realize that a young child or an elderly person may react adversely to a mushroom that is perfectly edible to teenagers and adults.
4. Certain digestive upsets commonly associated with mushrooms are usually the result of the overuse of butter or cooking oil rather than the mushrooms themselves.
5. Do not assume that a given mushroom is generally not poisonous because it comes from a species that is not poisonous.
6. For reasons yet little understood, some species of mushroom may be toxic in one locale and safe in another. The same looking mushroom on Vancouver Island may be safe yet those growing in Ontario may be lethal. European mushroom lovers who have immigrated here should double check any similar looking mushrooms that they find in this country before they use them.
7. There are a few people who will react violently to a mushroom that is safe to everyone else.
8. In some species a fresh mushroom may be quite safe, yet in an old or decaying state it is toxic. Use only fresh mushrooms; discard everything else.

9. Some mushrooms are toxic raw but perfectly safe cooked. Do not assume that all edible mushrooms may be eaten raw.
10. Some mushrooms become toxic if frozen.
11. It has been observed that some animals such as rabbits, squirrels and deer can safely eat certain poisonous mushrooms which would cause certain death to humans. Observing an animal eating a mushroom is no assurance that it is safe for people.
12. The presence of insects or worms in a fungus is no clue to its edibility.
13. The poisonous quality of a mushroom cannot be determined by whether or not silver tarnishes nor by any other simple chemical test.
14. The safe or poisonous quality of a mushroom cannot be determined by the ease of peeling the cap.
15. It is dangerous to assume that all or any poisonous mushroom may be neutralized by soaking or boiling in salt water. The worst mushrooms to start with are those that have some probability of being confused with dangerous types.
16. Do not experiment with mushrooms. Taking a small amount will not prove that a mushroom will be safe to eat in larger quantities. Your body may have the capacity to effectively deal with small quantities of certain toxic elements. Some mushrooms may be lethal in minute quantities. The toxicity in some mushrooms may vary considerably from place to place.
17. Unless you know what you are doing do not collect mushrooms in the button stage, because poisonous and non-poisonous mushrooms may appear very similar at the stage.
18. Beware of mushrooms with similar appearances growing intermixed with each other, singly and in clumps. Again: Pay Attention, Be Cautious, Be Prudent.

b) On Identifying Mushrooms

I am sure many more people would prepare mushrooms for the table if they only had the confidence to believe in their ability to positively identify the edible from the poisonous ones.

The mushrooms that are appropriate for the beginning collector are ones that are easy to identify positively. There are at least a dozen one can start with, and for most of us these are sufficient to provide a lifetime of enjoyment.

A common question that I have been asked is how to distinguish a poisonous mushroom from a safe one. There is no general rule or test that will help you separate one from the other except knowing each and every species of mushroom by its own characteristics. Until you are absolutely sure that you have properly identified a mushroom you are wise not to eat it.

I recognize my friend Joe by the many characteristics that combine to make him look like Joe: his ears, eyes, nose, hair, height, voice, the way he walks and so on. The same applies to the great majority of the mushrooms you may encounter in the field. There are also some mushrooms that tax the abilities of the most experienced of mycologists.

If you are anxious to use some mushrooms right away and you want to work alone you can start with the following list. The first four are so easy to identify that we call them "the foolproof four". They are abundant, widespread and good tasting.

IF YOU PAY CLOSE ATTENTION TO THE POSITIVE IDENTIFYING FEATURE AND THE DIAGRAM

THERE IS ONLY THE REMOTEST CHANCE OF ERROR.

The Morels: Taste: delectable

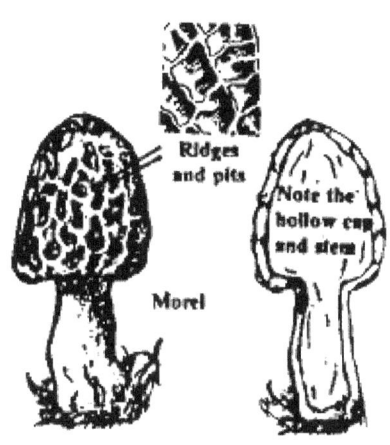

1. In early spring look for this mushroom in mature aspen forest.
2. The cap has irregular pits and ridges of a brown to tan colour. A similar mushroom found at the same time in the same environment is Verpa boehemica. Some people may encounter digestive problems with this mushroom.
3. The cap and stem are continuous and hollow as illustrated. The flesh of both cap and stem are brittle.

The Puffballs: Taste: good

1. Puffballs may be found at any time and especially in the fall. Look anywhere on the ground or on decaying wood.

2. The size may vary from that of a grape to that of a watermelon.
3. The shape is generally spherical or rounded.
4. When sliced in half, the interior must be white, uniform and firm. If the outline of a small mushroom is visible you may have an amanita, which could be poisonous.

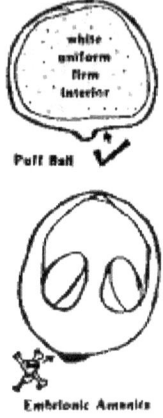

Puffballs

The Shaggy Mane: Taste: excellent

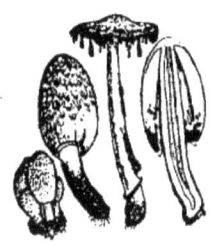

1. This mushroom is usually found in the same place, year after year. It appears after the first frost of the fall. The shaggy mane prefers sandy soil.

2. The coprinus family to which the shaggy mane belong are the only mushrooms that dissolve into an inky mass as they grow old.

Coral Fungus: Taste: a bit tough

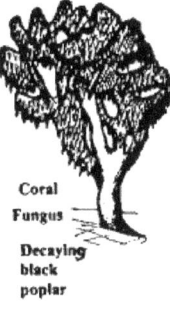

Coral Fungus

1. Usually found on fallen, decaying black poplar trees.
2. This fungus is seldom inhabited by insects.
3. This fungus forms irregular branched clumps showing multitudinous tapering teeth that point downward like icicles.

If you are more adventuresome, you might consider adding the following to your list:

- The false morel (Verba bohemica)
- Pasture mushroom (Agaricus campestris)
- Milky caps (Lactarius deliciosus)
- The King bolete (Boletus edulis)
- The orange cap bolete (Leccimum ausanticum)
- Spreading hedgehog mushroom (Denticum repandum)
- Honey mushroom (Armillariella mellea)
- Oyster mushroom (Pleurotus ostraetus)

These are all easy to identify if you look them up in any good book on mushrooms.

II Wilderness Survival

A) Defining Survival

An emergency situation is a setback or accident, life threatening or not, that can be handled without outside help.

A pure survival situation is one where there is an immediate or long term threat to life, where only feasible plan of action is to stay alive as long as possible, WITH THE HOPE OF BEING RESCUED.

The extent of your knowledge and how prepared you are will determine whether an emergency situation becomes a survival situation or vice versa.

1. Basic Existence Skills

Basic Existence Skills are the skills concerned with staying alive in any environment using the simplest, most fundamental techniques of existence, for day-to-day living. You may be in an urban, rural or wilderness environment. Techniques include fire lighting and shelter building.

Basic existence skills are taught to provide a working knowledge of the skills that relate to staying alive under short-term adverse situations and to begin the training process that will provide for a relatively comfortable existence under long-term conditions. Social unrest (war), environmental calamity, the cessation of energy supplies, or the avoidance of epidemic by evasion and wilderness seclusion, are some examples of long-term survival situations.

At one extreme one may wish to follow the program for simple recreational reasons; at the other extreme, the more paranoid may be preparing for the often prognosticated breakdown of present-day society, Apocalypse, Armageddon, or Ragnarok.

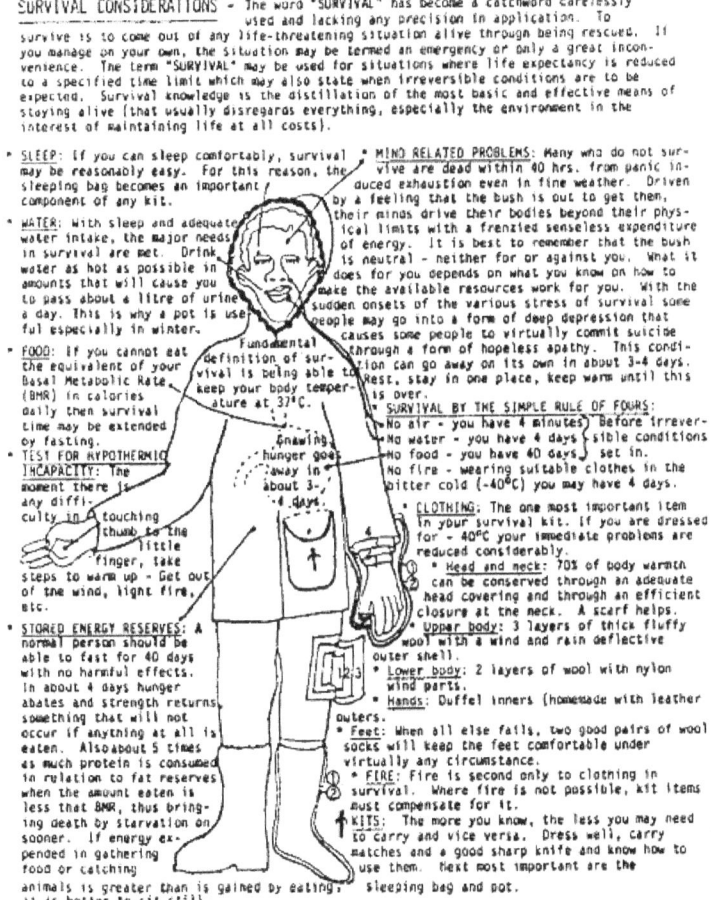

A specialized extension of basic existence skills is wilderness living skills. Wilderness living skills are that body of knowledge and skills that may allow you to live indefinitely in a wilderness environment without vulnerable dependence on modern industrial technology. Acquiring the relevant skills and knowledge may take years. Wilderness living skills and survival are usually erroneously defined as being one and the same.

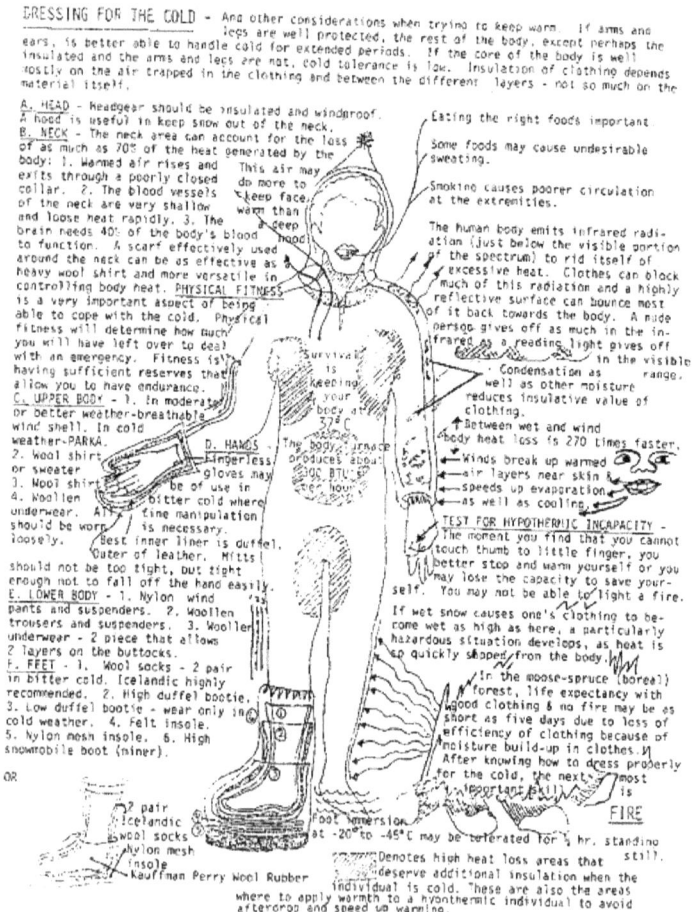

2. Wilderness Survival

Survival knowledge, in the modern sense, should be defined as being a very small and specialized portion of wilderness living skills that may take a relatively short time to master, and provide a large return for a small amount of input. You may have never seen a desert, yet through reading the right things about it you may learn enough about desert survival to find that information a significant factor in your being able to live through a desert survival episode.

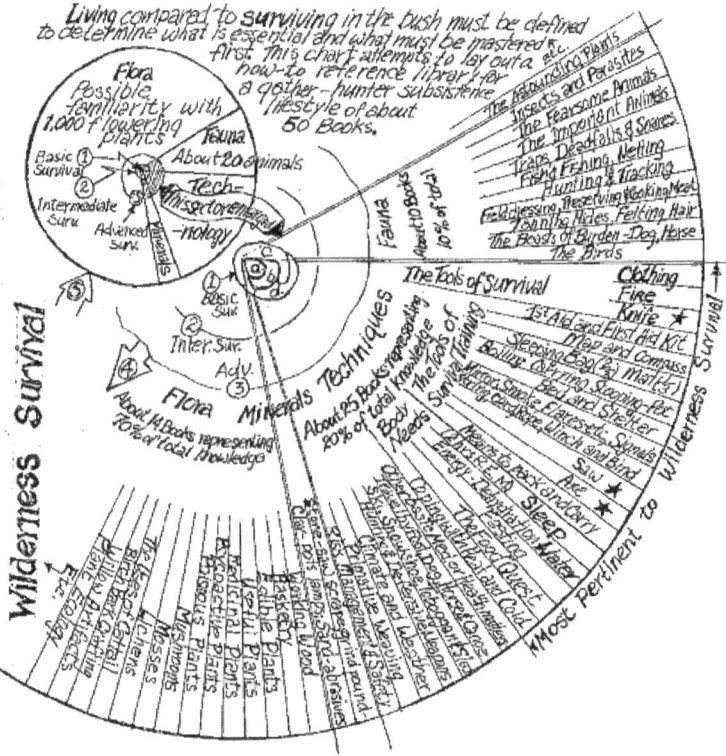

Survival experts, who were once sent to study the survival methods of the Sahara Arabs, were disappointed to find that the Sahara Arabs did not know any desert survival techniques. They only lived in the desert.

The wilderness that may seem so stressful in a so called "survival" situation may have met the daily needs of native peoples for eons of time. What seems "survival" to us may be just plain everyday living to others. It is conceivable that your knowledge can become so extensive that the term "survival" can no longer have any meaning. If you starve to death it is not because of lack of knowledge or skill on your part - it just happened that the vagaries of nature left nothing for you to eat.

There are other notions that should be woven into the meaning of survival. Four times out of five rescue will likely play a significant role in your survival. This means that survival techniques have to be directed towards keeping you alive as long as possible so as to increase your chances of being rescued before irreversible conditions develop. If you have survived a crash uninjured, your chances of being found alive may be significantly reduced through outright exhaustion, disorientation by attempting to walk out, or attempting anything beyond your knowledge and skill level. Your rescuers may find it easier to locate you at the crash site than halfway to the middle of nowhere. This means you may do best by waiting for rescue UNLESS YOU KNOW WHAT YOU ARE DOING. In cold water immersion, your heart may stop in twenty minutes when attempting to swim to a distant island. Using sound cold water survival techniques you may be alive an hour longer, thereby giving rescuers that much more time to save your life.

Knowing what you are doing means that you may not be able to use common-sense solution to certain problems because the outcome of a common-sense solution is often unknown and may result in death. For example, in crossing rivers or living off the land a common-sense approach can easily result in your death.

3. In Survival You Have No Guarantees

In a survival situation you have none of the following guarantees:

1. That you will not be injured. You may have to cope with a broken arm or a broken leg. In air crashes 68 out of 100 people are injured in some way.
2. That you will find any food in the way of wild animals or wild edible plants.
3. That you will find yourself in a survival situation in daylight. You have no way of knowing when you will have to survive, day or night, summer or winter, rain or shine.
4. That you will find yourself in an area where fuel and shelter materials are available. Fire may not be possible.
5. That you will not be ill during a survival situation. You may already have a cold, or a bad case of the flu, or be recuperating from some illness.
6. That you will have available that carefully chosen and well packed survival kit.

Points 1 to 5 are generally solved by having a good survival kit handy so that the need to relate to your environment is minimized. That is, you provide your own shelter, warmth, utensils, etc., with water being the only crucial item to be provided by the environment. A well chosen back-packer outfit could be an excellent survival kit in some circumstances.

Point 6 demands preparation for survival through knowledge. The more you know the less you will have to carry, until the point is reached that a kit is not an absolute necessity. The less you know the more you will have to depend on what your bring along for your comfort.

4. Living Off the Land

In attempting to live off the land, it is more preferable to only drink water, than to eat less than the minimum number of calories required each day. In not meeting the basal metabolic rate, which may be from 1100 to 1700 calories per day, there is such a disproportionate use of protein reserves in comparison to fat reserves that one may die of protein depletion in at least a quarter of the time as compared to fasting. In fasting there is a more balanced use of proteins and fats so that a healthy person of normal weight of 65 kilograms will not begin to suffer any irreversible deficiencies for at least six weeks. Overweight persons may get by for longer than this. The record stands at over a year.

5. The Advantages of Fasting (On Water Only)

By realizing that there is no need to eat for six weeks, panic may be more easily held in check. Fasting can act as the stop gap measure until you have had the time and opportunity to become competent in living off the land. You can learn fasting techniques in less time than you can learn to use one edible plant. In some instances you may have no choice but to fast. Unless you are reasonably expert and well practiced in hunting and trapping, and game is plentiful, or you happen to have a firearm, you may mismanage your energy budget. You could spend more energy catching and eating the animal than you would have saved by resting. This takes into account any fruitless attempts. If you are to subsist on plants you may have to know from 50 to 200 to have a workable number in your given area of survival.

Fasting usually brings on greater clarity of thought and improved recall that assists in making plans and decisions. In a true fasting state, within two to six days your energy reserves become available to be used at a more normal rate of expenditure. You may not feel like it, but you can now exert yourself to the point of expending four to five thousand calories per day. On a diet that is less than your basic metabolic rate you may collapse from exhaustion. If you are going to walk out, you will do better in a fasting state. In an experiment in Sweden ten people walked 320 miles in ten days ingesting only the spring water found enroute. On being examined by doctors after the walk, all were in a perfect state of health.

You generally heal more quickly in a fasting state and overcome any illness more readily. The ketosis in fasting usually brings on an euphoria, making the discomforts of survival more tolerable and any depression less acute.

To fast, simply eat nothing and drink far more water than you normally would. The water should be brought to a boil and drunk as hot as possible.

6. Problems with Fasting

Ketosis: This is the build up of undesirable levels of ketones in the blood. They are a by-product of fat reserve metabolism. This was once thought to be a dangerous condition to be avoided, probably because of the association of ketones with other often grave diseased states. The situations may be somewhat eased by drinking more water. One should attempt to make the urine as colorless as possible but still retaining a yellow tinge.

(Drinking too much water can make you ill as well). Some euphoric irrationality is also associated with the ketosis.

The general impression seems to be that the first major fast is the most uncomfortable one. Your past eating habits may also have a considerable influence on the ease of comfort experienced in your first fast. The body has a major detoxification job to do the first time. Once you have detoxified you find fasting to be relatively pleasant. The detoxification process works on the principle that your body will burn up first what it needs the least. The substances first burned up are those that accumulate in your body that can not be eliminated by the normal means. Uric acid and cholesterol are the first substances to go.

Some of the unpleasant and temporary side-effects that you might expect are: foul breath, severe headaches, aching joints and teeth, loose teeth, coated tongue, boils, foul odor about the body, pains of various levels of intensity in the esophagus, and fasting may also result in prescription glasses becoming too strong. These conditions are far more tolerable than the conditions associated with death in a quarter of the time.

B) Introduction to Wilderness Survival

1. Preparedness

Anticipate the problems you may have in the event of an emergency and train yourself in methods of coping with these problems. It is somewhat late to be learning how to swim when your boat is sinking in the middle of the lake. It is a little late to be wishing that you had brought a life jacket.

Your clothing is the most important survival tool you have. Dress properly and any emergency you may have to endure becomes more manageable.

Carry on your person a dependable means of fire lighting, a good knife, an appropriate first aid kit, and a map and compass and know how to use these items. Depending on your circumstances and background, a well chosen "survival kit" may be appropriate. The less you know, the more comprehensive your kit may have to be; the more you know the less you have to carry.

2. Panic

The bush is neutral. It is neither for or against you. The bush is not out to help or harm you. Your welfare depends on what you know and what you can do for yourself. You will only get out of the situation what you are able to put into it.

Your greatest success depends on a calm and collected attitude backed up by the resolve to do the best you can under the circumstances. If you are unable to develop a positive attitude about your ordeal, things are likely to become much more difficult to cope with. Cursing and striking out at inanimate objects is both mentally and physically exhausting. If you have taken the time to gain the proper knowledge and experience in wilderness survival you should have the confidence to cope with staying in the bush alone a few nights.

3. Survival in a Nutshell

The essence of survival is to be able to sleep comfortably when you need to and to drink enough water to maintain the bodily functions at an optimum level. Outside of life threatening injury, an immediate concern is maintaining a comfortable body temperature. In cold conditions this is accomplished by dressing adequately, knowing how to preserve or maintain the insulative integrity of your clothing and supplementing any inadequacy with fire and shelter.

4. Fire

One should have the means and skill to light a fire under any circumstances. In the cold it makes sense to light a fire immediately to keep warm, rather than later to thaw one's self out. Once a fire is established, the next concern is an adequate stock pile of fuel to last until the next day. If it is not raining or snowing there may not be any immediate need for a shelter outside of sleeping between the fire and fuel supply. A resilient bed can be made with just about anything at hand. In some circumstances it may be most convenient to sleep sitting up.

5. Shelter

Weather conditions may require the construction of a shelter. There are many shelters, each especially appropriate to a given circumstance. In essence, a shelter provides an improved micro environment wherein one may more comfortably work, rest and sleep. The most universally useful shelter is the open lean-to with a fire in front of it. It must block any movement of air on the three sides away from the fire, and it must be close enough to intercept at least some of the radiant energy from the fire to create a warmed micro environment.

6. Dehydration

With the immediate needs of warmth and shelter taken care of the next most important concern is to drink enough, preferably hot water, to maintain body processes and functions at their maximum effectiveness. The importance of preventing dehydration can not be overemphasized. It has a profound effect on every aspect of survival. Since thirst is a poor indicator of bodily needs, one should use additional means to ensure an adequate intake. Drink enough to pass at least a litre a day. The urine should be virtually colorless but still retaining a yellow tinge. Drinking enough water should help to avert headaches, strong hunger pangs and fatigue.

Drinking enough water will allow you to cope better with frostbite and hypothermia. If you must exert yourself, a correspondingly appropriate intake of water must be maintained or profound fatigue will likely prevent further exertion.

7. Hypothermia

Inadequate clothing, water and food intake, as well as cold, wet and wind can all contribute to a lowering of one's body temperature. This not only results in the physical discomforts associated with cold but also places you in danger by reducing the mind's ability to react and think adequately to meet the demands of the situation. When you cannot touch thumb to little finger of the same hand you should immediately seek respite from the cold, usually by building a large fire. If you begin to shiver violently your body is signalling its final warning to warm up.

8. Signals

You should know how to signal with a mirror, how to build signal fires and the standard ground to air signals. The standard signals are:

- the big "X": I am unable to proceed;
- 3 shots, 3 honks, or 3 blasts on a whistle: and
- two of anything means "please respond".

9. Conservation of Mental and Physical Energy

Do not rush things. Do tasks properly the first time so that you do not have to find the time to do them right the second time. Rest often. If you do not know where you are, stay put so that you do not waste energy becoming more lost. If you must move, mark your trail distinctly. Sit instead of standing, lay down instead of sitting up. If you plan to live off the land be sure you gained more energy from eating your fish than you used up in catching it. Take the time to allow your body and mind to adjust to your predicament before you go off half-cocked. You may choose to live by the rule of 4's.

- If you have no water, by knowing how to apply conservative measures you should live longer than 4 days.
- If you have no fire but you are adequately dressed for temperatures below -40°C or F you should be able to survival at least 4 days.
- Without adequate protection you can reach an irreversible state of hypothermia in less than 4 hours.
- If you have no food you should get by for at least 40 days with no permanent damage to your health.
- Allow yourself and your rescuers at least 4 days before you embark on any significant decision such as walking out.
- Think over anything you plan to do at least 4 times from 4 different angles if possible.

10. Lost? Finding Your Way

Any of a multitude of unforeseeable occurrences or circumstances can induce a sense of being lost even in the most experienced bush walkers. It may be that only after you yourself have become thoroughly disoriented that you begin to fully appreciate the unique nature of the mental turmoil that results when you have no idea where you are and in what direction you should take your next step. The novice should find, if they mentally or physically survive the ordeal, that each such episode should induce a firm determination to master the skill that counteracts or prevents future occurrences of a like nature.

The worst thing that you can do under these circumstances is to become excessively excited about your condition. The first thing you should attempt is to re-establish your correct sense of direction. This is easily done with a compass but it you do not have one, knowing the time of day and using the sun is a good alternative. If the sun is obscured you may have to wait until it shows itself. If you know how, you can locate the sun on the most overcast of days.

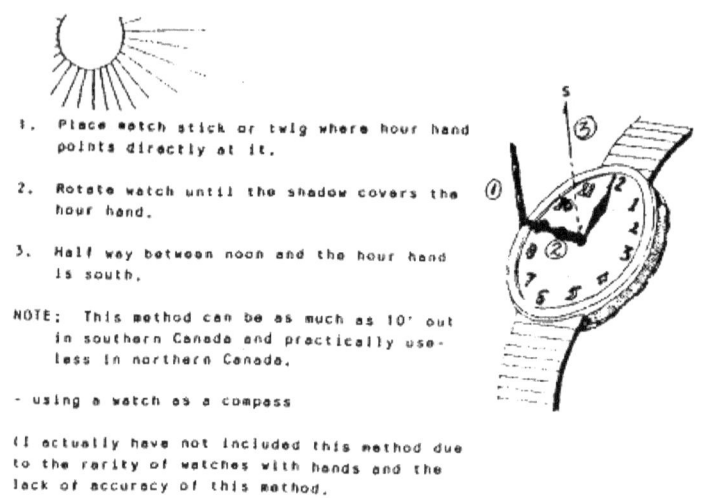

1. Place watch stick or twig where hour hand points directly at it.

2. Rotate watch until the shadow covers the hour hand.

3. Half way between noon and the hour hand is south.

NOTE: This method can be as much as 10° out in southern Canada and practically useless in northern Canada.

- using a watch as a compass

(I actually have not included this method due to the rarity of watches with hands and the lack of accuracy of this method.

The next step is to re-establish your position. One way is to backtrack until you relocate a familiar land mark. Another way is to identify a familiar land mark especially, with the aid of a map.

Once you have re-established your sense of direction and have pinpointed your location you can now continue on to your objective.

There is a possibility, however, that you are either not convinced that you have actually met either one or both conditions and the situation at best is a bit fuzzy. Worse still, you remain completely disoriented. Under these circumstances there is often an overwhelming compulsion to keep moving. If you can not fight it then you should mark your trail distinctly to help prevent you from becoming more disoriented or confused.

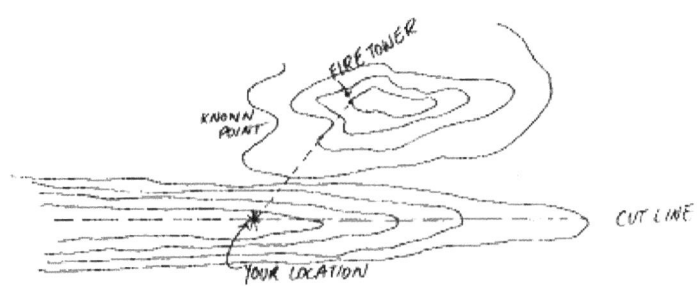

There are basically two convenient ways of marking your trail. The preferred method is to use wads or handfuls of moss; the other is by blazing trees. The wads of moss should be placed at approximately eye level in such a way that you should be able to see the last two wads as you place your third. If there is a sudden change of direction then three wads are placed in one tree to warn of a sudden direction change. Mark your starting point with five wads. From this point on you are not likely to make things worse by becoming more disoriented. You may have to return to your starting point and try other directions. If you are so lost that you have to be rescued you will provide a better target for searchers. You may establish other starting points but they should all be connected. Make pointers to show searchers which trail you are currently on.

If you must travel in as straight a line as possible, use a long thin pole to assist you. Point it in the desired direction and hold it so that a metre and a half of it is visible in front of you. Endeavour not to change the direction of the pole unless you purposely want to do so as you travel. If you come to dense bush blocking your way, snake the pole through first, go around and pick it up again. If you go around with it, a certain loss of accuracy of direction will result. In dense bush or darkness where you can only see a very short distance, this navigational ploy may be more accurate than a compass. Where accuracy is very important under such circumstances the use of the pole and compass together may be the answer.

Marking Trail When Lost

When you realize that you are lost, do not wander around becoming more lost.

Mark your trail with wads of moss or grass, blazes or broken branches, made at eye level. Each time a marker is put up, the last one, better still, the last two markers should be visible.

C) Water and Human Survival

The human body, which is close to two thirds water by weight, has an acute dependence on this precious substance. We lose water to our surroundings by evaporation and urination. One third of water is lost from the lungs, mouth and skin, and another two thirds of the water through urination. Under normal Boreal Forest conditions we generally cannot survive more than ten days without replacing the water lost through the above processes at a replacement rate of three to six percent (one to two litres) per day. This must result in the barest minimum of a half-litre of urine excretion, with a litre being more desirable. This water performs in the body's metabolism through the transport of nutrients, oxygen, enzymes and so on in one direction and the elimination of waste products in the other direction. It participates in muscle toxicity, temperature regulation and cellular upkeep. It seems to be an extremely important factor in combating fatigue.

When water loss significantly exceeds water intake, the condition known as dehydration occurs. The blood becomes more viscous, which slows down the circulation and which in turn hampers the flow of oxygen and nutrients to the brain. This results in a dulling of the mind, decreased rationality, tendency to disorientation, greater irritability and so on. The impairment of the circulation slows down the clearance of metabolic by-products from the muscles and results in fatigue and cramps. The mechanism for maintaining optional body temperature is disrupted and predisposes the human body to frost bite and hypothermia in cold weather and heat cramps, exhaustion, and stroke in hot weather.

1. Body Water Needs

As a simplistic rule, under survival conditions, drink enough water to eliminate a minimum of one litre of urine daily. This ensures that an adequate amount of water is being taken in to flush out the undesirable by-products of metabolism that are not removed in other ways. The actual quantity of water ingested to accomplish this may vary according to your physical exertion and the environmental conditions you are working in.

Your water intake must make up for water lost through a variety of usual and unusual means, such as (1) urination, (2) sensible and insensible sweating, (3) respiration, (4) tissue destruction, as in sprains, burns and crush injuries, (5) vomiting and (6) defecation, especially as diarrhea.

2. How Much Water?

The American scientist, Dr. E.F. Adolf, in his work "Physiology of Man in the Desert" made a careful analysis of water needs through working with volunteers and analyzing their reports. The follow table has been adapted from that work.

Dr. Adolf found three related factors that affected a person's capacity for survival:

   i. The temperature of the surroundings
   ii. The level of physical activity of the survivor
   iii. The amount of water available

Dr. Adolf's research led him to recommend that one should drink as much water as required every hour, regardless of how limited the water supply was, as rationing did not contribute to survival time.

WATER NEEDS

LIVING IN THE SHADE - NO PHYSICAL ACTIVITY - IN STILL AIR

Maximum Daily Temp. in °C	No Water	1.0 Litre	2.5 Litre	5.0 Litre	10.0 Litre	20.0 Litre
50	2.0	2.0	2.0	2.5	3.0	4.0
45	3.0	3.0	3.5	4.0	4.5	6.5
40	5.0	5.5	6.0	7.0	8.5	12.5
30	7.0	8.0	9.0	10.0	15.5	21.0
25	9.0	10.0	11.0	13.0	17.0	26.0
20	10.0	11.0	12.0	13.0	18.5	29.0
15	10.0	11.0	12.0	14.0	19.0	29.0
10	10.0	11.0	12.0	14.0	19.0	29.0

Expected Days of Survival

3. Thirst

Thirst is not necessarily a valid indicator of the state of the body's actual water needs. Will power can overcome the feeling of thirst to a certain extent. In spite of the body experiencing a chronic water deficit, you may find that you are still easily satiated and you have to use considerable will power to drink what you really need. Without knowledge and good judgement as a back-up, thirst alone has been proven a poor indicator as a means to deal with dehydration.

4. Local Thirst

Local thirst is centered around the esophagus and throat and is caused mainly by the drying out of the cells in that area. The feeling of thirst is alleviated by water rehydrating these cells, or by simply stimulating saliva flow by such means as sucking on a small object, such as a pebble or button. Although the sensation of thirst is being satisfied, body needs are far from being met.

5. Boiled Water Recommended

In the October 1978 issue of the Science Magazine, Vadim and Igor Zelepukhum reported that thoroughly boiled water with all the naturally entrenched gasses driven off, becomes much more biologically active and thus more readily assimilated by the body. By drinking degassed water, the body is spared the energy and effort of putting it into the required state for assimilation. It has been long observed that drinking hot water seemed to increase survival time about ten percent, and it was assumed that this was due to the conservation of valuable calories by the warming of the body core via the stomach.

6. Undetected Water Losses

A particular hazard exists when water loss occurs without being detected. Prolonged cold, as found in Canada's northern winters, usually has very low relative humidity's associated with it. This puts a heavy demand on the moisture in the breath and other avenues of insensible heat loss, and causes sweat to evaporate so quickly so as to go undetected. This condition can be further compounded by high altitudes, where low atmospheric pressure also promotes more rapid evaporation. The imposition on one's bodily water resources can be more severe in the cold of winter than would be found in the Sahara desert.

High heat and low humidity will likewise be deceptive, in that the evaporation of sweat is so quick that the wetness of the skin is not perceived and the temperature seems lower than it actually is.

7. Water Loss Through Lungs in the Cold

Cold, relatively dry air entering the lungs must be warmed and moisturized for the proper functioning of the breathing process. The air is warmed in the upper respiratory tract. For example, there are about five grams of water per cubic metre of air at 0°C. Warmed to the body temperature of 37°C, the air in the lungs requires about 43 grams of water for every cubic metre inhaled. The difference of 38 grams has to be made up from the body's resources.

The exhaled air, on passing through the parts of the upper respiratory tract, is cooled to about 30°C and releases about eight grams of moisture. Saturated air at 30°C contains 30 grams of moisture per cubic metre. The result is the all-too-familiar running nose.

Having breathed in air with a content of five grams of water and exhaled it with a content of 30 grams of water accounts for a 25 gram loss of water for every cubic metre of air breathed in. This loss becomes more evident when we breathe through a scarf or wear a beard.

At rest you may breathe a cubic metre of air in about fifteen minutes. Any exertion may easily double this figure. You can therefore require a half to a cup of water per hour for breathing alone.

8. The Mechanism of Water Absorption

Our body must continuously maintain a certain constant concentration of chemicals known as electrolytes. It is the concentration that is important rather than absolute amounts for determining proper chemical activity. If the total amount of body salt concentration is relatively high, water is readily absorbed. If the concentration is low, the kidneys will concentrate what remains and any additional water brought into the body will be made to continue out of the body through the kidneys.

Water will not be absorbed as fast as a solution that is similar in concentration to body fluids. This solution is called 'isotonic' and is sometimes called an electrolyte replacement solution or ORT (oral rehydration therapy). A proper, home-made electrolyte replacement solution is more appropriate than salt tablets by themselves.

For each litre of solution, premix and bag the following ingredients:

2.0 grams glucose (grape sugar)
3.5 grams table salt (sodium chloride)
2.5 grams baking soda (sodium bicarbonate)
1.5 grams potassium chloride

It is particularly important to use an electrolyte replacement solution when water loss has been caused by sweating. In other situations, the use of the electrolyte replacement solution should produce a more rapid, pronounced reduction of discomfort induced by low body water levels.

9. Dehydration

Dehydration is the unacceptable and life threatening condition which occurs when the body has to function with less water than it actually needs. Usually this is due to a lack of the availability of water, and occasionally it is due to not realizing that body water levels were sinking dangerously low, in spite of the fact that water was readily available.

Warning Signs of the Early Stages of Dehydration:

a. Early dehydration involves a deficit of about a litre of water. This is about a one to five percent loss of the body's weight of water.
b. An early sign is muscle fatigue. There is about a 25% impairment of ability.
c. The lips tend to be dry, the mouth may be dry and there may or may not be any sensation of thirst.
d. Urine output is noticeably reduced. It is of a strong orange color as opposed to the normal pale straw color.
e. A usual early sign of dehydration is a headache. As blood becomes less fluid, the blood vessels of the brain have to expand to accommodate the more sluggish flow. This in turn puts a strain on the nerves in the vicinity of the blood vessels. The solution is to drink three or four cups of water rather than taking a painkiller - providing the headache was not caused by smoke, sun or something else.
f. There may be vague discomfort in the form of depression, dizziness, drowsiness, lethargy or loss of appetite. Attempting to eat without making up the water deficit may bring on nausea.
g. There should be an increased pulse rate in reaction to the thicker blood being pumped through the system.

All further loss of water will lead to dehydration proper. Dehydration is cumulative: by not making up today's deficit, tomorrow's deficit will be greater.

Dehydration Proper:

a. There is an accentuation of most of the warning signals found in the early stages. The water deficit may be at least two litres, amounting to 6 to 10 percent of the body's weight.

b. The mouth is dry. Mucus or saliva may be scant or may no longer be produced.
c. The skin is numb or may show some signs of shrinking.
d. The victim may be mentally disorganized and disoriented. He or she may be irrational or exhibit inappropriate behavior.
e. Breathing may be laboured and difficult.

The appropriate action in this instance is to give the victim as much water, or preferably, the electrolyte replacement solution as much he/she can drink. The water must not be cold or the stomach may contract and further interfere with intake of water.

Fatal Dehydration

a. There is now a water deficit of three to five litres or from 11 to 20 percent of the body's weight.
b. A person's physical condition and familiarity with living in hot climates will determine how quickly a person reaches this stage.
c. The skin is shrivelled, the lips are cracked, the gums are shrunken, the tongue is swollen and the victim is unable to swallow.
d. Sight and hearing are diminished.

a. Delirium is followed by unconsciousness and then death due to hypothermia or hyperthermia. This is the final step.

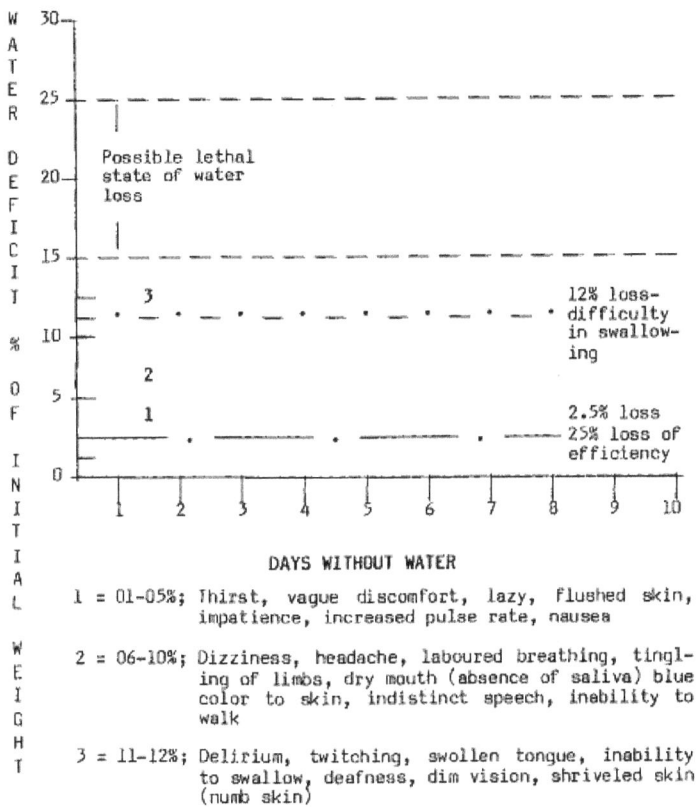

1 = 01-05%; Thirst, vague discomfort, lazy, flushed skin, impatience, increased pulse rate, nausea

2 = 06-10%; Dizziness, headache, laboured breathing, tingling of limbs, dry mouth (absence of saliva) blue color to skin, indistinct speech, inability to walk

3 = 11-12%; Delirium, twitching, swollen tongue, inability to swallow, deafness, dim vision, shriveled skin (numb skin)

D) Handling Stress

Increased personal and mental stress is likely the major problem you will have to cope with in bush survival. Having to take care of your needs yourself, by yourself, may put a serious strain on the confidence you have about your own ability. Many people seem to panic at this prospect and often succumb in as little as 36 hours.

Stress is the condition where you have to endure a greater or lesser level of stimulation and activity than you are usually accustomed to.

The body generally reacts in the same way to both pleasant and unpleasant stress. The body has to respond beyond a normal level in both cases. In perceiving a threat to the body, the brain sends messages to nerve cells and the nervous system. Hormones are released into the bloodstream and the organs ready themselves and the body for some form of combat to counter the threat.

Stress is nothing new, even in a survival situation, as the body is constantly under some form of stress or another. The only body not experiencing stress is a dead one. In fact, if properly handled and controlled, stress is what makes life exciting, interesting and worth living. It is only when stress runs out of control that our health, well-being or survival is threatened. By and large, the body's powerful nerve and hormone systems in their reciprocal checks and balances keep things from running out of control.

1. Responding to Stress

The pioneering scientist and professor in the area of the stress concepts, Dr. Hans Selye, states we respond to stress in a predictable sequence which he calls the General Adaptation Syndrome: (1) Alarm, then (2) Resistance, then (3) Exhaustion.

1. Alarm: The body reacts to a threat or stressor. The stressor can be severe enough to kill. If the stress not lethal, the body takes steps to mobilize the body's defense system in reaction to the stressor.
2. Resistance: If the stressor continues below the level of being lethal, the body's level of resistance rises above its normal level and adapts (at least momentarily) to this higher level.
3. Exhaustion: Your body has a limited amount of energy reserves to use in its efforts to resist. This is what fatigue is about, the body loses its ability to continue the fight.

2. Your Only Three Options

1. Fight: Attempting to destroy the stressor's impact.
2. Flight: Remove your presence from the influence of the stressor.
3. Ignore or tolerate the stressor.

3. Limiting Factor

It takes energy to respond to stress and Selye feels you have only a finite store of energy that has to last you a lifetime. Carefully spent, it goes a long way. Squandering correspondingly shortens the lifespan.

You can cope efficiently with survival stresses by:

1. Sorting out which are the stressors that have to be responded to
2. Determining how much energy reserve can be or is to be spent on the stress and determine if it is appropriate or worth it
3. Seeking out opportunities to rest or recuperate: give yourself deserved breaks
4. Assessing yourself as to whether you are:
    a. aggressive, competitive, impatient. If you are trying to achieve more in less time, you may find yourself in a survivalist's nightmare. You will likely be over concerned with everything and feel a heightened sense of impending doom if you are not doing something. If others are involved, you will tend to be domineering and constantly wanting to run the whole show your way.

    OR

    b. relatively free of time urgency, hostility and competitiveness. Your chances of coming through a survival situation are optimistic. You may even enjoy the survival episode.

E. Survival Kits

As far as survival expertise is concerned there are two extremes: The Wilderness Living Skills expert who can survive with the bare hands, and the Survivalist with a well chosen kit who is virtually a complete backpacker.

1. Survival Kits: The Basics

The design of survival kits is a complex topic. The well designed survival kit seems to be rather rare.

There are many poor kits on the market. The main hazard associated with them is that buyers develop a false sense of security in thinking they have acquired something that will properly meet their survival needs.

Comprehensive kits are closely tied to the bush life-style of the users and especially their modes of transportation. Cross-country skiers, canoeists, automobile drivers, snowmobilers and pilots all require their own unique kits.

Weight

Most kits are usually too heavy. The kit may be comprehensive but it is often abandoned because the user does not have the strength to carry it around.

Priorities

Kits should address how much they contribute to sleep and to meeting the water needs of the body before anything else. The survival priorities of the kit designer are often poorly sorted out. We see cups that are meant to take the place of pots, and wire saws as the major cutting implement. What can you do with a razor blade, when a good sturdy knife is needed?

Compactness vs. Effectiveness

The effectiveness of a kit's components is often sacrificed in the name of compactness. The choice and size of tools are a very important aspect of kit design. Many kits do not seem to take into account the physical fitness of the user, let alone the chance of the user being incapacitated by injury, lack of food and the cold. The survivor cannot be wasting valuable time and energy using tokens of the real thing, when the largest, best designed piece of equipment can barely be used with comfort. How many logs can you saw through with a wire saw, before the effort begins to incapacitate you? What can you do with a razor blade as opposed to a well chosen knife? Can you cut down a green tree the thickness of your wrist in a second or two with a razor blade?

A good survival kit should have the following qualities:

1. It will help keep you alive for at least 40 days by addressing the need for sleep and water.
2. It should be light and portable. If it has to be large or heavy, then it should be broken down into smaller packages.
3. It should take into account the physical fitness of the user. It may be very important to include shelter fabric and a sleeping bag.
4. It should take into account the expertise of the user. For example, a good saw and a light hatchet (350 to 400 grams) may be more useful than an axe. The use of a saw may be mastered in an hour or so whereas an axe may take days. A saw is infinitely safer to use and requires perhaps a quarter of the energy to cut through a

log as does an axe. An axe may be very dangerous to use after dark where a saw would be relatively safe.
5. It should meet a wide variety of conditions, and wherever possible have a multiplicity of uses built into the components. For example, a sleeping bag stuff-bag could double for a head net, nightcap or water bag.
6. Ideally the kit components should be designed to be useful even in the event of injury to the user. For example, a sleeping bag should unzip full length and the tent should be easily set up from a laying position by a victim who has one or both legs broken.
7. Field testing: Using a kit is like learning to swim. It is too late to be learning how to swim when you are in the middle of the lake and the boat is sinking. It is also a little late to find out that the life jacket you are using is inadequate.

Ideally, you should become thoroughly familiar with the contents of your kit before any actual survival situation occurs. Everyone having to place any reliance on a survival kit should personally field test it to determine its appropriateness and durability. A kit designed to be used by trained military personnel, may do very little for a nurse flying in the far north. If you use your kit until you wear it out, you may discover its shortcomings as well as what you need to know to use it effectively. It is easier to determine what you really need in a knife after you have used one for a few hours in a skillful way. You may underrate the importance of cord until you have had to use it in its various survival applications. You will have a more realistic notion of how fragile a Mylar survival blanket is, after wearing out a few.

Many kits are packed and sealed so that the user is assured that the items on the packing slip are not pilfered or mislaid. The user does not see the contents of the kit until an actual survival situation occurs. That is a poor time to discover that the compass is unserviceable, the knife or axe is dull, or the food is rancid, or be wondering how to effectively use a particular piece of equipment such as a signal mirror.

Note: The following information is meant to help you figure out what you need to consider. How to use these items is dealt with in greater detail throughout this guide.

2. The Personal Kit

When venturing anywhere into the wilderness on a short term basis you should be properly dressed for the occasion. The importance of clothing in survival has been proven time and time again. Nine-tenths of the information in this article will not be needed if you are properly dressed. When you are well dressed, you may dispense with any heroics because -40°C may be of little concern to you. Clothing should include well chosen headgear, scarf, and footwear. You should not travel in the out-of-doors without proper clothing any more than you would go to the moon without a space suit. Your clothing will have to cope with cold, moisture, wind, solar radiation, and biting insects. It should be non-restrictive and easily vented. Adequate headgear and scarf are very important because these may be used to conserve over half of the heat generated by the body.

a) Matches

Fire lighting is one of the more important bush survival techniques. Where all else is inadequate, fire may still keep you from freezing to death. Fire is also useful in smoke signaling.

One might consider carrying waterproof matches, windproof matches or the now available windproof-waterproof matches. For kits carried in aircraft there must also be safety matches. Certain disposable lighters would be prohibited on aircraft and could also be ineffective in extreme cold. Lighters of this type, under the right circumstances can have the same explosiveness as an equal quantity of dynamite. In sandy situations some lighters with pressurized fuel may drain rapidly because of sand particles getting into their valves.

People who do not fly should also carry ordinary strike-anywhere matches in case safety matches and strikers become separated. Matches should be carried in coat, pants, and the pack to assure their availability in need. Loose matches account for about 55 deaths a year in the U.S.A. Matches should not be packed loosely in a container or the heads may pulverize or disintegrate. Do not use match containers that cannot be opened with cold incapacitated hands. Many people have been found frozen to death, obviously having been unable to open their match containers. All so-called waterproof match containers should be tested regularly to prove their water tightness by emersion while upright.

A good, very compact backup for fire lighting is the metal or rare-earth element match, which is in reality a huge lighter flint. Its spark is so hot that it will ignite most fine kindling, such as toilet paper, fine shavings, dry grass, papery inner bark and so on. Gather up your fine kindling into a pile on a solid base. The metal match should be pressed down through the kindling to find support from the solid base. The metal match is given a good scrape with the scraper provided, or with anything sharp or with the back of your knife sharpened for that purpose. If you are using your knife, use only the part of the blade near the handle as the metal match is very hard on a good edge.

b) Knife

A good knife, although dispensable, makes life much easier and represents little investment for a large return. It is one of the most portable of tools. There is no excuse for not carrying a knife on you at all times, unless of course you do not know how to use it. The knife should be sharp, have a large enough handle to afford a good grip, be brightly colored and have an attachment for a lanyard to help prevent loss and be of carbon steel for easy sharpening and for lighting fire by the flint and steel method.

An inexpensive group of highly recommended knives are the laminated steel Swedish knives, made by Frosts, Mora or Sandvik. The edge holding capability of Swedish steel is well known. The blade is composed of a tool steel of a Rockwell hardness of 65(c) sandwiched between two layers of softer, more shock-absorbing steel. The hardwood handle is oval in cross section for a comfortable fit in the hand. The most highly recommended size is the one with a blade eight to ten centimetres long. The design of this knife goes back a few hundred years in the traditions of the Scandinavian peoples. The longer you use it the more you will realize its superior design for general bush work. Its major drawback is its weak handle design, which results from minimum expense-construction techniques.

If you prefer to carry a folding knife, it should be large enough and be of a sturdy design. The more universally useful blade point is the spay. The main blade should lock in the open position but use the knife as if it closes, not have the lock blade feature. A lock blade can close unexpectedly with heavy use. Ideally, you should be able to open the knife with one hand. The pivot pin should be sturdy enough to stand extensive use. Avoid knives that have squarish corners on the handle: these raise blisters very quickly with any amount of use. The use of a baton is not compatible with the pin of a folding knife blade.

c) Compass and Map

Carry any compass you are comfortable with. Do not carry one if you do not know how to use it as it will only be a waste of money.

d) First Aid Kit

A small first aid kit packed in a dustproof bag and carried in a shirt pocket should consist of:

1. 10 knuckle bandages (Elastoplast)
2. 10 Bandaid butterfly closures (large, medium and small) or more modern wound closures such as steri-strips.
3. 10 Telfa pads 7.5 cms. by 10 cms.
4. Small tube Polysporin opthalmic ointment.
5. Mirror – fore removing objects in the eye and signaling.
6. To supplement the above, elsewhere on your person or in your pack or survival kit, you should carry a roll of 5 cm. wide elastic adhesive plaster or "Tensor" type bandage.
7. Tweezers. A small pair of well designed sharp, pointed tweezers (spare no expense)
8. Needle or large safety pins with a well sharpened point.

It is important that this kit be carried on the person at all times. That is why the kit should be compact enough to carry in the shirt pocket. A larger (less portable) kit would double or triple the quantities of items a), b), c), and f) and in addition have a roll of Elastoplast rubber elastic bandage (non-sticking), 3 or 4 triangular bandages, two dozen assorted safety pins and a good pair of small scissors.

e) Sleeping Bag, Protective Cover and Mattress

A good survival kit could be a large pot with one hundred windproof-waterproof-strike-anywhere matches, a good knife and a Mylar tube tent combined with a clear poly drop sheet, a sleeping bag stuffed in, the lid taped shut with heating duct tape to waterproof and make it buoyant. A sleeping bag is very useful in the event of injury, illness, lack of food, and lack of fuel. The importance of proper rest and sleep and the difficulty in making an adequate substitute are points that give the sleeping bag a high priority. If you are going to spend a lot of money on a kit, spend it on a sleeping bag. In some circumstances where fire is impossible the sleeping bag ranks next to clothing in importance.

A bag, or combination of bags, should be effective for the lowest temperature you expect to encounter. Allow 22 centimetre loft for -40°C. A closed cell mattress (minimum of 1/2 centimetre thick) is very useful but not absolutely essential if you are well versed in bed making from natural materials. A protective nylon bag will protect your bag from sparks if you have to sleep near a fire (provided the bag is not synthetic, in which case it may be damaged by the heat of a fire).

f) Pot in a Protective Waterproof Bag

Most people who do not survive actually dehydrate to death. The adverse effect of dehydration on every aspect of the bodily functions can not be over emphasized. A thorough understanding of dehydration is a must in survival. A large pot (of at least eight litres capacity) with bottom edge corners that are rounded, a sturdy bail and a tight fitting lid are desirable. The pot should double as the container or one of the containers for a survival kit. For a one or two person survival situation, the Mirro Aluminum Coffee Pot, 10 cup size with bail handle and side grips is recommended. A bag should be provided to protect other items from the soot on the outside of the pot.

g) Shelter

Shelter is relegated to such a low position because some form or another of a shelter can usually be made from locally available materials such as poles, boughs, grass, snow etc. The prime intent of the shelter is to protect the sleeping bag and enhance its function. In the case of injury a shelter can be a more critical factor. Pilots should carry a large shelter and a stove especially if they have many passengers and may not have enough space to carry a sleeping bag for each one. In the far north where flies can be a problem a fly-proof shelter would be greatly appreciated. In certain situations there may be no shelter materials available so that survivors have to rely on what is packed in a kit.

Effective and inexpensive shelters can be made up of parachute fabric, mylar tube tents and thin polyethylene drop sheets providing the environment can contribute pegs, poles, arches or other materials for the framework.

In order to maximize on the effectiveness of your steeping bag you must have a good shelter. Commercially made shelters are usually prohibitively expensive for survival kit usage.

Speculation on the Ideal Survival Shelter

The ideal survival tent should have the following characteristics:

1. The user should be able to live in the tent for long periods of time with a minimum of adverse effect on health and morale. The tent should have proper ventilation, condensation control and color (green). Color can be important in a psychological sense and for the prevention of snow blindness in snow camping. The design should allow for cold usage and rain.
2. The tent should be capable of being erected by one person alone within five minutes in spite of any strong winds or other adverse conditions to be found in the area of expected usage.
3. The tent should be portable (low in bulk and weight).
4. The tent should be useable in a variety of situations. For example, you should be able to use it with an open fire in extremely cold conditions.
5. The tent should be durable and fireproof.
6. Ideally the tent should be self contained and able to be efficiently erected without any dependence on outside materials. If such a tent fulfilling all conditions as described above exists, it would be prohibitively expensive.

h) Signal Mirror

The signal mirror is best carried in the personal first aid kit. Another important use for the mirror is in assisting to remove a foreign object from the eye, especially when you are by yourself. A suitable mirror can be bought in most drug stores.

i) Cord

The recommended cord is the nylon braided camping cord sold in most sporting goods stores in 15 to 30 metre hanks. Better still is parachute shroud line. Carry one or two 15 metre hanks. This is very useful in making emergency snow shoes. If any room remains in a completed kit, fill it with paracord.

j) Tools

The axe, saw and knife are usually the first to be chosen. A versatile combination is a hatchet weighing 500 grams and a carpenter's saw with regular Swede saw teeth sometimes called a Swedish Board Saw. This saw is more compact and less fragile than a Swede Saw and can also be used to cut snow blocks. It is not as fast in cutting wood as a Swede Saw. Tools are items that should not be made less efficient in the interest of compactness. If you are to pack a miniature folding version of the real thing you might just as well do without for the actual amount of benefit you may derive from it.

In the Boreal forest, as far as cutting wood is concerned, there is nothing to compare to a well designed, properly sharpened Swede saw. You know you have one when the blade buries itself a blade width on the full forward and back stroke. The blade should be no shorter than the distance from your nose to your outstretched fingertip or about one metre. The throat of the saw at its narrowest part should be at least 30 centimetres wide. This saw combined with a 3/4 or full sized axe, providing you know how to use it, should allow you to get by with only a pot and no other kit components. A Swede saw blade can be carried and a saw frame made when needed. This would be superior to most folding saws or so called survival saws. Add to this a good sleeping bag and you should be surviving in the lap of luxary.

k) Miscellaneous Items

You can include the following items:

- Duct tape to repair tears in clothing, sleeping bags or shelter fabric; for first aid bandaging and splits; or for shelter building, lashing etc.
- More cordage.
- Log book and pencil.
- Candles, a minimum of 3 made of stearic acid wax that burn for 8 hours.
- Spare pocket knife.
- Matches.
- One to three hot water bottles or the liners of cardboard wine casks for storing and carrying water and treating hypothermia.
- Sewing kit with dental floss for thread.
- An aluminium saucepan of about a half-litre capacity with the handle cut down.

l) Food in Kits

In the strict definition of survival, food may play a minor role. When food is included in a kit it considerably increases the weight of the kit. Foods suitable for long term storage may be laced with preservative chemicals. Some foods purported to be designed for survival kits provide good habitats for bacterial growth. Properly nourishing food is difficult to pack in a kit. Improperly chosen food may sicken the survivalist rather than nourish. This is not an unheard of occurrence.

You have to make up your own mind on this topic. The stance in this manual is that fasting is a more effective ploy within the definition of the concept of survival and the provision of food it kits is a low priority.

m) Survival Manual

In case the survivor is not well versed in all aspects of survival a well chosen manual should provide the answers to many of the problems which may arise.

Note: The following lists may be a useful reference for vehicle and aircraft survival. At the barest minimum the basic two kilogram universal kit will suffice for up to six people for vehicle, light plane, helicopter and snowmobile.

3. The Basic (Two Kilogram) Universal Kit

The following kit is a home made affair that should compare favourably with any kit presently on the market and at a fraction of the cost. It is a compromise between what you can carry and what is available from the natural environment. In some circumstances, this may be a disadvantage. The basic kit provides a means to teach a fairly effective two day "survival" course by using all the items to the fullest.

1. Container: The container which doubles as a cooking pot is a three litre cooking-oil can that is about 215 cms. deep, by 190 cms. wide, by 85 cms. broad. The handle is made of snare wire that has been doubled over until it is about eight strands thick.
2. Knife: Choose a Swedish Mora knife, preferably with a blade at least 10 cms. long and a handle size that fits the user's hand well.

3. Hatchet: The hatchet (Norton) should weigh 450 to 500 grams, and be sharpened to a razor's edge. The edge should be protected with duct tape.
4. Saw: The saw components are: (1) a Swede saw blade at least 900 cms. long (36"), two small nuts and bolts at each end (threads slightly mangled so that the nuts do not unscrew easily by themselves, but still unscrew when and if needed, (2) a strong non-elastic cord (SISAL) at least seven times the length of the saw blade and (3) four nails about 4 cms. long.
5. Snowshoes: (optional component*) The snowshoe components consist of (1) either 4 metres of lampwick or one metre of lampwick and six 3 cm. wide elastics made from an old inner tube. The elastics are also used to keep the contents of the kit in the can as well as to attach the shoulder carrying strap, (2) 10 metres of 45 kg. (100 lb.) test nylon line or utility cord, and (3) 50 shingle nails.
6. Pack Frame: (optional component*) The pack frame components consist of (1) the pack strap which is about 1.5 metres long, which acts as the shoulder strap for the packed kit, (2) three pieces 45 kg test nylon cord for lashing the pack frame, (3) 10 metres of 1/4 cm. cord for lashing pack frame loads and (4) three shingle nails for nailing pack frame together.
7. Shelter: The shelter components of (1) Mylar tube tent (2) two 1/2 ml polyethylene drop sheets about 3 x 4 metres in size, (3) 24 large safety pins, (4) two metre duct tape neatly folded (optional) and (5) 2 by 3 metre sheet rip stop nylon (pack cover and door entrance on shelter).
8. Fire: (1) a box of waterproof matches and (2) metal match (1000 to 4000 lights).
9. Subsistence: (optional component*) (1) Roll #22 snare wire, (2) leather pouch for sling-shot, (if elastics are of suitable rubber), (3) 12 assorted hooks, 2 leaders, 12

weights and 30 metres suitable fish line, (4) all spare space in can filled with OXO cubes.
10. Signals: Signal mirror (two pieces of mirror 3 x 4 cms.), signal flares (very expensive, thereby optional - HOPPE recommended).
11. Plastic bags: Two good plastic bags to empty the kit, carry water, etc. Also a plastic liner from a cardboard wine keg for carrying water and as a flotation device.
12. First Aid: (1) Tube Polysporin Ointment, (2) 12 large Telfa pads, (3) 24 knuckle bandages, (4) 1 roll tensor bandage 4 cm. size, (5) Tweezers, (6) Dental floss.
13. Boat-Stretcher/Toboggan (Not a true "survival" component*) (optional): On outside of can a piece of 6 ml. polyethylene about 3 by 4 metres long. This component is not included in the weight of the overall kit.
14. Directions for the use of the kit in the form of a small booklet.

---

* How "Optional" is used in this list: In the austere definition of "survival" the victims should settle down, make themselves comfortable and await rescue. Therefore the need to travel (snowshoes), to carry anything (backpack) or the haul anything (boat, toboggan) is eliminated. Unless the victims are well versed in living off the land they may use up more energy in the gathering activity than may be gained back through eating the product of their efforts. Unless you KNOW WHAT YOU ARE DOING you may be far better off by fasting while waiting for rescue.

4. The Personal First Aid Kit

Someone once pointed out that fire extinguishers, life jackets, parachutes and first aid kits are in a way in the same category: you hope you will never have to use them. But when you do need them, you really need them.

a) The Basic Kit

An obviously important aspect of a personal first aid kit is that it needs to be immediately available when you need it. It should be light enough and small enough to fit in the shirt pocket. The following kit weighs under a 100 grams and makes a package 13 cms. long, 10 cms. wide and about 3 cms. thick.

The kit consists of the following items:
6 Curity Telfa Pads® 10 x 7.5 cms.
12 Elastoplast® anchor (knuckle) dressings
1 tube Polysporin® ointment (3.5 grams)
1 package (10) Steri-Strips 3M® (butterfly closures)
1 mirror (purse size 5 x 7 cms)
1 good tweezer, sharp pointed
2 sewing needles, medium size
3 metres dental floss

Detailed explanation of contents:

Telfa Pads: These pads are designed to be applied directly on cuts, burns and scrapes. One particularly useful feature of Telfa pads is that they do not stick to the wound. An important aspect of handling cuts is to avoid tearing them open when an old dressing is removed and a new dressing is applied.

Anchor Dressing: This is a type of "band-aid" that is shaped like a capital 'H'. It will conform to most contours, especially about the arms, hands and feet. A number of anchor dressings can be used together to complete a bandage. This takes the place of roll adhesive tape which is more awkward to pack in a small kit.

Polysporin: This is the antibiotic component of the kit. If a circle of Polysporin is drawn around the wound once or twice a day whenever a new dressing is applied there will likely be no pus formation. The cut itself may be of little consequence compared to the infection or blood poisoning that may result from it.

Polysporin is packaged in two forms: Topical First Aid antibiotic ointment (30 grams) and Sterile Opthalmic ointment (3.5 grams). The two can likely be used interchangeably. The Opthalmic ointment is specifically meant to be used for eye problems or injuries, which is obviously very useful in the bush.

Steri-Stripes: These are the modern replacements for stitches for holding gaping wounds together.

Mirror: This is used for removing objects from the eye and for signalling.

Tweezers: These would be the sharp-pointed type that can dig for a bad silver. Run the tips between a folded piece of fine sand paper to make them oppose each other more perfectly. The sharp tips should be taped up to prevent punctures to the rest of the kit.

Sewing Needles: For removing slivers, thorns and prickles.

Dental Floss: For removing anything wedged between the teeth and for sewing.

The tweezers, needles and floss should be taped to a 5 x 10 cm. card to prevent loss.

Packaging: The kit should be packed in a tough plastic bag such as 1 1/3 litre milk bag and taped shut to make it dust proof.

b) The Kit for Long Term Trips

Although the Personal First Aid Kit meets nine-tenths of one's needs in the bush, on long term trips it may be wise to carry a few supplementary items separately in the pack especially when working with a group.

6 Curity Telfa Pads® (extras)
24 anchor dressings (extra)
1 pack Steri-Strips (extra)
2 Tensor® bandages (5 x 170 cms.)
2 (compressed) Triangular bandages
1 roll Elastoplast® tape (5 cms wide)
24 assorted safety pins
Vitamin C 1000 mg tablets.
Vitamin E 400 mg tablets.
Antihistamine (Benadryl)
25 Asprins
1 vial 222's
1 small bottle Betadine
Sunscreen ointment
1 small vial oil of cloves
1 small pair sharp pointed scissors
Good quality polaroid sunglasses

Detailed explanation of contents:

Telfa Pads, Anchor Dressings and Steri-Strips: These are extras in case the components in the personal kit are used up.

Tensor Bandages: These elastic, non stick roll bandages can hold a compress or pad in place or can be used to support a sprained ankle.

You will find that the elasticity of the tensor bandage will allow it to be placed tightly enough to cut off circulation; you will have to guard against this in some cases.

Triangular Bandage: These cloth bandages (non-elastic) can sometimes be obtained in a compressed form that makes a remarkably small package. If necessary some items of clothing can be cut up for bandages to replace the triangular bandage.

Elastoplast Tape: The tape referred to here is the moderately elastic type that has only enough adhesiveness to grip well. It is a cross between adhesive tape and a tensor bandage. Tensor bandages are notorious for slipping out of place with movement, especially when used on the leg. Elastoplast may have to be safety-pinned to keep it from undoing. It is removed with relative ease and if clean enough can be reused.

Safety Pins: Safety pins have many uses around camp. In the kit they are used with tensor or triangular bandages. One should carry a large safety pin pinned to the shirt pocket or hat brim for instant access. Sharpen the point on this safety pin as ordinarily safety pin points are too dull for removing slivers.

Vitamin C: For your own use, carry about three pills a day. These are taken for colds, sore throat, cuts and loose or infected teeth. Vitamin C often stops a smoke induced headache faster than aspirins do.

Vitamin E: Same number of pills as for Vitamin C. Use Vitamin E ointment for cuts, scraps and burns. Apply it externally.

Antihistamine: Benadryl is suggested as a general antihistamine in case of allergic reaction to bee stings, wild edible plants, pollen or other drugs. You may need a prescription to get this.

People who may react adversely to bee stings or who are allergic to fruit in particular should carry a Bee Sting Prophylactic kit. It is usually obtainable by prescription.

Aspirin, 222 or Other Painkillers: The best approach is to carry on a lifestyle that does not require the use of pain killers. For example, many headaches are dehydration induced. After drinking three or four cups of water, the headache often goes away. For smoke use Vitamin C. For glare, use proper sunglasses. Codeine painkillers also help to relieve severe diarrhea.

Betadine: This is a disinfectant solution that may be used to cleanse the skin in the case of burns, cuts, abrasions and in preparing for injections.

Sunscreen Ointment: This may be something like zinc oxide which can also be used in connection with friction injuries.

Oil of Cloves: This is used to reduce tooth pain either from cavities, loose fillings or broken teeth. Any swelling of the gums can be kept under control with Vitamin C. Keep increasing the hourly dosage until the swelling goes away.

Scissors: Pointed scissors are especially useful in removing old bandages with a minimum of disturbance.

Sunglasses: There are times when good quality polaroid sunglasses are worth their weight in 222's.

F) Caching of Supplies and Equipment

The cache should be easily recognizable to oneself but not to would-be thieves.

Rodents: The cache should be rolled up in two or three layers of fresh polyethylene. Food odours tend to be masked by the polyethylene. Fabric of any kind may be used as nest material by rodents. Bury the cache deep enough in mineral soil to discourage rodents and coyotes. Try to bury the cache at the base of the dry side of a tree under overhanging branches. Dry airtight tin containers are especially appropriate for caching. Anything packed in polyethylene should be wrapped with clicken wire.

Permanent Springs: Can be used to cache canned goods to protect from freezing.

Rivers: As landmarks along a river's edge can become unrecognizable in a very short time, it is best to keep well away from a river bank.

Improperly Packaged: The contents of the cache can be damaged by dampness, mildew, rodent damage due to saltiness, freezing, and rusting if in a can. Anything that is prone to rust, coat with Vaseline or petroleum jelly. Pack your cache carefully.

G) Signalling with a Mirror

It's a good idea to always carry a mirror when travelling in the bush, whether it is somewhere remote or just off the beaten path. A convenient place to carry a small mirror of the drugstore variety is in your personal first aid kit. There it is readily available for its most important use: assisting in removing foreign objects from the eye.

The usefulness of a mirror for signalling in the bush is obvious. What may not be obvious is that the mirror could be as useful a few hundred metres from a well travelled road, or somewhere in the 'back forty' where you may be pinned under a fallen tree or have broken a leg. You could be immobilized a few hundred metres from a busy thoroughfare, yet your only recourse might be to get the attention of a passing aircraft. It is rare for an aircraft not to pass overhead daily in all but the remotest parts of the country, so your chances of attracting attention are reasonably good.

When aircraft are scarce, you could scan the horizon in the hope that you might flash an aircraft below the horizon due to the refraction of the atmosphere, or during the fire season you may get the attention of a fire tower that may not be visible to you. If you hope to attract a fire tower, use your mirror constantly between 2 and 4 pm.

The simplest way to use a mirror is to extend one arm with your thumb pointed up, and with your other hand to manipulate the mirror by holding it above or below your eye. Direct the reflected sunlight partly onto your thumbnail and partly onto your target aircraft or horizon. Because of the short distance between the thumb and eye compared to the distance from the thumb to the target, flash well above and below the target to ensure that you hit it.

For greater accuracy, the mirror should have a sighting hole in its centre. Just scrape away a small hole in the silver backing of an ordinary piece of cut glass mirror with the tip of a pocket knife.

Mirrors of this type are readily available at hardware stores, perhaps for free if you ask the storekeeper to save you some mirror trimmings.

Another way of signalling is to use two mirrors back to back. A one centimetre long vertical scratch is made in the centre of one and a horizontal scratch is made in the centre of the second. When the mirrors are put back to back, one can sight on a target through the hole that is found at the intersection of the two scratches. At the same time, the sun should be shining through this hole to produce a dot of light on your face. If it misses your face, catch the dot on the palm of your hand.

Watch the dot on your cheek or hand in the mirror facing you. As you maintain the target in view, tilt the mirror until the dot disappears back into the non-reflective hole. An observer at the target should see a steady beam of reflected light. A mirror five by five centimetres wide will produce a flash that might appear three by three metres across to an observer five kilometres away.

H) Signal Fires

A signal fire may be the only means of attracting attention in some circumstances. A good signal fire should fulfill the following requirements:

- It should produce a large volume of intense smoke.
- The smoke should reach the tree tops within three minutes, even in a wind.
- The fire should be easy to light.

There are various types of signal fires. Some are simple, quickly built and burn for a relatively short period of time. At the other extreme, a signal fire may take considerable effort to build but the end result may be quite spectacular.

1. The Choice of Site

If possible pick terrain that is apt to be checked first by searchers, such as the edges of lakes or rivers. Clearings are better than thick stands of trees. Avoid any monotonous type of setting. Other ideal requirements of a site are:

1. The site should provide an abundance of boughs for the signal fire.
2. The signal fire should be close to camp so that it can be lit at a moment's notice.
3. The signal fire should be built near water. If the fire hazard is high, build the fire on sandy or rocky ground.
4. Build the signal fire downwind and at least fifty metres away from your gear. Sleeping bags, clothing (especially nylon) and other equipment could be damaged by the burning needles the signal fire will produce.

Basic Safe Travel and Boreal Survival

2. The Simple Signal Fire

This fire requires no tools, and takes only minutes to build. This type of signal may be held in a reserve while the proper signal fire is being built. Also, if one is travelling or is expected to be caught away from camp it may be worth while to carry the bundle of twigs so as to be able to make the signal on the spot.

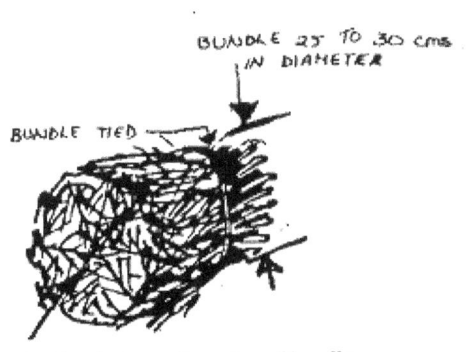

Hug sized bundle of twigs.

Kindling

Gather a large bundle about the size of a hug of fine, dry twigs, preferably (but not necessarily) spruce. The branches used should range from elbow-to-fingertip to armpit-to-fingertip in length. Have all the butt ends at one end of the bundle. When compressed the bundle would be at least twenty-five centimetres in diameter. For convenience of handling, the bundle is bound with spruce roots, grass cord or willow withes. The fine end of the bundle are folded inward into its center to concentrate the dispersed tips so that they will ignite more readily when a flame is applied.

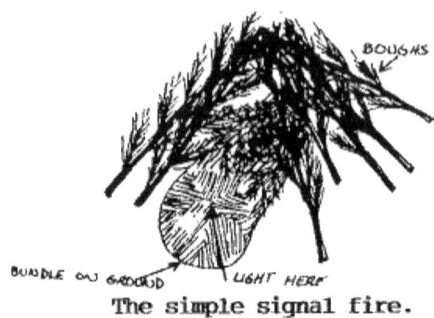

The simple signal fire.

Building the Signal Fire

Lay down the bundle, fine ends to the wind. Pile a few sticks, thumb-to-broom handle thick in teepee fashion over the bundle. Now cover this with ten to fifteen centimetres of spruce boughs, or leafy green branches, teepee fashion, with the Butt end down. If boughs are not available use moss or grass or the organic material on the forest floor. The fine ends of the bundle should be uncovered, or left uncovered, to provide easy access for lighting the signal fire.

3. The Standard Signal Fire

This signal fire produces a maximum of effect with a minimum of effort. If necessary this signal can be built without an axe or knife, because spruce boughs are easily broken off with the hands.

Kindling and Fuel Support

Select two dry or green poles that are approximately five centimetres in diameter at their thin ends. Set up the poles about twenty-five to thirty centimetres apart and roughly parallel to the ground at knee height. The poles should extend beyond their supports the length of the fingertip to the elbow. This can be done in a number of different ways, as illustrated below. This fuel support arrangement provides an easy access for lighting the kindling and allows for an unrestricted oxygen supply.

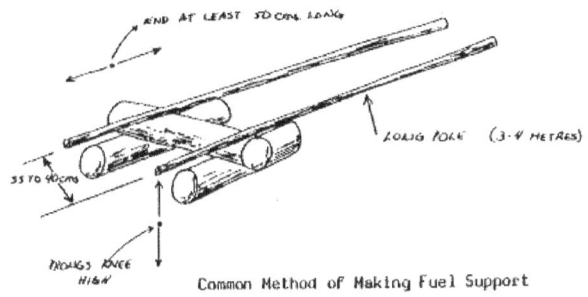

Common Method of Making Fuel Support

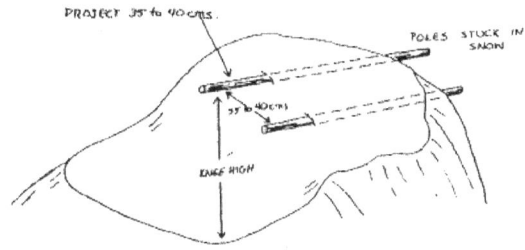

Method Of Making Fuel Support In Winter

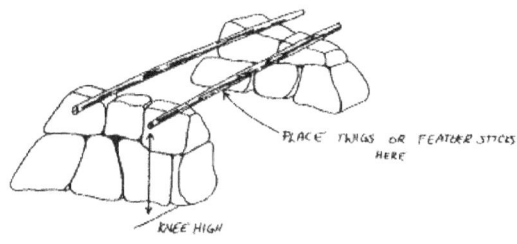

Using Rocks And Poles To Make The Fuel Support

Kindling and Fuel

The kindling can be a bundle of twigs as is used in the simple signal fire. If this type of kindling is used, a grate is made by laying four or five sticks of thumb thickness across the pole ends. This keeps the bundle from falling through as it burns. If a knife and axe are available the bundle can be replaced with fifteen to twenty feather sticks. The feather sticks can be stacked in log cabin fashion with the feathers to the inside. To help sustain the fire, thumb thick fuel is loosely stacked behind the feather sticks or bundle to help the signal last longer. Most signals last about ten minutes.

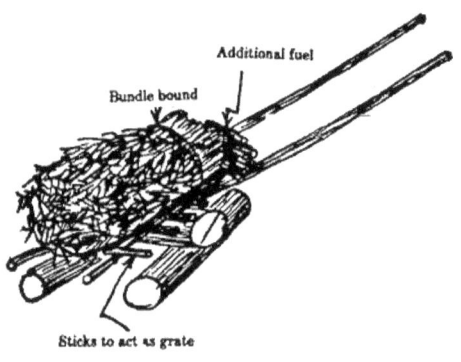

Bundle placed on grill.

The Framework

To support the boughs over the feather sticks, and to keep the signal fire from falling over as it burns, a framework is made with four larger boughs that are stood up teepee fashion with the stems pressed into the ground. If large boughs are not available, saplings or any straight poles can be used. Bend or snap any tips of the boughs projecting out of place so that they will lay down.

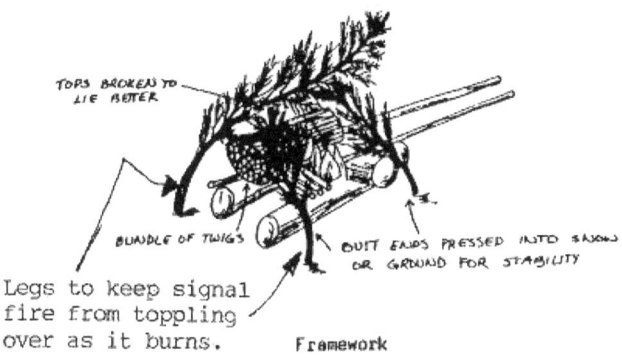

The Cover

The bough cover is now placed onto the framework. The boughs are placed stem upward with the underside of the bough to the outside as in shelter building. This protects the fire bundle from rain. About 75 boughs are required. The front of the cover generally does not extend below the kindling and the fuel. The cover should be about fifteen to twenty centimetres thick, with a cap to help keep the kindling and fuel dry in case of rain. The best cover of all is made from balsam fir boughs.

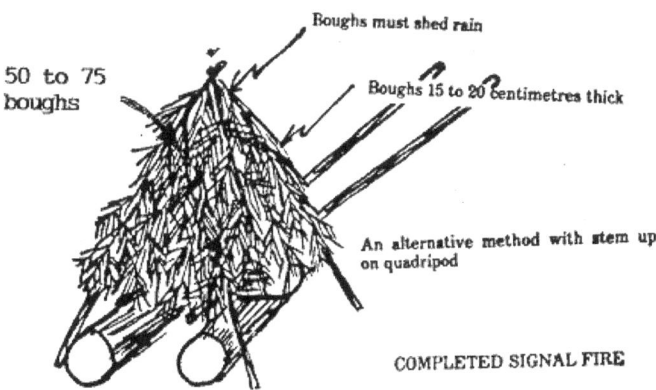

4. The Large Signal Fire

This signal fire requires more effort to construct and produces a correspondingly greater volume of smoke. This fire is more feasible if an axe is available and you are staying in one place for some time. It may be a more appropriate fire when you have to camp in featureless terrain, or in a rather tall and thick forest, or if you are attempting to attract the attention of a remote fire tower.

Kindling and Fuel Support

Construct this as described for the standard signal fire.

The signal can also be extended by the addition of more boughs. There should be a stockpile of boughs for this purpose, both for cramming into the hot spots that invariably develop and replenishing the boughs as they are consumed. Your bough bed and shelter cover may be considered as the reserve if circumstances demand it. Other materials can be added if boughs are in short supply. Any green vegetation such as brush, grass or clover can be used.

If time and energy permits, a number of signal fires may be built and kept in reserve. If the first signal is missed, another aircraft may pass overhead before you have built a new signal fire.

5. Other Tactics

On clear days you can light a signal fire in the mid-afternoon, to attempt to attract a fire tower or forestry personnel. If no one is aware of your plight (you may not be an air crash victim) you may have to light three signal fires in a triangular pattern or mark out a large "X" (I am unable to proceed) near your signal fire or camp, otherwise your signal fire can be mistaken for a large campfire.

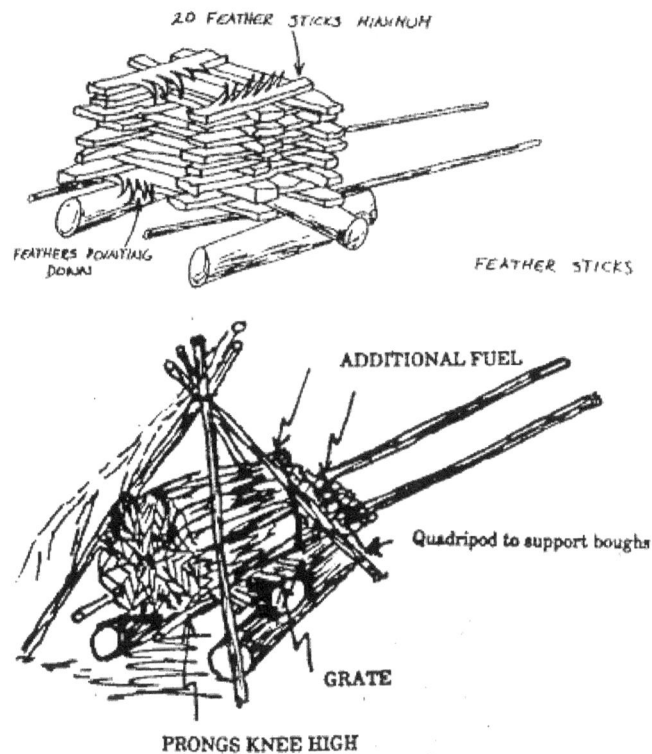

The Large Signal Fire

I) Vehicle Survival

1. Vehicle Operation Kit – circa 1985

You should have the following items in the vehicle:

1. Serviceable spare tire
2. Lug Wrench -- tire iron
3. Spare belts (fan, etc.)
4. Jack (safety, jackall or scissors)
5. Flares
6. Good spade for summer travel, scoop shovel for winter
7. Tire Chains
8. Tow cable or rope

In addition, if you are going well off the beaten path you might consider these in their order of importance:

1. Tire Pump
2. One or two spare tire tubes
3. Tire kit to consist of: 6 value stems, a tire patching kit with patches for tubes and tubeless tires and a hole plugging kit for tubeless tires.
4. Axe: 3/4 size, sharp, in a protective sheath.
5. Saw: 36 inch blade with a strip of wood taped to teeth to prevent damage to other items.
6. Chains or two cables (with hooks or ends and about eight metres long) or both. These are to be used with the jackall for pulling.
7. Basic Tool kit for: (a) replacing <u>fan belt</u>, (b) tightening battery cables, (c) removing spark plugs and gaping, (d) servicing or removing <u>thermostat</u>, (e) replacing <u>headlamps</u>, (f) tightening radiator and heater hoses, (g) replacing <u>gas filter</u> (h) plus underlined items.
8. 6 fuses of each kind used

9. 1 roll electrical tape
10. 1 roll radiator hose tape
11. 1 spare gas line filter
12. Spare fuel (5 gallons or 25 litres). Pack this item safely or you will have a bomb on your hands
13. Small roll of wire
14. Seal-all for leaks, emergency patches, etc.
15. Two large hose clamps
16. If you have an older vehicle or if the radiator hoses have not been changed recently take at least one spare upper (hot) hose
17. Spare oil
18. Spare coolant and radiator stop leak

In Winter you might also carry:

1. Large snow shovel (aluminum)
2. Jumper cables and protective eye goggles which are to be used whenever the jumper cables are used. Attach the eye goggles to the cables
3. Gas line de-icer (methyl hydrate, wood alcohol) one gallon or 5 litres.
4. Second Coleman lantern plus fuel. With two Coleman lanterns going under the hood and grill, and a tarp reaching to the ground a cold engine can be warmed to the starting point about as quickly as plugging in a block heater. This is only recommended when travelling at very low temperatures.
5. Surplus parachute or old blankets to insulate engine.

Optional but worthwhile to consider:

1. Spare spark plugs
2. Spare points
3. Spare condenser
4. Spare wiper blade

5. 1 sheet fine emery cloth
6. 2 alligator clips joined with 2 metres of electrical wire
7. Spare thermostat
8. Radiator sealant
9. Chain chocks, to facilitate putting on chains easily

2. Vehicle Survival Kit

Keep these items in your vehicle. Make sure you know how to use them:

1. A Coleman lantern with spare mantles, generator and a suitable wrench to replace the generator and to tighten all screws on the lamp. A small funnel to prevent spillage during filling. Spare matches. All of the above components should be packed in a protective box which is padded to prevent breaking the mantles and globe on the lantern. The lantern will provide light in the event of breakdown at night and will heat the interior of a vehicle more adequately than most other means. The lantern can also be used to warm an engine to start it in cold weather.
2. Three or four litres of white gas or other suitable fuel for lantern, or enough fuel to continuously operate the lanterns for 48 hours.
3. Two good wool blankets in protective cases or, better still, one blanket for each passenger.
4. Pot: recommended minimum size of 10 cups. The Mirro coffee pot is highly recommended. An aluminum saucepan small enough to fit in the pot will serve as a general eating utensil.
5. Three pairs new wool socks (Icelandic: 85% wool, 15% nylon).
6. Spare headgear such as a good toque or balaclava.
7. Water-proof tarp: woven polyethylene, canvas or polyethylene coated nylon approximately 3 x 5 metres.

An alternative is one or two parachutes, provided you can obtain them and know how to use them.
8. Large first aid kit as described elsewhere in this guide.
9. Food (optional if you choose to fast). In size 10 cans: (a) 1 fruit mix - 2 1/2 lbs., (b) 1 soup blend (vegetable mix) - 2 1/2 lbs., (c) 1 textured vegetable protein beef - 2 1/2 lbs., (d) Cereal fruit and nuts - 3 lbs., (e) 1 quart sealed tin of olive oil, (f) Tea, coffee or hot chocolate, (g) Fruit crystals for hot or cold drinks(h) hard candy like barley sugar (i)OXO cubes.
10. A pair of good sunglasses that is reserved for the use of the driver.

J) Aircraft Survival

Transport Canada in its flight information manual (1976) states that aircraft flying over sparsely settled areas must carry the following) (unconverted to metric).

1. Pamphlet--flight precautions in sparsely settled areas (and series #12)
2. 5 pounds suitable food for everyone on board
3. Cooking utensils and mess tins
4. Safety matches (suitable to be carried on aircraft)
5. Compass
6. Axe: minimum size of 2 1/2 lbs and 28 inch handle
7. 30 feet of snare wire
8. A jackknife or hunting knife
9. An assortment of fish hooks, lines and nets
10. A mosquito net for each one on board

In Addition for Winter:

1. Sufficient tents or shelter for all aboard
2. Sufficient sleeping bags for all aboard
3. Two pair of snowshoes

Also Recommended but not Mandatory:

1. Spare axe handle
2. Stone or file
3. Ice Chisel
4. Snow knife
5. Snow shovel
6. Flashlight with spare bulbs and batteries
7. Pack sack
8. Insect repellent
9. Copy of information circular title "Search and Rescue"

Note: For extended flight over water, additional mandatory equipment is required.

Two Approaches to Aircraft Survival

In my opinion there are two basic approaches in packing kits for aircraft survival. One entails providing an enclosed shelter that is kept warm with a wood burning stove. This is suitable for non-barren lands survival with trees to provide fuel and framework for shelters. The other entails providing sleeping bags for each person which can be used without the benefit of fire at any temperature. This should be considered when flying over the barren lands.

For the first approach consider the following equipment:

1. From one to three war surplus parachutes for shelter construction. Each two parachutes can provide an excellent shelter for 8 to 12 adults. Supplement with 6, 1-ml thick 8 x 12 foot polyethylene drop sheets. Or for every 3 or 4 people, 1/2 parachute plus one drop sheet plus two survival blankets to be made into a willow arch "super" shelter.
2. Five gallon pail for a stove, or a small airtight heater.
3. a small chisel to make the pail into a stove (optional)
4. Five sections of three or four inch diameter stove pipe. Unassembled plus a butterfly valve.
5. Items 2, 3 and 4 can be replaced with a commercially made woodstove which itself becomes the kit container.
6. Swede saw, 36 inch blade, non folding, Sandvik brand recommended.
7. Hatchet weighing 500 grams.
8. Good pot with a 10 litre or greater capacity.
9. 75 x 75 cm. sheet of aluminum for stove-pipe hole, precut for the proper fit.
10. Small roll stove wire.

K) Helicopter Safety

Helicopters are frequently encountered in bush operations. Knowing the proper conduct around them could prevent injury, death or costly damage.

1. The most dangerous area is where the pilot cannot see you approaching. Always approach the helicopter in a way that allows the pilot to clearly see you.
2. The tail rotor is easy to walk into because it is so low.
3. On level ground the main rotor blades may clear the ground by a little more than two and a half metres. The slower the blade is rotating the more dangerous it is, because it may dip without warning as low as a metre and a half. This is on level ground, so if you cannot wait for the main rotor to stop walk very crouched down.
4. Always exit down slope or you may be shortened the amount that the ground rises. Tools such as axes, shovels, etc. should never be carried on the shoulder when you are near a helicopter. Headgear should be clasped to the chest or use chin-straps. If your hat is blown off you may automatically react by reaching up with your hand into the blade.
5. Loose objects such as tarps, tents, polyethylene sheets, canvas water buckets, articles of clothing, and folded sleeping bags may be swept up into the rotor if they are near it while you are unloading. Keep this in mind.
6. The loading and unloading of cargo should be done very carefully without dropping or jamming them. It is very easy to damage a helicopter. Unload fairly close to the helicopter if possible, then let it fly away.
7. A helicopter door is not meant to be slammed shut. It is not made to support any weight, so do not swing on it.

Basic Safe Travel and Boreal Survival

8. Pilots are very happy when no one touches the plexi-glass bubble in any way. Touching it smears it. Anything sharp will easily scratch or crack it. It is very easy to stick a boot through it from the inside.
9. Trees that have been burned at the trunk may have their roots burned through. The wind from the rotor may be enough to blow the tree over on the machine itself or on persons nearby. Consider this when selecting the landing pad.
10. A helicopter that flies low or hovers over campfires can blow ashes around. People or their equipment may be burnt or an uncontrollable fire could be started.

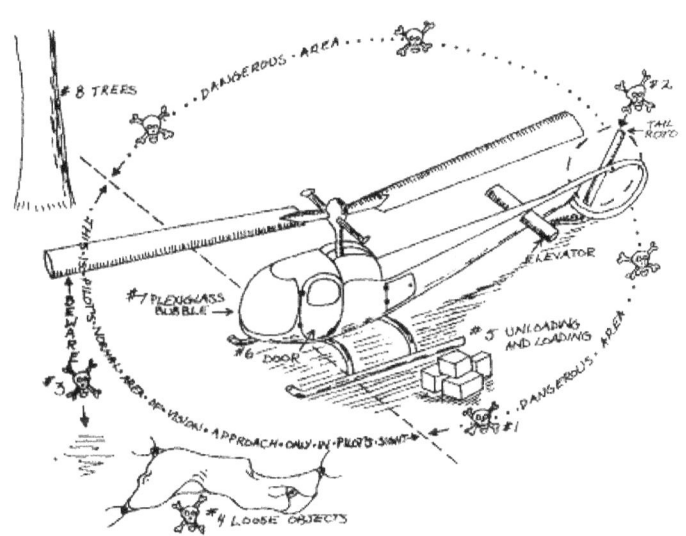

III Wilderness First Aid

A) Cold Injuries

1. Introduction

There are four cold injuries that tend to keep each other company in the cold out-of-doors: Frostnip, Frostbite, Dehydration and Hypothermia.

If you have an accident or are detained in the bitter cold (-40°C in a stiff breeze), expect these to be your major enemies.

Frostnip

The skin turns white and becomes numb. It should be rewarmed immediately with your hand. No real skin damage is usually expected. Frostnip should be looked upon as a forewarning of frostbite.

Frostbite

Expect skin damage. If possible, do not attempt to rewarm a frostbite case, unless you know what you are doing and no doctor or hospital is available.

Dehydration

Moisture loss through sensible and insensible means may be greater at -40°C than in the Sahara. Reduced circulation due to a lack of body fluids may eventually result in dehydration induced fatigue.

Hypothermia

The condition where the human body temperature drops below the normal of 37°C.

HYPOTHERMIA*

STAGES	SYMPTOMS		TREATMENT
Early Warning Signs	Shivering	37°	Stop Exposure
	Slow Speech	36°	Remove Wet Clothing
	Uncharacteristic Behavior	35°	Put on Dry or Extra Clothing
Hypothermic Signs	Loss of Appetite	34°	
	Incoherence of Mental Processes	33°	Give Warm, Sweet Liquids
	Immobile, Fumbling	32°	Expose to Heat Source
Danger Signs	Stumbling, Loss of Shivering	31°	
	Extreme Irrationality	30°	Sleeping Bag With Two People Together
	Collapse	29°	
Death Signs		28°	Hot Packs in Thigh, Torso, Liver
	Unconsciousness	27°	Slow Rewarming
	Stoppage of Breathing	26°	Commence C.P.R.
	D E A T H	25°	

* Harvey Scott's notes, University of Alberta

At 35°C: Shivering.
At 34°C: Inability to help yourself.
At 33°C: Violent, uncontrollable shivering.
At 32°C: Coordination, concentration and thinking are all slowed down.
At 30°C: Shivering stops. Irrational behaviour. Muscles

stiffen.

At 25°C: The air temperature for a comfortable summer day. When the body temperature drops this low, it means death.

How to Combat the Major Enemies:

1. Stay healthy and eat properly. It is difficult to stay warm in cold weather if you haven't eaten properly. When you are tired, rest before venturing into the cold. If you are suffering from a cold or the flu, get better before venturing on a major trip out-of-doors in the cold.
2. Drink adequate amounts of water to eliminate at least a litre of fluid a day.
3. Poor fitting, inadequate clothing, especially your footwear, could be a significant hazard. Clothing is your first and most significant line of defence in combating the four major enemies.
4. As soon as you start to overheat, vent off excessive moisture and warmth before you become wet from sweat. Strive to use your energy efficiently.
5. When you come to a stop, do you know how to keep warm? Do you have clothing to change into if you are wet with sweat? Can you light an adequately large fire? Do you know where to find a wind protected spot?
6. It may be wise not to travel in unusually strong winds. If you do, make sure your clothing is up to the task.
7. Take action when you feel the effects of the cold. There is no time more convenient than right now to take care of the problem. Build a windbreak of snow blocks, build a fire, make some hot drinks, or put on more clothing. Act!
8. The use of coffee could compound your problems in coping with the cold. Coffee increases the heart rate and causes the blood vessels to constrict; this may promote

frostbite. Coffee also causes you to eliminate fluids more rapidly which in turn could contribute to dehydration, which will contribute to frostbite and hypothermia.
9. If you are a smoker you are likely to have more problems in coping with frostbite, especially to your feet.
10. If you have had frostbite previously, the altered circulation will give you problems in coping with frostbite.
11. Uncontrollable shivering is your last warning! STOP FURTHER HEAT LOSS if it is not already too late.

2. Hypothermia

a) The Dangers of Hypothermia

Hypothermia is the term used to describe the condition where the body temperature has dropped to below 36.5°C. The normal temperature range for people is anywhere between 36.5 and 39.5°C.

The hypothermia centre of the brain harmoniously plays heat loss against heat production in the mammalian body so that it stays at the temperature where most enzymatic systems tend to reach maximum activity.

Hypothermia frequently occurs in somewhat mild temperatures (from -1 °C to 10 °C) especially in wet and windy conditions in the spring and the fall. In the foothills and the mountains, hypothermia can occur at any time of the year.

Brain function can be affected by the slightest cooling of the body core. This results in an increasing irrationality that keeps pace with the cooling. This is insidious because the person suffering from hypothermia does not comprehend what is happening. Alteration of personality generally occurs so that quiet people becoming argumentative or pugnacious and loud people becoming quiet. Your best guide is to follow your observations of the victim's physical condition and behaviour rather than relying on what the hypothermic victim tells you.

This "irrational" effect of hypothermia may explain the puzzling behaviour of some people who have become lost. In many instances, people have been found frozen, with dry matches, knives and axes in their possession, and in areas where there was ample firewood. These people did not die from freezing, but from hypothermia: the cooling of internal body organs which impairs rational thinking and muscular co-ordination, and which, unless arrested, will lead to heart stoppage. Freezing the limbs, if such ever occurs, may happen during lower night temperatures after the victims were dead. If the outside temperature is 25°C it is considered a warm day, but a human dies if the body temperature drops this low.

Heat loss from the outside of the body must be replenished from the interior to restore warmth. A defensive mechanism, which restricts the circulation of blood to the body's extremities, takes over when exterior heat loss is too great to be restored without lowering body core temperature.

The temperature of the body core is maintained but the restriction of the circulation in the fingers, toes, hands and feet, may result in these parts freezing first. Continued exposure, whether or not the temperature is below the freezing point of water, results in the further cooling of the inner core.

Freezing to death from outright cold conditions is not unusual but the majority of deaths occur in air temperatures considerably above freezing. In temperatures well below freezing, the air is dry and people are usually suitably dressed for the cold.

Setting aside certain variables, a temperature drop in the body core from the normal 37 °C to 34 °C usually impairs reasoning and co-ordination to the point where you are not capable of assisting yourself. A further reduction of 3 to 6 °C will usually leave the individual on the verge of collapse, at which point physical activity stops and body heat production is reduced by as much as 50 percent. Thereafter, body heat loss is accelerated, until a further drop of 2 to 3 °C results in the failure of the cardiac control centres in the brain, and the heart stops.

Neglecting to keep yourself comfortable is inviting loss of hands or feet or death by hypothermia.

b) Coping with Hypothermia

Your first and most important defense against hypothermia is the clothing you wear. In cold weather you must have a sufficient thickness of air entrapped in the clothing to provide the required insulation. For example, for light work in still air at zero Celsius you should have 2 cms., for minus 20°C-3.5 cms., and for minus 40°C-5 cms. For heavy work at the same temperatures you need .5, .9, and 1.3 cms. respectively. When you change from light to heavy work you must be able to adjust the insulative effectiveness of your clothing or you may become just as wet as if someone poured cups of water down your back. Wind will tend to be a big problem in protecting yourself from hypothermia. It is important that outer garments be windproof when strong wind is expected.

Cotton is a poor choice for winter clothing in that it becomes limp when wet, thereby collapsing any air cells entrapped in it. Cotton promotes quick evaporation which causes considerable surface heat loss from the skin.

Wool is a good durable fabric albeit heavy for winter clothing. Wool pants should be considered a must even though all the other items may be of some other fabric.

Stay dry. If this is not possible, light a fire as soon as possible and dry out. In melting snow in thaw conditions it is easy to become soaked to the crotch. Even if the snow is not deep it may be appropriate to build emergency snow shoes to stay drier. You can experience considerable heat loss in the inner thigh area because so many large blood vessels are near the surface.

Protect the head and neck from heat loss. Estimates of heat loss in this area range from 20 percent to 70 percent of total body heat loss. The surface blood vessels located in the neck circulate almost half of the body's blood through the brain. A good scarf that covers the neck and helps to close off the top opening of your coat plus a cap that covers the ears, combine to produce the equivalent effectiveness of an additional heavy wool shirt at a fraction of the weight.

Realize the role of body water loss (dehydration) in hypothermia. Few people realize how easy it is to lose vital body water through breathing and sweating in the cold. When the body has to do work with inadequate amounts of water in the system, the blood gets thicker, and moves slower with greater effort. Heat transportation and transferral become more difficult. The results are pronounced fatigue, colder extremities and all kinds of other undesirable disadvantages.

Force yourself to drink. Use fatigue as an indicator of your water needs because thirst becomes completely unreliable under most adverse conditions. It may be difficult to comprehend and believe, but if you feel very tired you simply may not be drinking enough water. As a starter, drink enough water to pass at least a litre a day.

c) Pay Attention to the Symptoms of Hypothermia

Persistent or Violent Shivering: Shivering can double and even triple body heat production. However, shivering hastens exhaustion because it required additional oxygen and energy. Shivering is the signal to terminate hypothermia when there is still reserve energy for building a fire and shelter or taking other steps to warm yourself.

Vague, Slow, Slurred Speech: An early sign of hypothermia is the tendency to move, talk and act in a slow motion.

Uncharacteristic Behaviour: Normally quiet people may become loud and argumentative and loud people quiet. This is a sign of significant amounts of cooling.

Loss of Appetite: As the body temperature lowers, all body systems, including the digestive system, work less efficiently. The hypothermic person may not feel hungry, even though he or she has not eaten for some time.

Incoherence: This is more noticeable in others than in yourself.

Fumbling Hands: A practical test that is used by some natives in Northern Canada is to touch the thumb and little finger of the same hand. If this is difficult to do, they know that it is time to seek shelter and to build a fire.

Frequent Stumbling and Lurching Gait: By this stage, the victim is beginning to lose touch with reality, and is unable to assist him or herself.

Drowsiness: A hypothermia victim must be kept awake, for sleep means death. The body's heat production is reduced by 50 percent or more when physical activity ceases. This causes a rapid drop in body temperature. However, staying awake when you are not hypothermic is pointless.

Exhaustion: The victim is unable to get up after a rest and is in serious condition. At this stage, the blood is undergoing a chemical change because of its lower temperature, and the victim's recovery will be very difficult.

Unconsciousness: Recovery of the victim at this stage is very unpredictable because of a further drop in the core temperature of the body while you are attempting to warm the victim.

d) Treatment of Hypothermia

Treatment must be given immediately; treatment of hypothermia is generally difficult in its advanced stages. A hypothermic victim who is at the point of exhaustion may be minutes from death. The treatment given depends upon the stage that the victim has reached. There are, however, some general procedures that apply to all stages:

- Stop exposure. Get the victim out of the wind and rain.
- Strip off all wet clothing. Get the victim into dry clothing and into a dry, warm (eg. warmed in front of the fire) sleeping bag.

- Give warm, preferably sweetened drinks. If the victim is fully conscious. A semi-conscious or unconscious person will be unable to swallow and may drown.
- Build a fire to warm the victim.
- Warm the victim. The buddy system of warming a hypothermia victim has been recommended in the past and may be the only practical method on the trail. One or two donors donate warmth to the victim by direct skin contact inside a single or double sleeping bag. However, the following precautions should be taken:
    - The donors themselves must not be on the verge of hypothermia or the treatment may backfire.
    - Applications of external heat can cause a semi-conscious victim and an unconscious victim to lapse into death because of afterdrop. Afterdrop occurs because of the cold blood from the body extremities reaching the heart. Restoration of blood circulation to a victim in the extreme stages of hypothermia must be done very slowly.
    - Try to keep the victim awake. If the semi-conscious victim lapses into unconsciousness, discontinue the buddy system of warming. It the victim responds favourably to treatment, apply hot packs such as a canteen filled with hot water and wrapped in cloth to the inner thighs, torso, liver and kidney areas. Do not try to warm the hands and feet.
- Treat the unconscious victim so that afterdrop is minimized. Unconscious hypothermia victims should be allowed to recover by their own metabolic heat because of the danger of afterdrop. The victim should be placed in the "unconscious position" (eg. on the side with the upper leg comfortably bent and the lower leg

straightened. The upper arm is bent comfortably at the elbow and lower arm is pulled out from under the body. The victim's head is laid sideways and the chin is tilted slightly upward).
- The head should be kept slightly lower than the rest of the body. The victim should be well insulated from the cold ground.
- The unconscious position allows the victim to breathe more easily, an important precaution when the victim is very weak and could suffocate on the phlegm in the throat. First, wrap the victim in a Mylar survival blanket to trap as much body heat as possible and then insulate the victim with wool blankets or sleeping bags.
- Reduce handling to a minimum, as handling seems to be one of the prime factors in causing cardiac arrest.
- Get the victim to a hospital as soon as possible.

3. Cold Hazards: Frostnip and Frostbite

When the temperature of the surface of the skin drops below minus 1°C, the fluid around the cells of the skin begins to form ice crystals. During their formation the crystals will draw water out of the cells through the yet-intact cell membrane. If the ice outside the cells can be thawed soon enough, the water moves back and the delicate physical and chemical balance of the cell is returned. If the temperature drops low enough to freeze the fluid within the cell, irreversible damage occurs and the cell dies.

Frostnip or superficial frostbite can be easily recognized and immediately treated with about as much injury as a mild sunburn. The area affected is usually white or waxy and feels cold with a tingling pain or 'nip' at first, then quickly becomes numb. The frozen spot becomes stiff and is easily detected by touch.

Frostnip should be expected and one should be on constant guard against it. The simplest remedy is to run your warm bare hand over the afflicted part - be it the nose, cheek, or ear lobe. Hold the hand on the frozen spot for a few moments until the stiffness and whiteness is gone.

Handle your face gently so as to not scratch or damage the numb skin. Your hand may have to be rewarmed in the armpit before further thawing or putting your hand back into your mitt.

In the cold, you should get into the habit of constantly grimacing and exercising the muscles of the face. This will tend to stave off frostnip, as well as signal to you that some part of your face is developing a stiff spot. If there are others with you, you should watch out for each other's welfare by keeping a lookout for the tell-tale waxy white spots on each other's faces.

You may thaw your face a dozen times an hour with no permanent ill effect.

Frostnip becomes Frostbite when more than just the epidermis is affected. Deep frostbite kills tissue. In frostnip, the pain you feel signals you that your nerves are not damaged. In frostbite, the lack of pain or a sensation of cold indicates that the nerves are also frozen. This is not good. If no other alternative is available, you are now stuck with a slow warm up at room temperature with at minimum an expectation of skin damage, or at worst, damage to the underlying tissues.

If Possible, Do Not Attempt To Rewarm A Frostbite Case, Get To a Doctor Or Hospital Immediately.

4. Dehydration

Most of us don't drink enough water. Both in bush survival and in day-to-day living, one of the more poorly understood physiological processes is the role of water in our body.

When the body has to operate under a water deficit there can be profound implications for bush survival. The term 'dehydration' describes the condition where the body has to labour under a shortage of water.

It is readily understandable that someone lost in the desert may have to deal with life threatening dehydration. However, ignorance of dehydration tends to make it a rather common occurrence even where there is more than adequate water available such as in the boreal or spruce-moose forest.

Some authorities claim that most people who have perished in survival situations may have actually died of dehydration rather than from seemingly more obvious conditions such as freezing or starvation. Dying of 'exposure' is more likely dying of dehydration.

Drinking water, like breathing, is done more or less unconsciously. We usually do not keep track of how much or how often we drink, but simply drink when the need arises in response to thirst and our habits. Habit may determine how adequate or inadequate our approach to drinking water is.

Those of us who suffer frequent headaches, constipation, and constant fatigue amongst many other related ailments may be flabbergasted to learn that these conditions may stem from something as simple as not drinking adequate amounts of water.

It would be a rather rare situation to not find adequate amounts of water anywhere throughout Canada's sparsely settled areas. The last thing we need to die of is dehydration. The directions on how to avoid dehydration are quite simple.

1. Force yourself to drink enough water frequently, so as to eliminate at least a litre of urine daily.
2. Thirst should not be relied on as the only signal to drink more water. Hunger, fatigue and cold should also serve to remind you to drink more water.
3. If possible bring the water to a boil and drink it as hot as possible.

Why should you force yourself to drink water? Under the duress of survival you may not even feel any thirst. For most people thirst has been proven to be a poor indicator of water lack. You are better off not to thrust it. You may find that thirst may be all to easily alleviated by a mouthful of cold water when you should have consumed two or three cups full.

Why pass as much as a litre of urine? Regardless of how much you may lose through perspiration and respiration and how readily you may quench your sensation of thirst, you should be taking in enough water for your body to function properly and to flush out your system. Your urine should then be rather pale in colour. If it is bright orange you are likely at an early stage of dehydration.

The usually adequate intake of eight cups of water per day is recycled by that marvelous organ known as the kidney. The less water you ingest below the required minimum, the harder your kidneys have to work.

Can drinking water alleviate hunger? In my personal experience, drinking seemed to reduce hunger pangs to the point where they were hardly noticeable.

What is the relationship of dehydration to fatigue? C.G. Pitts, a Harvard physiologist, tested trained athletes on a treadmill at three and a half miles per hour. One group was given no water, and instructed to walk until exhaustion would not allow them to continue. They lasted about three and a half hours. A second group were allowed to drink as much as they desired. They lasted six hours. A third group were calibrated for their water losses which were replenished at a rate of about a cup every 15 minutes. At seven hours this group terminated their treadmill walk with virtually no sign of fatigue.

This would seem to be a very useful bit of knowledge in any emergency situation. By replenishing lost water frequently you may maintain a high level of energy expenditure without the expected chronic fatigue.

Through maintaining a high level of energy, you can stand the cold better, avert frostbite and hypothermia, and have enough energy to walk. Cold injuries are not improved by thicker blood and a sluggish circulation.

Cold tends to numb the sensation of thirst. The cold air entering the lungs is humidified with moisture from the lungs as it is brought to body temperature. The relative humidity of cold air is usually very low.

The difficulty of drinking cold water and the exertion of cold weather living can create a water demand greater than that imposed by the Sahara desert.

Why should you drink hot water? Water that has just been boiled has been degassed. That is, the bond between certain gasses, especially oxygen and the water molecules have been broken by boiling, and as a result they are more readily absorbed by the body. This not only saves energy, but warms the stomach and averts the bloated feeling that results from drinking large amounts of cold water. Some survival specialists claim that drinking hot water as suggested may increase survival time by at least ten percent.

In survival, if you can sleep well at night and have all the water you need, you have it made.

5. Snow Blindness

Early spring is the time when 'snow blindness' is most apt to occur. The great expanses of reflective snow, combined with the increasing intensity of the sun, direct more than the usual amount of ultraviolet radiation into the eye. Ultraviolet radiation is a form of electromagnetic radiation that has a wavelength between that of visible light and x-rays. It can produce burns, skin cancers and kill many organisms.

The effect of the glare of the sun off the snow is easily understood. The glare itself is enough to cause the eyes to squint against it, making it a relatively minor contributor to snow blindness. What is very insidious about ultra violet radiation is that it can be as intense on an overcast day as it is in glare conditions.

When the cloud cover is thick enough to hide the sun but not thick enough to produce a heavy overcast, the diffused light plus the whiteness of the snow combine to produce an effect that virtually eliminates shadows. As the pupil of the eye opens wider in the shadier condition and strains to detect images in the shadowless terrain, comparatively large amounts of ultraviolet rays are admitted.

If unprotected for a day the eye can sustain enough ultraviolet damage to develop 'snow blindness'. This is a severe intolerance of any form of light entering the eye, rather than true blindness.

If your eyes have been exposed to excessive amounts of ultraviolet radiation, not only from the sun but from welding, electric arcing, ultraviolet lamps and lightning, you will probably not to be aware of it at first. Hours later your will begin to realize something is wrong when your eyes feel as if they are full of grains of sand and begin to water excessively. Smoke of any kind becomes intolerable. Poultices made of used tea bags, or if nothing else, a cold water soaked cloth, will afford some relief at this stage. Eventually any light entering the eye seems to produce a pain that you may feel to be many times worse than any severe headache.

Keep the eyes well covered and the room as dark as possible. You are truly unfortunate if you have no pain killers to take. Doing anything other than lying on your back is out of the question. Without medication, it is too painful to walk, and if you can walk, you are virtually blind until the condition clears up.

The pain may come and go in waves: at each peak only moaning seems to ease the situation somewhat.

If the exposure was light you may be over the pain by next morning. If severe, it may last up to three days.

Eventually snow blindness heals by itself without complications unless you have rubbed your eyes enough to cause an infection. Medication can speed up the healing process in severe cases and help to reduce the pain. The most intelligent approach is knowing how to avoid it simply by using the right type of sunglasses.

The glasses should filter out at least 90 percent of the ultraviolet light or any light below 3200 angstroms. The glasses should be close fitting and have side shields that will keep out any light from the sides. There are many sunglasses that are adequate for driving, but not on high altitude snowfields. In extreme conditions, goggles specifically designed for the purpose are more appropriate. I would consider these glasses an important component of any outdoors first aid kit.

You can improvise goggles out of paper, bark or wood with only a narrow slit to look out of. Darken the inside of the goggles and around the eyes with charcoal if possible. The light entering the eye will then be at more acceptable levels.

B) Diarrhea

The amount of normal water loss in feces is about 100 c.c.'s per day unless it is in the form of diarrhea. Diarrhea is the term used for the condition where fluid stools are passed with abnormal frequency. The condition is recognized as a source of serious water loss that may aggravate dehydration. There are many causes for the condition. It may simply be the body's way of rapidly eliminating material that may be unsuitable for absorption of the intestine. It is often the first sign of any digestive disturbance brought on by any of the following conditions:

Unaccustomed Food: The digestive system will have an established flora for a particular type of eating habit. A sudden change in the type of food eaten, such as a hearty Christmas dinner, may require a significantly different flora.

Stimulating Food: Some foods, such as green vegetables or fruits if taken in excess, will cause the gut to react.

Diseased Condition: Many diseases such as giardiasis, amebiasis and those of the typhoid group, certain kidney, pancreatic and metabolic diseases, cancer and nutritional deficiencies, have diarrhea as one of their major symptoms.

Poisoning: Ingesting many toxic substances such as heavy metal compounds or spoiled food will invariably result in diarrhea.

Drugs: Antibiotics that affect the normal flora of the intestine generally cause diarrhea. Laxatives are compounds that are specifically used to induce the bowel to move. If used excessively or in large doses they may cause a persistent diarrhea known as catharsis habituation.

Excitement: Certain forms of excitement and mental stress can result in short term diarrhea.

If there is a distinct cause for the diarrhea, it must be correctly diagnosed before it can be cured. To treat the diarrhea itself is to treat one of the symptoms and not the cause.

When engaged in backpacking, canoeing or other wilderness activities it is assumed that none but the pertinent causes of diarrhea may apply. There may be a change from a normal diet to one of freeze dried food, more than the normal exertion, psychological stresses such as canoeing a dangerous part of a river or undertaking some risky mountain walking.

These forms of diarrhea usually cease on their own especially if some knowledgeable steps are taken.

1. Prevent dehydration. Any excessive water lost through the gut should be replenished by drinking extra water. A litre and a half of electrolyte replacement solution should be drunk every six hours.
2. Take nothing but water or liquid foods for a day and see if the condition improves. When food is taken, eat bland, un-spiced foods.

C) The Heat Illnesses

1. Introduction

Heat Fatigue

Heat fatigue is primarily induced by not adequately replacing the water lost to heavy sweating. Fatigue should be interpreted as a sign that the water intake is inadequate. The victim should drink enough water for the fatigue to go away.

Heat Cramps

Heat cramps are caused by painful muscle contractions, usually in the abdominal area. Water that should be reserved for other bodily processes is used for heat regulation with a resultant loss of electrolytes. Sodium and potassium depletion result. The treatment is to rest in a cool place and replenish the lost electrolytes.

Heat Exhaustion

This condition is more severe than heat cramps and is implicated in the rare death. Having ignored heat cramps, the victim now suffers from nausea, headache, dizziness and weakness. Any further dehydration can actually bring on a form of shock. The gradual diminishing of the blood volume in circulation produces a shock like state where pallor and a cold and clammy skin is associated with great weakness. The victim is often irritable and argumentative.

The treatment is rest in a cool place and to drink lots of water or replacement electrolytes. Give drinks slowly and soak down the skin to keep it moist and cool.

Heat Stroke

This is a very serious condition characterized by a high body temperature (40°C) that may lead to a severe depletion of body fluids and damage to the nervous system. This is due to an overloading or hindering of the function of the sweat glands. The condition is often brought on when the external temperatures are higher than the body temperature. There is a characteristic lack of sweating with the victim exhibiting signs of being chilled and running a high fever. The skin may be dry and red.

The treatment is to keep the victim in the shade, remove most of the clothing, wet the body down and speed up the cooling by evaporation by fanning as well as the usual replenishment of electrolytes. This condition could sometimes be mistaken for a heart attack.

2%	Thirst
2.5%	A 25% loss of physical efficiency accompanied by considerable metal deterioration. Significant judgement impairment may occur before noticeable fatigue sets in in some individuals.
3%	Heat Cramps
5%	Heat Exhaustion-the body stops sweating
7.5%	Hallucinations
10%	Heat Stroke-permanent damage may result within a few hours unless water is restored. This condition can be lethal to many people.
12.5%	The individual is unable to swallow. Water loss has to be made up intravenously to save the victim's life.
15-25%	A point of no return can be reached within this range for all but the exceptional individual.

2. Water Loss

The following is a rough guide to the symptoms related to water deficiency by percentages of body weight:

Avenues of Water Loss

A healthy, moderately active person under normal circumstances would take in daily about 1450 cubic centimetres of water and beverages and another 1150 cubic centimetres of food and internal metabolism. One hundred grams each of fat, carbohydrate and protein produce 107, 55 and 41 cubic centimetres of water each respectively. This makes a total of 2.6 litres.

This is balanced by the amounts eliminated by the kidneys (1,500 c.c.), skin (700 c.c.), lungs (300 c.c.) and the feces (100 c.c.).

Urination

The amount of urine excreted in 24 hours varies greatly depending on the amounts of fluids drunk and the amount lost in other ways. Under normal conditions, the kidneys may account for about two thirds of the total that is eliminated. However, when the body needs water for other purposes such as temperature regulation, the lungs and keeping the skin supple, the urinary output is reduced. Some authorities claim that the barest minimum that should be eliminated from the bladder is 500 c.c. daily, so that the undesirable by-products of metabolism are carried away. In survival and in the stresses and exertions involved in wilderness living, the minimum should be set at two or three times this amount. A simple method of monitoring water intake is to eliminate at least a litre of urine daily, regardless of what losses may be incurred by other means.

The urine should be a light straw color; any stronger color is an indication to increase water intake.

Diuretics

A diuretic is a substance that causes the kidney's to excrete more urine than normal under the circumstances. Diuretics play a vital role in managing some medical conditions, however, their inadvertent ingestion may contribute to dehydration in some circumstances. Coffee and alcohol are diuretics. If you attempt to maintain fluid intake with either, under some conditions you may only make matters worse by causing the body to excrete what is already in short supply.

Respiration

Under normal conditions the lungs may need from 300 c.c.'s to a litre a day to moisturize the air in the lungs. It has already been mentioned that cold air, with its low relative humidity, may require up to a half cup of water per hour for this one purpose alone.

Loss through the Skin

The healthy skin must give off a certain amount of moisture to function properly. This may be termed insensible perspiration because it is not felt or noticed. The body uses the mechanism of sensible perspiration for cooling the body: the all too familiar sweating. Under normal conditions this may account for a third of the moisture given off by the body. Under conditions of severe heat stress a phenomenal amount of water is given off by the skin.

Sweating also tends to deplete the body of essential chemicals such as sodium and potassium, the excessive loss of which results in painful muscle contractions known as cramps. If allowed to continue, depletion can lead to heat exhaustion or heat stroke.

Water alone will not improve the situation much once electrolytes are depleted. It is crucial that electrolyte concentrations be maintained for the proper functioning of the body. If electrolytes are low, the kidneys will excrete water to compensate. The water will then be ineffective as a means to relieve conditions brought on by electrolyte deficiency.

3. Burns, Scalds and Fluid Loss

A burn victim may die from burn shock brought on by the loss of fluid from the circulation by a large burn. A large burn would involve at least 18 percent or more surface area in a normally healthy adult or 9 percent or more in children and the elderly. A rule of thumb for estimating the size of a burn is "Wallace's Rule of Nines". This states that various regions of the body are multiple of 9 percent. The head and neck is 9%; each arm 9%; the back 18%; the front 18; each lower limb 18%.

Where transfusion by blood plasma or plasma substitutes is not possible in the field (a dire need in the case of a 54% burn) it is very important to give fluids by mouth as soon as possible in small frequent drinks. For each 9% of body surface burned give 60 c.c. or two ounces every 20 minutes for 3 hours and half the amount every 20 minutes for the next 16 hours. If possible use a quarter teaspoon of sodium bicarbonate for each cup of water; in hot climates a quarter teaspoon of salt for each cup of water used or use the electrolyte replacement solution.

D) Knife Cuts: How to Avoid Them

Outdoor living and survival in the spruce-moose forest, at times depends heavily on three important cutting tools: the knife, the axe and the saw.

Although it is definitely possible, you have to be quite negligent to cut yourself with a Swede saw.

It is obvious that cuts from an axe could be serious because of the bone shattering violence with which the tool is used. If you have any wits about you at all, one near miss usually instills a cautious from of mind with regard to that particular way of misusing an axe. Combining some healthy respect with some good training should make axe cuts virtually non-existent. In some 25 years of bushwhacking I doubt if I have seen more than a half dozen axe cuts; two were truly horrendous.

For every minute that you may use some form of axe you may end up using a knife for ten. A well chosen, unobtrusive knife is capable of helping you meet your survival needs in the spruce-moose forest at any time of year. The knife can also provide hours of everyday enjoyment through carving and crafting.

Quality Training

There was a time when I accepted knife cuts as inevitable in my students as part of their learning process. However, over the years I realized that the number of cuts was closely related to the quality of training given to the learning knife user.

Essentially, the first objective is to instill a healthy respect for the knife by recounting the various gory ways that a cut may occur. The second step is to systematically instill the techniques that prevent cuts, especially on how to apply any force behind the cutting edge so that any inadvertent follow through will miss all parts of the body. The learner should always be asking "what may happen if a slip occurs", until this becomes an automatic reaction. When there is any doubt about what may happen then the cut must be made with great care and attentiveness.

A training device used to demonstrate how to safely make any complex cut with a knife is the Try Stick. This could be a knot free stick of broom handle thickness that is the length of the extended arm.

Cut Safely

There are two main considerations in using a knife. One is making your cuts efficient with a minimum of awkwardness. The other is to make the cut with perfect safety. Usually the two are not one and the same. To make a cut safely, efficiently and fast can result in some unusual contortions that may seem awkward at first. Extensive knife use may prove that there is only one perfect way to execute a given cut safely and efficiently in a given circumstance. The sooner you learn to make that cut the better as far as your safety in remote wilderness is concerned.

If you cut yourself while learning how to use a knife, the only excuse you really have is that you have obviously broken some rule. You can't say that the knife slipped, the wood split or broke unexpectedly and so on.

In all aspects of living (not necessarily confining oneself to wilderness camping and survival) it is likely more sensible to first master the technique of avoiding injury rather than focusing on the methods of patching up after the fact. The more you may know on handling the knife, the less you will have to worry about handling knife cuts.

But human nature, being what it is, a wise person should also know enough first aid to properly handle any cut in the field that may result from any tool you may be using, be it a pen knife or a power saw.

IV. Wilderness Travel Skills

A) Leading Your Group

1. Travel Hints

1. During your climb, establish a steady rhythmic pace.
2. To help conserve energy, do not swing arms unnecessarily.
3. Look for level foot placements.
4. Ascending 400 metres/hour is a good pace. You may ascend 600 metres if you are in good physical condition.
5. Try to place your whole foot on ground rather than just your toe. The upward thrust then comes from the thigh and stomach muscles rather than the calf.
6. Take short steps on unsure ground.
7. While travelling in groups do not get ahead of the leader or fall too far behind. The slowest moving person should be behind the leader and everyone should follow their pace.
8. At obstacles, pause long enough to keep the group together.
9. Do not crowd the person in front of you. This invites injury from snapped back branches.
10. The leader should be made aware of any problems with equipment etc. The group should keep together while adjustments are made.
11. Develop the habit of looking in all directions around yourself. Look behind yourself every few hundred feet of travel. Frequently scan the skyline and the distance of visual penetration into the bush. The moment you

enter a clearing completely scan its perimeter: you may see a bear in time. You may not feel as lost on the return journey, and it is easier to maintain your orientation in this way. Most people see the toes of their boots and a patch of ground extending a few metres in front of them.

12. Sort frequent rests are better than infrequent long ones. An important part of navigation is to keep track by pacing. Stop and rest 10 minutes every kilometre (1000 paces where 2 steps equal 1 pace).

River Crossing

1. Crossing on Foot

If you are in a hurry to cross a river, you are asking for trouble before you have even stepped into the water. Never cross flooded rivers - the risk is too great. You should never cross a river when trees are floating down it or boulders are heard rolling in it. Wait until the river subsides. The character of a river may change completely with a few inches rise in water level. Each time the depth doubles, the velocity also doubles. On each doubling, the water can shift objects sixty times greater in weight previous to the doubling. Skill at crossing rivers is acquired through experience and practice. Those who need to cross rivers should gain the necessary experience by practicing in a river or part of a river where it is absolutely safe to do so. You first have to learn how to overcome the feeling of dizziness caused by the moving water. With practice, most people become used to this feeling. The middle of a stream that is trying to sweep your feet away is a poor place to start getting use to this feeling.

Choice of Ford

1. You should take time to study a considerable stretch of the river to find a safe crossing.
2. Find a high spot to survey large sections of river to get a better appraisal on the speed, turbulence, width of the river, and the nature of its bottom.
3. The river bank often gives clues as to what the bottom may be composed of. A smooth gravel bottom is the most desirable.
4. Look for a widening in the river as the water will usually be shallower and flow slower.
5. There is often shallow water just before a change in gradient of a river.
6. A river that breaks up into many braids is usually easier to cross.
7. Avoid curves as the water is deeper and stronger on the outside of the bends.
8. A point halfway between a bend and its reverse is a good place to consider for your crossing.
9. The river below the crossing should also be safe. In the event that your footing is lost, lost equipment or drowning could result. A safe run out will facilitate any rescue.
10. The entrance and exit of a ford should be easy to navigate.
11. The nature of a river bottom can change beyond recognition in a short time. Assume nothing. Treat a familiar crossing as if you are seeing it for the first time.
12. The nature of a river bottom can change beyond recognition in a short time. Assume nothing. Treat a familiar crossing as if you are seeing it for the first time.
13. In the mountains, the rise of water level can fluctuate considerably. Rain in catchment areas results in a rise

shortly after. Streams fed by melting snow will be at their lowest in the early morning.
14. Camping and starving on a riverbank may be far more desirable than death by drowning.

Before Crossing

1. Do Not Remove Footwear. Without footwear it is far easier to lose your balance and injure your feet. It is permissible to remove socks.
2. Pants, however, should either be tight fitting or be removed because they offer a great deal of drag.
3. Heavy coats, parkas, etc., should not be worn as they will prove cumbersome when wet.
4. Undo the waistband on your pack, so it will be easier to drop you pack. Crossing with one shoulder strap undone will contribute to your imbalance.
5. Close up your pack to make it as waterproof as possible. Enclosing everything in waterproof plastic bags, especially sleeping bags, will enable your pack to provide flotation in the event of a mishap.
6. In deep water, a pack may be better held in front of you. On your back it may not hold your head above water.

Crossing Alone

1. A pole can be used on the upstream side to help to maintain your balance. Use a pole two to two and a half metres long. Place the pole slightly ahead and upstream so that the water forces the tip against the bottom. Lift the pole clear of the water to a new position and then move up to it. Present your body sideways to the current to minimize the drag.
2. Systematically feel for the bottom with your feet.
3. Avoid looking down at the water swirling around you. Fix your gaze onto the point you are walking toward.

4. The crossing may be made easier by allowing the current to carry you a little diagonally downstream.
5. How deep you can go depends on the swiftness of the current. You may reach a point where it is impossible to maintain your footing.
6. If your footing is lost and you feel yourself being swept away, turn to face downstream and take big strides to regain some control, to get past obstacles and to return to shore. If you are being carried by the water, lead with your feet so that you can fend off rocks and boulders. When you are crossing alone it is especially important that your run out is safe.

Group Crossing

1. A green pole up to 8 centimetres in diameter can be used for groups of 3 to 6 people.
2. The pole is clasped firmly against the chest with the upstream arm under the pole and the downstream arm over the pole.
3. If only a thin pole is available everyone could interlock arms.
4. The weakest people are placed in the middle of the group.
5. No one should let go in case of a slip because each person contributes to the safety of the whole group.
6. The pole must always be kept in line with the flow of the water. Never turn in midstream.
7. If a decision is made to retreat and walking backwards is impossible, then one individual at a time should try changing position or direction.

2. Rope Crossing

1. A rope twice as long as the river is wide is required.

2. The most adept person crosses with one end of the rope at a point where a safe run out will allow them to be swept back to shore with the assistance of the rope.
3. A loop is made in the middle of the rope and the second person to cross is tied around the waist or chest.
4. The first person ties the end to an immovable object, or at worst his own waist. A third person ties the rope's end around his or her waist and plays it out as needed. The first person takes it up. If the first person stands a ways upstream, should the person crossing stumble, the belayer (first person) will more or less be swung into shore.
5. When the rope is submerged, there is considerable drag put on it by the current. Remaining members could go as far as possible into the water and hold the rope above their heads or set up tripods for this purpose.
6. The person crossing should endeavour to make it without being pulled. A pull by either the first or third person will surely pull them off balance and then the two of them have far more work to do.
7. The first person to cross should build a good fire for those coming across to get warmed up and dried. A steam bath on both sides may be a good idea.

Rope Stretched Across River

This should only be used as a convenience where a very shallow river is crossed frequently and perhaps has a slippery bottom. In dangerous crossings, the rope will put you under severe strain when your foothold is lost. My Australian and New Zealand sources of information indicate this method has resulted in many fatalities.

Being Towed Across

Especially in the case of weak members of the party, it is recommended that a deep pool is preferable to a swift rapid. Buoyant packs could be used to advantage for added support.

Where a large group has to cross and the water is deep but not exceptionally swift a coracle-raft ferry may be appropriate.

C) Effects of Travelling at Higher Elevations

The higher the elevation the harder the lungs, heart and circulatory system have to work and therefore the greater the chance of heart attack for some people. Time is required to adjust to the new elevation. Some individuals may require at least two weeks to acclimatize to higher elevations. The effects may range from irritability, dullness and lethargy to loss of judgement and reasoning. All of the effects of increased altitude work against survival in the event of an emergency.

At 6,000 metres (18,000 feet) half of the normal volume of oxygen is present. The brain begins to show the effects of oxygen starvation. There is not enough oxygen to go around. Digestion will rob oxygen from the muscles and the brain. Exertion will rob from the digestive system and the brain. High elevation travel is very demanding. The effect of altitude manifests itself in headache, shortness of breath, insomnia, lack of appetite, and nausea. High altitude living is not within the scope of this article.

1. Conditions Resulting in High Altitude Pulmonary Edema

If proper acclimatization procedure has not been taken, after a day or two at 3000 metres (9000 feet) elevation the following symptoms may occur.

a. Unusual tiredness
b. Shortness of breath, dry cough and pneumonia like symptoms.
c. Heart Failure

Treatment: Immediate and rapid decent. Administer oxygen.

2. Conditions Above Tree Line

It is only within the scope of this article to suggest that inexperienced persons refrain from excursions to high elevations until they are intelligently, mentally and physically prepared. Above the tree line there is little fuel, few plants, few identifiable features, sudden and violent weather changes, scant shelter from the wind, glaciers and on top of this, there is a rarified oxygen atmosphere that tends to make some people giddy. To this add snow and another group of hazards have to be understood:

- Crevices and cavities on the lee side
- Rocks absorbing heat and melting snow to make cavities
- Water flowing under the snow
- Avalanches
- Ultraviolet radiation: its effect is stronger at higher elevations because there is less filtering of sunlight by the atmosphere, particularly of ultraviolet rays.

Glaciers and snowfields may reflect three quarters of the ultraviolet so that the effect is nearly doubled. Ultraviolet is not significantly filtered out on overcast days so that you can still experience a burn and snow blindness.

Lapse Rate

A 2 or 3 °C temperature drop per 35 metres (100 feet) elevation is usually experienced in ascending a mountain.

Wind

Winds generally blow more strongly at higher elevations.

Visibility

In heavy rain, fog and thick cloud, you may have to refer to a compass frequently. Under these conditions it is easy to lose all sense of time and have night come on before you realize it, especially if a watch is not carried.

V. Wilderness Environment

A) Annoying Insects

Canada's northland is well known for its biting insects. Not only are flies a distracting annoyance but they may drive some people to madness with their bites. These bites may become seriously infected.

A serious menace is the omnipresent black fly (simuliidae). These flies have the habit of crawling inside pant cuffs, shirt sleeves and open collars. They have a painless bite which may go undetected for some time. The bites soon itch and are further aggravated by scratching. The resultant sores may then become infected and are slow to heal. All openings in your clothing should be snugly buttoned down. If repellent is used, an effective barrier can be created by applying it a few inches under the cuffs or collar before buttoning up. Boot laces should be extra long to tie the pant cuffs tightly around the ankle. The cuff should be gathered at the back of the leg, as there it is always higher than the rest of the cuff. Tied at the back it allows more room to bend the knee.

When no repellent is available the simplest method of dealing with mosquitoes and black flies is by using a smudge. A gallon can is sufficient to make an effective and portable smudge. A smoldering fire can be maintained in the can very effectively with dried animal dung such as horse, moose or elk. Otherwise punky (rotten dry) wood is useful. The density of the smoke is maintained by adding moss, leaves, grass or humus. Such a smudge carried at the head of the line will make life more tolerable for at least a dozen people.

In a tent certain fungi such as the false tinder fungus can be ignited to produce a similar effect on a smaller scale. Outside of the smudge or smoke type methods there are really no effective natural means for repelling insects.

B) Bears are Dangerous

"A Bear-wise person, upon meeting a bear continues to go about his business, being careful that his business carries him away from the bear".   M. Kochanski

1. The Black Bear

The bear, a fairly recent development in the animal kingdom, is a close relative of the dog. Once very common in many parts of the world, it is now mainly restricted to remote areas, as a result of encounters with man and rifle. Virtually all of Canada is still blessed by the presence of the black bear especially in areas with high wilderness recreation potential. This large, rather numerous animal has readily adapted to the presence of people, sometimes much to the consternation of those wishing to use the same areas it inhabits.

W.H. McDonald in his article "Bears and People" in Volume 8, issue Number 4 of Land, Forest, Wildlife, Winter 1965-66, classified black bears into three broad groups:

1. The Most Common: The ordinary wild shy bear that has detected you long before you have had a chance to spot it. It has the good sense to avoid all humans as much as possible.
2. The Less Common: The park or camp bear: the scavenger whose native shyness has been lost with its closer association with humans. These bears are hopefully becoming more rare - they can be a thorough nuisance.
3. The Least Common: The basically 'vicious' bear which will kill or maim for a variety of (perhaps) understandable, or even valid reasons. The bears include the injured, old, sick, malformed, starving, wounded, the protective mother with cubs or the bereaved mother.

2. A Brief Natural History of The Bear

Terminology: A boar is an adult male bear. A sow is an adult female bear. The cub is a young bear with tracks 15 centimetres or less long.

Conception: These normally solitary animals pair for a short time during mating season from late June to early July. The female will remain in heat from late May to mid August. A nursing bear will not conceive so a female usually bears cubs every second year, unless lactation is disturbed or the cubs are lost.

Gestation: 220 days.

Basic Safe Travel and Boreal Survival

Birth: Usually one cub is born on the first birth to a sow. Sometimes as many as four are born to a litter. The newborn cub may weight from 150 to 300 grams, and be from 20 to 23 centimetres long. The naked, blind and toothless cub is usually born sometime in January or February.

At 40 Days: The rapidly growing cub now measures 30 centimetres, weighs about a kilogram, has grown a coat and has cut his first teeth.

Leaves Winter Den: Sow and cub leave their den in April or early May. The weight of the cub is now almost two kilograms.

Enter Fall Den: Sow and cub will den up again at or before the first severe cold snap and heavy snowfall. The summer's foraging will have brought the cub's weight up to 13 or 14 kilograms. A cub 5 1/2 to 6 months old could survive the loss of his mother. Generally, bears in northern climates will have a dormant period of at least three months even in mild winters.

Spring Exit: The cub is definitely not able to forage for itself. It may weigh from 25 to 45 kilograms. Mother and off-spring generally part company in the second year. A lactating mother usually will not mate.

Maturity: Both females and males attain sexual maturity in four to five years. A male will attain full growth in about seven years. All females are fully mature at 5 1/2 years. Sows with cubs represent about 10 percent of the total bear population. The approximate mean weight for males is about 100 to 150 kilograms and 65 to 70 kilograms for females. There is usually equal numbers of females and males in the population.

Territory: Bears usually remain in the same area from year to year: emigration is uncommon. A boar may occupy an area of 30 square kilometres and a sow an area of 10 square kilometres. There is no overlap of areas occupied by males. Females overlap male areas and even other female areas with no conflict.

There may be one bear per square mile of good bear habitat (state of Washington). Preferred habitat is mixed coniferous-deciduous forest.

Colour Phases: The familiar black is a dominant colour for bears. Depending on where bears are geographically located the populations vary from totally black to about half black and half brown. I have seen a few bears with distinctive white markings on the chest, and which have a different coloration on the back and the stomach.

Nocturnal Habits: Bears are most active from dusk to dawn. At peak berry season they are about at all hours.

Eating Habits: Bears are omnivorous. The greater part of their diet is vegetation; berries of all sorts rate highly. Where vegetable food is scarce, there is a greater dependency on flesh. Carrion is the preferred form of meat. As bears like to drink frequently, they must stay reasonably close to water.

Part of understanding bears and their habitats is knowing what they tend to eat. Depending on geography and other circumstances a wild bear may eat about 10% animal matter (fish, fowl and mammal), about 5 to 10% insect material (such as carpenter ants and wasp nests), and about 10 to 15% inert material (such as wood fiber, evergreen needles and dirt), with the remaining 65% to 75% being vegetable material (leaves, blossoms, berries, roots, grasses, lichens, fungi, etc.).

Life Expectancy: In the wild a bear may live to be 10 years old, with some bears reaching age 30.

Coat Condition: A bear's coat is at its best just after leaving its den in the spring and just at entering the den in the fall. The coat condition for most bears studied is an indicator of general physical condition. A poor coat just after leaving the den and on entering it might be considered an indication of poor physical condition.

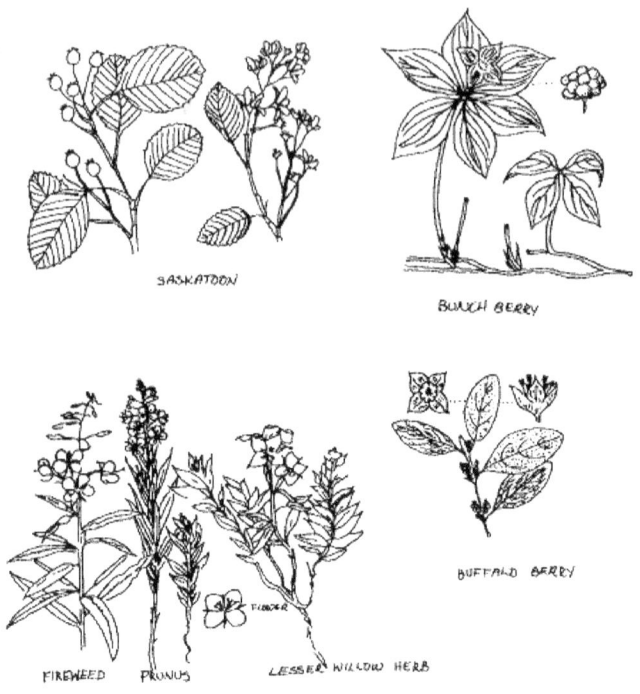

Common and Typical Plants Eaten By Bears

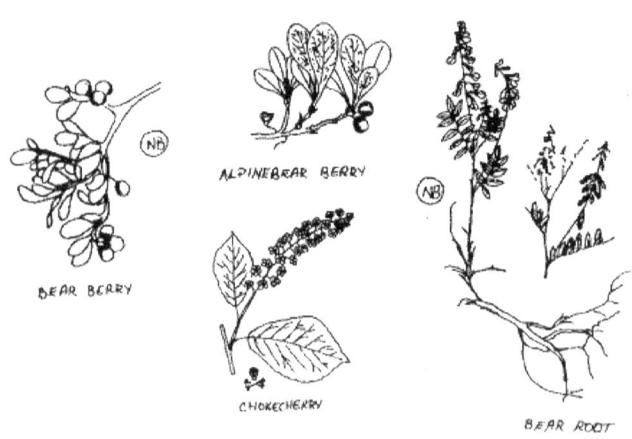

Common and Typical Plants Eaten By Bears

3. Your Food ... Your Bear

The following statement will summarize the biggest problem with bears:

"PEOPLE FOOD PLUS BEARS -- MEANS -- TROUBLE FOR PEOPLE"

With the increased numbers of people presently using the bush, there is a greater opportunity for bears to sample human food through their own opportunism or through intentionally being fed. A bear's single-mindedness about getting at food it detects will leave you with little opportunity to get out of the bruin's way. If no one would ever feed a bear, or if garbage dumps were made inaccessible or unattractive to bears, encounters would likely be rare. There are other circumstances where you may experience a problem with bears, but these are by far the most common ones that affects campers.

The most effective way of dealing with bears, in my opinion, is to become thoroughly versed in the natural history of the animal. The more you know about the animal, the more likely you are to act correctly when encountering a bear.

The bear is an intelligent, adaptable animal and one of the greatest opportunists around. It learns very fast, especially if that learning has something to do with food. One of its most noteworthy characteristics is its persistence when it is after food. It does not take a bear long to come to the conclusion that when a person is around, food is nearby, and therefore public campgrounds are worth patrolling as a good source of tasty food.

When a bear knows you have food, he immediately assumes that he has every right to it, and in his single-mindedness to get at it he is often interpreted to be very contemptuous of the rightful owner and very impatient with anything that stands in his way. Before you try to deter bruin from taking your food with sticks and stones, think of how a bear raiding a beehive will endure thousands of stings to get its fill of honey.

The intentional feeding of bears along roadsides is a gross act of ignorance as it may result in injury to other wilderness users and the necessity to destroy the bear that has become accustomed to the handouts. The feeder may simply be fined, but the bear may pay the ultimate price.

4. Minimizing Bear and Food Problems

Never store food in a tent. This includes potato chips and chocolate bars. Unopened cans are no guarantee that the contents are undetectable to bears. I once saw a can of unopened sardines chewed up into a round ball about the diameter of a 50 cent piece.

Use odor-tight containers where possible. Avoid the use of odoriferous foods that may tend to smell up your equipment or clothing. Sardines and bacon may be prime culprits here. Never cook bacon in or near a tent because the fabric will retain the odor. The bears may not distinguish between canvas and bacon rind and their consequent investigation could prove costly and alarming. If any clothing has been soiled by odoriferous food (like sardines), keep the clothing with the food. If you expect to spend a lot of time in bear habitat, choose food with this point in mind. Freeze dried foods may be the most appropriate. Bears are after sweet and smelly foods more than anything else. Honey, jam, and strong smelling candies are apt to be zeroed in on by bruin. Children accustomed to carrying chewing gum or candies may be roughed up.

Cook food far enough away from you tent so that is does not acquire any cooking smell. Try to have your cooking, dishwashing and other food related chores done by early evening, well before sunset. Bears tend to get more active around dusk and may present more of a problem when attracted by late evening cooking smells. Cooking odors may carry further under early evening conditions.

Wash your dishes immediately after use. Pour the dishwater into the ashes at the edge of your fire or dispose of it some distance from camp. Store your dishes with your food.

Wash out tin cans thoroughly to cut down any bear attractive odors. The smell of burning garbage may carry further than the smell of an unwashed can. Bears that are familiar with the smell of burning garbage dumps may zero in on your camp from miles away. In campouts with larger groups it is advisable to package garbage well and haul it to the nearest dump rather than incinerating it locally. Carefully handled polyethylene bags (4 to 6 mil thickness) should effectively seal in food odors. Clear polyethylene has been observed to make food packaged in it virtually undetectable to bears. Normal garbage bags may be too thin. It is possible that bears associate the black bags with something edible.

You may consider avoiding altogether the areas where bears may have had the opportunity to associate humans with food.

When fishing, be careful to confine any contact with the fish to your fingertips. A bear that is following you may only be after the fish in your creel, or the smell of fish on your clothing.

Leave no garbage whatsoever for bears to get into. Stow your garbage with the same care that you stow your food. It's more smelly, so it may be a stronger attraction for bears. It may be wise to adopt a wilderness use lifestyle that produces no garbage.

5. Characteristics Almost Human

A close study of the bear personality reveals that it shares many traits with us, thereby making it easier for us to understand it better.

Besides being an intelligent, adaptable opportunist, the bear has other characteristics that are easy to comprehend. People closely associated with bears feel they are cunning and that they have a good memory. They are one of the few animals that display a sense of humour, a sense of curiosity, a sense of revenge if wronged, and a sense of remorse (as with a mother that has lost her cub). On occasion, they seem to be sensitive to a loss of face when they have been startled or when their personal space is disturbed in their own territory. Their affinity for sweet tasting food is another characteristic they share with humans.

Although some people tend to explain the dangerous aspect of bears by saying that they are unpredictable, I would tend to agree with Andy Russell that the term "unpredictable" is just a poor way of saying "misunderstood". If you take the time to try to understand the bear and its personality you may find that it is quite predictable in its actions and any unhappy encounter could be either a case of bad luck or could be attributed to someone else's mishandling of the animal. In its "wild" state, the bear is a naturally shy animal even though it has only two enemies: another bear or a person with a rifle or trap. One attribute of their intelligence is that bears will prefer to avoid any encounter where they are not exactly sure of the consequences.

6. What a Bear Might Worry About

If we were to become a bear for a while we would likely find that our greatest fear would be connected with our own kind (which should also be the case, perhaps, with us humans).

A male bear finding its territory violated by a smaller bear may kill it and make a meal of it. A male bear will readily kill and eat a cub. A mother bear will viciously attack any bear that comes to close to her cubs. She may even attack another mother and adopt her cubs. Male bears are somewhat anti-social but may tolerate each other at garbage dumps. In the forest they seem to respect each other's territory religiously.

It is little wonder that an intelligent bear hastily takes flight when it encounters something it can't see. This fear of one bear for another may partly explain the often encountered mad dash to get away and the (defensive) attack on occasion.

D.R. Wooldridge of Simon Fraser University, Burnaby, B.C. has developed a very effective polar bear deterrent by using an amplified and enriched tape recording of a polar bear threat roar. Something similar may be effective with the black bear.

Mother and Cub

7. Action in the Event of Encountering a Bear

In travelling through the bush, your greatest concern is in encountering a bear and surprising it in such a way that it feels its only defense is to attack. Compared to humans the bear has poor eyesight, has very keen hearing and possesses a superior sense of smell. If it has to act on a split second's warning, on what it thinks it sees, it might identify you as another bear. There is possibly an imaginary boundary around the animal within which the expected response will be an immediate direct attack first, with positive identification second.

Robert Sommer in his book "Personal Space" describes the phenomenon of personal space as being an invisible boundary surrounding a person or animal into which the uninvited, unfamiliar, or the unaccepted are not allowed. A closely related, more easily measured boundary that affects or is affected by personal space is the spacing between members of the same species known as individual distance. Individual distance and personal space interact to establish the distribution of the animals. A well known example are the storks of Amsterdam that have been observed from time immemorial to space themselves no closer than a certain interval when uncrowded and at a precise minimum interval when crowded. Violation of the animal's personal space may in itself be irritating and may invite aggressive behaviour or attack.

Any study as to the size of the personal space of bears has not been located thus far, and likely such a study has not been done as yet. The personal space of a mother with cubs may be considerably greater than that of a single bear. Likely, if you are within 20 metres of a bear you are encroaching upon its personal space. With a mother bear and cubs you would do well to stay 100 metres away. As yet I have not found any data to support these figures, and at present they are strictly conjecture on my part.

Your problem is to stay out of the bears personal space. You might do this by watching where you are going and by being particularly vigilant when you see a bear sign. Watch for scat, profuse bear forage such as berries and bear root, and especially for ground that is rooted up in the search for bear root (Alpine hedysarum). Knowing what bears eat is important. Do you know what bear root looks like? You should continually scan the penetration-of-sight distance ahead and to both sides of your direction of travel. You may also give the bear forewarning especially when travelling at night, by making a noise such as wearing a bell or beating on a pot, or perhaps turning on a noisy transistor radio. Resorting to such ploys may make your fellow travellers strongly hope you are eaten by a bear. You may still have some problems if you are in dense bush, if it is very windy, if you are near noisy water, or if the bear is sleeping.

If you have startled a bear, your first reaction should be to STAND STILL AND REMAIN ABSOLUTELY MOTIONLESS. This will give the bear time to sort out his confusion and to not react until he has identified you by scent, hearing and sight. After a minute or so, you may reassure the bear of your lack of aggressive intentions by speaking softly to let it know exactly where you are. Its likely reaction will be to leave the vicinity faster than you can.

Because bears use smell for guidance and warning, the wise person attempts to maintain a position upwind of any bear encountered. By this means any scent is carried to the bear and its curiosity is thereby often satisfied.

8. Action in the Event of a Charge

There are two forms of charge:

The Sudden or True Charge

This charge may be triggered if you have entered the animal's personal space so that the bear reacts instantly to your intrusion. The charge usually is accompanied by the sound of the jaws snapping, or by growling and by raised hackles and flattened ears. A vertical, head-high posture is usually the first part of the threat display of most bear species. Here you may expect some rough treatment. The worst reaction is to attempt to run.

It was at one time considered the best action to drop to the ground and assume a tight fetal position (the passive, feigned sleep or unconsciousness position with the vulnerable stomach protected by drawing the knees up to the chin and the neck at least partly protected with the interlocked fingers) or laying flat on your stomach, with your hands interlocked and covering the back of your neck, passively accepting anything the bear might deal out and laying very still and quiet.

Where there is absolutely no other alternative, no weapon, no tree to climb, if the encounter is very sudden, or in the instance where children encounter a bear, the fetal protective position may be the last resort. It may take considerable nerve to remain completely passive. It may be advisable to drill children who are unable to defend themselves effectively in reacting to a bear charge by assuming this position instantly. The leader should pretend to be a bear and test the participants ability to maintain the stance. A child would have to be thoroughly convinced that the fetal protective position is the best way to cope with a bear attack.

Opinions are changing, however. Although we may attribute many human-like traits to a bear we may be going too far in some cases. It is perhaps natural to think that any resistance whatever may infuriate the animal more and make matters worse. However, being completely passive allows the bear to do whatever it wishes. You may fare better by fighting back. For example there are camp cooks who have effectively dealt with bears for years, and who swear by the effectiveness of a good baseball bat. It seems that those who have chosen to fight back feel that they have fared better than if they had taken a passive stance.

There is a possibility that a standing human may have the general appearance of presenting what is known as the standing-bear challenge. It may be appropriate to assume some other posture.

The Sham Charge

If you have encountered a bear, stood perfectly still and have given it the opportunity to determine where and what you are, the bear may still charge in your direction. Put away your 357 Magnum, as you will needlessly kill or maim the bear and then get your just reward to boot. You will likely find that the bear will brush by you and keep going. Wounding the bear could result in a bad or lethal mauling. With the sham charge the bear is only paying you back for the fright you gave it.

9. On Bear Trail

Bears are very fond of trails. It is as if they have tender feet. If you encounter a bear on the trail and it does not react in the expected way, it likely means that it is your turn to get off the trail today. However, be very slow and methodical and continue to face the bear. Talk quietly, continually and soothingly. Assume a lower profile by stooping. Sudden movements are disconcerting to bears. If you find yourself being observed while walking, do not stop or speed up, but smoothly change your direction away from the bear. It is not a good idea to set up camp on any animal path, especially ones that might be used by bears. Any unusually distinct trail could very likely be a bear trail.

10. Bear Crossing Path (Mother with Cubs)

If you notice a bear crossing your path ahead of you, it is time for a break. It may be a mother with cubs and with their usual cavorting, wrestling and examining of everything, they may be a hundred metres or so behind her. There is nothing that is more maternally protective than a mother bear, especially one with her first cub. The frolicsome youngsters are irresistibly attractive but an alert audience and a quiet withdrawal is desirable. Keep a wary eye open for the mother bear and the relative positions of all participants. Adult males often look upon cubs as good eating and the mother will attack an adult male with murderous fury if he gets too near the brood. If you find yourself within the much larger personal space that is found around a mother and her cubs, you may pay dearly for your lack of vigilance. Remain very still, retreat very methodically and very quietly. Be instantly ready to assume the stomach protective, neck protective fetal position.

11. For the Injured or Senile Bear (Passive Reaction May Not Be The Answer)

In its precarious relationship with its own kind, and in encounters with humans and our trapping devices, a bear may become maimed or crippled in some way. You may also come across an old bear who has patronized his fair share of garbage dumps. Bears with teeth or claws missing or which are otherwise debilitated may have to be more opportunistic and may have to depend heavily on depredation to make up for their injuries. These bears usually look very lank and bedraggled. If you see a bear in this state, you are likely going to have some problems with its persistence. In this case you may have to climb a tree or use whatever other resistance you can muster.

Bears injured by gunshot or trap seem to take on a vengeful attitude toward people and our property, and often cause considerable damage that cannot be attributed to any other apparent reason. If you hear of a "gut-shot" bear in your area, it might be very prudent of you to leave immediately unless you are capable of defending yourself.

12. Park Bears

The increasing incidents with bears may be the result of the increasing numbers of people taking to the parks, many of whom are unschooled in the bear etiquette. Some park bears seem to develop a "contempt" for people. Their association with humans while marauding for human food has likely resulted in have to endure some stone and stick throwing and yelling. If you want to avoid this type of bear, you may have to stay out of parks. You may also unexpectedly encounter park bears outside the park if the Park Authorities live-trap nuisance bears and release them in remote areas. On a heavily used pack trail, how are you to know that just a half hour ago someone pelted and aggravated that bear that is standing in front of you now?

13. Mating Season

Bears tend to be out of sorts and short-tempered in the peak mating season, which is in June and early July. While otherwise preoccupied, they may be a little oblivious to what is going on around them. Being disturbed at this time may elicit a stronger than usual response from a male if you are misconstrued as a rival.

14. Bear Haunts, Kills and Carrion

If you come across a bear-kill or carrion, you may have to be as cautious as if encountering a mother and her cubs. It is well known that the grizzly looks upon this as one of the worst kinds of intrusion and black bears seem to be of a similar mind. If you notice great amounts of fresh droppings, especially in heavy berry patches (bearberry, Saskatoon, choke cherries, blue-berries and huckleberries), torn up logs, bark ripped off spruce (for the sap), and signs of digging for bear root (Alpine hedysarum), you may be in a bear's favorite haunt and it may not appreciate the intrusion. It may expect you to move out on encountering it, rather than vice versa. Occasionally, however, berry pickers have been known to share a thicket with a bear and remain unmolested, with the bear maintaining a wary eye on them.

15. Other Factors That May Trigger An Attack

Evidence indicated that bears may be aggressive towards women wearing certain cosmetics or deodorants. Bears may also attack women who are menstruating.

Enjoying connubial relationships in bear habitat may be very dangerous as an analysis of some attacks seem to suggest. This point is supported by some native informants. The man often suffers the main brunt of the attack. In association with the sexual act are the formation of prenomes which are highly detectable by the sense of smell by such animals as stallions or bears, etc. Detection of prenomes by many animals can cause rather violent reactions on their part.

Running: Most sources of information indicate that running will only invite pursuit and attack. A bear can travel as fast as the best sprinters. If you must move, do so very slowly and always facing the bear.

Spring Encounter: A bear may be very short-tempered in the spring, but it is not as voraciously hungry as might be supposed. Bears do not normally break their fast by eating flesh, as they prefer certain herbs, possibly because flesh might cause a violent reaction.

Dogs have been known to rile bears and then lead the bear to their master. Some people who have encountered bears feel that their dog saved the day. The size and experience of the dog may make the difference. A bitch in heat may also arouse a bear. On the other hand I have known of dogs so adept at dealing with bears that it has no choice but stay clear of the dog.

Possibly one of the best protections against any bears is a dog, especially a small, nimble footed, yapping dog. By aggressive annoyance a dog claims the bear's attention first, allowing time for its owner to retreat. A nimble dog can often then escape, though it may get a cuffing if it is very daring. Small terriers are excellent companions for this purpose.

Though bears are often hidden from unwary intruders, if they are accompanied by a dog or a horse, they are usually warned well in advance of a meeting. The delicate senses of even domestic animals can detect a bear's presence. The riders claim this advantage if they remain attentive to their mount's behaviour.

Climbing Trees: Unless you have a good head start, you may be pulled down before you are out of reach. Black bears will climb after you and give you a bad time, although you are at a far greater advantage than on the ground. The bear travelling 50 k.p.h. hardly breaks step when it scoots up a tree.

Whistle: Most people feel that a shrill whistle will frighten away bears. It may do one of two things - either frighten it away or make it madder.

Hiking in a Group: The references proposing this do not give the minimum size of a group. A larger group will make more noise to fore-warn a bear. If you get mauled, there will at least be someone to help or get help. A group of people may deter a bear by virtue of its size.

Fear of Fire: Some sources indicate that bears have no fear of fire. They will walk between your shelter and your fire if you have a nice string of trout hanging on your ridgepole.

Railroad Fuses: Some sources indicate that flares with their brilliant light and sulphurous smell will deter even a grizzly. If for nothing else, it may be valuable for the peace of mind it brings as it sits under your pillow ready for instant use.

T Gee of Grande Prairie has these observations:

"We all know about hanging our packs well out of reach from a cross-bar or branch that is sturdy enough for the pack but not the bear. Bears have learned to climb the tree, walk the branch regardless of size and, if it doesn't break under their weight, to drop on the pack breaking the rope or ripping the contents free, at some discomfort to themselves when they stun themselves on hitting the ground.

Bears are expert climbers as is often seen by their claw marks on aspen

The Bullroarer: The ethnographic literature indicates that bullroarers were used to frighten away polar bears. If you have no other recourse you may try this method providing you have the room to use it.

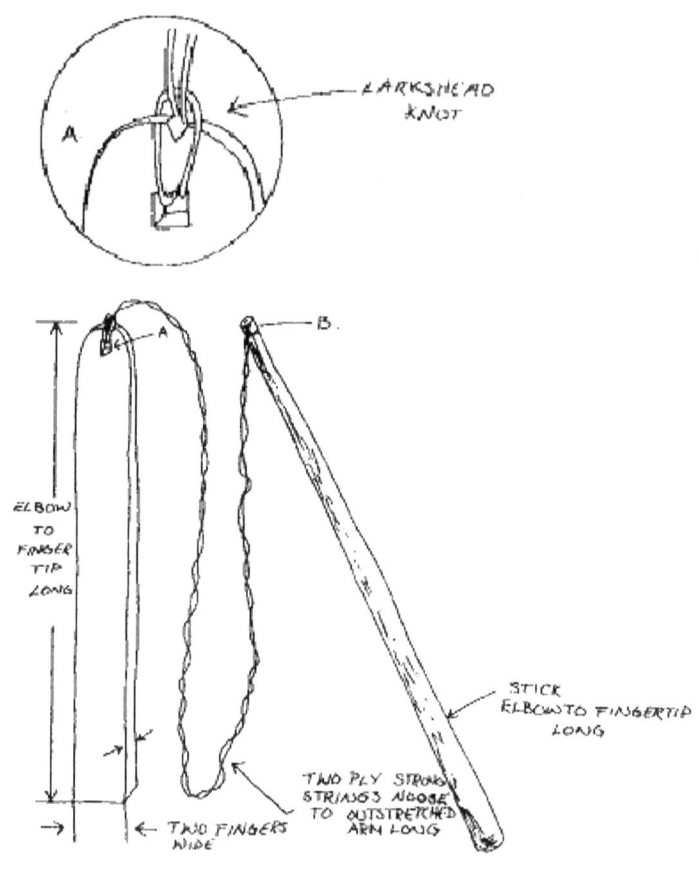

The Bull Roarer

After many canoe trips through bear country, I have made a discovery that saves me a lot of time and frustration and has, thus far, been bear-proof: bears can't detect backpacks wrapped in polyethylene.

Use the polyethylene tarps to keep the rain off your packs in the canoe. Equipped with grommets in the corners and at the positions of tent pole entry, they also make excellent flysheets. At night, lean two or three packs together or against a tree and wrap the entire bundle with the polyethylene, tucking it around the edges and the bottom and anchoring it with firewood. Put a pot containing a couple of spoons on top so any disturbance will be heard. This takes five minutes and since I began three eight-day trips ago (involving a total of 40 packs) there hasn't been a bear in my campsite, even though they had a heyday on more than one occasion at neighbouring campsites".

16. Effective Bear Stoppers

If the need to protect yourself from a bear arises a 12 gauge shotgun with number 00 shot will work. Any rifle suitable for deer is adequate for black bears: 30/06, 30/30, .303 and .270 calibers.

Target Area on Bear

17. Masking the Scent of Food with Moth Crystals

In the April 1970 issue of Field and Stream, Gabby Barrus described the experiments that Richard Hatfield of Cody, Wyoming, carried out using strong moth crystals (paradiclorobenzene) for discouraging bears from rummaging in garbage by masking the smells of human food.

Black bears and grizzlies will give the exposed crystals a wide berth if placed near your tent, in a garbage can or around a garbage dump. Once exposed the crystals have useable life of about a week.

Wash your hands if you have handled the chemical directly and keep it out of the reach of children. It is no small reason that bears wish to avoid it. Skunks cannot tolerate the smell of the crystals either.

The evaporation rates for the crystals given by Barrus seem high. The paradiclorobenzene also comes in blocks to be used in bathrooms and closets.

C) Lightning

As soon as you are aware that a lightning storm is approaching the best idea may be to immediately look for shelter. The safest place to be is inside a metal container such as a car or metal building. The next best is to be in a dry environment such as a house or cave.

If Caught Outside in a Thunderstorm:

1. Seek a dry place if possible.

2. Avoid any object that may attract lightning such as isolated tall trees (especially the most lightning struck tree: Populus balsamifera or black poplar), the tallest trees in a clump, wire fences, clothes lines, telephone and power poles and lines, hilltops, ridges and sky lines and anything of an open metal framework. You are in danger while riding a bike, tractor, ATV or horse.
3. Seek a level clearing, at least a tree length away from the nearest tree and get as near as possible to the ground.
4. Lay aside metal objects, such as rifles, axes etc.
5. You are safest in a ditch, ravine, under a cliff, in thick timber or flat on the ground.

If Caught on Water

If you are swimming or boating your chances of being struck are considerably increased. The hint of a distant thunder storm should cause you to seek shelter.

Persons Struck by Lightning

A person struck by lightning does not retain any charge. The victim may be stunned and knocked unconscious. If the respiratory muscles are paralyzed then artificial respiration must be applied immediately.

Higher elevations have their special problems in electrical storms. Mountains and any high points, especially exposed ridges and summits may be frequently struck by lightning. If you are on a mountain get as far down the mountain and as far away from exposed ridges as soon as possible. If you can, avoid wet ground. Do not sit under solitary trees or under the tallest trees in the general area. Hair rising or buzzing sounds emanating from surrounding rock or from your equipment may indicate a lightning strike building up.

D) Breaking Through the Ice

1. When you break through the ice, contrary to instinct to lean forward, throw yourself backwards.
2. If possible push on the opposite edge of the hole. If the hole is wide then bring legs vigorously together for propulsion.
3. Bear down slightly on head and shoulders and push away from hole.
4. Using a backstroke, maneuver away from the hole until safe ice is reached.

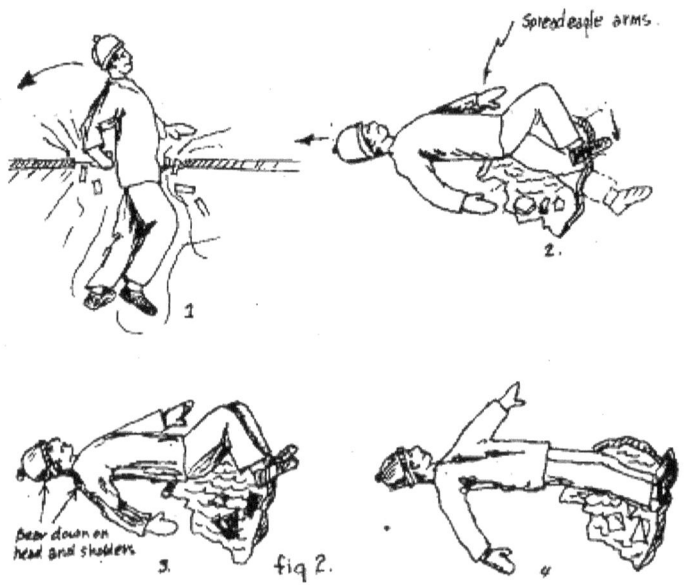

fig 2.

E) Quicksand or Mud

Quicksand is a very rare condition in the North Temperate Zone. It may be encountered near some beaver dams or springs or in certain mountaineering terrain. Immediately on stepping into quicksand one should fall flat and swim or roll out of the area. Quicksand or mud does not create suction. Soil of this condition offers little support to weight concentrated on small areas, so a standing person will sink easily. To remove a person stuck in the sand, build a raft out to him and pass a rope under his armpits. Apply a slow gentle pull with the victim moving about as much as possible.

Horses should be removed out of quicksand or mud as quickly as possible as they have difficulty breathing when they are neck deep in the sand or mud. Pass a rope around the neck and to the Spanish Windlass. Cattle could be pulled out the same way but may be dangerous as they may attack the rescuer out of panic.

Some seismic lines can be chewed up by large tracked vehicles, especially in permafrost areas. These can be found in unexpected places anywhere in muskeg. Becoming stuck is a possibility.

VI. Ropework

There are a great many ropes on the market suitable for almost every situation. It is not within the scope of this article to delve too deeply into the various types of ropes. Information about special ropes usually can be obtained at the source of purchase.

Some Types of Ropes:

Manila is the strongest rope made of natural fiber. This is a popular all-purpose rope that is smoother than most other natural ropes.

Sisal is a natural fiber rope that is about three-fourths as strong as manila, but less expensive. It is less flexible and is less abrasion resistant than manila. Sisal has been a popular fiber for baler and binder twines but is largely being replaced by synthetics as it has recently become somewhat scarce. The stiff fibers tend to splinter and hurt the hand.

Nylon is a synthetic fiber rope, twice as strong as manila and more expensive. It is slippery and hard to work with when wet and tends to be difficult to tie. Nylon rope acts like an elastic and suffers no damage if stretched up to eight percent of its length. This property allows it to withstand sudden jerks well. It deteriorates if left in the sun and is easily damaged by paints.

Dacron is a synthetic fiber rope that is as strong as nylon but has no stretch. It is impervious to moisture and is especially resistant to heat and insect damage.

Polyethylene is a synthetic fiber rope slightly stronger than manila but impervious to water and buoyant in it. It tends to melt easily near flame.

Taking the Kinks Out of New Rope:

Rope is made by twisting fibers together in a certain way. The main reason for doing so is to hold the rope's strands together when a strain is applied. In making a rope it is very necessary to make the tension equal on the strands, and on the yarns comprising the strands, or kinking results. If the kinkiness of new rope is bothersome, it may be removed by dragging it on the grass. Dragging a rope on gravel or cement will cause undue wear. Most kinks can be worked out with the hands.

To avoid damage, a kink should not be removed with force but be carefully untwisted with the hands. A rope is also often kinked by a knot tied in it. The set in the rope caused by a knot should be carefully unbent with the hands. The rope may also be rolled underfoot to relocate the strands and yarns.

Protecting Rope from the Elements:

The greatest deterioration of natural fiber ropes is usually caused by direct sunlight, damp and heat. A few months of exposure to the weather may weaken a rope from twenty to fifty percent.

Wet rope should be thoroughly dried in the shade with good air circulation. Rope is best stored hung in loose coils from a peg.

Coiling:

Rope should be coiled in the same direction as the twist of its strands. A rope with a right hand twist should be coiled clockwise.

To avoid twisting in a rope taken from a coil one must begin with the end last laid down at the center of the coil.

Start by laying the outer circle first and wind inward in a clockwise direction. A half turn is given to the rope as each loop is made. If the rope is a long one, it is coiled in layers from the outside inward.

Figure 1
Coiling a Right Hand Laid Rope

Relaying Stands:

If the end of a rope is unwound, use the same technique as outlined in the making of grass or other rope in the article on primitive binding materials, elsewhere in this issue.

Whipping:

To prevent the end of a rope from unwinding, it should be "whipped" as illustrated in Figure 2. Whipping is perhaps a more sensible, economical way to finishing the end of a rope in comparison to back splicing. Taping the end of a rope is another alternative.

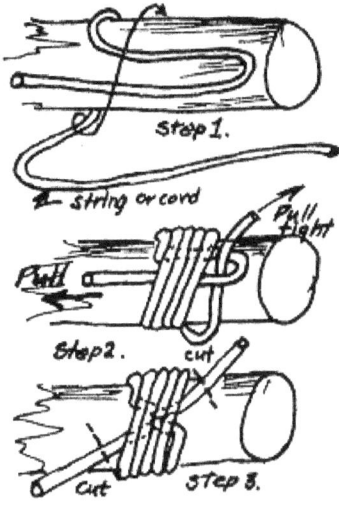

Figure 2
Simple Whipping

Sharp Corners:

Rope is very easily damaged by being pulled across a sharp corner, or especially, across another rope. Any form of chafing or abrasion damages a rope. Sharp corners should be padded if possible with some suitable frictionless material, or the use of pulleys where needed.

Weakening Effects of Knots:

Any knot or hitch will affect the tensile strength of a rope. An overhand knot may reduce the strength of a rope by more than one half. Needless knots are therefore to be avoided. As certain knots weaken a rope far more than others, the choice of a suitable knot becomes very important.

Safety Factor:

To minimize wear, extend rope life, and in the interests of safety, a rope should be five times as strong as the load it is expected to bear.

Some Principles behind a Good Knot or Hitch:

The knot must not weaken a rope more than necessary or damage the rope through being used. Because rope is expensive, knots tied in it generally have to be untied when they have served their purpose, so that the rope can be used again. If the knot jams, the rope may be damaged and further damage occurs in the process of untying the difficult knot. Knots tied in cordage, (anything less than 3/16 of an inch in diameter), which is considered expendable, may be cut off and discarded when they have served their usefulness. Hence a knot appropriate to cordage may not be appropriate to rope. The knot must be easy to untie, to minimize damage and inconvenience, and must fulfill its purpose efficiently. It should not fail under stress and strain. In the realm of knots, there is always one knot that will serve a particular purpose better than any other knot.

In tying a knot it is important to realize that it is unlikely to be properly made by merely pulling at the two ends. Knot illustration often have to be drawn up to exhibit clearly how the knot is tied and the fully adjusted knot may appear quite different. After the knot is tied according to a given illustration, it must then be judiciously and carefully pulled into shape. It is very important in some circumstances to snug a knot up tight before putting it under strain.

Some Knot Terminology:

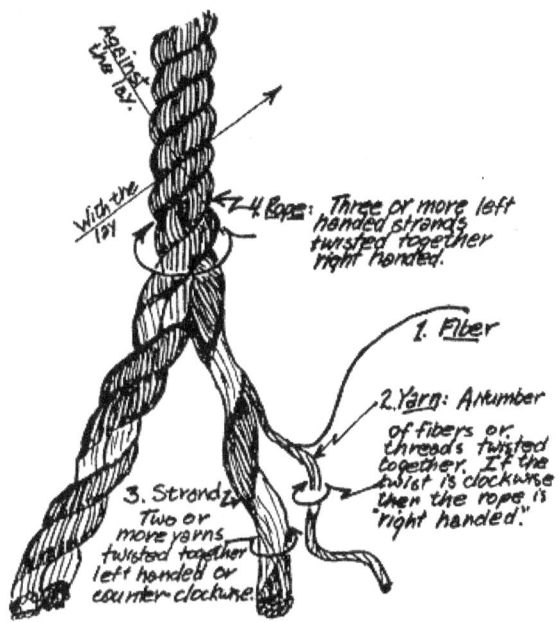

Figure 3
Rope Construction Terminology

The turn: This is also a basic component of many knots but is seldom used by itself.

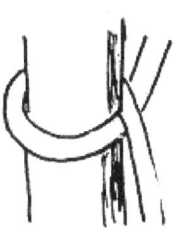

Figure 4 Turn

Round Turn: A round turn around a post will resist a considerable pull if the end is held by hand as illustrated in Figure 5.

Figure 5 Round Turn

Half Hitch: This is a basic component of many knots, but it is seldom used by itself.

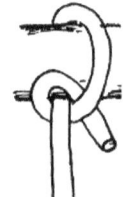

Figure 6 Half Hitch

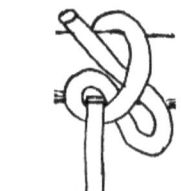

Figure 7 Slippery Half Hitch

Basic Safe Travel and Boreal Survival

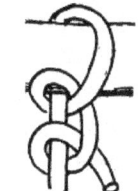

Figure 8 Two Half Hitch

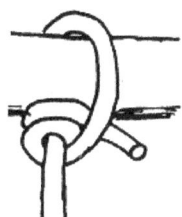

Figure 9 Double Half Hitch

The bight, loose end and standing part: These are the parts of a rope as illustrated in Figure 10.

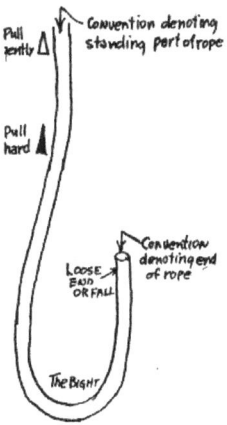

Figure 10 Rope Terminology

Slipping a Knot:

In order to untie a knot by means of a pull, it may sometimes be slipped, and the word slippery added to the name of the knot. For example, a slippery figure of eight is illustrated in Figure 11(a) and a slippery sheet bend in Figure 11 (b).

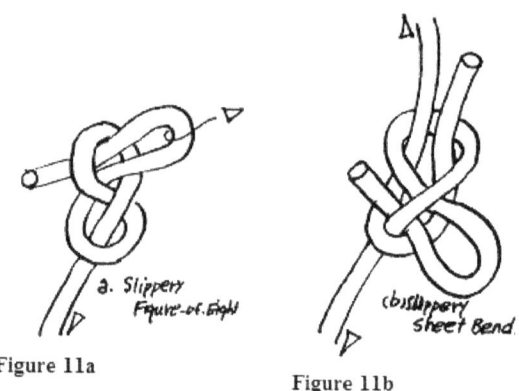

Figure 11a

Figure 11b

Figure 11 Slipping a Knot

Knot Configuration:

Some knots can be tied in a number of different ways and yet look the same. The most commonly met situation is the right-hand and left-hand versions of the same knot. There may be no noticeable functional difference between the right-hand and the left-hand versions, as in the left-hand and the right-hand bowline, as far as strength and security is concerned. With other knots, one or the other version may be inferior and even dangerous. It is therefore very important to tie the knots as illustrated in their correct configurations.

The Basic Knots

The Overhand Knot:

The overhand knot is a very difficult knot to untie, either by itself or as a component of other knots. It places a severe strain on the fibers of a rope, reducing its strength as much as fifty percent.

Figure 12 OVERHAND KNOT

The Figure of Eight Knot:

Wherever the overhand knot is called for it should be replaced by the Figure Eight knot. This knot is mostly used as a stopper knot, where it is desirable not to allow a rope to slip through a hole or out of a pulley.

Figure 13 FIG. 8 KNOT

The Reef Knot:

This knot should only be used in tying bundles or bandages but never as a bend (a knot used to tie the ends of two free lines together). Under a sharp pull or strain the knot may fail by capsizing into a lark's head as illustrated in Figure 14(3). This knot should never be used where your life may depend on it.

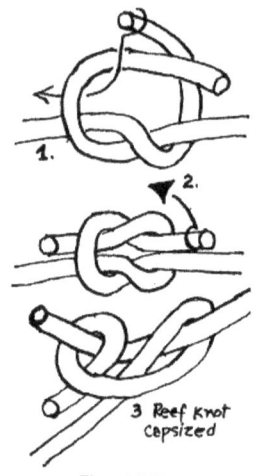

Figure 14 THE REEFKNOT

The Bends:

The Sheet Bend:

This is an excellent knot as it holds well with a wide variety of sizes of rope and ropes of different materials. The knot must be tied with the ends on the same side as illustrated. The sheet bend can be made more secure by taking another turn to make a double sheet bend.

Basic Safe Travel and Boreal Survival

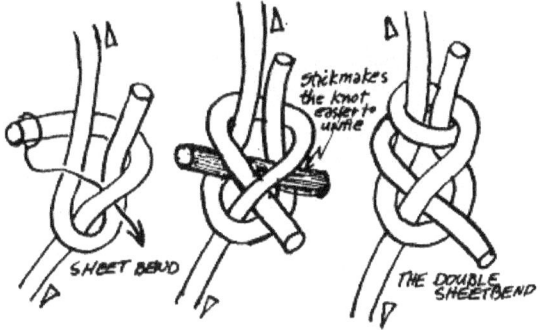

Figure 15 THE SHEET BENDS

The Carrick Bend:

This bend should be used instead of the reef knot. It is a general heavy duty bend of special use with large rope. It is strong, and secure and easily untied even when wet. It is necessary to seize the ends (lash together) when used with a very large rope (hausers). In this knot the ends must be diagonally opposite. When the knot is tightened, the transformation of appearance it undergoes (upset) is no cause for concern as the knot continues to retain its full effectiveness. This somewhat complicated looking knot is not as well known as it ought to be.

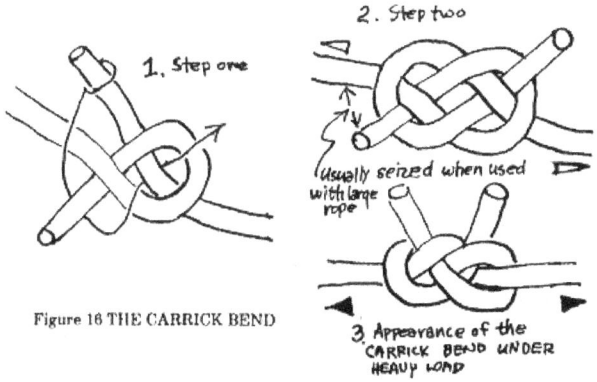

Figure 16 THE CARRICK BEND

The Bowline Bend:

Ropes tied together by interlocking two bow-lines is almost as strong as the straight rope itself. This is probably the strongest bend of all.

Figure 17 THE BOWLINE BEND

The Strap Knot:

This knot is also known as the grass or wire knot. It should be used only for bending together straps, grass or wire.

Figure 18 STRAP, WIRE OR GRASS KNOT

The Nooses and Loops

The Bowline Family:

The Bowline: The simple bowline is an ideal knot for making a fixed loop. It is simple, strong, does not slip or jam, and the left-hand version is as strong as the right-hand version. If the bowline is double knotted (double bowline) it is even more secure and stable.

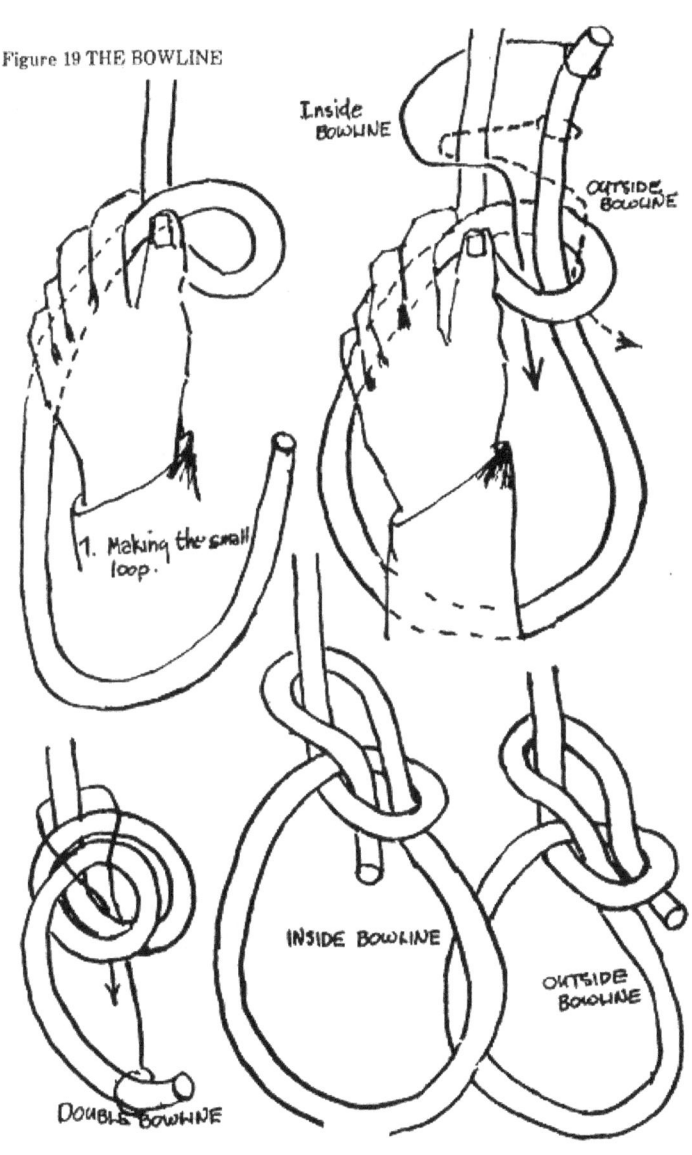

The Running Bowline: This is a free running noose made by simply tying a bowline and a rope or passing the end of the rope through a small bowline.

The Bowline on a Bight: This knot is often used for a sling or chair. It must be tied well when used on the body or it may capsize into a double noose. The bowline with a bight may be more secure. (An ordinary bowline tied with the bight end of a doubled rope).

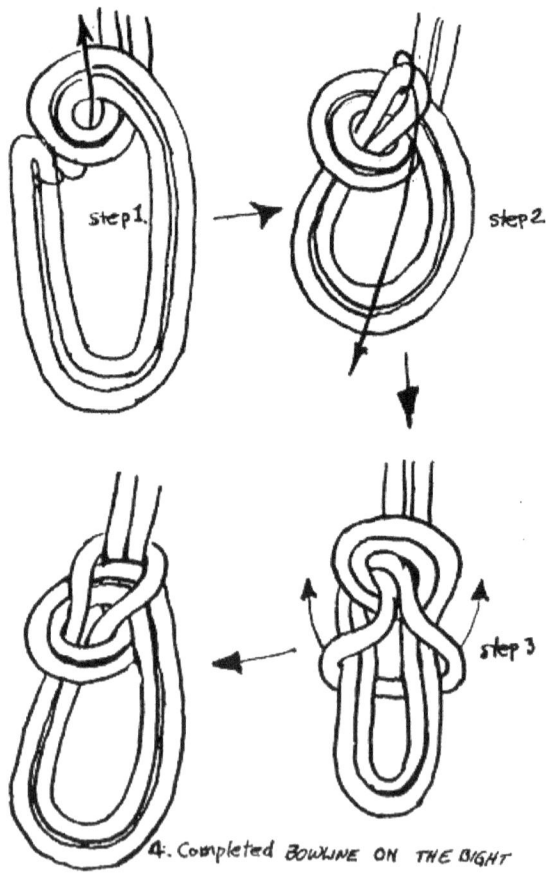

Figure 20a The Bowline on a Bight
The Bowline Family

The Bowline with a Bight: This bowline, when tied as illustrated in Figure 20, provides three loops to be used in a sling or for any other purpose.

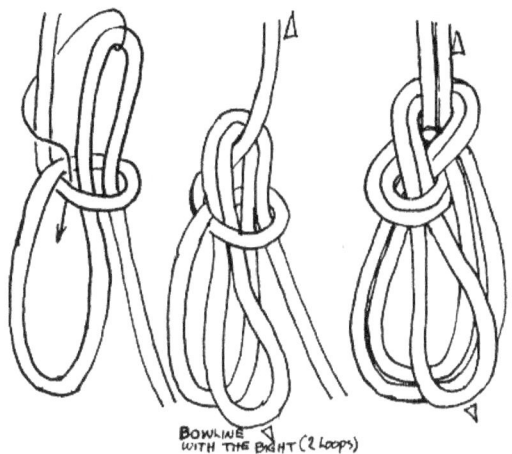

Figure 20 b BOWLINE WITH THE BIGHT

Other Loops:

The Honda Knot:

This is the smallest of the most open of the loop knots. This knot may be used for the eye of a lariat or the end of a bow string.

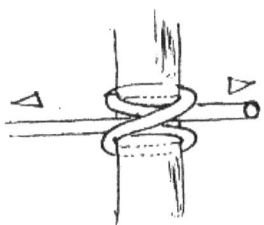

Figure 25 THE CLOVE HITCH

The Figure of Eight Loop:

This is one of the better single loops in the bight. It is far superior to the overhand loop which is perhaps more useful on cord.

Figure 21 FIGURE-OF-EIGHT LOOP

Making a Simple Coil:

When a rope has to be stored or carried about, it may be convenient to coil the rope so that it is compact to handle and does not get tangled. There are multitudinous methods to coil a rope. One simple method is shown in Figure 41.

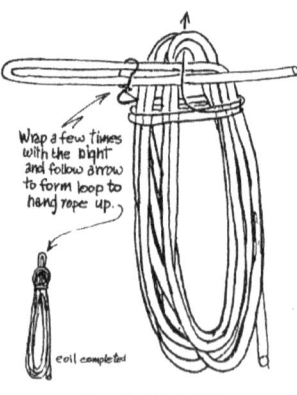

Figure 41 A Simple Coil

The Butterfly Knot or Lineman's Rider:

This is one of the best of the single loops in the bight, much trusted by mountaineers.

- ➢ Step One: Make two clockwise loops.
- ➢ Step Two: Take the first loop and place it between the other two as shown in Figure 22(b).
- ➢ Step Three: Take the loop that is now first and bring it through the loops as shown in Figure 22(c).

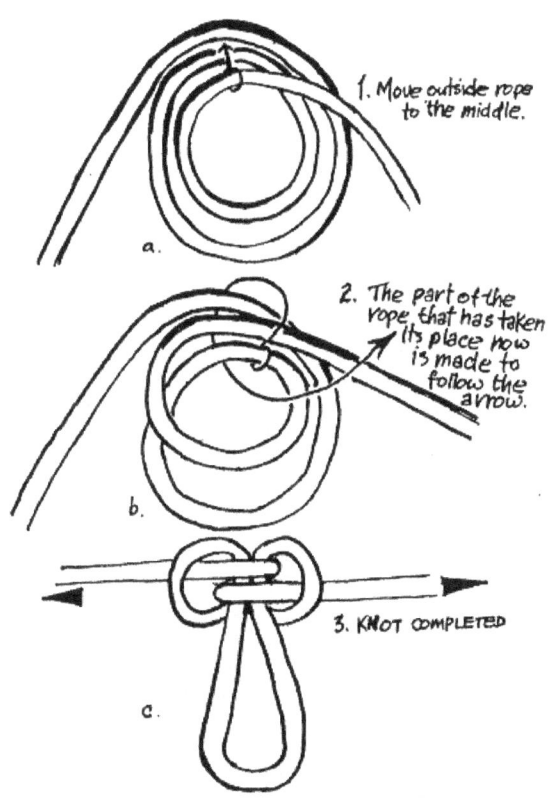

Figure 22 THE BUTTERFLY KNOT

The Hitches - Knots tied directly to or around an object:

The Fisherman's Bend:

This is a hitch that cannot slip or jam and has a high breaking strength.

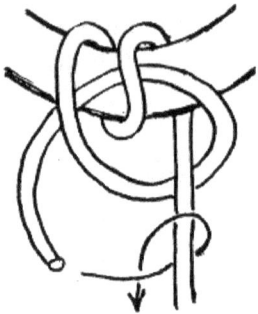

Figure 24 THE FISHERMAN'S BEND

The Clove Hitch:

This is secure fastening only when under constant tension. It is easily untied.

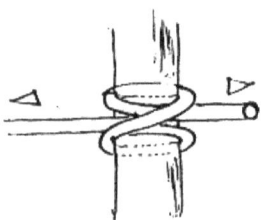

Figure 25 THE CLOVE HITCH

The Constrictor Knot:

This is the most secure of all binding knots as long as it is tied around a convex surface. The tenacity of the knot makes it somewhat difficult to untie. If it is essential to untie the knot quickly, it may be "slipped". Generally, this knot should replace the clove hitch. (In fact the knot is a clove hitch with an overhand knot tied under the crossing part). The knot may find practical applications in seizing, whipping, clamping, closing bags, hoisting objects and attaching a line or rope to a post, spar or another rope. The knot can also be tied in the bight as shown in Figure 26.

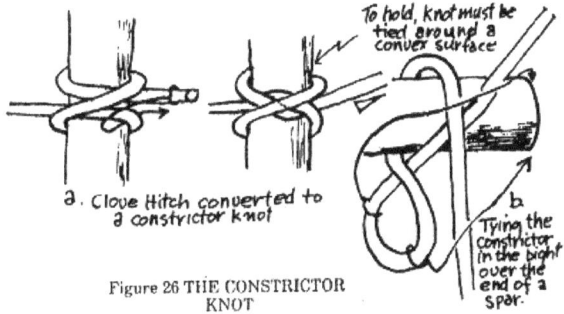

Figure 26 THE CONSTRICTOR KNOT

The Timber Hitch:

This hitch is used for towing or lifting a log or spar. It has a high breaking strength and is impossible to jam. The end must be twisted around the other part in the same direction as the lay.

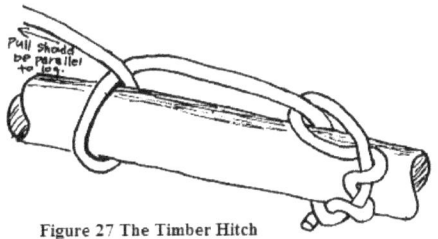

Figure 27 The Timber Hitch

The Rolling or Taut Line Hitch:

This is used where a line is to be secured to another or to a spar where the strain is expected to be nearly parallel. The two round turns are made on that side of the standing part from which the strain will come, before crossing the end over to make the jamming half hitch. This hitch should always be put on a rope against the lay.

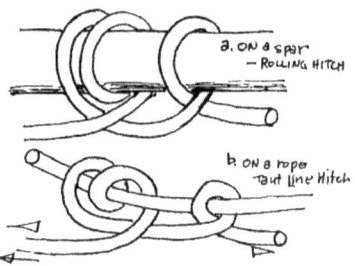

Figure 28 The Taut Line Hitch

The Midshipman's Hitch:

In this hitch the rolling hitch is tied with equal sized rope or cord or upon itself. The hitch should only move when moved by hand. This knot is often used for tightening tent guy ropes. If tied as in Figure 29(b) it may be used for tying parcels.

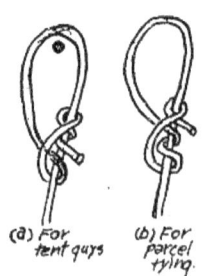

Figure 29 THE MIDSHIPMAN'S HITCH

Basic Safe Travel and Boreal Survival

Turk's Head Knot

The Turk's Head Knot-Spruce Root Ring & Coaster
First learn to make this knot with stiff string to reduce frustration.

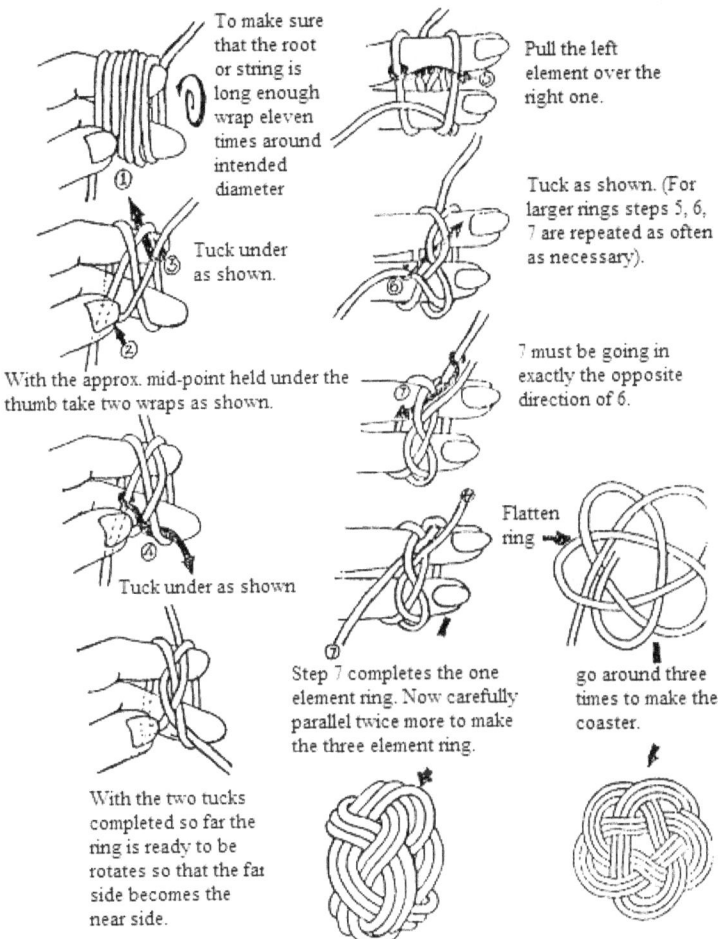

The Nylon Taut Line Hitch:

This knot is similar to the taut line hitch, but is altered to hold better when used with nylon cord.

Fig. 30 NYLON TAUT LINE HITCH

The Splices

Preliminaries:

When making splices, there are a number of things to keep in mind.

To prevent the strands of the rope from unraveling, they should be whipped or melted if the rope is synthetic, and to prevent the rope from unraveling more than necessary, a constrictor knot may be tied at the required point.

A fid (a pointed, usually conical, tapered tool made of wood) is used for opening a rope when splicing. A tool with similar function made of steel is the marlin spike.

Rolling under the foot smooths out the surface of the splice and helps to even up the strains within the splice. Like rolling under the foot, gentle pounding helps to even out the adjustment of the strands.

When Trimming the ends, if the ends are cut off to closely, they are apt to work out. Tapering is achieved by cutting away a portion of each strand as the splice continues, in order to reduce the bulk of the splice. This is usually done more for appearance than for anything else. The strength and security of the splice is likely not enhanced.

The Short Splice:

Unravel both ends of the ropes being spliced about five to seven centimetres. Crotch the unravelled ends as shown in Figure 31(a) and bind (perhaps a constrictor knot). Tuck all strands at the same longitudinal point and then remove the binding and do the same in the opposite direction. Six tucks altogether should make an adequately strong splice.

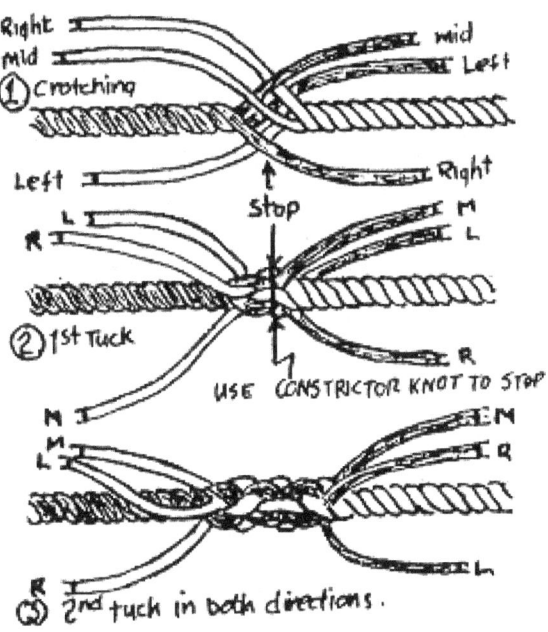

Figure 31 The Short Splice

The Eye Splice:

The eye splice is important to know as it is called for more frequently than any of the other splices. The strands are unlayed five to seven centimetres. The middle strand is tucked under the strand against the lay. The left hand strand enters where the middle strand exits and is tucked under the next strand. The work is flipped over and the third strand is tucked under the remaining strand. All three strands must be at the same longitudinal point on the rope. The strands should now be tucked at least twice more. The ends may be trimmed to leave a centimetre protruding or the ends may become untucked under train. For added security the strands may be halved and the halves of adjoining strands tied together. For a neater appearance the strands may be halved and one half trimmed away and tucked twice more.

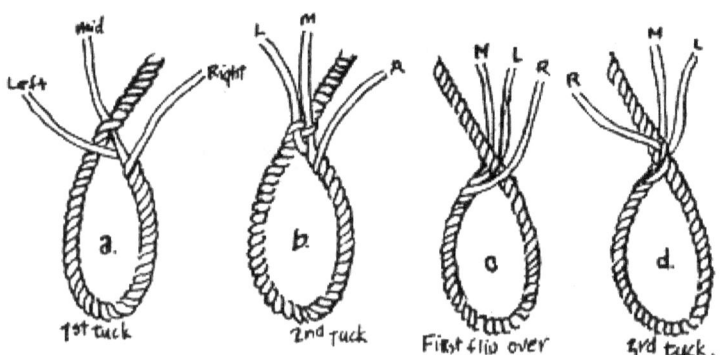

Figure 32(a) The Common Eye Splice

Another variation of the eye splice, involving unraveling the rope is illustrated in Figure 32. This may be a more secure form of eye splice.

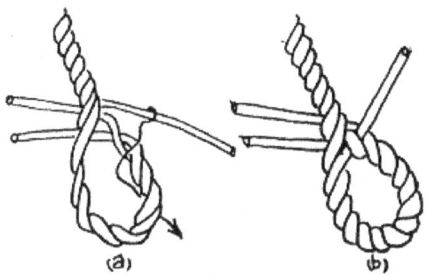

Figure 32(b) The Unravelled Eye Spice

The Tuck Splice:

This splice is used to make an eye in the bight of a rope. Where a loop is desired, raise two strands and pass the first end through the opening formed at a right angle to the strands. Adjust the loop formed to the desired size. Next, pass the second end under the two strands of the first end above and adjacent to the loop. The natural position of the loop should be in line with the end of the rope first used.

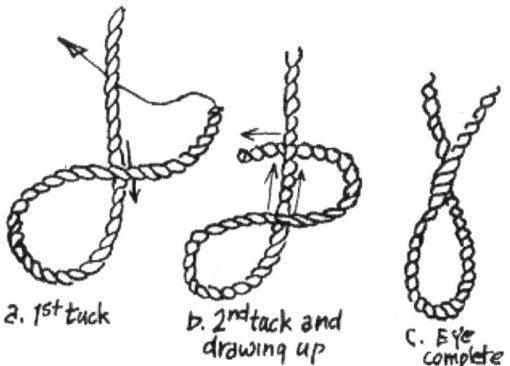

a. 1st tuck   b. 2nd tack and drawing up   c. Eye complete

Figure 33 The Tuck Splice

The Lashings

Preliminaries:

In making lashings one end of the lashing rope is attached with a clove hitch or constrictor knot to one of the poles. In completing the lashing, the end of the lashing rope is attached to a pole other than the one started on. The lashing is also completed with a clove hitch or constrictor knot.

Pole Lashing:

This lashing can be used where poles have to be lashed together end to end. One particular application is where a gill net has to be put out from shore without the use of a boat.

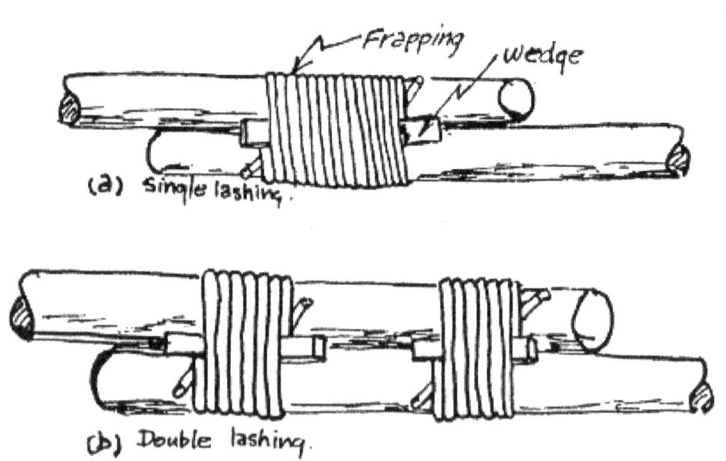

Figure 34 Pole Lashing

Round Lashing:

This lashing is used for making a bi-pod or shear legs.

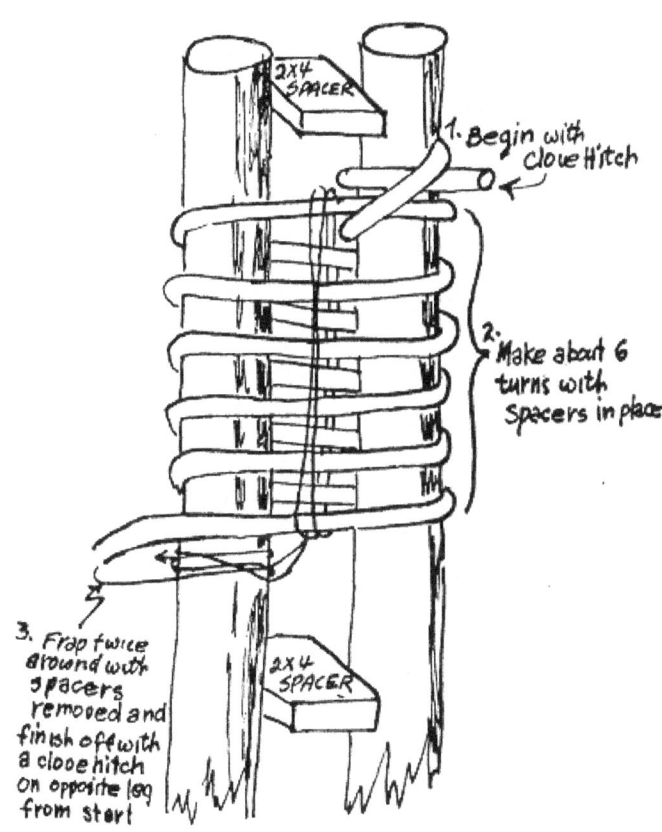

Figure 35 Round Lashing

Tripod Lashing:

This lashing has to be made loosely, otherwise too much tension may develop in the lashing rope.

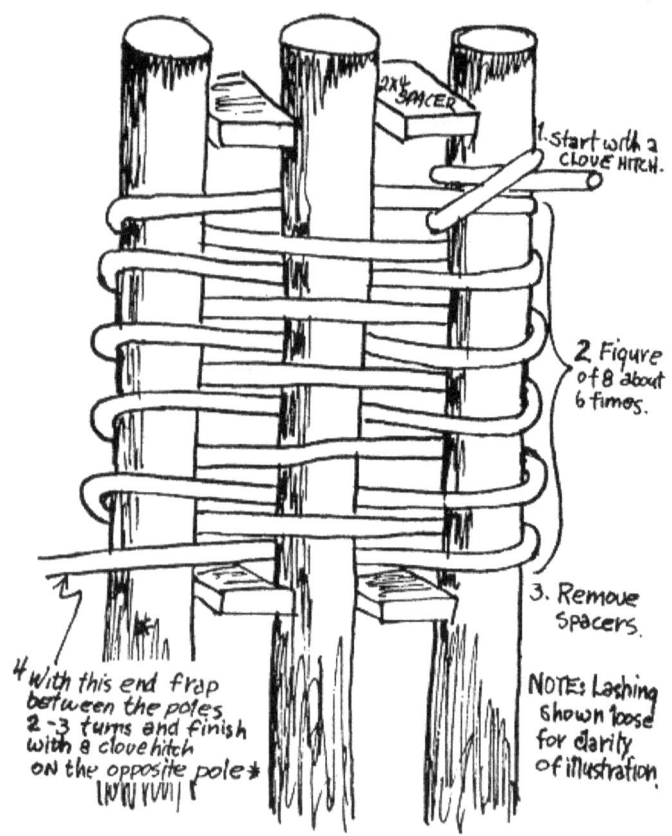

Figure 36 Tripod Lashing

Basic Safe Travel and Boreal Survival

Square Lashing:

This lashing is used for securing two poles crossing each other at 90 degrees.

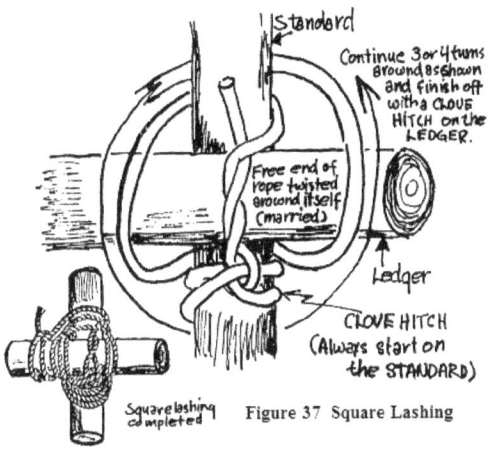

Figure 37 Square Lashing

Diagonal Lashing:

This lashing is used to secure poles that cross each other diagonally.

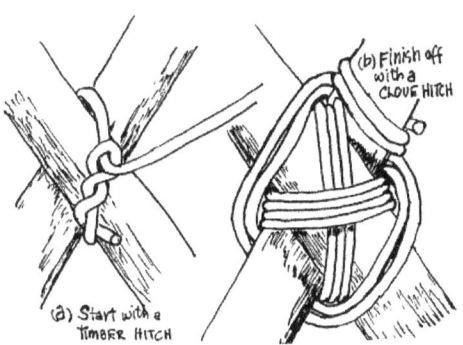

Figure 38 Diagonal Lashing

The Jam Knot:

This is the most useful knot in survival. This knot is designed to be used with nylon cord, specifically parachute shroud line. The knot is very useful wherever something has to be tied together very tightly and where loosening of the binding is not desirable. Another feature of the knot is that when it is to be untied, the first overhand knot is cut off, causing the knot to come off easily with a minimum of wastage of cord. An alternative is to substitute a slip knot for the overhand knot.

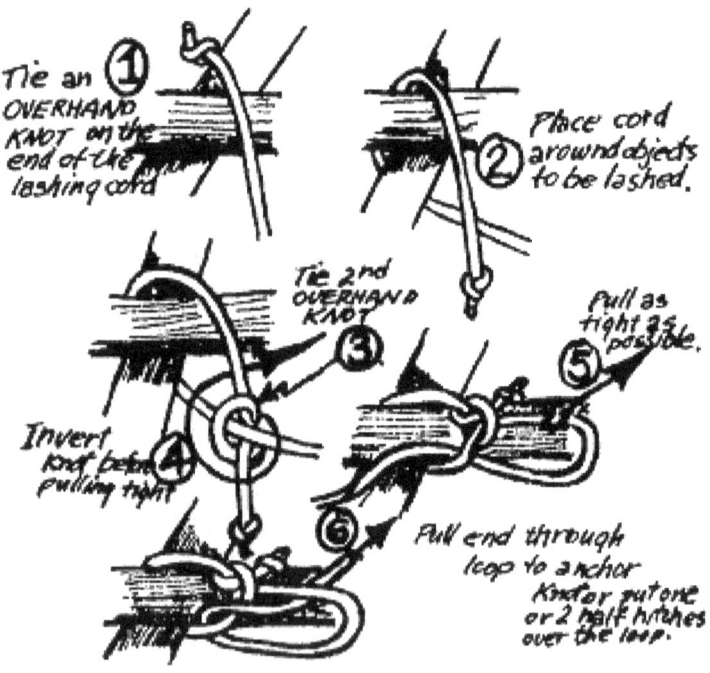

Figure 39 The Jam Knot

Basic Safe Travel and Boreal Survival

Rope Harness - The Alberta Hitch:

This somewhat complicated looking knot is a very secure method of making a rescue harness for hoisting or lowering a conscious or unconscious person. The knot is used by Alberta's Disaster Services agency.

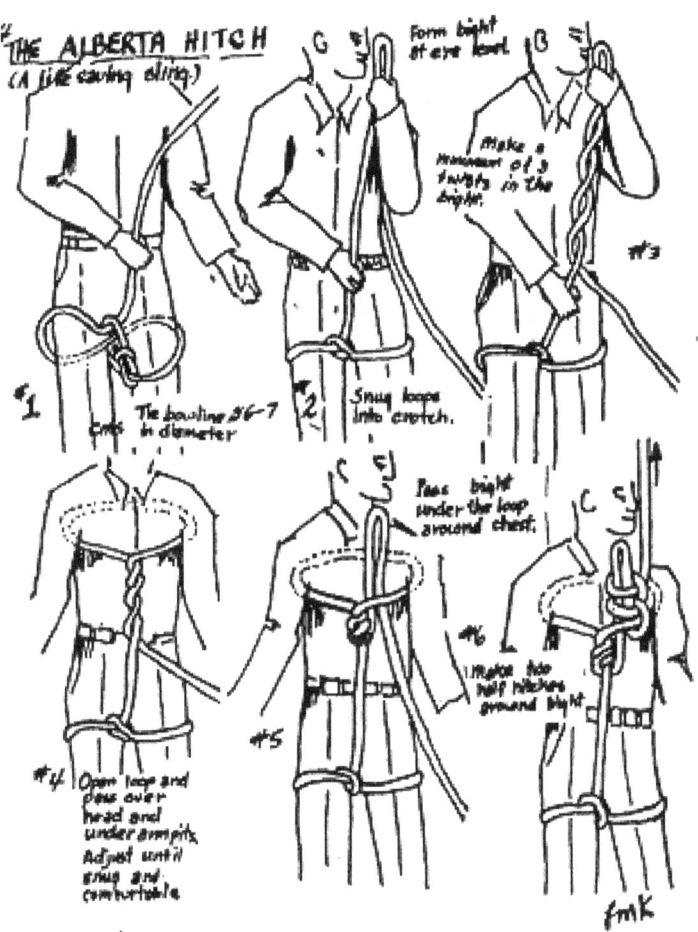

Figure 40 THE ALBERTA HITCH

Emergency Halter:

For horses or cattle. The Australian Quick Halter is a quick, secure, dependable halter. Follow the illustrations as outlined in Figure 42.

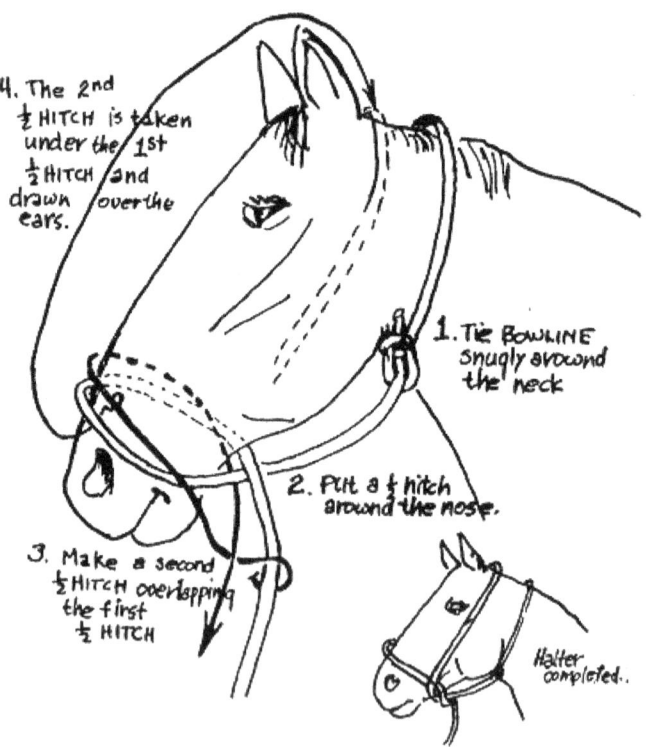

Figure 42 The Australian Quick Halter

Spanish Windlass:

The device illustrated in Figure 43 is a form of winch or capstan that provides a considerable power gain. This will also work with light steel cable. Be sure the rope used is strong and in good condition. It is hazardous to stand near the ropes near the vertical post, in that, if the rope breaks in the right way the post could deal quite a blow. This device can be used to move buildings, and pull vehicles out of mud holes, etcetera.

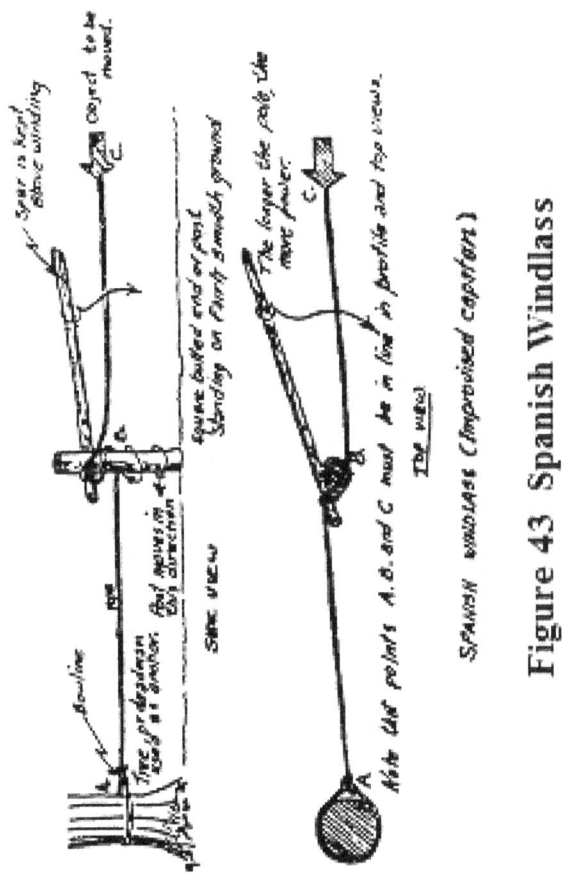

Figure 43 Spanish Windlass

Holdfasts:

When no trees are available to provide an anchor for using a windlass to move a vehicle or other heavy object, a trench may be dug ninety degrees to the direction of pull and a log placed in it as illustrated in Figure 44.

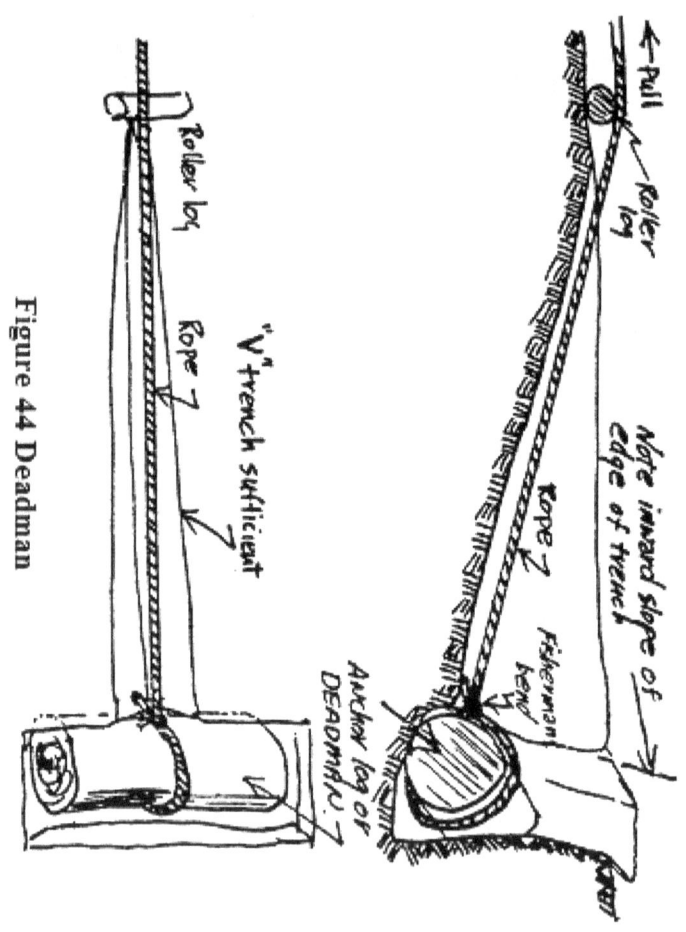

Figure 44 Deadman

Basic Safe Travel and Boreal Survival

An alternative is to use iron or wooden posts as shown in Figure 45.

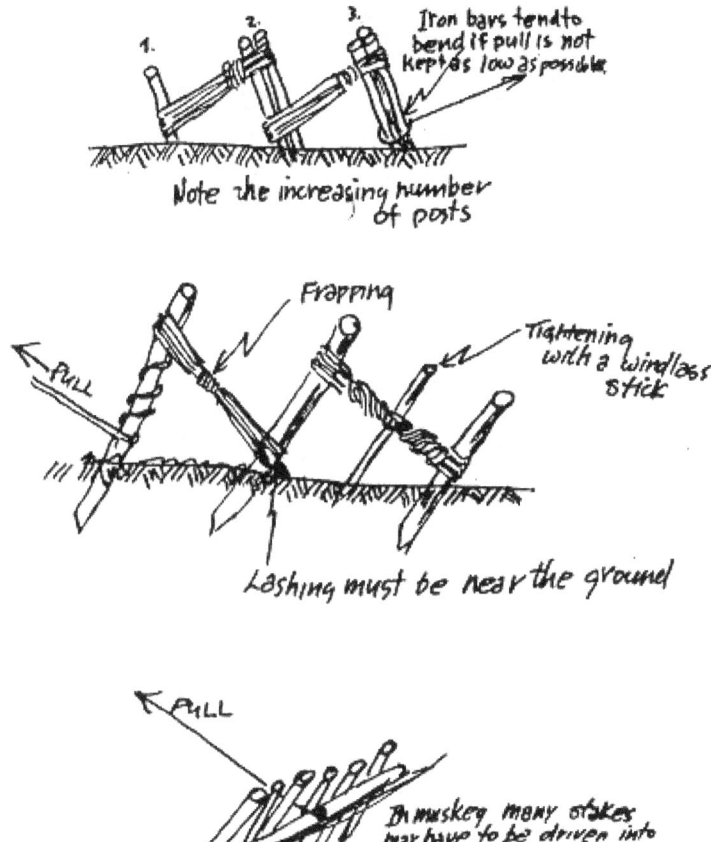

Figure 45 Peg Holdfasts

Climbing Poles, Trees or Masts with a Sling:

Make a loop for each foot with a piece of rope about a metre long - depending on the diameter of the object being climbed. Using two slings, set one about 1 1/2 meters above the other. Step into the higher sling, keeping the knee bent, reach down and bring up the lower sling until it comes up against the first. Transfer the weight to the lower sling and move the higher one up.

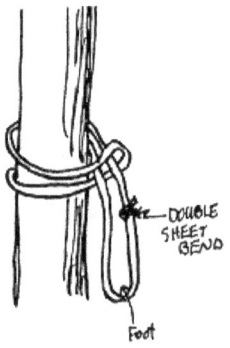

Figure 46 Climbing Sling

Miscellaneous Operations with Rope and Cordage:

Snarls: There is a systematic approach in dealing with snarled line or cord:

1. Anchor the longest free end.
2. Loosen the snarl.
3. Find the uppermost bight and open it, and work it downward so that the whole snarl and the end of the line passes through it.
4. Step 3 is repeated until the snarl is undone.

ABOUT THE AUTHOR

Mors is widely known throughout North America and Europe for his extensive work in outdoor education, survival and wilderness living. His passion for the Northern Forest and his desire to learn everything about it has made him one of the world's foremost authorities on Boreal Wilderness Skills and Survival.

He popularized the term 'Bushcraft' and coined the familiar saying "the more you know, the less you carry". Bushcraft, published in 1987, is a foremost text on that subject with the skills you really need to know, including; Firecraft, Axe Use, The Bush Knife, Cordage, Shelter Concepts, Trees and Animals. It is evident that Mors is teaching from experience rather than regurgitating knowledge.

Mors is truly the "Old Dog" of the forest being one of those unique individuals that not only knows his subject but is also able to teach what he knows.

A resident of Peers, Alberta, he is most familiar to outdoor enthusiasts of Northern and Central Alberta where he has lived and worked for the past 48 years. Kochanski was an outdoor education instructor at the university of Alberta for 23 years.

He still participates in the intensive week long wilderness living-survival courses as a Master Instructor with Karamat Wilderness Ways.

Mors has been involved with the Junior Forest Warden Program for the last 30 years inspiring wardens and leaders for which he received the JFW Lifetime Achievement Award in 2008.

www.ingramcontent.com/pod-product-compliance
Lightning Source LLC
Chambersburg PA
CBHW050118170426
43197CB00011B/1628